Episodes *of the* Cuban Revolutionary War

Ernesto Che Guevara

Episodes *of the* Cuban Revolutionary War *1956-58*

PATHFINDER

NEW YORK LONDON MONTREAL SYDNEY

Edited by Mary-Alice Waters

ISBN 0-87348-824-5
Library of Congress Catalog Card Number 95-72958

Manufactured in Canada

First edition, 1996
Sixth printing, 2005

COVER PHOTO: Guevara addressing people of Fomento in Las Villas province following the city's liberation by the Rebel Army, December 18, 1958. (Courtesy of Council of State Office of Historical Affairs, Havana)
COVER DESIGN: Eric Simpson

Pathfinder
www.pathfinderpress.com
E-mail: pathfinder@pathfinderpress.com

PATHFINDER DISTRIBUTORS AROUND THE WORLD:

Australia (and Southeast Asia and the Pacific):
Pathfinder, Level 1, 3/281-287 Beamish St., Campsie, NSW 2194
Postal address: P.O. Box 164, Campsie, NSW 2194
Canada:
Pathfinder, 2238 Dundas St. West, Suite 201, Toronto, ON M6R 3A9
Iceland:
Pathfinder, Skolavordustig 6B, Reykjavík
Postal address: P. Box 0233, IS 121 Reykjavík
New Zealand:
Pathfinder, Suite 3, 7 Mason Ave., Otahuhu, Auckland
Postal address: P.O. Box 3025, Auckland
Sweden:
Pathfinder, Bjulevägen 33, kv, S-122 41 Enskede
United Kingdom (and Europe, Africa, Middle East, and South Asia):
Pathfinder, First Floor, 120 Bethnal Green Road
(entrance in Brick Lane), London E2 6DG
United States (and Caribbean, Latin America, and East Asia):
Pathfinder Books, 306 W. 37th St., 10th Floor, New York, NY 10018-2852

Contents

PORTRAITS OF REVOLUTIONARIES

THE LAS VILLAS CAMPAIGN, SEPTEMBER–DECEMBER 1958

LETTERS ON THE CUBAN REVOLUTIONARY WAR

GLOSSARIES AND CHARTS

MAPS AND SKETCHES

Ernesto Che Guevara

ERNESTO "CHE" GUEVARA was born in Argentina on June 14, 1928. Both before and after graduating from medical school in 1953, he traveled extensively through the Americas. While living in Guatemala in 1954, he became involved in political struggle, opposing the CIA's eventually successful attempts to overthrow the government of Jacobo Arbenz. Following the ouster of Arbenz, he escaped to Mexico. There, in the summer of 1955, he was selected by Fidel Castro as the third confirmed member of an expeditionary force being organized by the Cuban July 26 Movement to overthrow dictator Fulgencio Batista.

In late November 1956 the eighty-two expeditionaries, including Castro and Guevara, set sail from Tuxpan, Mexico, aboard the yacht *Granma.* The rebel forces landed on Cuba's southeastern coast in Oriente province on December 2 to begin the revolutionary war from the Sierra Maestra mountains in the eastern part of the island. Originally the troop doctor, Guevara was named commander of the second Rebel Army column (Column no. 4) in July 1957. At the end of August 1958 he led Column no. 8 toward Las Villas province in central Cuba. The Las Villas campaign culminated in the capture of Santa Clara, Cuba's third largest city, and helped seal the fate of the U.S.-backed dictatorship.

Following Batista's fall on January 1, 1959, Guevara carried a number of responsibilities in the new revolutionary government, including president of the National Bank and minister of industry, while continuing his duties as an officer in the armed forces.

He frequently represented Cuba internationally, including at the United Nations and in other world forums. As a leader of the July 26 Movement, he helped bring about the political regroupment that led to the founding of the Communist Party of Cuba in October 1965.

Guevara resigned his government and party posts, including his military commission and responsibilities, in early 1965 and left Cuba in order to return to South America to help advance the anti-imperialist and anticapitalist struggles that were sharpening in several countries. Along with a number of volunteers who would later join him in Bolivia, Guevara went first to the Congo (now Zaire) where he aided the anti-imperialist movement founded by Patrice Lumumba. From November 1966 to October 1967 he led a guerrilla movement in Bolivia against that country's military dictatorship. Wounded and captured by the Bolivian army in a CIA-organized operation on October 8, 1967, he was murdered the following day.

Introduction

WITHOUT PRETENSION OR EXAGGERATION Ernesto Che Guevara provides a firsthand account in these pages of the final two years of the revolutionary struggle in Cuba that culminated January 1, 1959, in the destruction of the brutal U.S.-backed dictatorship of Fulgencio Batista.

The workers and farmers government consolidated in the following months rapidly became what Guevara calls "the hope of the unredeemed Americas." It opened the door to the first socialist revolution in the hemisphere, a reality that almost four decades later still stands at the center of world politics.

Episodes of the Cuban Revolutionary War, written with clarity and humor, is also about the education of Ernesto Che Guevara, the young Argentine rebel who became one of the central leaders of the Cuban revolution. It is a book that reveals Che's political coming of age—often to his own surprise—as he is transformed from a serious student of Marxism with little practical political experience into a seasoned combat leader of men and women. We watch him as he takes on greater and greater responsibilities. We follow his growth, his education, and his transformation by the Cuban workers and peasants alongside of whom he is engaged in a life-and-death struggle. From a determined revolutionary intellectual imbued with a spirit of adventure, a self-described Quixote, one of the great communist leaders of the twentieth century begins to emerge.

"Some time ago," Guevara wrote to his parents from Mexico in July 1956, "I met a young Cuban leader who invited me to join his movement, dedicated to the armed liberation of his country. I of course accepted." Guevara's letter, which appears here in full for the first time in English, continued, "My future is linked to the liberation of Cuba. Either I will triumph with it, or I will die there."

The young Cuban leader was Fidel Castro, twenty-nine years old but already a well-known political figure in Cuba. As a student leader at the University of Havana law school in the late 1940s he had begun to assume growing leadership responsibility within the Latin American anti-imperialist student movement. In 1947 Castro became a founding member of the Cuban People's Party—the Orthodox Party, or *Ortodoxos*, as it became known—which campaigned on a platform of opposition to Yankee domination and rampant government corruption and graft. He was a leader of the party's student-based youth organization, which led its left wing. That same year he volunteered for an armed expedition to the Dominican Republic aimed at overthrowing the dictatorship of Rafael Leónidas Trujillo. The operation, led by bourgeois forces, was aborted, however, before even leaving Cuba.

A year later Castro was in Bogotá, Colombia, helping to organize a Latin American student conference to coincide with a meeting of foreign ministers from North and South America, when opposition Liberal Party leader Jorge Eliecer Gaitán was assassinated. The city erupted in a mass popular uprising soon known as the *Bogotazo*. Joining with thousands of others who rushed to the police stations and seized arms, Castro found himself helping to organize the resistance to the impending military assault on the working people and youth who had poured into the streets.

While a student at the university, Castro came in contact with Marxist literature, including the *Communist Manifesto* and other classic works by Marx, Engels, and Lenin, and he began to develop a materialist world outlook and a revolutionary perspective.[1]

1. "As a result of studying capitalist political economy, even before I discovered Marxist literature, I started drawing socialist conclusions and imagining a society whose economy would operate more rationally. I started off as utopian communist. I didn't come in contact with revolu-

In 1952 Castro was running as an Orthodox Party candidate for the house of representatives when Batista and his generals seized power on March 10 and scuttled the scheduled elections. Within weeks of the coup, Castro began putting together an armed movement to overthrow the dictatorship, an underground organization that grew, in little more than a year, to twelve hundred men and women.

On July 26, 1953, 160 of these combatants carried out simultaneous armed assaults on the army garrisons in the eastern Cuban cities of Bayamo and Santiago de Cuba, hoping to create the conditions for an armed popular uprising in Santiago, the island's second-largest city and a historic center of anti-imperialist activity in Cuba. If Santiago could not be held, the plan was to retreat to the Sierra Maestra mountains and regroup a force of several thousand combatants to dig

---

tionary ideas, revolutionary theories, the *Communist Manifesto,* and the first works by Marx, Engels, and Lenin until I was a junior in the university. To be quite frank the simplicity, clarity, and direct manner in which our society are explained in the *Communist Manifesto* had a particularly great impact on me.

"Naturally, before becoming a utopian or a Marxist communist, I was a follower of José Martí. . . . I always wholeheartedly admired our people's heroic struggles for independence in the past century. . . . I'm absolutely convinced that if Martí had lived in the same environment as Marx, he would have had the same ideas and acted in more or less the same way. Martí had great respect for Marx. . . . I think that Martí s thinking contains such great and beautiful things that you can become a Marxist by taking his thought as a starting point. Of course Martí didn't explain why society was divided into classes, though he was a man who always stood at the side of the poor and who bitterly criticized the worst vices of a society of exploiters.

"When I first got hold of the *Communist Manifesto* I found an explanation. In the midst of that forest of events, where it was very difficult to understand phenomena and where everything seemed due to the wickedness of men—their defects, perversity, and immorality—I started to identify other factors that weren't dependent on man, his morals, and his individual attitude. I began to understand human society, the historic process, and the divisions that I saw every day." *Fidel and Religion: Conversations with Frei Betto* (Pathfinder, 1986), pp. 112–13.

in and continue the armed insurrection.

The attacks were crushed. Nearly half of the revolutionaries were captured, brutally tortured, and murdered. Twenty-eight of those who escaped this slaughter, including Castro, who had headed the assault force in Santiago, were tried and sentenced to up to fifteen years in prison. Castro's defense speech before the court, later reconstructed by him in prison and smuggled out, was published under the title *History Will Absolve Me* and initially circulated in some 100,000 copies as part of a growing popular amnesty campaign in Cuba.

In May 1955, in response to this campaign, Castro and other veterans of the attacks on the Santiago and Bayamo garrisons were released from prison. Together with other groups moving in a revolutionary direction, they founded the July 26 Movement. Then, with persecution mounting in Cuba, Castro left the island for Mexico in July 1955 to prepare an expedition that would establish a base that could be defended in the Sierra Maestra mountains of Oriente province and relaunch the armed struggle against the Batista dictatorship.

In Mexico City, Castro soon met Ernesto Guevara and signed him up as the third confirmed member of the expedition. Raúl Castro, Fidel's brother, had been the second. In the closing weeks of 1956, eighty-two combatants with relatively few weapons returned to Cuba aboard the yacht *Granma,* and the revolutionary war whose episodes are recounted in these pages began to unfold.

Che, as Ernesto Guevara was called by his Cuban comrades, was twenty-seven at the time, two years out of medical school in Buenos Aires, Argentina, when he met Fidel Castro. He had spent most of the preceding three and a half years traveling through the Americas. Riding a motorcycle, then hitching transportation in trucks, boats, rafts, and planes, bumming food wherever possible, Guevara immersed himself in the lives, culture, and, increasingly, the struggles of the peoples of the Americas.

In December 1953 Guevara arrived in Guatemala, drawn by the popular upsurge that accompanied the limited land reform program being advanced by the government of Jacobo Arbenz. In pre–land reform Guatemala, counting each imperialist-based corporation as one person, 98 percent of Guatemala's cultivated land was owned by 142 people.[2] The United Fruit Company, one of the biggest landowners, and its government in Washington responded to the threat that even this timid land reform represented to propertied interests by organizing a mercenary army to overthrow the Arbenz regime in 1954.

Along with thousands of Guatemalans, Guevara volunteered to fight, but Arbenz rejected arming the population and resigned. As the mercenary troops entered Guatemala City and began massacring supporters of the Arbenz regime, Guevara took refuge in the Argentine embassy, and in September 1954 escaped to Mexico.

In Guatemala Guevara had become friends with Ñico López, a veteran of the assault on the "Carlos Manuel de Céspedes" army barracks in Bayamo in 1953. López and several other participants in the Bayamo action had escaped arrest and fled Cuba, ending up in Costa Rica and Guatemala.[3] López and Guevara found themselves together again in Mexico, where the Cuban fighter introduced his Argentine comrade to Raúl Castro and then Fidel Castro. As Fidel recalls in the 1971 speech that opens this book, he met Che a few days after arriving in Mexico:

> Because of his state of mind when he left Guatemala, because of the extremely bitter experience he'd lived through there—that cowardly aggression against the country, the interruption of a process that had awakened the hopes of the

2. The figure is cited from John Gerassi, *The Great Fear: The Reconquest of Latin America by Latin Americans* (New York: Macmillan, 1963), p. 164.
3. Of the twenty-one veterans of the 1953 actions who later joined the eighty-two-man *Granma* expedition, four had been part of the assault on the Bayamo garrison: Antonio "Ñico" López, Calixto García, Enrique Cámara, and Antonio Darío López. Guevara had met Calixto García and another Bayamo veteran in Costa Rica before arriving in Guatemala, where he met Ñico López and his comrades.

> people—because of his revolutionary vocation, his spirit of struggle, we can't say it took hours, we can say that in a matter of minutes Che decided to join the small group of Cubans who were working on organizing a new phase of the struggle in our country.[4]

"Che wasn't Che then," Castro added. "He was Ernesto Guevara. It was because of the Argentine custom of calling people 'Che' that the Cubans began calling him Che." That was how he got the name he later made famous.

Throughout this period, in addition to holding down a number of odd jobs, Guevara worked on and off at hospitals and other places related to his medical training. But, as letters to his family attest, he found himself drawn more and more to a serious study of Marxism. "My path seems to diverge gradually and firmly from clinical medicine," he wrote his mother in August or September 1956. "St. Karl," as he humorously referred to Karl Marx, "has won a studious adherent."[5] On the eve of departure aboard the *Granma,* he explained:

> I'm in the process of changing the direction of my studies. In the past, for better or worse, I concentrated on medicine while devoting my free time to an informal study of St. Karl. The new stage of my life demands a change in the direction of my studies as well. St. Karl now comes first. He is the axis of my studies and will remain so for the years that remain to me in the outermost layer of this spheroid. . . .
>
> In addition, I was beginning to draw a series of conclusions that clashed sharply with my trajectory as fundamentally an adventurer. I decided to tackle first things first, to enter into battle against the way things are, a shield upon my arm, full

4. See page 65.
5. Ernesto Che Guevara, in Ernesto Guevara Lynch, *Aquí va un soldado de América* (Here goes a soldier of the Americas) (Buenos Aires: Editorial Sudamericana/Planeta, 1987), p. 149.

> of dreams; and then, if the windmills didn't crack my skull, to write.[6]

Guevara departed Mexico as the troop's doctor. In the battle of Alegría de Pío, the first episode of the revolutionary war described here, he tells how he had to choose between rescuing a knapsack full of medicine or salvaging a box of ammunition. After brief hesitation, he picked up the ammunition.

Six months later he became the first combatant to earn the rank of commander, leading the first column separate from the nucleus directed by Fidel. Within two years, as columns led by Commander in Chief Fidel Castro closed the encirclement of Santiago, Che commanded the Rebel Army campaign in Las Villas province to the west that cut the island in two, capturing Santa Clara, Cuba's third largest city. The fate of the Batista dictatorship was sealed.

■

"The war revolutionized us," Guevara wrote to Ernesto Sábato, a prominent Argentine novelist, in 1960:

> There is no more profound experience for a revolutionary than the act of war; not the isolated act of killing, or of carrying a rifle, or of undertaking a struggle of this or that type. It is the totality of the war itself, knowing that an armed man is worth something as a combat entity, and is worth as much as any other armed man, and no longer fears other armed men.
>
> It is the process of continuing to explain to the defenseless peasants how they can take up a rifle and prove to the soldiers that an armed peasant is worth as much as the best of them; of continuing to learn how the efforts of one are

6. Guevara, letter from Mexico to his mother, October 1956, in Guevara Lynch, p. 152.

> worthless if not surrounded by the efforts of all.
>
> It is the process of continuing to learn how revolutionary slogans have to reflect the deep aspirations of the people, and of continuing to learn from the people what their most deeply felt desires are, and to transform these into banners of political agitation.
>
> This we have all been doing, and we understood that the peasants' yearning for land was the most powerful motive of struggle that could be found in Cuba.[7]

As Guevara explained on several occasions, he did not foresee the opening of the socialist revolution in the Americas as the outcome of the revolutionary war in Cuba. Based on his knowledge of the history of Latin America, and his reading of books, including those written by Marxists, he was convinced that the forces being assembled under the leadership of Fidel Castro could bring down the Batista tyranny, one of the bloodiest yet seen in the long list of Latin American dictatorships. That was an objective for which he was willing to give his life. But he thought that imperialist dollars and bourgeois greed would then once again assert their dominance, and the revolution would go the way of all movements trying to reform capitalism.

The workers and peasants of Cuba would teach Che that a different outcome was possible.

As the war transformed the Rebel Army, and the July 26 Movement as well, Guevara's assessment of the social and class dynamics of the revolution, including the course of the central leadership of the movement, changed also. The turning point came in December 1957, as he explains in the chapter "One Year of Armed Struggle." That was when Fidel Castro, speaking for the leadership of the July 26 Movement, publicly repudiated an agreement among bourgeois opposition forces, known as the Miami Pact, after its drafters falsely claimed that the document, which contained both public and secret clauses, had been signed

7. See page 407.

by authorized representatives of the July 26 Movement.

Throughout the *Episodes*, Guevara tells much of the story of the July 26 Movement's unceasing, though generally unsuccessful, efforts to secure arms and money from the parties that opposed the Batista dictatorship but had come to fear even more the growing organization and confidence of the armed workers and peasants. "The opposition groups were varied and dissimilar," Che wrote, "even though most had as a common denominator the wish to take power (read: public funds) for themselves. This brought in its wake a sordid internal struggle to win that victory."

The July 26 leadership fought throughout the revolutionary war to win political leadership of the broadest possible forces influenced by the bourgeois parties. The stakes were high: preventing those parties from coalescing and mobilizing Washington's support behind them in order to usurp the victory being won by the Rebel Army at the head of a popular insurrection.

Fidel Castro's December 14, 1957, letter, on behalf of the July 26 Movement, repudiating the Miami Pact—printed in full by Guevara in the single longest chapter of the *Episodes*—was the turning point in the political battle. Thousands of copies were produced by the fledgling print shop (a mimeograph machine brought up to the Sierra) and propaganda apparatus of the Rebel Army under Guevara's command. Then, during a window of opportunity when press censorship was briefly lifted by the Batista regime, *Bohemia*, the most widely circulated weekly magazine in Cuba, published the letter in full in a print run of half a million copies.

While the long record of negotiations with all the diverse forces made clear that compromise on many points of difference was possible in order to maintain unity, "what is important for the revolution is not unity in itself, but the principles on which it is based," Castro's letter stated.

> No matter how desperate our situation in face of thousands of the dictatorship's troops mobilized to annihilate us, and

> perhaps with more determination because of it (since nothing is more humiliating than to accept an onerous condition under trying circumstances), we would never accept the sacrifice of certain principles that are fundamental to our conception of the Cuban revolution.[8]

Those conditions had been contained in an earlier agreement with some of the forces behind the betrayal of the Miami Pact, especially former National Bank head Felipe Pazos, who thought he deserved praise for not being corrupt, and the "absolute mediocrity" Raúl Chibás. Guevara colorfully describes them both as "two Stone Age mentalities" imbued with deep antipathy to the peasants' demands for agrarian reform.

Two principles were omitted from the Miami document, Castro wrote: first, "the explicit declaration that we reject every form of foreign intervention in the internal affairs of Cuba," that is, not only aid to Batista but any other attempt to determine the course of events in Cuba; and, second, "the explicit rejection of any kind of military junta as a provisional government of the republic," that is, rejection of any government that did not derive its legitimacy, authority, and composition from the hard-won victory of the insurrectionary forces.

Moreover, the secret clauses of the Miami Pact provided that "the revolutionary forces are to be incorporated, with their weapons, into the regular armed bodies of the republic," a condition the July 26 leadership categorically repudiated as an invitation to "gangsterism and anarchy."

"The July 26 Movement claims for itself the role of maintaining public order and reorganizing the armed forces of the republic," Castro responded, with a conviction born of hard-won experience in the mountains dealing with banditry and crime unleashed by the disintegration of the old repressive order, and often carried out by those camouflaging themselves as part of the guerrillas. No other force could guarantee the revolution-

8. See page 277.

ary victory and maintain public order.

With the rejection of the Miami Pact, the deepening social revolution in the Sierras, led by the vanguard forces of the Rebel Army, was strengthened, and the march toward the establishment of a popular revolutionary government of the workers and peasants accelerated. But these two factors were intertwined. Without the victories of the first year of struggle in the Sierras, without the growing support of the peasantry, without the increasing political homogeneity of a battle-tested cadre committed to deep-going social transformation, the uncompromising rejection of the Miami Pact would not have been possible either.

■

Throughout the *Episodes* we can follow the birth of the first free territory of the Americas, high in the Sierra Maestra, as the guerrilla forces grew strong enough to win the confidence and collaboration of the peasants, and as the declining morale of the dictatorship's troops enlarged the terrain the army treated as a no-go zone.

Out of the poverty, hopes, and dignity of the men and women of the Sierra, out of the struggle for change, new social relations began to emerge, at the center of which was the land reform, the right of each peasant family to the land they tilled. Military Order no. 1, issued by Guevara as the commander in chief of the Las Villas region during the closing months of the war, reprinted here as part of the documents from the Las Villas campaign, underscores the place of land reform in the revolutionary program of the advancing Rebel Army: "Every peasant who for at least two years has been paying rent, either in cash or in kind, for working a parcel of land in the territory covered by this military order is hereby declared free of all payment obligations and is invited to claim his rights over the land he works."[9]

The new legal system emerged as a reflection of already chang-

9. See page 374.

ing social practice, Guevara noted, before any written law of the Sierra had been promulgated. The land reform, for example, had begun well before Law no. 3 of the Rebel Army was issued on October 10, 1958, granting land to the tillers.

"The execution of antisocial individuals who took advantage of the prevailing atmosphere in the area to commit crimes was, unfortunately, not infrequent," Che writes. But such severe measures had the "full public blessing" of the local residents, Fidel points out in the letter rejecting the Miami Pact.

> The local residents, accustomed in the past to viewing agents of authority as enemies of the people, offered protection and shelter to those fleeing from the former system of justice. Now, when they see our soldiers as defenders of their interests, the most complete order prevails; and the best guardians of it are the citizens themselves.[10]

The great miracle of the revolution, Guevara writes, is "the rediscovery by the Cuban peasant of his own happiness." The happy, hearty laughter that can be heard in the new Sierra flows from "the self-confidence that the awareness of his own strength gave to the inhabitant of our liberated area."

Guevara's description of El Hombrito, the base where his column took steps to establish the first industries—a forge and crude armory, an oven for baking bread, a leather goods shop, preparations for hydroelectric generation of power, a newspaper, *El Cubano Libre*, and later the increasingly important Radio Rebelde—provide a glimpse of life in the liberated Sierra. The total destruction of that base in a matter of hours by the forces under the command of Ángel Sánchez Mosquera, "the bravest, the most murderous, and one of the most thieving of all of Batista's military chieftains," was a bitter lesson in the limits imposed by war, as well.

The Sierra peasants longing for land to till, the exhausted

10. See page 281.

women condemned to too much work on too meager a diet, and the children whose bellies were distended with parasites, taught Che in the course of day-to-day struggle that revolutions are not born directly of a set of ideas or from the history of previous revolutions, but from the line of march of a class fighting for its liberation.

The opening of the socialist revolution in Cuba turned out to be much closer than any of the revolutionary combatants thought when they began their struggle. It came about because—with growing political clarity and leadership capacity forged in battle—they refused to be diverted from that line of march and the confrontation with imperialism it provoked.

In the eyes of the North American rulers, Guevara wrote in a 1960 letter printed in these pages, "we constitute the great fraud of the century: we stated the truth in an attempt to deceive." To Washington

> the words "We will nationalize public services," were to be read as "We will prevent this from happening if we receive a reasonable amount of support." The words "We will eliminate the system of large landed estates," were to be read as: "We will utilize the large landed estates as a good source of funding for our political campaigns, or for our personal enrichment." And so on and so forth. It never entered their heads that what Fidel Castro and our Movement were saying so candidly and sharply was what we actually intended to do.[11]

■

Throughout the *Episodes of the Cuban Revolutionary War*, Guevara also describes his evolution as a political leader among the cadre of the July 26 Movement. Working together with Fidel Castro, Che learned the revolutionary art of uniting diverse

11. See page 408.

forces around the central objective of taking power, while avoiding premature conflicts and allowing time and experience in struggle to create the conditions in which differences could be settled in practice if not superseded. Fidel's course was to fight from a political base in the Sierra to win the uncontested leadership of those social forces that, unlike the bourgeois parties, *were* committed to the insurrectional struggle to overthrow the Batista regime.

Throughout the book, we see how the leadership of the July 26 Movement charted a course to forge a revolutionary united front with the student-based Revolutionary Directorate, which maintained its own political and military structures during the war. We follow this political evolution from the Mexico Pact signed by Fidel Castro and José Antonio Echeverría in August 1956; to the assault on the Presidential Palace in March 1957, in which Echeverría and other Revolutionary Directorate leaders were killed; to the split in the Directorate's forces that gave rise to the current known as the Second National Front of the Escambray, whose cattle rustling and thievery, Guevara said, was responsible for "sowing more terror than Batista's army"; to the Pedrero Pact between the July 26 Movement and Revolutionary Directorate during the final push toward victory in December 1958.

With careful precision, Guevara also sketches the relations between the July 26 Movement and the Popular Socialist Party, the name taken in 1944 by the Communist Party. "The PSP joined with us in certain concrete actions, but mutual distrust hampered joint action and, fundamentally, the party of the workers did not understand with sufficient clarity the role of the guerrilla force, nor the place of Fidel in our revolutionary struggle," Guevara writes.

Guevara recounts a discussion he once had with a PSP leader during the war. "You are capable of creating cadres who can silently endure the most terrible tortures in jail," Guevara told him, "but you cannot create cadres who can take a machine gun nest." This PSP leader, Guevara writes, later repeated this observation to others "as an accurate characterization of that period."

"As I saw it from my guerrilla vantage point," Guevara continued, "this was a consequence of [the PSP's] strategic conception: a determination to struggle against imperialism and the abuses of the exploiting classes, together with an inability to envision the possibility of taking power."[12]

Each of these three forces—the July 26 Movement, the Revolutionary Directorate, and the Popular Socialist Party—was put to the test in the course of the deep-going revolution described in these pages, and a process of political differentiation and transformation took place within and among them. Following the defeat of the Batista regime, and under the leadership of the July 26 Movement and Rebel Army that had organized the victorious popular revolution, the forces that emerged from these organizations and from this experience came together to form a united party that in 1965 took the name Communist Party of Cuba.

Guevara's most concentrated political education took place within the July 26 Movement itself. In the chapters "One Year of Armed Struggle" and "A Decisive Meeting," Che explains how Fidel successfully worked to bring about a revolutionary political resolution of differences between "two quite clearly defined tendencies" within the July 26 Movement, known as the *Sierra* [mountains] and the *Llano* [plains]. "Differences over strategic conception separated us," Guevara notes, above all over counterposed assessments of the vanguard position of the Rebel Army in creating the political and military conditions for victory. The Llano current saw the work in the cities, Guevara says, "as having greater relative importance than the Sierra."

The frictions were ongoing, and sometimes intermixed with differences within the July 26 Movement over broader class and political perspectives. As Guevara describes in the chapter "The

12. See pp. 268–69.

Second Battle of Pino del Agua," when a broadening polemic threatened to erupt, Fidel stepped in to prevent it and allow the differences to begin being resolved in a revolutionary direction, as the entire leadership of the July 26 Movement united around a public repudiation of the Miami Pact. This was an important leadership lesson for Che. "It is important to point out," he emphasizes, "that the fighters against the dictatorship in both the Sierra and Llano were able to hold opinions on tactics that were at times diametrically opposed, without having this lead to abandoning the insurrectional struggle."

The resolution of the conflicts came later in 1958, following the disastrous outcome of the April 9 general strike called by the July 26 Movement's National Directorate, despite the strong reservations of the Sierra about the adequacy of its preparation. At a May 3 gathering of the National Directorate held in the Sierra Maestra, which Guevara describes in the chapter "A Decisive Meeting," those who had been centrally responsible for the April 9 action were replaced in their Llano responsibilities and reassigned to the Sierra. The national leadership was reorganized.

Fidel Castro was elected general secretary of the July 26 Movement and was named commander in chief of all armed forces, including the Llano militias. The Sierra leaders assumed undisputed political guidance of the movement, their authority having been won as a consequence of "their accurate interpretation of events."

The defeat of the April 9 general strike led to some dark days for the rebel forces, as Guevara describes, and opened the door to the final "encircle and annihilate" offensive mounted in the Sierra by the Batista regime. On May 25 an invasion column some 10,000-strong was sent into the mountains to wipe out the combatants of the Rebel Army—at that time numbering 300, with 200 usable weapons.

The Batista army's advance into the Sierra did prove to be its final offensive, but it did not succeed in encircling the Rebel Army, let alone annihilating it. With the victory by the revolutionary forces at El Jigüe in July, the tide turned once again, and the rebels' retreat was over. "Once the regiments that assaulted the Sierra Maestra had been wiped out, once the front had returned to its normal level, and once our troops had increased their strength and morale," Guevara recounts, "it was decided to begin the march on the central province of Las Villas." Guevara was placed in command of that new front.

The final march toward victory accelerated toward New Year's Day 1959.

■

The Rebel Army was a political vanguard organization, built around an expanding cadre that was painstakingly selected and tested in battle. As the revolutionary war advanced, these cadres became more educated and more politically homogeneous in the process.

Out of the eighty-two combatants who participated in the *Granma* expedition, Fidel Castro told Italian journalist Gianni Minà in 1987, "there were many young men who, had they survived the initial expedition, were well suited to become leaders. At least fifteen or twenty outstanding leaders could have emerged from our group—because a man needs both the opportunity and responsibilities to distinguish himself." The accuracy of this judgment, Fidel noted, was confirmed by the fact that "out of those few who survived, several brilliant leaders emerged," men such as Che, Raúl Castro, and Camilo Cienfuegos.[13]

Fidel, like Che, first "looked for men and women who are made of good timber," is the way a former Rebel Army combatant, today a brigadier general in Cuba's Revolutionary Armed Forces, explained it. If the human material is there, "it can be

13. Fidel Castro, interview June 28–29, 1987, in Gianni Minà, *Un encuentro con Fidel* (An encounter with Fidel) (Havana: Oficina de Publicaciones del Consejo de Estado, 1987), p. 318.

shaped. Leaders who are forged in adverse conditions develop a deep sense of fraternity, of comradeship, knowing that human beings need each other, cannot live as hermits like Robinson Crusoe. In order to withstand the hostile environment of the Sierra, to really be able to fight, one has to be part of a collective effort. In such a context human qualities are born, allowing future leaders to be forged."[14]

Throughout the pages of the *Episodes*, we are introduced to hundreds of the men and women whose courage and capacities made possible the Cuban revolution; and we see in turn, how they grew into the fighters and leaders they became.

"Men may contribute to the making of history," Castro tells the people of San Miguel in Santiago de Chile in the speech about Che at the opening of this volume, "but history also makes men."

Among those we meet are some of the legendary heroes and heroines of the Cuban revolution. People like Frank País, leader of the Santiago underground, whose "calm lesson in order and discipline" made such an impression on Che when País visited their camp in the Sierra; Celia Sánchez, organizer of the July 26 Movement's first peasant cells in the Sierra before the *Granma* landing, the person responsible for the urban supply and recruitment network for the Rebel Army, and the first woman to join the Rebel Army and then the Sierra leadership; Camilo Cienfuegos, *Granma* expeditionary and rebel commander whose bravery and good humor made him one of the most beloved of the guerrilla leaders.

Even more centrally, however, we learn how "the revolution has been built on many sincere efforts on the part of simple men." We watch as those who join the Rebel Army are tested, the human material sifted, and those who are made of good tim-

14. Interview with Harry Villegas, brigadier general of the Revolutionary Armed Forces of Cuba, in the *Militant*, December 18, 1995. Villegas was one of the young Rebel Army recruits who distinguished himself in the war. He later accompanied Che to the Congo and Bolivia.

ber distinguish themselves.

Che refers to the daily "struggle against the lack of physical, ideological, and moral preparation among the combatants" newly arrived. He describes how many were discharged and sent away after a period of testing. Others, he notes, developed what the combatants called "the hunted look." That look was "incompatible with guerrilla life," Guevara says—a sure sign that someone was getting ready to "shift into third" and risk the death penalty for desertion, rather than continue to face the psychological and physical hardships of life in the mountains.

Che tells the story of one of the many whose departure served to strengthen, not weaken, the fighting morale of the troops: "He had an attack of nerves, there in the solitude of the mountains and the guerrilla camp," Che writes. "He began to shout that he had been promised a camp with abundant food and antiaircraft defenses, but instead the planes were hounding him and he had neither permanent quarters, nor food, nor even water to drink.

"This was more or less the same impression that all new guerrillas had of campaign life." Guevara continues. "Afterward, those who stayed and passed the first tests grew accustomed to dirt, to lack of water, food, shelter, and security, and to a life where the only things one could rely on were a rifle and the cohesion and resistance of the small guerrilla nucleus."

The high level of discipline and fighting morale of the guerrilla fighters was not sustained on the basis of coercion, however. As Guevara explains in the chapter "An Unpleasant Incident," discipline was effective above all as it became a byproduct of the growing political homogeneity and commitment to the social program that was being implemented in practice as the revolution deepened its roots among the peasants of the Sierra. Che writes:

> Our revolutionary war was already beginning to acquire new characteristics. The consciousness of the leaders and the

> combatants was being deepened. We were beginning to feel in our flesh and blood the need for an agrarian reform and for profound and integral changes in the social structure that had to be carried out in order to cleanse the country. But this deepening consciousness among the best and the most numerous part of our fighters provoked clashes with those elements who had joined the struggle solely out of a lust for adventure, or perhaps not just for laurels, but for material gain as well.[15]

It is not surprising that among those who not only stayed and fought but rose to become lieutenants, captains, and commanders before the end of 1958, one recognizes the names of a strikingly large percentage of those who have been in the front ranks of leadership of the Cuban revolution for almost forty years.

The power of the events Che recounts comes in greatest measure, however, from the portraits of the ordinary men and women who joined in the revolutionary struggle, risking and often giving everything, including their lives. Men and women like Julio Zenón Acosta, Che's first pupil who, like hundreds of other combatants, was learning to read as part of becoming a Rebel Army cadre; Oniria, the very young woman combatant who demands to know if she too has the right to vote like the fighters who are men; Vaquerito, the head of the courageous and youthful "suicide squad" who is killed in the final days of the battle for Santa Clara; Crucito, the guerrilla bard whose ballads die with him at Pino del Agua; and hundreds more.

■

Every social movement lives within the channels of its own history and continuity. To mine the richness of the events Gue-

15. See page 226.

vara describes in *Episodes of the Cuban Revolutionary War,* the reader is obliged to enter the world of the Rebel Army combatants themselves. We need to learn a few of the often-cited names and places and events that are part of the revolutionary history and traditions of Cuba's century-long struggle to eradicate slavery, win freedom from Spanish colonial rule, and then break the stranglehold of U.S. imperialist domination.

Legendary figures abound: Simón Bolívar, hero of Latin America's struggle for independence from Spain; José Martí, great leader of Cuba's final struggle for independence, killed in battle in 1895; Máximo Gómez, Dominican-born general who was commander in chief of the independence forces in two wars against Spain; Antonio Maceo, the Bronze Titan, as he is known in Cuba, who led a military column from eastern to western Cuba in the independence war of 1895–98. Often a simple reference to a name such as these is sufficient to an audience in Cuba to imply an entire political course or military strategy, or to provide a timely warning that needs no further elaboration.

To aid the reader in politically understanding this world of the Cuban revolutionary struggle, extensive footnotes and glossary entries have been provided.

Episodes of the Cuban Revolutionary War is also a book about war, written by a military leader of exceptional ability. In the letter reprinted here repudiating the Miami Pact, Fidel Castro criticizes the signers for their "regrettable underestimation of the military importance of the struggle in Oriente," pointing out that "what is being waged at present in the Sierra Maestra is not guerrilla warfare but a war of columns," and explaining the political significance of that evolution of the rebels' military organization.

Guevara's accounts both give and demand attention to the details of war: to the weapons used; to the sounds of battle; to questions of military tactics and strategy and their interconnections; to the differences between guerrilla warfare and regular warfare; to command structure and order of battle;

to military training, discipline, and morale; to the political education of the troops; and much more. The reader learns in almost every battle, for example, what weapons combatants are carrying, and why it is sometimes a life-or-death matter who has a Thompson submachine gun, who a Springfield bolt-action rifle, and who a Garand semiautomatic. We learn how the best soldiers have earned the best rifles available by their conduct in battle *before* they possessed those rare and precious weapons.

The reader also sees what happens as the fighting morale of a dictatorship's army declines. Che describes how, in the twilight of the U.S.-backed tyranny, Batista's soldiers became "deaf to every suspicious sound," thereby easing the movement of the Rebel Forces. He recounts how, out of fear of ambush and improved accuracy of the rebel riflemen, the regime's soldiers more and more refused to take the point on patrol.

Numerous maps, battle sketches, and diagrams have been provided, to make it easier to follow the military campaign, along with charts that show the command structure and the branching-off of new columns and fronts as the Rebel Army grew and its zones of operations and political influence expanded.

■

Episodes of the Cuban Revolutionary War was written as a series of articles that appeared in the pages of *Verde Olivo* [Olive Drab], the weekly publication of the Revolutionary Armed Forces (FAR). The first article, on the battle of Alegría de Pío was published in February 1961; the last of the *Verde Olivo* articles, "A Decisive Meeting," appeared in November 1964.

A few months later, in March 1965, Guevara resigned his leadership responsibilities and posts in Cuba and left, first for the Congo (today Zaïre) and then, after returning to Cuba for several months, Bolivia.

In Bolivia, Guevara led an eleven-month campaign to begin

forging a fighting movement of workers and peasants that could advance the revolution in the Americas. In October 1967 he was wounded in battle, captured, and murdered by the Bolivian Army under Washington's guiding hand. The story of that campaign is told in Guevara's *Bolivian Diary,* also published in English translation by Pathfinder.

The first collection of Che's articles on the Cuban revolutionary war to appear in book form was published in 1963 by Ediciones Unión, the publishing house of the Union of Writers and Artists of Cuba, even before the *Verde Olivo* series had been completed. The first edition in English followed in 1967, published in Cuba by the Cuban Book Institute.

In addition to the articles that appeared as part of the *Episodes* series, Guevara wrote dozens of other contributions on many subjects for *Verde Olivo* between 1959 and 1964. As head of political education of the Revolutionary Armed Forces during part of that time, he took a special interest in the materials that appeared in the magazine and worked with the editorial leadership responsible for its production.

In Guevara's introduction to the *Verde Olivo* series that appeared in February 1961 along with the first installment, "Alegría de Pío," Guevara explains his intention to make a contribution to the monumental task of recording the history of the insurrectional struggle before an accurate memory of those events, "which already belong to the history of the Americas," dissolves into the past.

By beginning to put down his own reminiscences of the major events in which he participated, Guevara hoped to encourage other survivors of the revolutionary war to contribute in a similar way. They did so, week after week in the pages of *Verde Olivo.*

"I ask only that the narrator be strictly truthful," Guevara charged. "He should not present any inaccuracy in order to clarify his own role, exaggerate it, or claim to have been where he was not."

Che's insistence on historical accuracy, his war on exaggeration and retrospective self-aggrandizement, is a theme that runs throughout the pages of the book, including the letters to other veteran combatants. His October 1963 letter to *Granma* expeditionary Pablo Díaz González, for example, is a gem of Che's bluntly humorous style:

> Pablo: I read your article. I must thank you for how well you portray me; too well, I think. Furthermore, it seems you portray yourself pretty well too. The first thing a revolutionary who writes history has to do is stick to the truth like a finger inside a glove. You did that, but it was a boxing glove.

Guevara's concern for accuracy was reflected in the way he worked on preparing these articles. They were not quickly thrown together recollections, as someone might innocently assume from their brevity and transparent clarity; they were carefully prepared and thoroughly researched contributions. Luis Pavón, the editor of *Verde Olivo* during the period the *Episodes* were written, described how Che prepared them.

The first articles by Che, Pavón wrote, "were based fundamentally on his diary, on photographs taken in the Sierra Maestra, and on his own personal memory.

"Demanding in everything—and above all with himself—he constantly revised his opinions, compared them with those of other comrades, and in that way assembled his narratives in his own mind. Later he dictated them into a tape recorder that his secretary, Comrade Manresa, would transcribe. Che would then edit them over and over again with exemplary rigor."[16]

In drafting the articles from the September 1957 battle of Pino del Agua onward, Che had no diary to refer to. Those articles were "based on his recollections and those of other combatants.

16. Luis Pavón, in *Días de combate* (Days of combat) (Havana: Instituto del Libro, 1970), p. vi.

On various occasions he assembled together, in a meeting room of the Ministry of Industry, combatants who had been participants in the action to be related. Amid jokes and anecdotes, he would start to piece together maps and diagrams, spread out over the table, noting down people's responses. . . . In this way he reconstructed the battle, submitting to analysis each individual version, correcting them, eliminating exaggerations, until the most exact version was obtained."

All this was done while Guevara was carrying an enormous leadership load of other party, government, and military responsibilities. As a leading public spokesperson for the revolutionary government, he was deeply involved in internationalist work. And throughout these years, based on direct experience in beginning to transform the factory system and economic management in Cuba, Guevara was also putting down on paper the most valuable contributions on the practical connection between economics and politics that the workers movement has had since those of the leadership team forged by Lenin in the course of the Bolshevik-led revolution in Russia.

Che, as Pavón recounts, was "president of the National Bank and head of the Department of Instruction (today the Political Directorate) of the Revolutionary Armed Forces; minister of industry and head of the Army Corps of Pinar del Río; Cuba's representative at international events of special importance, etc; in addition to being a tireless student of political economy and of the classics of Marxism, constantly working in agriculture, promoter of scientific and cultural initiatives, etc. In the midst of this activity he continued writing his narratives, although the time gap between articles grew longer and longer."

As Guevara says in his 1961 introductory note, in preparing these episodes, he was not trying to write the history of the war. The legacy he left was something more important: the political history of the maturing of the Rebel Army as a modern revolutionary leadership of the workers and peasants, reflected through the coming of age of Che, as he gains unshakable confidence in the men and women who are capable of remaking the world.

■

Episodes of the Cuban Revolutionary War is a masterpiece of narrative writing in the Spanish language, some of the beauty of which survives even in English translation. The terrible eloquence of Guevara's description of the rout at Alegría de Pío is hard to forget:

> Then everything became a blur, as low-flying planes strafed the field. This only added to the confusion, with scenes ranging from the Dantesque to the grotesque—such as a comrade of considerable corpulence desperately trying to hide behind a single stalk of sugarcane, while in the midst of the din of gunfire another man kept on yelling "Silence!" for no apparent reason.

Che was "a magnificent writer and understandably paid careful attention to the literary structure of his works," Pavón noted. "But I dare to assert that for him this was secondary. What interested him was *historical truth*. If his writings are astonishing for their style and fluidity, if they are justly categorized by commander Fidel Castro as classics of our language, this is precisely because what motivated him was not merely literary concerns. He wrote not to show his hand as a writer—an art he mastered and loved—but because he had something to say."

■

Numerous editions of *Episodes of the Cuban Revolutionary War* have appeared in both Spanish and English since the original volume in 1963. No two have had exactly the same contents. This edition largely follows the version published in volume 2 of *Escritos y discursos* (Writings and speeches) of Ernesto Che Guevara, published in Havana by Editorial de Ciencias Sociales in 1977, as well as a new Spanish-language edition being prepared by Editora Política for publication in 1996.

Two previous English-language editions, both published in 1968—one by International Publishers, the other by Monthly Review press—have long been out of print. A special run of the Monthly Review edition appeared under a co-imprint with Merit Publishers, predecessor of Pathfinder Press.

This new and expanded Pathfinder edition is the first in English to include the entire *Verde Olivo* series. It also incorporates several articles written by Guevara for other publications and considerable additional material never before published in English.

Among the ample collection of historical photographs in these pages are a number that appear here in print for the first time.

The last of the *Episodes* Guevara completed for *Verde Olivo* was "A Decisive Meeting." The narrative "From Batista's Final Offensive to the Battle of Santa Clara" was written well before the *Verde Olivo* series began, in May 1959, for the Brazilian magazine *O Cruzeiro*. Similarly the opening chapter in this edition, "A Revolution Begins," also appeared in that Brazilian publication in 1959. The chapter "War and the Peasant Population" was originally published in *Lunes de Revolución*, the Monday cultural supplement to the Havana daily *Revolución*, the newspaper of the July 26 Movement. It was later incorporated into Guevara's book *Guerrilla Warfare: A Method.* "The Murdered Puppy," previously unpublished in English, first appeared in the magazine *Humanismo*.

Articles written for the *Episodes* series that have not before appeared in any English-language edition include "The Battle of Mar Verde," "Interlude," and "A Decisive Meeting." "The Second Battle of Pino del Agua" is published here in full for the first time in English.

The articles have been arranged chronologically, based on the events described. The three "Portraits of Revolutionaries," which are not part of the narrative sequence of events, have been included here as a separate section.

Two additional sections have been added. One presents reports, letters, and other documents written by Guevara during the course of the Las Villas campaign from September to December 1958. These provide a more detailed account of this decisive chapter of the revolutionary war, which is briefly dealt with in the 1959 article "From Batista's Final Offensive to the Battle of Santa Clara."

We have also included a number of letters by Guevara related to the events covered in his narrative, written both during and after the revolutionary war.

Other items appearing in English translation for the first time include Guevara's Military Order no. 1 on the agrarian reform in Las Villas and the letters by Che to Enrique Oltuski, Alfredo Peña, the Las Villas Provincial Committee of the July 26 Movement, Ernesto Sábato, and Ezequiel Vieta.

Translation work for this new edition has been done by Pathfinder editor Michael Taber, who did the lion's share of the work on the notes, chronology, glossary, and index, and gathered much of the information necessary for the maps. Monthly Review press gave permission to make use of its 1968 translation by Victoria Ortiz, which has been carefully checked and substantially revised. A major part of the work has been newly translated.

Book design, as well as the cover, photo sections, and maps, were done by Eric Simpson.

Photographs and reference materials were provided by Lee Lockwood, who as a young reporter found himself in Havana on January 1, 1959, and captured for all time the faces of the revolution at the moment of victory.

This new and extensively annotated edition of *Episodes of the Cuban Revolutionary War* could not have been prepared without the generous and enthusiastic collaboration of numerous individuals and institutions in Cuba.

The aid of Editora Política, the publishing house of the Central Committee of the Communist Party of Cuba, was indispensable, beginning with the support and encouragement of Editora Política's director, Hugo Chinea.

Special appreciation, above all, goes to Iraida Aguirrechu of Editora Política, whose long hours of work, attention to detail, and determination to provide accurate information made it possible to assemble the documents, photographs, and historical data incorporated into the notes, glossary, maps, photo captions, and other special features of this edition. María Cristina Zamora and Nora Madan, both members of the Editora Política team preparing a new edition of Guevara's *Episodes* in the Spanish original, assisted in collecting and cross-checking innumerable facts, as did the Council of State Office of Historical Affairs, and Ela Hernández in the Library of the Central Committee.

Numerous veteran fighters of the Rebel Army and the July 26 Movement, many of them today officers in the Revolutionary Armed Forces of Cuba, gave generously of their time and their own personal recollections to identify names and faces, locate places on maps, and clarify historical details, large and small.

Brigadier General Harry Villegas, who fought in Guevara's column not only in the revolutionary war, but later in the Congo and Bolivia as well, was unstinting in his aid and support. Colonel Enzo Infante, historian, combatant in the November 30, 1956, uprising in Santiago de Cuba, at various times in charge of propaganda work nationally or leader of the July 26 Movement in Oriente, Camagüey, and Havana, gave many hours of his time to clarify innumerable questions.

Brigadier General Miguel Lorente, Colonel Enrique Dorta, Colonel Raúl Izquierdo, Rafael Salas, and Commander Julio García Oliveras also gave invaluable help in reviewing maps and photos and clarifying other details. Hermes Caballero, adviser to the executive committee of the Council of Ministers, and veteran of the November 30 Santiago uprising, graciously gave his time and good humor to act as courier and collaborator, as well as providing firsthand knowledge of the work of the July 26 Movement in Santiago de Cuba throughout the revolutionary war.

Historian and author Mario Mencía provided information on the leadership responsibilities of various members of the July 26 Movement.

The extensive selection of historic photographs and battle sketches, which help make the events Guevara writes about come alive, is the product of collaboration from numerous sources. Special appreciation goes to the Council of State Office of Historical Affairs; to Luis Serrano and Margarita Hernández, of the Institute of Cuban History; Frank Agüero Gómez, director of the periodical *Granma,* and Delfín Xiqués, director of *Granma's* archives; and Manuel Martínez, head of the archive department, and archivist Irelia Rivera, of the magazine *Bohemia.*

To all those who helped make this book possible, the editors extend their deepest thanks.

■

Episodes of the Cuban Revolutionary War deals with the greatest challenge facing humanity at the dawn of the twenty-first century: it chronicles the forging of a revolutionary cadre able—and willing—to lead a mass armed insurrection to power and establish a popular revolutionary government.

The war whose episodes are the subject of this book was not the end but the beginning of the greatest historic event of the second half of the twentieth century, the opening of the socialist revolution in the Americas. The story of that revolution is still being written by the creativity of millions of women and men determined to remake the world and transform themselves in the process. Almost forty years after they confidently set out on that road, the words of Che Guevara at the end of this book remain true. We Cubans have begun the struggle for our territory's total freedom, he wrote:

> We know it will not be easy, but we are all aware of the enormous historic responsibility of the July 26 Movement, of the Cuban revolution, of the nation in general, to be an

> example for all peoples of Latin America, whom we must not disappoint.
>
> Our friends of the indomitable continent can be sure that, if need be, we will struggle no matter what the economic consequence of our acts may be. And if the fight is taken further still, we shall struggle to the last drop of our rebel blood.[17]

This book is dedicated to a new generation of fighters around the world for whom the example of the Cuban revolution and the line of march of its victorious Rebel Army still show the way.

Mary-Alice Waters
January 2, 1996

17. See pp. 333–34.

HAVANA
HAVANA
MATANZAS
MATANZAS
GUANIGUANICO MTNS.
PINAR DEL RÍO
PINAR DEL RÍO
SANTA CLARA
LAS VILLAS
CIENFUEGOS
PLAYA GIRÓN
ESCAMBRAY MTNS.
ISLE OF PINES

Cuba 1956–58

ATLANTIC OCEAN
GULF OF MEXICO
Bahamas
Tuxpan
Puerto Rico
Cuba
Jamaica
Haiti
Dominican Republic
Mexico
Br. Honduras (Belize)
Honduras
Guatemala
El Salvador
CARIBBEAN SEA
Nicaragua
Costa Rica
PACIFIC OCEAN
Panama
Colombia
Venezuela

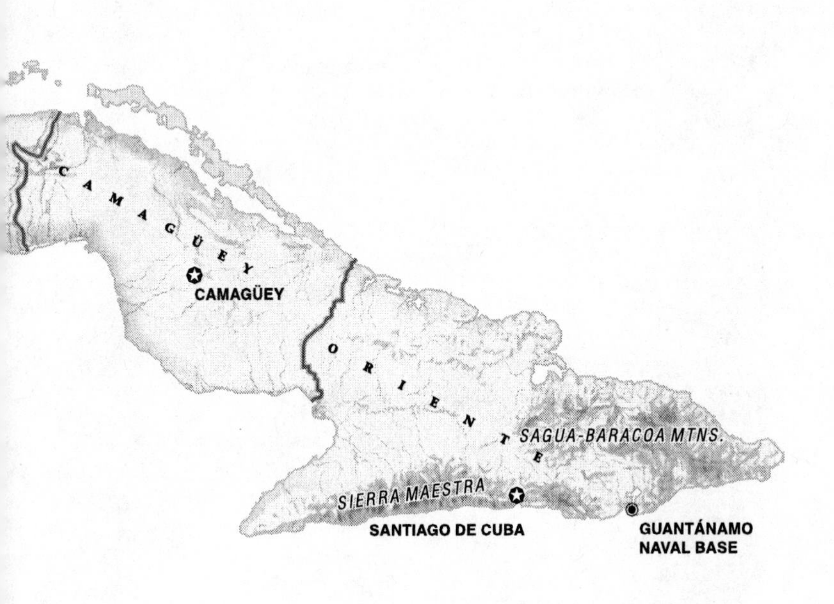
C A M A G Ü E Y
CAMAGÜEY
O R I E N T E
SAGUA-BARACOA MTNS.
SIERRA MAESTRA
SANTIAGO DE CUBA
GUANTÁNAMO
NAVAL BASE

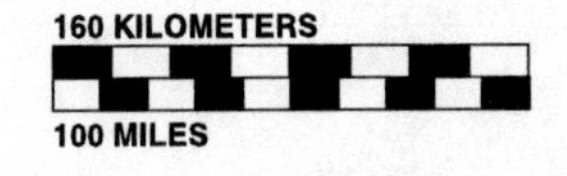
160 KILOMETERS
100 MILES

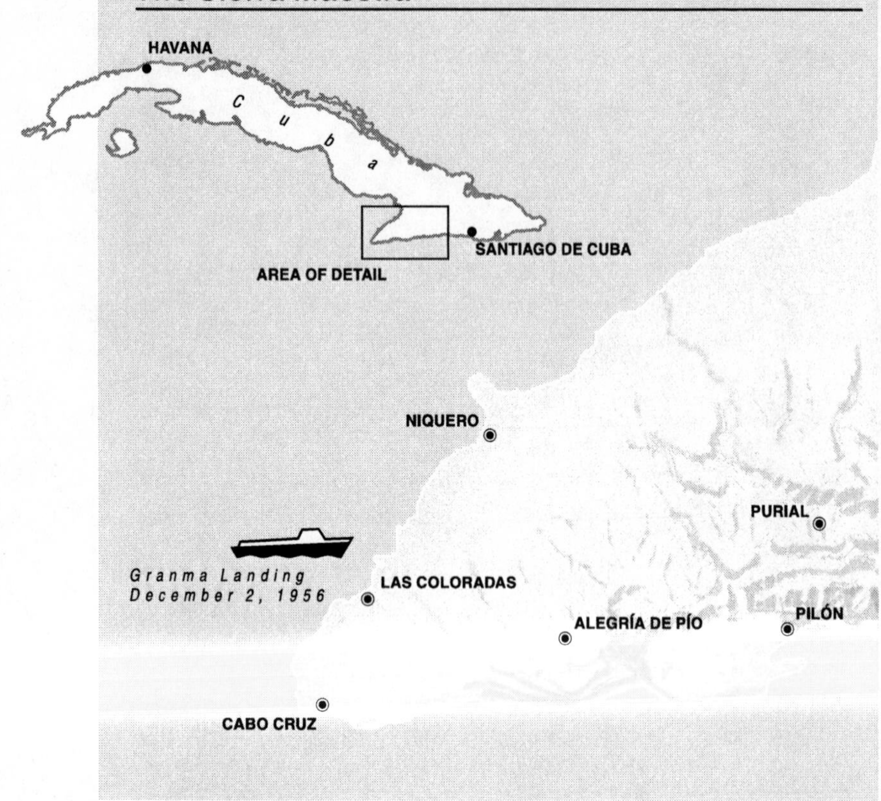
The Sierra Maestra
HAVANA
Cuba
SANTIAGO DE CUBA
AREA OF DETAIL
NIQUERO
PURIAL
Granma Landing
December 2, 1956
LAS COLORADAS
ALEGRÍA DE PÍO
PILÓN
CABO CRUZ

40 KILOMETERS
25 MILES

BAYAMO
MANZANILLO
VEGUITAS
YARA
GUISA
BUEYCITO
EL JÍBARO
ESTRADA PALMA
LOMA DEL BURRO
SAN PABLO DE YAO
EL ORO DE GUISA
LAS MERCEDES
La Botella Peak
PINO DEL AGUA
LA MONTERÍA
MOMPIÉ
ALTOS DE CONRADO
EL HOMBRITO
LA MESA
Bayamesa Peak
MINAS DEL FRÍO
EL JIGÜE
Turquino Peak
MAR VERDE
EL LOMÓN
Caracas Peak
La Plata
Palma Mocha
La Mula
Peladeros
LA DERECHA
Magdalena
ARROYO DEL INFIERNO
Altos de Espinosa
CUEVA DEL HUMO
LAS CUEVAS
EL UVERO
LA PLATA
TO SANTIAGO

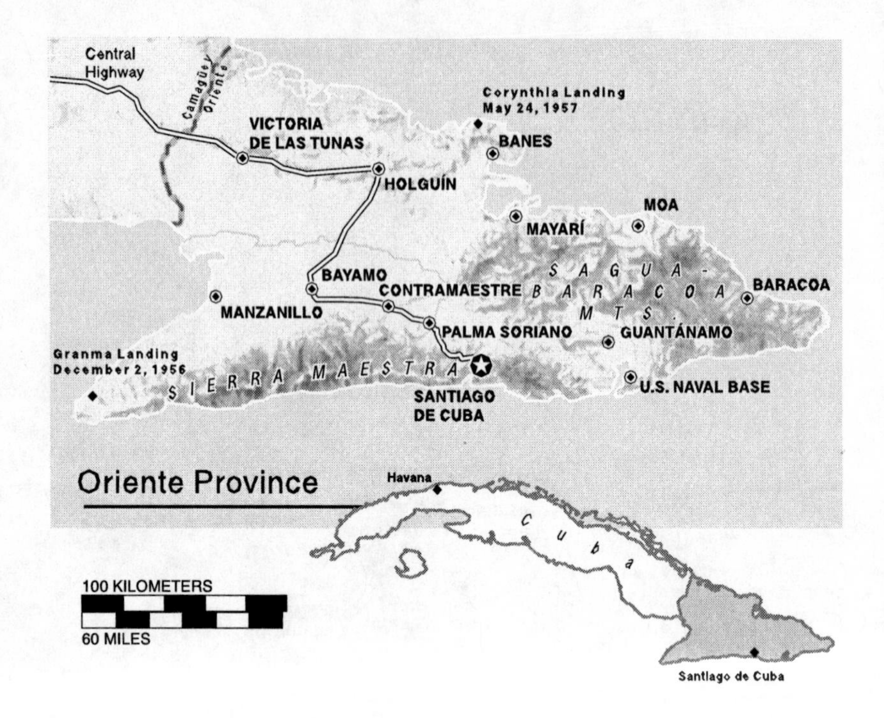
Central
Highway
Camagüey
Oriente
VICTORIA
DE LAS TUNAS
Corynthia Landing
May 24, 1957
BANES
HOLGUÍN
MOA
MAYARÍ
SAGUA-
BARACOA
MTS.
BAYAMO
CONTRAMAESTRE
BARACOA
MANZANILLO
PALMA SORIANO
GUANTÁNAMO
Granma Landing
December 2, 1956
SIERRA MAESTRA
SANTIAGO
DE CUBA
U.S. NAVAL BASE
Oriente Province
Havana
Cuba
100 KILOMETERS
60 MILES
Santiago de Cuba

Chronology

1926

August 13 – Fidel Castro is born into landowning family in Oriente province. At home, he observes contrast between his family's wealth and the impoverished conditions of peasants and immigrant Haitian and other farm workers on his father's lands. He also learns firsthand about the domination of politics by monied interests in Cuba.

From childhood, Castro attends private, all-white boarding schools in Santiago de Cuba and Havana, run by Jesuits, many with outspoken right-wing political views. In secondary school, Castro takes little interest in politics, concentrating on sports and his studies.

1928

June 14 – Ernesto Guevara is born in Rosario, Argentina, to Ernesto Guevara Lynch, a construction engineer and small businessman, and Celia de la Serna. He spends much of his elementary school years at home due to bouts with asthma and allergies. In secondary school he becomes involved in athletics and outdoor activities to limit the effects of his ailments, and begins broad reading in literature and history.

In the late 1930s his father is active in support of Spanish republic in that country's civil war and in Argentine Committee against Fascism.

1945

October – Fidel Castro enters University of Havana and becomes active in anti-imperialist student movement. He campaigns against U.S. domination of Cuba and inequalities and corruption of Authentic Party regime of Ramón Grau San Martín. As his political involvement deepens, he also begins to study works by José Martí and other Latin American revolutionary figures, as well as the *Communist Manifesto* and other Marxist literature.

1947

May 15 – Founding of Cuban People's Party—also known as Orthodox Party—a bourgeois oppositionist organization led by Eduardo Chibás. Castro is only student leader who attends founding meeting; he becomes leading figure in party's student-based youth group, which also becomes leadership of party's left-wing.

Summer – Castro joins armed expedition organized by bourgeois forces preparing to overthrow dictatorship of Rafael Leónidas Trujillo in Dominican Republic. Invasion plans are aborted as the expedition, penetrated by Trujillo's agents, is abandoned.

December – Ernesto Guevara enters medical school at University of Buenos Aires. Interested in politics, he continues his reading of works by Karl Marx and Frederick Engels he had begun in secondary school.

1948

April 9 – While organizing a Latin American student conference in Bogotá, Colombia, Castro participates in *Bogotazo*, a popular uprising, helping resist armed assaults by police and troops against the Colombian people.

October 10 – Authentic Party leader Carlos Prío succeeds Grau as president of Cuba.

1951

Fall – Castro campaigns as candidate for house of representatives on ticket of Orthodox Party in elections scheduled for 1952.

At age 26, he is already a nationally known political figure in Cuba.

December – On break from medical school, Ernesto Guevara begins hitchhiking through Latin America.

1952

January–August – Guevara's travels take him through Chile, Peru, Colombia, and Venezuela. Spends August in Miami.

March 10 – Fulgencio Batista, a retired general, carries out coup d'état against government of Carlos Prío. With Washington's support, Batista establishes brutal military dictatorship. The scheduled elections are canceled.

Following coup, Castro begins organizing a revolutionary movement, recruited primarily from Orthodox Party youth, to overthrow the Batista tyranny by force of arms.

Numerous student-led demonstrations are organized in Havana to protest the coup. Participants include José Antonio Echeverría, Raúl Castro, Armando Hart, and others.

1953

July 6 – Guevara graduates from medical school and begins second trip through Latin America. Visits Bolivia, where impact of 1952 revolution is still strong. Arrives in Guatemala December 20, drawn by political and social struggles accompanying land reform initiated by regime of Jacobo Arbenz.

July 26 – Some 160 fighters led by Fidel Castro launch insurrectionary attack on the Moncada army garrison in Santiago de Cuba and the garrison in nearby Bayamo. The attacks fail, and over 50 captured revolutionaries are murdered. Castro and 27 other fighters are subsequently rounded up and put on trial.

October – Castro and the other jailed Moncada and Bayamo veterans are sentenced to up to 15 years in prison.

1954

May – A Cuba-wide campaign for amnesty of Moncada prisoners is organized. Supporting the campaign over the next 12 months are relatives of the combatants; Moncada veterans Haydée Santamaría and Melba Hernández after their release from prison; and other revolutionary-minded young people including Celia Sánchez, Frank País, and Vilma Espín.

June 17 – Mercenary forces backed by CIA invade Guatemala to oust government of Jacobo Arbenz. Guevara is among those who volunteer to fight the imperialist-organized attack. Arbenz refuses to arm the people and resigns 10 days later; mercenary forces enter Guatemala City in August.

September 21 – Guevara, forced to flee Guatemala, arrives in Mexico City.

October – Defenders of July 26 combatants and supporters of amnesty begin campaign to circulate "History Will Absolve Me," Castro's courtroom speech reconstructed by him in prison and smuggled out. Tens of thousands of copies are distributed in coming months.

1955

May 15 – Faced with growing campaign for amnesty, Batista releases Castro and the other Moncada prisoners.

June 12 – Political supporters of revolutionary movement identified with Moncada assault and "History Will Absolve Me" reorganize themselves as July 26 Movement. Also joining the new organization are other revolutionary forces, including Santiago-based Revolutionary National Action led by Frank País, veterans of Revolutionary National Movement such as Armando Hart and Faustino Pérez, and other currents. Repression and provocations against revolutionaries intensify.

July 7 – Castro arrives in Mexico to begin preparations for expedition to launch insurrectionary struggle against Batista regime. Guevara meets Fidel Castro in Mexico City shortly after the latter's arrival and joins the combatants' nucleus as troop doctor.

1956

June 24-July 3 – Twenty-eight expeditionaries and their supporters are arrested by Mexican police. Castro is released July 24; Guevara a week later.

August 30 – Fidel Castro and José Antonio Echeverría sign Mexico Pact, agreeing to coordinate armed action by July 26 Movement and Revolutionary Directorate to oust Batista.

November 25 – Castro and 81 other members of July 26 Movement, including Guevara, depart from Tuxpan, Mexico, aboard the yacht *Granma* to initiate the revolutionary war.

November 30 – July 26 Movement organizes uprising in Santiago de Cuba led by Frank País to coincide with scheduled arrival of *Granma*. The rebellion is crushed. In its wake, Batista's police begin a wave of arrests and murders, especially in Santiago and throughout Oriente province.

December 2 – Delayed by storms, *Granma* reaches Cuba at Las Coloradas in Oriente province.

December 5 – Rebel combatants are surprised by Batista's troops at Alegría de Pío and dispersed under enemy fire; the rebels are hunted down and half are murdered or imprisoned.

December 18 – Two groups of survivors led by Fidel Castro and Raúl Castro, consisting of eight combatants altogether, reunite at Purial, in the foothills of the Sierra Maestra mountains.

December 21 – Group led by Juan Almeida, including Guevara, reunites with others at Purial. At this point there are 15 fighters in the Rebel Army with 7 weapons. They head higher into the mountains.

December 24 – Meeting of July 26 Movement leaders in Santiago de Cuba discusses support and aid to the combatants in the Sierra Maestra.

December 28 – After the arrival of other dispersed *Granma* expeditionaries and initial peasant recruits, the Rebel Army consists of 24 combatants.

1957

January 6 – Nine recruits join Rebel Army, sent by the July 26 Movement in Manzanillo, which is led by Celia Sánchez.

January 15 – Batista suspends civil liberties throughout Cuba and imposes press censorship.

January 17 – Rebel Army, with 23 usable weapons, overruns Batista army outpost at La Plata, in coastal region of Sierra Maestra.

January 21 – Lt. Ángel Sánchez Mosquera leads elite company of 45 Batista troops into Sierra Maestra to combat guerrillas. He is followed by unit of 300 troops under Maj. Joaquín Casillas.

January 22 – Rebels ambush government column at Arroyo del Infierno.

January 24 – A second group of eight Rebel Army recruits reaches Sierra Maestra, sent by July 26 Movement in Manzanillo.

January 30 – Guided by an informer, army planes bomb rebel positions on Caracas hill.

February 9 – Batista troops attack guerrillas at Altos de Espinosa, dispersing Rebel Army forces for three days.

February 12 – After several of the scattered units regroup, the Rebel Army consists of 18 combatants.

February 17 – National Directorate of July 26 Movement meets in the Sierra.

New York Times correspondent Herbert Matthews interviews and photographs Castro in the Sierra Maestra. The interview is published in the *Times* several days later. After Batista officials declare the interview a fake, the *Times* publishes a photograph of Matthews with Castro, providing sensational evidence that the guerrillas have not been wiped out.

February 18 – Castro drafts "Manifesto to the People of Cuba," analyzing military situation in the Sierra since *Granma* landing and explaining why army will be unable to defeat revolutionary forces.

February 26–March 2 – Censorship lifted. *Bohemia* and other Cuban periodicals publish reports on Matthews interview with Castro, giving Cuba's people the first independent confirmation of rebels' existence. A new 45-day censorship decree is imposed on March 2.

March 11 – Frank País is arrested in Santiago on charges of participating in November 30 uprising.

March 13 – Armed units of Revolutionary Directorate attack Presidential Palace in Havana in attempt to assassinate Batista; the attack fails and a number of revolutionaries are killed, including the Directorate's leader, José Antonio Echeverría, killed in an attempt to seize Radio Reloj.

March 16 – Fifty reinforcements, sent by July 26 Movement in Santiago de Cuba, reach rebel troops in Sierra Maestra.

March 30 – Batista tells the press there are no guerrilla encampments in the Sierra Maestra.

April 12 – Col. Pedro Barreras informs the press that the army's presence is no longer necessary in the Sierra Maestra.

April 15 – Censorship is lifted briefly following expiration of 45-day decree, then reimposed shortly after.

April 20 – Four leaders of Revolutionary Directorate who survived attack on Presidential Palace are gunned down in Havana in what became known as 7 Humboldt St. massacre.

April 23 – Castro is interviewed and filmed in Sierra by U.S. journalist Robert Taber; the interview is shown in May by CBS-TV.

May 9 – Crescencio Pérez arrives at guerrilla camp with group of 18 new peasant recruits. Fourteen more soon arrive.

May 10 – In a Santiago de Cuba courtroom, 22 arrested *Granma* expeditionaries are sentenced to up to nine years in prison. Judge Manuel Urrutia votes against verdict. Dozens of other political prisoners on trial, including Frank País and other participants in November 30 Santiago uprising, are acquitted.

May 18 – Over two dozen automatic weapons and 6,000 rounds of ammunition reach Rebel Army in the Sierra, sent by July 26 Movement in Santiago.

May 24 – Twenty-seven armed combatants, organized by supporters of Authentic Party, land on northern coast of Oriente province aboard the *Corynthia*. The expedition is quickly routed, evidently betrayed before landing; 16 are captured and executed. One makes his way to Sierra Maestra and joins Rebel Army.

May 28 – Rebels overrun well-fortified army garrison at El Uvero.
July 26 Movement members in Havana conduct sabotage action, cutting off electricity for 57 hours.

June – Guevara commands small Rebel Army group tending fighters wounded at El Uvero. Reunites with main column in early July.

June 4 – A United Press International dispatch announces that 800 U.S.-trained and -equipped Cuban troops will be sent to the Sierra to combat Rebel Army.

June 12 – Two more small groups of Rebel Army recruits arrive in the Sierra, sent by July 26 Movement in Manzanillo.

July – The Rebel Army now consists of 200 fighters; Batista's armed forces number over 30,000.

July 12 – Manifesto of the Sierra Maestra is issued, signed by Fidel Castro, Felipe Pazos, and Raúl Chibás. It calls for broad opposition front to support Rebel Army and overthrow Batista.

July 21 – Guevara is first combatant promoted by Castro to commander, named head of a second Rebel Army column, Column no. 4, nicknamed the "Dispossessed Peasants."

July 27 – Rebel Army attacks garrison at Estrada Palma, marking fourth anniversary of July 26, 1953, attack on Santiago and Bayamo garrisons.

July 30 – Frank País is murdered by Batista henchmen in Santiago de Cuba.

July 31 – Sixty thousand attend funeral march for Frank País in Santiago. U.S. ambassador Earl Smith goes to Santiago that same day, and is met by street protest of women demanding end to U.S. support to Batista.

August 1 – A general strike begins in Santiago to protest the murder of País. It rapidly spreads throughout Oriente province and then to the entire island.
Guevara's column attacks army post at Bueycito.

August 20 – Rebel Army Column no. 1, led by Fidel Castro, defeats army at Palma Mocha, in Las Cuevas region.

August 29 – Guevara's column, now numbering 100, ambushes army troops at El Hombrito. Following the battle, the two Rebel columns meet up and march, sometimes together, sometimes separately, toward Pino del Agua.

September 5 – Anti-Batista military conspirators at naval base in Cienfuegos rise up and seize city, with support from local cadres of July 26 Movement and other civilians. The rebellion is crushed the same day.

September 17 – Rebel forces under Guevara's command ambush government troops in first battle of Pino del Agua.

October – Guevara's column establishes base at El Hombrito, constructing an oven for baking bread, crude armory and leather goods shop, and other supply facilities. Camilo Cienfuegos is assigned to the column, heading up the forward detachment.

October 12 – Batista army launches another offensive to crush Rebel Army in Sierra Maestra.

November – The July 26 Movement and Rebel Army organize to sabotage the annual sugar harvest by burning cane belonging to owners of large landed estates. On orders from Fidel Castro, cane fields belonging to Castro's family are among the first targets.

Revolutionary Directorate establishes guerrilla base in Escambray mountains in Las Villas province, led by Eloy Gutiérrez Menoyo; later takes the name Second National Front of the Escambray.

November 1 – Miami Pact is signed by Authentic Party, Orthodox Party, Revolutionary Directorate, and others; among the signers is Felipe Pazos pretending to represent signers of Sierra Manifesto, including Castro. The Pact creates the Cuban Liberation Junta, dominated by bourgeois opposition forces; it does not oppose U.S. intervention and encourages military coup to replace Batista.

November 4 – Guevara publishes first issue of Rebel Army newspaper *El Cubano Libre,* produced on mimeograph machine brought into Sierra.

November 8 – Rebel troops led by Ciro Frías of Column no. 1 clash with army at El Mareón.

July 26 Movement activists in Havana set off 100 bombs as part of a campaign of sabotage actions.

November 20 – Forces from Rebel Army Column no. 1 clash with government forces at Mota, San Lorenzo, and Goviro.

News of Miami Pact reaches Fidel Castro and Rebel Army command.

November 29 – Guevara's column conducts ambush at Mar Verde; Rebel captain Ciro Redondo is killed, posthumously promoted to commander.

December 6 – Rebel troops led by Lt. Lalo Sardiñas clash with army at El Salto.

December 8 – Guevara's column ambushes army troops at Altos de Conrado. Following battle, the army occupies and destroys facilities at El Hombrito camp.

December 14 – Castro repudiates Miami Pact in name of July 26 Movement; letter is later mimeographed by Guevara's column for distribution.

December 27 – July 26 combatants conduct a sabotage action against ESSO Standard Oil Company installations.

1958

Mid-January – Armando Hart and other July 26 Movement leaders are arrested leaving the Sierra and jailed. Evidence of debate over strategy between Llano and Sierra sections of July 26 Movement is publicized by progovernment media.

January 27 – Censorship lifted briefly in all provinces except Oriente. *Bohemia* publishes interview with Rebel Army leaders done by journalist for *Paris Match* magazine.

February – *Look* and *Coronet* magazines in the United States publish widely read articles on guerrilla struggle in Cuba by U.S. reporter Andrew St. George, based on his visit to the Sierra.

February 2 – *Bohemia* publishes full text of Castro's letter repudiating Miami Pact, in special run of half million copies.

February 8 – Fighters of Revolutionary Directorate led by Faure Chomón land on northern coast of Camagüey. Some head to Escambray mountains of Las Villas. By summer, Gutiérrez Menoyo's Second National Front of the Escambray is expelled from Revolutionary Directorate.

February 16–17 – Rebel victory at second battle of Pino del Agua marks decisive shift in military relation of forces, opening several months of expanded operations by Rebel Army.

February 24 – Radio Rebelde begins transmission from Sierra Maestra.

March 1 – Columns led by Raúl Castro and Juan Almeida, branching out from Column no. 1, set out from Sierra Maestra to establish two new Rebel Army fronts in Oriente province, the Second and Third Eastern Fronts, aimed at encircling Santiago de Cuba.

April – Guevara is assigned to set up school, named after Ciro Redondo, to train new recruits at Minas del Frío in the Sierra; Ramiro Valdés replaces him as commander of Column no. 4.

April 9 – July 26 Movement calls general strike throughout Cuba; announced without adequate preparation, the strike fails. Batista forces step up repression and offensive action.

May 3 – Meeting of July 26 Movement National Directorate in Sierra Maestra assesses April 9 strike failure; center of national leadership of July 26 Movement is shifted from Havana and Santiago to Sierra Maestra, and Fidel Castro is chosen general secretary.
"Ciro Redondo" Column no. 8 is created, with Guevara as commander; many of its members come from the Minas del Frío school.

May 25 – Rebel Army holds first peasant assembly in Sierra Maestra; the meeting, attended by 350, is addressed by Fidel Castro, Guevara, and others. Meeting discusses approaching harvest and adopts plan for agrarian reform.
Seeking to take advantage of April 9 rebel setback, Batista launches "encircle and annihilate" offensive, sending 10,000 troops into the Sierra Maestra. Rebel Army, then with 300 fighters and 200 usable rifles, concentrates forces around command post of Column no. 1, drawing in government troops.

July 11–21 – Battle of El Jigüe. Decisive Rebel Army victory marks defeat of government offensive and constitutes turning point in war. Between May 25 and July 21 battles fought in Santo Domingo, Meriño, Las Vegas de Jibacoa, Las Mercedes, El Jigüe, and other skirmishes inflict over 1,000 casualties on Batista forces. Rebels, now 800 strong, capture 600 weapons and 100,000 rounds of ammunition. Rebel Army plans counteroffensive.

July 20 – Radio Rebelde broadcasts text of Caracas Pact, signed by Fidel Castro for July 26 Movement and by broad range of other opposition forces. The document calls for armed insurrection to establish provisional government and an end to U.S. support to Batista.

August 21 – Cmdr. Camilo Cienfuegos leaves Sierra, leading Rebel Army Column no. 2 toward Pinar del Río province on the western end of Cuba.

August 31 – Column no. 8, with 140 combatants commanded by Guevara, leaves from Sierra Maestra; marches on foot toward Las Villas province in central Cuba.

September 1–2 – Hurricane Ella hits Oriente province, making roads and rivers impassable.

September 4 – Mariana Grajales platoon, consisting of women fighters, is formed in the Sierra. The unit is part of First Rebel Front led by Fidel Castro. Women combatants have been members of Rebel columns since March 1957.

September 7 – Guevara's column crosses Jobabo river into Camagüey province.

September 9 – Column no. 8 is ambushed by government troops at La Federal.

September 14 – Guevara's column clashes with army at Cuatro Compañeros.

September 18 – Rebel Army Column no. 1 successfully attacks Batista forces in Yara, in foothills of Sierra.

September 21 – Rebel Army Second Eastern Front commanded by Raúl Castro organizes congress of peasants in Soledad, Mayarí Arriba.

September 27–28 – Columns 1 and 12 destroy Batista military garrison in Cerro Pelado, in Oriente province. The Mariana Grajales platoon participates in the action.

Column no. 3 ambushes 200 army troops near Loma Blanca.

October 9 – Rebel Army creates Fourth Front, commanded by Delio Gómez Ochoa, to operate in northwest Oriente province.

October 10 – Rebel Army issues Law no. 3 of the Sierra Maestra, granting tenant farmers, squatters, and sharecroppers title to the land they work.

October 12 – Column no. 8 crosses Jatibonico river into Las Villas province.

October 16 – Guevara's column establishes camp at Caballete de Casa in Escambray mountains of Las Villas.

October 23 – Column no. 7 ambushes government convoy between Bayamo and Guisa in Oriente.

October 26–27 – Column no. 8 captures army garrison at Güinía de Miranda.

October 31 – Column no. 2 under Cienfuegos, operating in northern Las Villas, wages successful assault on garrison at Venegas.

November 2 – Column no. 6 captures army garrison at Alto Songo in Oriente province.

November 3 – Batista regime holds general elections, in attempt to give legal cover to dictatorship. July 26 Movement calls for boycott and voter abstention is massive. Batista's candidate for president, Andrés Rivero Agüero, is declared elected.

November 8 – Guevara issues Military Order no. 1, an agrarian reform decree in the Escambray.

November 10 – United National Workers Front (FONU) formed, grouping supporters of July 26 Movement, Popular Socialist Party, Revolutionary Directorate, and other revolutionary-minded workers and unionists.

November 13 – Guevara's column founds *Patria* as Rebel Army newspaper in Las Villas; it later establishes a second Las Villas paper *El Miliciano*.

November 20–30 – As opening step in drive to surround and seize Santiago de Cuba, Rebel Army columns in Sierra Maestra defeat Batista's troops at battle of Guisa.

December 1 – July 26 Movement and Revolutionary Directorate issue Pedrero Pact, calling for unity of revolutionary forces in Las Villas.

December 7 – Rebel Army Second Eastern Front holds First Provincial Plenary of Revolutionary Workers in eastern Oriente province.

December 9 – Baire and San Luis in Oriente fall to Rebel Army.

December 15–18 – Battle of Fomento, waged by Guevara's column, ends in rebel capture of the city.

December 19 – Jiguaní falls to Rebel Army First and Third Fronts, led by Fidel Castro and Juan Almeida respectively.

Caimanera falls to troops of Second Front, which is commanded by Raúl Castro.

Column no. 2 captures Mayajigua in northern Las Villas.

December 21 – Camilo Cienfuegos's column organizes congress of agricultural workers and sugar workers in northern Las Villas.

December 22–23 – Guayos and Cabaiguán fall to Column no. 8.

Sancti Spíritus is captured after an attack by Column no. 8 and Revolutionary Directorate, sparking popular insurrection there.

December 23 – Placetas and Manicaragua fall to Guevara's column.

December 24–25 – Cumanayagua, Camarones, Cruces, and Lajas fall to units of Column no. 8 and Revolutionary Directorate. Sagua de Tánamo is captured by Rebel Army Second Front in Oriente. Members of Fourth Front capture Puerto Padre.

December 26 – Column no. 8 captures Caibarién and Remedios.

December 28 – Palma Soriano, near Santiago, captured by Columns 1 and 3.

December 29 – Rebels under Guevara's command launch attack on Santa Clara, capital of Las Villas province and Cuba's third-largest city; population mobilizes in massive show of support to the Rebel Army.

Revolutionary Directorate forces under Faure Chomón capture Trinidad.

December 30 – Maffo is taken by rebels, completing circle around Santiago de Cuba.

Jobabo taken by Column no. 12 on Fourth Front.

December 31 – Yaguajay, the last army bastion in northern Las Villas, falls to Camilo Cienfuegos's column.

Rebel Army tightens grip on Santa Clara; by nightfall the city is almost entirely in rebel hands.

Fourth Front tightens siege of Holguín and Las Tunas.

1959

January 1 – Batista flees Cuba at 2:00 A.M., ceding power to a military junta.
Army garrison in Santa Clara surrenders to Guevara.
Speaking over Radio Rebelde, Commander in Chief Fidel Castro opposes new junta, calls for nationwide general strike, and orders Guevara's and Cienfuegos's columns to march on Havana.
Faced with Rebel ultimatum, the army's garrison at Santiago de Cuba surrenders.

January 2 – Cuban workers respond to call for revolutionary general strike with massive uprising.
Rebel columns led by Cienfuegos and Guevara enter Havana and occupy principal army garrisons.
Military junta collapses.

January 2–8 – Fidel Castro and main rebel columns march from Santiago de Cuba to Havana.

January 8 – Rebel forces commanded by Fidel Castro enter Havana.
At conclusion of war, there are 3,000 fighters in Rebel Army.

'Men contribute to the making of history, but history also makes men'

by Fidel Castro

AUTHORITIES AND RESIDENTS of the Pedro Aguirre Cerda district and of the three communities, in particular the San Miguel community:

A few days ago, when I visited the statue of José Martí, I said I would come a few days later to visit the statue of Che and meet with the residents of this community.

Today you have honored me with the title "Illustrious Son" of this community, and I thank you for it.

My task here is to give you my impressions and memories, to present some of the characteristics of Che's personality and life.

When I came here and placed flowers in front of the monument, many thoughts went through my mind. First, the memory of one who was a comrade in struggle and a brother of our people and our fighters; the impact of seeing, transformed into bronze, a man I once had the privilege of knowing, at whose side I once had the privilege of fighting.

This is the first time I've seen a monument to someone I've known in life. Usually, when statues are created by artists in memory of men who distinguished themselves for their feats and accomplishments in the struggle for humanity, they symbolize individuals who lived a long time ago, hundreds and even thousands of years ago. Possibly only in very special circum-

---

This speech was given November 28, 1971, during a trip by Cuban president Fidel Castro to Chile. He spoke in the working-class community of San Miguel in Santiago de Chile, where residents had erected a statue to Guevara.

stances does one have the chance to see a statue of someone one has known, because usually history sees fit to erect these monuments after the passage of many years. But in this case the revolutionary proletarian community of San Miguel wanted to erect a monument to Che. And so, three years after his death, in October 1970, this monument was unveiled.

I met Che in Mexico in 1955. An Argentine by birth, he was Latin American in spirit and in heart. He had just come from Guatemala.

About Che, as about all revolutionaries, many tales have been invented. They try to present him as a conspirator, a shadowy subversive dedicated to devising plots and revolutions. As a young man, like so many other young students, as a graduate of his country's university, like so many other graduates—in his case, as a doctor—Che, who had a special curiosity and interest in things related to Latin America, a special interest in study and knowledge, a special desire to see all our nations, made a tour of several countries. He had nothing more than his degree.

At times on foot, at times on motorcycle, he went from country to country. In fact, when we were in Chuquicamata [in northern Chile] we were shown the place he had stopped for a day on the first trip he made outside his country. He had no money. He wasn't a tourist. He went to see the work centers, the hospitals, the historic sites. He crossed the Andes, took a boat or a raft, and went as far as a leper hospital in the Amazon, where he worked for a time as a doctor.

He continued his journey. He arrived in Guatemala after passing through—if I remember correctly—Brazil, Venezuela, and Colombia. And he arrived in Guatemala when a progressive government headed by Jacobo Arbenz was in power. An agrarian reform was being carried out. Also there at the time were some survivors of the 1953 attack on the Moncada garrison.[1]

1. On July 26, 1953, some 160 revolutionaries launched an insurrectionary attack on the Moncada army garrison in Santiago de Cuba, and a simultaneous attack on the garrison in Bayamo, marking the beginning of the revo-

They established a friendship with Che. He was working there—if I remember correctly—as a doctor.

As one who was interested in the Guatemalan process, a studious man who thirsted after knowledge with an inquiring spirit, a revolutionary vocation and disposition, and a clear intelligence, he had of course read the books and theories of Karl Marx, Engels, and Lenin. And although he wasn't a member of any party, Che was already a Marxist in his thinking.

But it was his lot to live through a bitter experience. While he was in Guatemala the imperialists intervened with an invasion led by the CIA—that is, the CIA organized the invasion of that country from neighboring territory, with arms, planes, and all kinds of equipment. It was something similar to what they later tried to do at Girón.[2] But in Guatemala, they attacked without any risk. Using their planes and then advancing on the ground, they overthrew the revolutionary government.

The Cubans and other Latin Americans who were there and

---

lutionary armed struggle against the Batista dictatorship. After the attack's failure, Batista's forces massacred more than fifty of the revolutionaries they held. Fidel Castro, the central leader of the group and commander of the Moncada assault, and twenty-seven others were captured, tried, and sentenced to prison. They were released in May 1955 after a public defense campaign forced Batista's regime to issue an amnesty.

In Guatemala Guevara had met some survivors of the attack: Antonio "Ñico" López, Mario Dalmau, Antonio Darío López, and Armando Arencibia. Prior to arriving in Guatemala, Guevara had also met other Moncada survivors in Costa Rica.

2. On April 17, 1961, 1,500 Cuban-born mercenaries invaded Cuba at the Bay of Pigs on the southern coast. The action, organized by Washington, aimed to establish a "provisional government" to appeal for direct U.S. intervention. However, the invaders were defeated within seventy-two hours by Cuba's militia and its Revolutionary Armed Forces. On April 19 the last invaders surrendered at Playa Girón (Girón Beach), which is the name Cubans use to designate the battle. The day before the abortive invasion, at a mass rally called to honor those killed or wounded in U.S.-organized air attacks on Havana, Santiago de Cuba, and San Antonio de los Baños, Fidel Castro had proclaimed the socialist character of the revolution in Cuba and called the people of Cuba to arms in its defense.

who had supported the government, who had carried out simple tasks of a practical nature—not even political tasks—had to leave the country. They went to Mexico.

In 1955 the first Moncada combatants who had just come out of prison had to leave Cuba. One of the first comrades subjected to persistent harassment and persecution was Raúl [Castro], who left for Mexico. I arrived a few weeks later.

Raúl had already made contact with other comrades who had not been in prison, and he had also met Che. A few days after my arrival in Mexico I met Che in a house where some Cubans were staying on Emparan Street, if I remember the name correctly—but I can't remember the number of the house now.

Che wasn't Che then. He was Ernesto Guevara. It was because of the Argentine custom of calling people "che" that the Cubans began calling him Che. That was how he got that name, a name he later made famous, a name he turned into an emblem.

That's how we met.

As he himself related in one of his writings, he joined the Cuban movement immediately, after a few hours of discussion.

Because of his state of mind when he left Guatemala, because of the extremely bitter experience he'd lived through there—that cowardly aggression against the country, the interruption of a process that had awakened the hopes of the people—because of his revolutionary vocation, his spirit of struggle, we can't say it took hours, we can say that in a matter of minutes Che decided to join the small group of Cubans who were working on organizing a new phase of the struggle in our country.

We spent a little over a year in Mexico, working under difficult conditions, with very few resources. But that really doesn't matter, that's what was to be expected of the struggle, as with all struggles. Then at last, on November 25, 1956, we left for Cuba.

Our movement had launched a slogan against the skeptics, against those who doubted the possibility of continuing the struggle, against those who disputed our position that in this situation there was no other solution. We had declared, "In 1956 we will be free or we will be martyrs." That declaration was simply a reaffirmation to the Cuban nation of our determination to struggle, of our confidence that the struggle would be renewed without delay.

It is true that many people—not the people in our organization, for they understood perfectly the meaning of that slogan—did not understand why we made that promise to return to Cuba practically on a fixed date. It was because of the state of mind of many people in our country who, because of the frustrations, because of the tricks by the traditional politicians, had become somewhat skeptical. Moreover, there were many people representing vested interests who were engaged in political maneuvering, making great efforts to obtain political agreements with the Batista tyranny and to extinguish the people's faith in revolutionary struggle.

That was why we were forced to launch that slogan. Right or wrong, we aren't going to discuss it now. It may serve as material for theoretical research. Men don't always go strictly by a diagram. Men don't make history at their own whim or to their own liking. Men may contribute to the making of history, but history also makes men. So, for better or worse, the slogan was launched. And for better or worse, we were determined to carry it out.

Special circumstances could and did arise, and there were very serious complications on the eve of our departure. But we always had a small number of arms hidden, and we said that if we can't all go, some of us will, no matter what. So eighty-two fighters left aboard a small yacht called the *Granma*. We sailed 1,500 miles and arrived at the coast of Cuba on December 2, 1956. Two or three days from now our country will be celebrating the fifteenth anniversary of that landing, which marked the birth of our small army; December 2 is now our Armed Forces Day.

That's the way the struggle began.

I don't propose to give you an entire history—far from it. I simply want to provide you with a clear understanding of the circumstances in which this contingent began the struggle.

And what was Che? Che was the doctor of our contingent. He wasn't the commissar, and he didn't yet have any troops under his command. He was simply the doctor.

Because of his seriousness, his intelligence, and his character, Che had once been assigned as leader of a group of Cubans in a house in Mexico. One day a small, disagreeable incident took place. There were about twenty or thirty Cubans there in all, and some of them—it must have been two or three, but sometimes two or three are enough to create a disagreeable situation—challenged Che's leadership because he was an Argentine, because he was not a Cuban.

We of course criticized such an attitude that ignored human qualities, this ingratitude toward someone who, although not born in our land, was ready to shed his blood for it. And I remember the incident hurt me a great deal. I think it hurt him as well.

He was, in addition, a man without any desire to exercise authority. He did not have the slightest ambition, he was not self-centered in any way. He was instead a man who became inhibited if anyone contradicted him. When he came to our country, he came—I repeat—as our troop doctor, on the general staff.

The interesting thing is how Che became a soldier, how he distinguished himself, and what his characteristics were.

A few examples: On December 5, because of tactical errors, our small detachment was the victim of a surprise attack and was completely dispersed. After overcoming tremendous difficulties, a small number of men regrouped in the midst of an encirclement and heavy pursuit. There were three groups: one with Raúl, another group that included Che, who wasn't in charge of anything yet—Comrade Almeida was in this group too—and the group with me. Almeida's group rejoined mine first, and Raúl's did so a few days later. We continued the struggle.

Our first battle took place January 17, 1957; we had seventeen men. At the beginning, of all the weapons we had brought with us, we were able to round up only seven. December 5 was what we might call the baptism by fire for Che and many other comrades. But the first small battle we won was on January 17.

By the second battle Che had already begun to distinguish himself, to show he was Che.

In a confrontation with forces that were pursuing us, he showed his personal bravery. In a practically individual battle with an enemy soldier, in the midst of general combat, he shot the adversary and crawled forward under a hail of bullets to take his weapon. He carried out that brave, outstanding, and special deed on his own initiative, and it earned him the admiration of all.

Barely six or seven days later, at the end of January, we suffered the consequences of a betrayal. Our small contingent had grown to some thirty men, five or six of whom were peasants who had asked for and received permission to go visit their families—discipline was still not very strong in that small group. They left their weapons there, with the detachment. One day at dawn, a squadron of fighter planes and bombers attacked the exact spot where the detachment was located with a very heavy barrage—at least that's how we viewed it at the time. We had already had some experience along these lines, but this was the hardest we had ever been hit.

I'm going into this because when the combatants were trying to get away from the spot where the fire was concentrated—we were going up a hillside—at that moment we remembered the weapons that belonged to the five or six peasants who were visiting their homes. Those weapons had to be retrieved and I called for volunteers. Immediately, without thinking or hesitating for an instant, Che was the first to say, "I'll go." He and another comrade went quickly to the place being bombed, got the weapons, hid them in a safe place, and then rejoined the rest of our forces.

Different episodes took place. Che was still the doctor; he did not command any troops. But in May of that year, on May 28, something else happened. Our column by then had some one hundred men, if I remember correctly, and a group of Cuban revolutionaries from another political organization had landed in the northern part of the province.[3] We remembered our own landing and the difficult moments we had gone through; we wanted to help that group by carrying out a support action. So we started for the coast, where an enemy infantry company held positions with fortifications and trenches.

Basing ourselves on the information we had received, we scheduled the attack for dawn and organized it very quickly. But when we were about to start combat at dawn the situation became complicated. It turned out our information was not very accurate: the enemy positions were not where we thought they were. It was a complicated situation, but there was no turning back.

Our small units—platoons and squads—were scattered in a circle whose perimeter was at least a kilometer and a half long. We could not retreat. We had no choice but to attack.

At the time of that battle, Che was a part of the general staff; he already had some responsibilities. We had to carry out two or three actions. We had to ask Almeida's platoon to advance to the front quickly to get as close as possible to certain enemy positions. The advance was very risky and cost us a number of casualties.

We also had to have a group move toward the west. And while we were sizing up the situation and analyzing the necessity of that action, Che immediately volunteered. He asked for a group of men and an automatic rifle, and said he would march to the west. We gave him a group of men and an automatic rifle, belonging to the general staff, and he quickly began the advance toward that position.

That was the third time Che had immediately stepped forward when we needed a volunteer. In any difficult situation he would act at once, and that's what he did then.

3. Castro is referring to the landing of the *Corynthia* on May 24, 1957, organized by the Authentic Party. Guevara's account of this expedition can be found in "The Weapons Arrive," p. 164, and "One Year of Armed Struggle," p. 261.

That battle was a hard fought one. It lasted three hours, and almost 30 percent of the forces on both sides were killed or wounded. It had been motivated by the desire to help those who had landed in the north. Despite our efforts, however, they had been surrounded, captured, and killed. When we occupied the enemy camp, after three hours of fighting, there were a large number of wounded—enemy wounded and our own men. Che was the doctor who attended quickly to both our wounded and those of the enemy. That was always the practice and the rule throughout our struggle.

Later, logically, the battle gave rise to a concentration of enemy forces, a huge manhunt directed against us. And we had to solve the problem of our many wounded. After we took care of the enemy wounded—we left them there at the scene of the battle so that, as we withdrew, they could be picked up by their own side—Che as the doctor stayed behind in an isolated place with our wounded. He took care of them in a difficult situation in which sizable enemy forces in the area were trying to corner us.

The column marched through difficult, rugged terrain. We broke through the encirclement. But Che stayed behind with the wounded, with only a very few men. He stayed with them several weeks until they had recovered. The small group was then able to rejoin the main column, which had been reinforced by the weapons we had captured during the battle.

So the first time we organized a new column—the second column—we gave command of that column to Che. And we made him commander, the second commander of our forces. With his small new column, he began to operate in a specific area, in positions not far from where the first column was based.

That was how Che became a soldier and was named commander of a small column.

And, of course, he continued to display the same character, the same attitude, to such an extent that it can be said we had to watch out for him.

What do I mean by watching out for him? Well, his aggressiveness, his audacity led him to plan very daring operations.

And when he entered combat during the following stage, which lasted several months—a stage where his small group still lacked sufficient forces and experience in the region they were operating in—he displayed great tenacity and perseverance as a soldier. Sometimes he insisted on fighting with the enemy for a position. And there he would stay and fight for hours, even days.

We could say that, in a way, he even violated the rules of combat—that is, the ideal norms, the most perfect methods—risking his life in battle because of that character, tenacity, and spirit of his. He would obstinately refuse to surrender a position even though his little column was very small and the advancing enemy forces very numerous, even when there wasn't much sense in defending that particular position. That was his character; that was his perseverance; that was his combative spirit.

Logically, therefore, we had to lay down certain rules and guidelines for him to follow.

What was it that we admired in him, that impressed us? What was that characteristic that gave the precise measure of Che's spirit and soul? It was his moral qualities, his altruism, his absolute selflessness. He had met a group of Cubans; he became convinced of their cause; and from the very first moment he showed great selflessness and generosity. From the first moment, he was absolutely willing to give his life, regardless of whether it was in the first battle or the second or the third. Here we had a man born in a place thousands of kilometers from our country, a man some Cubans had even once objected to because he was giving them orders and had not been born in Cuba. But for that country and for that cause, he was the first at every moment to volunteer for something dangerous, for a mission with great risks.

He was a man who had no personal ambitions whatsoever. There was nothing he wanted except to do his duty and to do it well. He sought to respond quickly in any situation, to immediately and unhesitatingly set an example of what he thought a revolutionary fighter should be.

During those early days, Che could certainly never have imagined that one day, in this community, there would be a meeting such as this and we would be standing in front of a monument honoring him!

Che did not fight for glory, for material possessions, or ambition. He never fought for fame. He was a man who right from the outset, from the very first battle, was ready to give his life; who could have been killed as just one more soldier. If he had died in the first battle, he would have left behind the memory of his personal qualities, his personality, and the characteristics we knew him by, and nothing more. The same if he had died in the second, third, fourth, or fifth battle. He could have died in any of those battles; many men did.

Therefore, we can say that Che thought of nothing but duty and sacrifice, with the most absolute purity and with the most complete selflessness.

We can say that Che survived the battles in the Sierra Maestra because we followed the principle that whenever a man distinguished himself as a leader, we would not expose him in minor battles but would save him for more important operations.

At the end of May 1958, the army launched its last offensive against us. Some 10,000 men advanced against our forces—at the time we had at most 300 soldiers, including Che's column and some other forces we had managed to get together. After a battle that lasted seventy consecutive days, our soldiers, who were already combat-tested veterans—in spite of being at a disadvantage with regard to weapons and numbers—managed to smash the offensive, capture a sizable number of weapons, and organize different columns. When the battle began, we had 300 men; when it ended we had 805 armed men.

It was then that we organized two columns—one commanded by Camilo and the other by Che—equipped with the best weapons we had, and they carried out what was truly a feat. Starting from the Sierra Maestra—Camilo with 90 men, Che with 140—they marched toward the west, toward Las Villas province, across more than five hundred kilometers of flatlands, uninhabited in many places. The two columns left the Sierra Maestra around September. They advanced, many times having to fight their way through, with the enemy close on their heels, over difficult terrain, and carried out their mission of reaching the center of the island.

When, at the end of December, our forces were virtually in control of Oriente province, and the island was cut in two through Las Villas province, Che performed one of his last military feats in Cuba. He marched on the city of Santa Clara with 300 combatants, attacked an armored train stationed on the outskirts of the city, cut the tracks between the train and the main headquarters of the enemy, derailed the train, surrounded it, forced the troops inside to surrender, and captured all the weapons there. In short, he attacked the city of Santa Clara with only 300 men.

When the Batista regime finally collapsed on January 1, and there was an attempt to cheat the Cuban revolution of its triumph, the columns of Camilo and Che were ordered to advance rapidly on Havana. They carried out their mission; on January 2 both columns were inside the capital of the republic. Victory was consolidated on that day, and a long road began.

Everybody's life changed. Many tasks cropped up, and many combatants had to take on administrative responsibilities.

At the end of several months, Che was named minister of industry and began to carry out the work that occupied him for several years.

I have spoken of Che as a soldier, but he was endowed with outstanding qualities in many areas. First of all, he was a man of extraordinary culture; he had one of the most penetrating minds I have known, one of the most generous spirits, one of the most revolutionary characters. His feelings—his concern for other people, his concern for the movement in Asia, in Africa—extended to the whole world.

At the time the Algerians were fighting for their independence. At the time, the poor and underdeveloped countries in other continents were engaged in different struggles. He saw with complete clarity the need to establish contact with these worlds.

He visited many countries on different missions, seeking to improve relations, seeking closer relations and commercial trade, working hard to overcome the consequences of the economic blockade imposed on our country.[4]

When the Playa Girón invasion took place, Che was in command of the forces of Pinar del Río province. When the attack against Playa Girón began, in the south-central part of the island, we didn't know at first where the direction of the main attack would be. Generally speaking, the most experienced leaders assumed command of specific military zones. And even though he was in charge of the Ministry of Industry, as soon as the mobilization against the attack began, Che was sent to Pinar del Río province. Similarly, when the October crisis occurred in 1962—another moment of very grave danger—Che again assumed command of that military region.[5]

Thus, a number of times and under different circumstances, we were obliged to confront certain grave dangers. And he continued to serve as a combatant, he assumed his responsibilities, he continued studying military science assiduously.

He was an extremely studious man who, in the hours in which he could manage to free himself from his intense work, sacrificed sleep and rest to study. Not only did he work interminable

4. On February 3, 1962, following over two years of escalating economic warfare by Washington, President John F. Kennedy imposed a total embargo on trade with Cuba. The brutal embargo has been maintained, with bipartisan support, by eight U.S. administrations.
5. Amid escalating preparations by Washington for a new invasion of Cuba in the spring and summer of 1962, the Cuban government signed a mutual defense agreement with the Soviet Union. In October 1962 President Kennedy demanded removal of Soviet nuclear missiles installed in Cuba following the signing of that pact. Washington ordered a naval blockade of Cuba, stepped up its preparations to invade, and placed U.S. armed forces on nuclear alert. Cuban workers and farmers mobilized in the millions to defend the revolution. Following an exchange of communications between Washington and Moscow, Soviet premier Nikita Khrushchev, without consulting the Cuban government, announced his decision to remove the missiles on October 28.

hours in the Ministry of Industry, but he also received visitors, wrote accounts of the war and about his experiences in the countries he visited on one or another mission. He related his experiences in an interesting, simple, and clear style.

Many episodes of the revolutionary war have been preserved because Che wrote them down, because of his interest in making available for our people the experiences written down by their compatriots at various times.

Che was the originator of voluntary work in Cuba. He was a man who maintained close contact with the workplaces that were under the responsibility of the Ministry of Industry. He visited them, talked with the workers, analyzed the problems. Every Sunday Che went to some workplace—sometimes to the docks to load freight with the longshoremen; sometimes to the mines to work with the miners; sometimes to the cane fields to cut cane; sometimes he met with construction workers. He never kept a Sunday for himself.

What's more, all this and his previous feats must be viewed in the light of his own health, for he suffered from certain allergy problems that produced severe attacks of asthma. With asthma, he fought during the whole campaign. With asthma, he worked day and night. With asthma, he wrote. With asthma, he traveled throughout the country and the world. With asthma, he went down into the mines, went to work in the fields, went everywhere without ever allowing himself a moment's rest. When he wasn't working at his responsibilities in the ministry, he was studying during hours stolen from sleep, or he was out doing voluntary work.

Che was a man with infinite confidence and faith in man. He was a living example. It was his style to be the example, to set the example. He was a man with a great spirit of self-sacrifice, with a truly Spartan nature, capable of any kind of self-denial. His policy was to set the example.

We could say that his entire life was an example in every sphere. He was a man of absolute moral integrity, of unshakably firm principles, a complete revolutionary who looked toward the future, toward the man of the future, toward the humanity of the future, and who above all stressed human values, man's moral values. And above all, he practiced selflessness, renunciation, self-denial.

None of the words I use about him involve the slightest exaggeration, the slightest overestimation. They simply express what the man we knew was like.

Here is his monument, here is his figure as the artist saw it. But it is impossible for a monument to capture the overall conception of the man. We have Che's writings, his narratives, his speeches. Those who knew him have their own memory of Che. And we have seen how proudly the workers in many of our factories recall the day Che visited their workplaces, the places where Che did voluntary work.

Not very long ago, we visited a large textile plant whose machinery was being upgraded; we were accompanied by an illustrious foreign visitor. The workers there took us to a shop where they kept, almost like a family treasure, the looms on which Che had done voluntary work. The mines Che visited and the places where he worked and talked with the workers are other monuments to his memory, which our workers cherish with extraordinary affection.

But Che did not live for history; he did not live for honors or glory. Like every other true revolutionary, like every other thoroughgoing revolutionary, he knew what that extraordinary man, that great patriot José Martí— whom you have also honored here—meant when he said, "All the glory of the world fits into a kernel of corn."

Revolutionaries do not struggle for honor or glory, or to occupy a place in history. Che occupied, occupies, and will always occupy a great place in history because that was not important to him, because he was ready to die from the first battle on, because he was always absolutely selfless. And so his life became an epic, his life became an example. We say to our people—and this has become a basic idea, a watchword—if we were to describe what we want our children to be like, we would want them to be like Che. There is no Cuban family, no Cuban parent, no Cuban child who doesn't hold Che up as the model for his life.

If today's world—this contemporary world that is writing a new history of humanity, that is trying to build a better, more humane society, that confronts very complex problems and difficult struggles—if today's world is seeking an example, and if you consider the qualities this example requires, we who knew Che, we who had that great privilege, understand why our people and our country have chosen this model for our children. And we believe it is an extraordinarily worthy one.

How wonderful it would be if we were to succeed in making this model a reality in the generations to come, so that in the future we would have generations like Che!

Future societies will be made of generations of men like Che! From generations of men like Che a better society, communism, will arise! [*Applause*]

He left us his example. And as the final fruit of his clear mind, his Spartan character, his heart of steel—steel for self-sacrifice, for suffering—of his noble, sensitive, and generous spirit of giving himself to a cause and struggling for others, sacrificing himself for others, of his intelligence, his heart, and his calm hand, he left us, finally, his diary, in which he narrated the epic of the last days of his life. And in his concise, straightforward, terse style, reflecting the last moments of his life, he wrote a true epic of literature, containing extraordinary merit in every sense: his diary.[6]

That is why the youth of the world see Che as a symbol. And just as he identified with the cause of the Algerians, the Vietnamese, the Latin Americans, so Che's name and figure are viewed with tremendous respect, admiration, and affection on all con-

6. Guevara's day-by-day account of the 1966–67 guerrilla struggle is available in English translation in *The Bolivian Diary of Ernesto Che Guevara* (New York: Pathfinder, 1994). This edition also contains excerpts from diaries and accounts written by other combatants.

tinents. The name and figure of Che are emblazoned even there in the very heart of U.S. society itself. Civil rights fighters, fighters against the war of aggression, fighters for peace, progressives, all citizens who struggle for any cause whatever within the United States itself, have taken up Che's name and banner. He has therefore become a gigantic figure, and so he is. But nobody's imagination, nobody's fantasy, nobody's self-interest created this.

Never has a banner been raised on a more solid pedestal, never has an example been raised on firmer ground.

Che himself turned his figure into this symbol during his brief but intense life, his brief but creative life. This was not his aim; this was not what he sought. But because of his life, his selflessness, his nobility, his altruism, his heroism, he became what he is today. He became a banner, a model, a fighter. He became a guide. He became a monument to all that is noble, to the spirit of justice. Che is, in short, a model as a revolutionary, as a fighter, and as a communist for all the peoples of the world.

Thank you very much. [*Applause*]

Episodes *of the* Cuban Revolutionary War *1956-58*

Prologue

For a long time we have considered how to write a history of our revolution that would encompass all its many facets and aspects. The leaders of the revolution have often privately or publicly expressed their desire to write such a history, but the tasks are many, the years pass, and the memory of the insurrectional struggle is dissolving into the past. We have not yet clearly set down these events, which already belong to the history of the Americas.

For this reason I am beginning a series of personal reminiscences of the attacks, skirmishes, and battles in which I participated. It is not my intention that this fragmentary history, based on remembrances and a few notes, should be taken as a full account. On the contrary, I hope that all those who lived through these events will develop them further.

The fact that I personally was limited to the fighting at a given point on the map of Cuba during the entire struggle prevented me from participating in battles and events in other places. I believe that to make our revolutionary actions understandable and to do so in an orderly manner, I can best begin with the first battle, the only one Fidel participated in that went against our forces: the surprise attack at Alegría de Pío.[1]

There are many survivors of this battle and each of them is

1. In this volume, the account of the battle at Alegría de Pío is preceded by the chapter "A Revolution Begins." (All footnotes have been added by the editor.)

encouraged to contribute his recollections so that the story may be filled out. I ask only that the narrator be strictly truthful. He should not present any inaccuracy in order to clarify his own role, exaggerate it, or claim to have been where he was not. I ask that after writing a few pages to the best of one's ability, in line with one's education and disposition, the author then criticize them as thoroughly as possible in order to remove every word that does not stick to the absolute facts, or in which the author is not fully certain. With this aim I begin my recollections.

Ernesto Che Guevara

PUBLISHED IN VERDE OLIVO, FEBRUARY 26, 1961

1955–1956

A revolution begins

THE HISTORY OF THE MILITARY TAKEOVER on March 10, 1952—the bloodless coup led by Fulgencio Batista—does not of course begin on the day of that barracks revolt. Its antecedents must be sought far back in Cuban history: much farther back than the intervention of U.S. ambassador Sumner Welles in 1933; much farther back still than the Platt Amendment in 1901; much farther back than the landing of the hero Narciso López, direct envoy of the U.S. annexationists.[1] We would have to go back to the times of John Quincy Adams, who at the beginning of the nineteenth century announced his country's consistent policy toward Cuba: it was to be like an apple that, torn away from

1. In the midst of the 1933 revolutionary upsurge against Cuban dictator Gerardo Machado, Sumner Welles was sent as ambassador by President Franklin Roosevelt to mediate an agreement between Machado and the bourgeois opposition. When that failed, Welles helped engineer Machado's resignation and the installation of a new pro-U.S. regime.

   The Platt Amendment, incorporated into a U.S. military appropriations bill, was approved by Congress in 1901. The Cuban government established during the U.S. military occupation of the island following the Spanish-American War incorporated the provisions of the Platt Amendment in the new Cuban constitution. Washington was given the right to intervene in Cuban affairs at any time and to establish military bases on Cuban soil. Cuba eliminated these provisions from its constitution in 1934.

   Narciso López, a former Spanish officer, organized an expedition, with backing from allies in the United States, that landed in Cuba in 1850. López was taken prisoner by Spanish forces and executed.

Spain, was destined to fall into the hands of Uncle Sam. These are all links in a long chain of continental aggression that has not been aimed solely at Cuba.

This tide, this ebb and flow of the imperial wave, is marked by the fall of democratic governments and the rise of new ones in the face of the uncontainable pressure of the multitudes. History exhibits similar characteristics in all of Latin America: dictatorial governments represent a small minority and come to power through a coup d'état; democratic governments with a broad popular base arise laboriously, and frequently are already compromised, even before coming to power, by a series of concessions they have had to make beforehand to survive. Although in this sense the Cuban revolution marks an exception in all the Americas, it is necessary to point out the antecedents of this whole process. It was due to these causes that the author of these lines, tossed here and there by the waves of the social movements convulsing the Americas, had the opportunity to meet another Latin American exile: Fidel Castro.[2]

I met him on one of those cold Mexican nights, and I remember that our first discussion was about international politics. Within a few hours—by dawn—I was one of the future expeditionaries. But I would like to clarify how and why it was in Mexico that I met Cuba's current head of state.

It was during the ebb of the democratic governments in 1954, when the last Latin American revolutionary democracy still standing in the area—that of Jacobo Arbenz Guzmán—succumbed to the cold, premeditated aggression carried out by the United States of America behind the smoke screen of its continental propaganda. The visible head of that aggression was Secretary of State John Foster Dulles, who by a strange coincidence was also the lawyer for and a stockholder of the United Fruit Company, the main imperialist enterprise in Guatemala.

I was returning from there, defeated, united with all Guate-

2. See the glossary at the back of the book for information on individuals, organizations, and publications mentioned in the text.

malans by the pain, hoping, searching for a way to rebuild a future for that anguished country.

And Fidel came to Mexico looking for neutral ground on which to prepare his men for the great effort. An internal split had already occurred after the assault on the Moncada garrison in Santiago de Cuba. All the weak-spirited had left its ranks—all those who for one or another reason left it to join political parties or revolutionary groups that demanded less sacrifice. New recruits were already joining the freshly formed ranks of what was called the July 26 Movement, named after the date of the 1953 attack on the Moncada garrison. An extremely difficult task was beginning for those in charge of training these people under necessarily clandestine conditions in Mexico. They were fighting against the Mexican government, against agents of the United States FBI and those of Batista, against these three forces that in one way or another joined together, where money and buying people off played a large role. In addition, we had to struggle against Trujillo's spies and against the poor selection made of the human material—especially in Miami.[3] And after overcoming all these difficulties we had to accomplish an extremely important thing: depart . . . and then . . . arrive, and all the rest, which, at the time, seemed easy to us. Today we can weigh all the costs in effort, sacrifice, and lives.

Fidel Castro, helped by a small team of intimate collaborators, gave himself over entirely, with all his energies and his extraordinary spirit of work, to the task of organizing the armed fighters that would leave for Cuba. He almost never gave classes on military tactics, since for him time was in short supply. The rest of us were able to learn quite a bit from Gen. Alberto Bayo. Lis-

3. Rafael Leónidas Trujillo was dictator of the Dominican Republic from 1930 until his assassination in 1961. The July 26 Movement had denounced Trujillo's ties with figures close to Batista, and revolutionary forces in the two countries collaborated with each other.

A number of the *Granma* trainees had been sent by exile organizations in the United States. Some of these did not share the July 26 Movement's revolutionary perspectives and abandoned its ranks.

tening to the first classes, my almost instantaneous impression was that victory was possible. I had thought it quite doubtful when I first enrolled with the rebel commander, to whom I was linked from the beginning by a liking for romantic adventure and the thought that it would be well worth dying on a foreign shore for such a pure ideal.

Several months passed in this way. Our marksmanship began to improve, and the best shots emerged. We found a ranch in Mexico where, under the direction of General Bayo—with me as head of personnel—the final preparations were made. We aimed to leave in March 1956. Around that time, however, two Mexican police units, both on Batista's payroll, were hunting for Fidel Castro, and one of them had the good fortune, in financial terms, of capturing him. But they made the absurd error, also in financial terms, of not killing him after taking him prisoner. Within a few days many of his followers were captured. Our ranch on the outskirts of Mexico City also fell into the hands of the police and we all went to jail.

All this postponed the beginning of the last part of the first stage.

Some of us were imprisoned for fifty-seven days, which we counted off one by one, with the perennial threat of extradition hanging over our heads (as Cmdr. Calixto García and I can attest). But at no time did we lose our personal confidence in Fidel Castro. Because Fidel did some things for the sake of friendship that we might say almost compromised his revolutionary goals. I remember that I explained to him my specific case: a foreigner, illegally in Mexico, with a whole series of charges against me. I told him that by no means should the revolution be held up on my account, and that he could leave me behind; that I understood the situation and would try to make my way to the battle from wherever they sent me; and that the only effort on my behalf should be to have me sent to a nearby country and not to Argentina. I also remember Fidel's sharp reply: "I will not abandon you." And that's what happened. Precious time and money had to be diverted to get us out of the Mexican jail. That personal attitude of Fidel's toward people whom he holds in esteem is the key to the fanatical loyalty he inspires. An adherence to principles and an adherence to the individual combine to make the Rebel Army an indivisible fist.

The days passed as we worked in clandestinity, hiding ourselves where we could, shunning any public presence to the extent possible, hardly going out into the street. After several months, we found out that there was a traitor in our ranks, whose name we did not know, and that he had sold an arms shipment. We also learned that he had sold the yacht and a transmitter, although he had not yet drawn up the "legal contract" of the sale. That first installment showed the Cuban authorities that the traitor in fact knew our internal workings. But it was also what saved us, since it showed us the same thing.

From that moment on, we had to undertake feverish preparations. The *Granma* was put into shape at an extraordinary speed. We piled up as many provisions as we could get—very few, in fact—along with uniforms, rifles, equipment, and two antitank guns with hardly any ammunition. At any rate, on November 25, 1956, at two o'clock in the morning, we began to make a reality of Fidel's words, scoffed at by the official press: "In 1956 we will be free or we will be martyrs."

With our lights out we left the port of Tuxpan in the midst of an infernal heap of men and equipment of every type. Although navigation had been prohibited due to very bad weather conditions, the river's estuary remained calm. We crossed the entrance into the Gulf of Mexico and shortly thereafter turned on the lights. We began a frantic search for the antihistamines for seasickness and could not find them. We sang the Cuban national anthem and the July 26 Hymn for perhaps five minutes total, and then the whole boat took on a ridiculously tragic appearance: men with anguished faces holding their stomachs, some with their heads in buckets, others lying immobile on the deck, in the strangest positions, with their clothing soiled by vomit. With the exception of two or three sailors, and four or five others, the rest of the eighty-two crew members were seasick. But after the fourth or fifth day the general panorama improved a bit. We discovered that what we thought was a leak in the boat was actually an open plumbing faucet. We had already thrown overboard everything unnecessary in order to lighten the ballast.

The route we had chosen involved making a wide turn south of Cuba, bordering Jamaica and the Grand Cayman Islands, with the landing to be someplace close to the village of Niquero in Oriente province. The plan was being carried out quite slowly. On November 30 we heard over the radio the news of the uprising in Santiago de Cuba that our great Frank País had started, aiming to coincide with the expedition's arrival. The following day, December 1, at night, we set the bow on a straight line toward Cuba, desperately seeking the Cabo Cruz lighthouse, as we ran out of water, food, and fuel.

At two o'clock in the morning, on a dark and stormy night, the situation was disturbing. The lookouts walked back and forth, searching for the ray of light that was not appearing on the horizon. Roque, an ex-lieutenant in the navy, once again got up on the small upper bridge, to look for the light from the cape. Losing his footing, he fell into the water. Shortly after continuing on our way, we saw the light. But the labored advance of our boat made the final hours of the trip interminable. It was already daylight when we reached Cuba at a place known as Belic on the beach at Las Coloradas.

A coast guard boat spotted us and telegraphed the discovery to Batista's army. No sooner had we disembarked and entered the swamp, in great haste and carrying only what was absolutely necessary, than we were attacked by enemy planes. Naturally, walking through the mangrove-covered marsh, we were not seen or harassed by the planes, but the dictatorship's army was already on our trail. It took us several hours to get out of the swamp, where we had ended up due to the inexperience and irresponsibility of a comrade who said he knew the way. We wound up on solid ground, lost, adrift.

We were an army of shadows, of ghosts, who walked as if

following the impulse of some dark psychic mechanism. It had been seven days of continuous hunger and seasickness during the crossing, followed by three more days, terrible ones, on land. Exactly ten days after the departure from Mexico, in the early morning hours of December 5, after a night march interrupted by fainting, exhaustion, and rest for the troops, we reached a point known—paradoxically—by the name of Alegría [joy] de Pío. It was a small grove of trees, bordering a sugarcane field on one side and open to some clearings on the other, with a dense forest starting further back. The place was ill-suited for an encampment, but we stopped there to rest for a day and resume our march the following night.

PUBLISHED IN O CRUZEIRO OF RIO DE JANEIRO, BRAZIL,
JUNE 16, JULY 1, AND JULY 16, 1959

DECEMBER 1956

Alegría de Pío

ALEGRÍA DE PÍO is a place in Oriente province, Niquero municipality, near Cabo Cruz. There, on December 5, 1956, the dictatorship's forces took us by surprise.

We were exhausted from a trek not long so much as painful. We had landed on December 2, at a place known as Las Coloradas beach. We had lost almost all our equipment, and with new boots we had trudged for endless hours through saltwater marshes. As a result, almost the entire troop was suffering from open blisters on their feet. But boots and fungus infections were not our only enemies. We had reached Cuba following a seven-day voyage across the Gulf of Mexico and the Caribbean Sea, without food, in a boat in poor condition, with almost everyone plagued by seasickness, unaccustomed to sea travel as we were. We had left the port of Tuxpan November 25, a day when a stiff northern gale was blowing and any navigation was impossible. All this had left its mark upon our troop made up of novices who had never seen combat.

All that was left of our war equipment was our rifles, cartridge belts, and a few wet rounds of ammunition. Our medical supplies had disappeared, and most of our knapsacks had been left behind in the swamps. The previous night we had passed through one of the cane fields of the Niquero sugar company, owned by Julio Lobo at the time. We had managed to satisfy our hunger and thirst by eating sugarcane, but due to our lack of experience we had left a trail of cane peelings and bagasse all over the place. Not that the soldiers looking for us needed any trail to follow our steps, for it had been our guide—as we found out years later—who had betrayed us and brought them there. We had let him go the night before—an error we were to repeat several times during our long struggle until we learned that civilians whose backgrounds were unknown to us had to be closely watched in dangerous areas. We should never have permitted our false guide to leave.

By daybreak on December 5 hardly anyone could go a step further. On the verge of collapse, the men would walk a short distance and then beg for a long rest. Because of this, orders were given to halt at the edge of a cane field, in a thicket close to the dense woods. Most of us slept through the morning hours.

At noon we began to notice unusual signs of activity. Piper planes as well as other types of small army planes together with private aircraft began to circle overhead. Some of our group went on peacefully cutting and eating sugarcane without realizing they were perfectly visible from the enemy planes, which were circling slowly at low altitudes. I was troop physician at the time, and it was my duty to treat the blistered feet. I recall my last patient that morning: his name was Humberto Lamothe and it was to be his last day on earth. I still remember how tired and worn-out he looked as he walked from my improvised first-aid station to his post, still carrying in his hand the shoes he could not wear.

Comrade Montané and I were leaning against a tree talking about our respective children, eating our meager rations—half a sausage and two crackers—when we heard a shot. Within seconds, a hail of bullets—at least that's the way it seemed to our sagging spirits during that baptism of fire—descended upon our eighty-two-man troop. My rifle was not one of the best; I had deliberately asked for it because I was in very poor physical condition due to an attack of asthma that had bothered me throughout our ocean voyage, and I did not want to be responsible for wasting a good weapon. I can hardly remember the

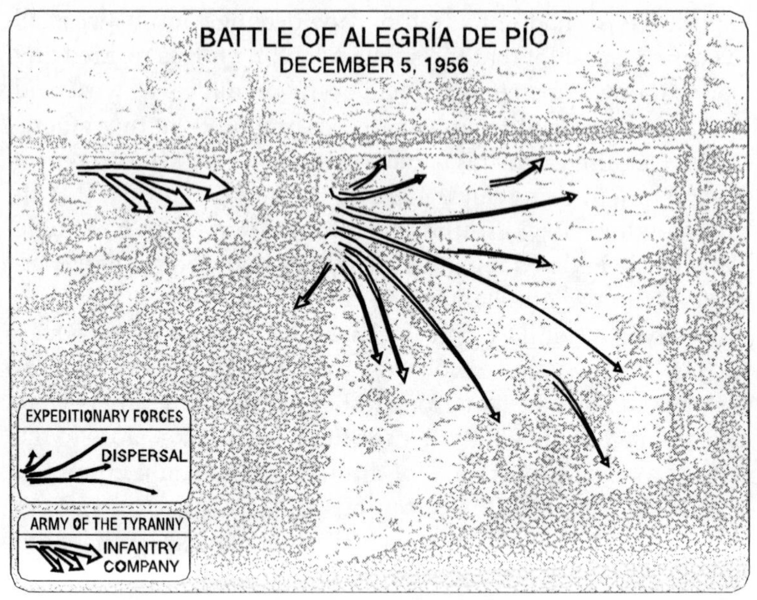

COUNCIL OF STATE OFFICE OF HISTORICAL AFFAIRS

sequence of events. I recall that Almeida, then a captain, came beside me to get orders, but there was nobody there to issue them. Later I learned that Fidel had tried vainly to get everybody together into the adjoining cane field, which could be reached by simply crossing a path. The surprise had been too great and the gunfire had been too heavy. Almeida went back to take charge of his group. At that moment a comrade dropped a box of ammunition almost at my feet. I pointed to it, and he answered me with an anguished expression, which I remember perfectly, that seemed to say "It's too late for ammunition boxes," and immediately went toward the cane field. (He was murdered by Batista's henchmen some time later.)

Perhaps this was the first time I was faced in real life with the dilemma of choosing between my devotion to medicine and my duty as a revolutionary soldier. There, at my feet, were a knapsack full of medicine and a box of ammunition. I couldn't possibly carry them both; they were too heavy. I picked up the box of ammunition, leaving the medicine, and started to cross the clearing, heading for the cane field. I clearly remember Faustino Pérez, kneeling and firing his submachine gun. Near me, a comrade named Albentosa was walking toward the cane field. A burst of gunfire hit us both. I felt a sharp blow to my chest and a wound in my neck, and I thought for certain I was dead. Albentosa, spewing blood from his nose and mouth and from a deep wound made by a .45-caliber bullet, shouted something like, "They've killed me!" and began to wildly fire his rifle at no one in particular. Flat on the ground I turned to Faustino, saying, "I'm hit!"— only I used a stronger word—and Faustino, still firing away, looked at me and said it was nothing, but I could read in his eyes that he considered me as good as dead.

Still on the ground, I fired a shot in the direction of the woods, following an impulse similar to that of the other wounded man. Immediately, I began to think about the best way to die, since all seemed lost. I recalled an old Jack London story where the hero, aware that he is bound to freeze to death in the wastes of Alaska, leans calmly against a tree and prepares to die in a dignified manner. That was the only thing that came to my mind at that moment.

Someone on his knees shouted that we had better surrender, and I heard a voice—later I found out it was Camilo Cienfuegos—shouting: "Nobody surrenders here!" followed by a four-letter word. Ponce approached me, agitated and breathing hard, and showed me a bullet wound, apparently through his lungs. He said, "I'm wounded," and I replied indifferently, "Me too." Then Ponce, and other comrades who were still unhurt, crawled toward the cane field. For a moment I was left alone, just lying there waiting to die. Almeida approached, urging me on, and despite the intense pain I dragged myself into the cane field. There next to a tree I saw Comrade Raúl Suárez, whose thumb had been blown away by a bullet, being attended by Faustino Pérez, who was bandaging his hand. Then everything became a blur, as low-flying planes strafed the field. This only added to the confusion, with scenes ranging from the Dantesque to the grotesque—such as a comrade of considerable corpulence desperately trying to hide behind a single stalk of sugarcane, while in the midst of the din of gunfire another man kept on yelling "Silence!" for no apparent reason.

A group was organized, headed by Almeida, including Lt. Ramiro Valdés, today a commander, and comrades Chao and Benítez. With Almeida leading the way, we crossed the last path among the rows of cane and reached the safety of the woods. The first shouts of "Fire!" were then heard in the cane field and columns of flame and smoke began to rise. I cannot say this for certain, however, since I was thinking more of the bitterness of defeat and the imminence of my death than of the events that were occurring. We walked until the darkness of night made it difficult to go on, and we decided to sleep, all huddled together in a heap. We were starving and thirsty, and the mosquitoes added to our misery.

This was our baptism of fire on December 5, 1956, on the outskirts of Niquero. Such was the beginning of forging what would become the Rebel Army.

PUBLISHED IN VERDE OLIVO, FEBRUARY 26, 1961

DECEMBER 1956

Adrift

THE DAY AFTER THE SURPRISE ATTACK at Alegría de Pío, we were marching through the brush in an area where red earth alternated with "dogtooth" rock.[1] A few isolated shots could be heard, coming from all directions. We were following no particular route. Chao, a veteran of the Spanish civil war, pointed out that by walking in this way we would surely fall into an enemy ambush. He proposed to find a place where we could wait for nightfall and continue on under cover of darkness.

We were virtually without water and had suffered a mishap with our only container of milk. Benítez, to whom it had been entrusted, had slipped it into his pocket with the little drinking holes upside down. When we went to serve our rations—consisting of an empty vitamin tube filled with condensed milk and a drop of water—we realized with dismay that it had spilled all over Benítez's pocket and uniform.

We succeeded in installing ourselves in a kind of cavern, which offered a broad view to one side. Its defect, however, was that it would be impossible to see the enemy advance from the other side. But since we were more concerned with not being seen than with defending ourselves, we decided to stay there throughout the day. All five of us made a formal pledge to fight to the death. Those who did so were Ramiro Valdés, Juan Almeida, Chao,

1. A type of sharp, porous rock found mainly in coastal regions.

Benítez, and the author of this account. All five of us survived the terrible experience of the defeat and the subsequent battles.

Night fell and we set out again. Drawing on my recollections of astronomy, I identified the North Star, and for two days we guided ourselves by it, moving eastward toward the Sierra Maestra. (Much later I would learn that the star we used to find our way eastward was not the North Star at all. It was simply good luck that we went approximately in the right direction and arrived at dawn in front of some cliffs very near the coast.)

Between us and the sea below we could see a cliff, about fifty meters high. On the other side there rose into view the tempting sight of a pool of water below, fresh water it appeared to us. Our biggest torment was thirst. That night a swarm of land crabs crawled around us and, driven by hunger, we killed some. Since building a fire was out of the question, however, we swallowed raw the gelatinous parts, which made us terribly thirsty.

After much searching, we found a passage by which we could descend to the pool of water. But in the confusion of our coming and going, we lost sight of the pond we had spotted from above. We had to make do with some little puddles of rain water, found in the hollows of the "dogtooth" rock. Using the tiny pump of an antiasthma vaporizer, we extracted the water, but there were only a few drops for each of us.

We marched on, in no particular direction, demoralized. From time to time a plane flew over the sea. Walking among the rocks was extremely tiring; some of us suggested that we move along the coastal cliffs, but there was a serious drawback to that: the enemy could see us. So we remained in the shade of a cluster of shrubs, waiting for sundown. At nightfall, we found a small beach, where we bathed.

I tried to replicate something I had once read about in a popular science magazine or in some novel, where it was explained that two-thirds fresh water mixed with one-third salt water makes very good drinking water and increases the quantity of liquid. I experimented, using what remained in a canteen. The result was lamentable: a brackish concoction that earned me

GRANMA

COUNCIL OF STATE OFFICE OF HISTORICAL AFFAIRS

Left, police chief Quirino Uria confronts Fidel Castro (left) during November 1950 demonstration in Havana, one of numerous student-led protests against the corrupt government of Carlos Prío and its subordination to Wall Street and Washington.

Right, an organizer for the Orthodox Party youth, Castro was one of the party's candidates in elections scheduled for 1952; these were canceled following Fulgencio Batista's coup d'état of March 10, 1952.

Cuban troops occupying streets in Havana on day of Batista coup, March 10, 1952.

AIN

Above, student-led demonstration in Havana shortly after Batista's coup; Raúl Castro, then a university student, is carrying Cuban flag at head of action.

Above, left to right, Antonio "Ñico" López, Abel Santamaría, and Fidel Castro, three leaders of July 26, 1953, assault on army garrisons in Santiago de Cuba and Bayamo that initiated the armed struggle against Batista regime. Santamaría, along with 54 other combatants, was murdered by his captors. López, a *Granma* expeditionary, was captured and murdered by Batista's troops after the battle of Alegría de Pío.

Below, the Moncada army garrison in Santiago following July 26, 1953, assault.

BOHEMIA

Above, Batista police occupy and sack University of Havana, April 21, 1956; in front, with sunglasses, is Rafael Salas Cañizares, one of regime's most notorious murderers. The university remained shut down until the Batista regime fell January 1, 1959.

Top right, visit by U.S. vice president Richard Nixon (right) in February 1955 gave Washington's stamp of approval to regime of Fulgencio Batista (left); Cuban president Andrés Domingo Morales is at center. Below, members of Cuba's capitalist class celebrate New Year's Eve at Biltmore Yacht and Country Club in Havana, January 1958. Batista himself was denied membership in country club due to his partly Black ancestry.

Right, before revolution, millions of working people lived in slums like these with little hope of change.

COUNCIL OF STATE OFFICE OF HISTORICAL AFFAIRS

GRANMA

COUNCIL OF STATE OFFICE OF HISTORICAL AFFAIRS

COUNCIL OF STATE OFFICE OF HISTORICAL AFFAIRS

GRANMA

BOHEMIA

Above, top, José Antonio Echeverría, leader of student-based Revolutionary Directorate, addressing a rally probably 1955; also in photo are student leaders José Machado and Onil Fuentes, second and third from left.

Bottom, student demonstration in Santiago de Cuba 1952 or 1953; future July 26 Movement leader Vilma Espín is at right.

Facing page, University of Havana students demonstrate November 27, 1956—two days after the Granma set sail from Mexico—marking a traditional day of student protest going back to Cuba's independence struggle from Spain. The march was attacked and broken up by the police.

Right, strike by over 200,000 sugar workers in December 1955 to protest government move to lower wages; a number of towns in Las Villas province were virtually taken over by strikers and supporters.

BOHEMIA

Top, Fidel Castro arriving in Havana, May 16, 1955, following release of Moncada prisoners after a mass amnesty campaign. A few weeks later, July 26 Movement was founded. As government repression mounted, Castro and others left for Mexico to prepare armed expedition to overturn Batista regime. (GRANMA)

Bottom, future Granma expeditionaries and supporters in prison in Mexico City, June 26, 1956. Standing, with sunglasses, is Fidel Castro; next to him is María Antonia González. Seated, second from left, Ernesto Che Guevara; fourth and fifth from left are Juan Almeida and Ramiro Valdés; kneeling at right is Calixto García. (WIDE WORLD PHOTOS) criticism from all the men. Somewhat refreshed by the swim, we resumed our march. It was night and, if I remember correctly, there was quite a good moon. Almeida and I, marching at the front, suddenly noticed that in one of the little shanties that fishermen put up at the sea's edge to protect themselves from bad weather, there were shadows of sleeping men. We thought they were soldiers, but we were already too close to retrace our steps so we strode ahead. Almeida was going to demand they surrender, but we had a pleasant surprise: it was three comrades from the *Granma*—Camilo Cienfuegos, Pancho González, and Pablo Hurtado. At once we began to exchange impressions, news, opinions about the little bit each of us knew concerning the other comrades and the battle. Camilo's group offered us sticks of sugarcane, which they had pulled up before fleeing. The sweet and juicy substance was good for fooling one's stomach. Meanwhile, they were chewing crabs avidly. They had found a way to appease their thirst by drawing water directly from the little hollows in the rocks with a little tube or a scooped-out stick.

We continued our march, all together. The surviving combatants of the *Granma* army numbered eight at that point,[2] and we had no information about the existence of other survivors. We deduced that there had to be other groups such as our own, but we had not the slightest idea where they were. All we knew was that by marching with the sea to our right we were going east, that is, toward the Sierra Maestra, where we were to take refuge. We did not try to hide from ourselves the fact that in case of an encounter with the enemy, trapped as we were between the craggy cliffs and the sea, our chances of flight were nil. I no longer remember whether we marched along the coast for one day or two. I only know that we ate a few little prickly pears that grew along the shore, one or two apiece, which did not assuage our hunger. And we were tortured by thirst, since we had to ration our few drops of water with the greatest strictness.

2. Juan Almeida, Ramiro Valdés, Che Guevara, Rafael Chao, Reynaldo Benítez, Camilo Cienfuegos, Pancho González, and Pablo Hurtado.

One morning at dawn we arrived, dog-tired, at the sea coast; we stopped there to doze, while waiting to see clearly enough to find a passage before facing the too-steep cliffs.

When it was light, we began to explore. Before our eyes there appeared a big house made of palmwood, which appeared to belong to some fairly well-off peasant. My immediate reaction was that we should not approach a house of that sort, since its inhabitants would probably be hostile to us; indeed, the house might even be occupied by the army. Benítez disagreed and we ended up going toward the house together.

I stayed outside while he climbed over a barbed-wire fence. (Someone else was with us, I don't remember who.[3]) Suddenly I noticed, in the dim light, a clearly outlined silhouette of a uniformed man holding an M-1 rifle.[4] I thought this was curtains for us, at least for Benítez, but since he was closer to the man than he was to me, I was unable to warn him. Benítez went almost right up to the soldier before turning around and coming back the way he came. With complete naïveté he told me that he had returned because he saw "a man with a gun" and that it seemed wiser not to ask the man any questions.

In actual fact, Benítez and all of us felt like we had been raised from the dead. But our odyssey did not end there. After a discreet inspection of the area, we saw that it would be necessary to scale the cliffs, which were not so steep at this point. We were coming close to the zone called Ojo de Buey [eye of the ox], so named because of a small stream of water that flowed down to the sea, cutting right through the cliff.

Daybreak came upon us before the end of our climb. We had time only to find a cave, a magnificent spot for observing the entire panorama. Absolute calm reigned on the landscape. We saw some men come ashore from a navy skiff and others embark, in what appeared to be a relief operation. We counted about thirty of them, and learned later that these men were

3. Ramiro Valdés.
4. See the glossary of weapons beginning on page 457.

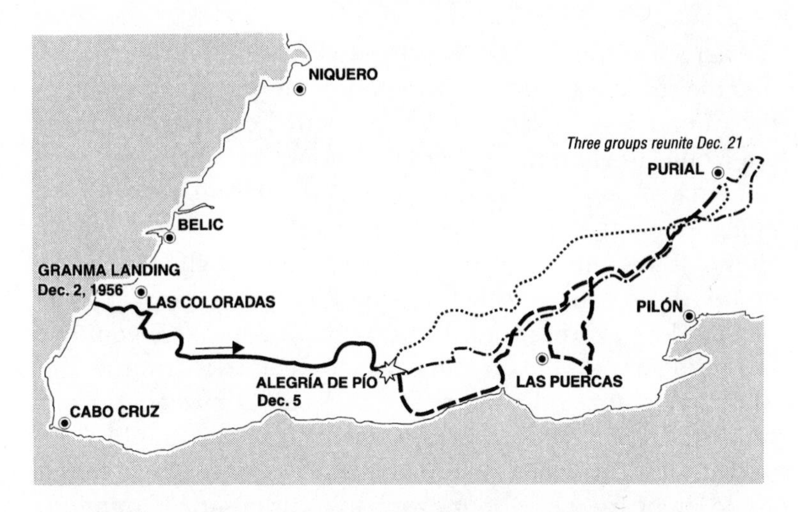

GRANMA LANDING TO DEC. 21 REGROUPMENT OF REBEL FORCES

ROUTE OF EXPEDITIONARIES FROM GRANMA LANDING TO ALEGRÍA DE PÍO ———
FIDEL CASTRO'S GROUP OF 3. ARRIVES AT PURIAL DEC. 16 ....
RAÚL CASTRO'S GROUP OF 5. ARRIVES AT PURIAL DEC. 18 _._._._._._._._.
JUAN ALMEIDA'S GROUP OF 8 (WITH GUEVARA). ARRIVES AT PURIAL DEC. 21 — — —

Laurent's, that fearful navy murderer who, having accomplished his mission of executing a group of our comrades, was engaged in relieving his men.[5]

Before the astounded eyes of Benítez the "men with the guns" appeared, in all their tragic reality. The situation was not good. If we were discovered, there was not the slightest chance of escape; we would have no alternative but to fight to the very end.

We had not eaten a mouthful all day; we strictly rationed our water, distributing it in the eyepiece of a pair of field glasses; nothing could be fairer.

At night we resumed our march, aiming to distance ourselves from this locality where we had spent some of the most anguished days of the war, victims of hunger and thirst, of a sense of defeat, and the imminence of real and present danger, which gave us the feeling of cornered rats.

5. Julio Laurent was a major in the Naval Intelligence Service.

After some wandering, we came upon a stream that emptied into the sea, or of one of its tributaries. Throwing ourselves to the ground, we drank for a long time with the avidity of horses; we would have continued but our stomachs, empty of food, refused to absorb another drop. We filled our canteens and kept going. At dawn we reached the top of a hillock crowned with a clump of trees. In order to resist and hide most effectively, the group spread out; we spent the entire day watching small planes passing low overhead, equipped with loudspeakers emitting incomprehensible noises. Almeida and Benítez, veterans of the Moncada, realized they were calling on us to surrender. From time to time, unidentifiable noises came from the forest.

That night our wanderings led us near a house where music could be heard. Once more we had a difference of opinion. Ramiro, Almeida, and I were of the firm opinion that we must absolutely avoid showing ourselves at a dance or anything like it because the peasants would immediately make our presence known far and wide, simply through normal indiscretion. Benítez and Camilo Cienfuegos felt that we had to enter, at any price, so we could eat. Finally Ramiro and I were chosen to go to the house, find out what was going on, and procure food. As we approached, the music stopped and we heard in the distance the voice of a man saying something like, "And now, let us drink to our comrades-in-arms whose exploits were so brilliant," etc. That was enough for us; we did an about-face, stealthily but on the double, and reported to our comrades who was celebrating at the party.

We resumed our march but the men increasingly refused to walk. That night, or perhaps the following one, virtually all the comrades decided they did not want to continue. We were obliged, at that moment, to knock at a peasant's door near the road, at a place called Puercas Gordas, nine days after the surprise attack at Alegría de Pío.

We were warmly received, and that peasant hut became the scene of endless feasting. Hours passed and yet we ate, until daybreak came upon us and it was not possible to leave. During the morning peasants arrived who had learned of our presence. Filled with curiosity and friendly concern, they came to make our acquaintance, offer us food, or bring us some gift.

Then, the little house that sheltered us turned into an inferno. Almeida was the first to be overcome by diarrhea; and, in a flash, eight inappreciative intestines gave evidence of the blackest ingratitude, poisoning our small refuge. Some of the men began to vomit. Pablo Hurtado, exhausted by days of seasickness, marching, thirst, and hunger, could no longer stand up.

We decided to leave that night. The peasants told us that according to news they had picked up, Fidel was alive. They proposed to take us to a place where he would presumably be, together with Crescencio Pérez. But we would have to leave our weapons and uniforms behind. Almeida and I kept our two machine pistols. The eight rifles and all the cartridges were stored in the peasant's hut for safekeeping. We planned to make it to the Sierra Maestra in stages, staying in the houses of peasants; we divided into two groups, one of three men, one of four.

Our group, if I remember correctly, was composed of Pancho González, Ramiro Valdés, Almeida, and me. In the other were Camilo, Benítez, and Chao. Pablo Hurtado was too sick to leave the house.

We were scarcely on our way when the owner gave in to the temptation of passing on the news to a friend, asking his advice on where to hide the weapons. The latter convinced him to sell them. They had dealings with a third person, and it was he who denounced us to the army. As a result, a few hours after our departure from the first hospitable Cuban hearth, there was an enemy raid; they took Pablo Hurtado prisoner and seized our weapons.

We were staying with an Adventist named Argelio Rosabal, known by everyone as "Pastor." This man, hearing the bad news, promptly got in touch with another peasant who knew the zone thoroughly and was a rebel sympathizer. That same night we left for another, safer shelter. The peasant we met on that occasion was named Guillermo García: today he is head of the Western Army and a member of the national leadership of our party.

Subsequently we were welcomed at several other peasant homes: Carlos Mas, who later joined our ranks; Perucho [Carillo]; and other comrades whose names I have forgotten. One morning at daybreak, after crossing the road to Pilón and after marching without any guide at all, we reached the farm of Mongo Pérez, Crescencio's brother. There we found all the surviving expeditionaries who were free as of then: Fidel Castro, Universo Sánchez, Faustino Pérez, Raúl Castro, Ciro Redondo, Efigenio Ameijeiras, René Rodríguez, and Armando Rodríguez. A few days later we were joined by Morán, Crespo, Julito Díaz, Calixto García, Calixto Morales, and Bermúdez.

Our small troop was without uniforms and without weapons, since the two machine pistols were all we had salvaged from the disaster. Fidel reproached us bitterly.

For the duration of the campaign, and even today, his words of admonition remain engraved in my memory: "You have not paid for the error you committed, because the price for abandoning your weapons under such circumstances is your life. Your only hope of survival, in the event of a head-on encounter with the army, was your weapons. To abandon them was criminal and stupid."

PUBLISHED IN VERDE OLIVO, DECEMBER 8, 1963

JANUARY 1957

The battle of La Plata

OUR FIRST VICTORY was the result of an attack on a small army garrison at the mouth of the La Plata river in the Sierra Maestra. The effect of our victory was electrifying and went far beyond that craggy region. It was a clarion call, proving that the Rebel Army really existed and was ready to fight. For us, it was the reaffirmation of our chances for final victory.

On January 14, 1957, a little more than a month after the surprise attack at Alegría de Pío, we came to a halt by the Magdalena river, which is separated from La Plata by a ridge originating at the Sierra Maestra and ending at the sea. Fidel gave orders for target practice as an initial attempt at some sort of training for our troop. Some of the men were using weapons for the first time in their lives. We had not washed for many days and we also seized upon the opportunity to bathe. Those who were able to do so changed into clean clothes. At that time we had twenty-three weapons in operating condition: nine rifles equipped with telescopic sights, five semiautomatic rifles, four bolt-action rifles, two Thompson submachine guns, two machine pistols, and a 16-gauge shotgun.

That afternoon we climbed the last hill before reaching the environs of La Plata. We were following a not-well-traveled trail marked specially for us with a machete by a peasant named Melquiades Elías. This man had been recommended by our guide Eutimio [Guerra], who at that time was indispensable to us and seemed to be the prototype of the rebel peasant. He was later apprehended by Casillas, however, who, instead of killing him, bribed him with an offer of $10,000 and a rank in the army if he managed to kill Fidel. Eutimio came close to fulfilling his bargain but lacked the courage to do so. He was nonetheless very useful to the enemy, since he informed them of the location of several of our camps.

At the time, Eutimio was serving us loyally. He was one of the many peasants fighting for their land in the struggle against the landowners of the region, and anyone fighting them was also fighting against the Rural Guards, who did the landowners' bidding.

That day we captured two peasants who turned out to be our guide's relatives. One of them was released, but we kept the other one as a precautionary measure. The next day, January 15, we sighted the La Plata army garrison, under construction, with its zinc roof. A group of half-naked men were moving about, but we could nevertheless make out the enemy uniform. Just before sundown, about 6:00 P.M., a boat came in; some guards landed and others got aboard. We did not quite make out the maneuver, so we postponed the attack to the following day.

At dawn on the sixteenth we began watching the garrison. The coast guard had disappeared during the night; scouts were sent out, but no soldiers could be seen anywhere. At 3:00 P.M. we decided to approach the road along the river leading to the garrison and take a look. By nightfall we crossed the shallow La Plata river and took up our positions on the road. Five minutes later we took two peasants into custody, one of them with a record as an informer. When we told them who we were and that they had better speak clearly with us, they gave us some valuable information. The garrison held about fifteen soldiers, they said. We also learned that Chicho Osorio, one of the region's three notorious overseers,[1] was to go by at any moment. These overseers worked for the Laviti family plantation. The Lavitis

1. The others were Miro Saborit and Honorio Olazábal.

had established an enormous fiefdom, holding onto it by means of a regime of terror with the help of characters such as Chicho Osorio. Shortly afterward, Chicho showed up, astride a mule, with a little black boy riding "double." Chicho was drunk. Universo Sánchez gave him the order to halt in the name of the Rural Guard and immediately Chicho replied: "Mosquito." That was the password.

We must have looked like a bunch of pirates, but Chicho Osorio was so drunk we were able to fool him. Fidel stepped forward and, looking very indignant, said he was an army colonel who had come to find out why the rebels had not yet been wiped out. He bragged about going into the woods, which accounted for his beard. He added that the army was "botching things up." In a word, he cut the army's efficiency to pieces. Sheepishly, Chicho Osorio admitted that the soldiers spent all their time inside the barracks, eating and doing nothing but occasional useless rounds. He emphasized that the rebels must be wiped out. We began asking discreetly about friendly and unfriendly people living in the area, and we kept tab on his replies, naturally reversing roles: when Chicho called somebody a bad man we knew he was one of our friends, and so on. We had about twenty-odd names by now, and he was still jabbering away. He told us how he had killed two men in the area, adding: "But my General Batista set me free at once." He spoke of having slapped a few peasants who "had gotten a little out of hand," adding that the soldiers would not do such a thing; on the contrary, they let the peasants talk without punishing them. Fidel asked Osorio what he would do if he ever caught Fidel Castro, and Osorio, with a very expressive gesture, replied: "We'll have to cut his — off." He said he would do the same thing to Crescencio. "Look," he said, showing us his shoes (they were the kind of Mexican-made shoes our men wore), "these shoes belonged to one of those sons of — we killed." Without realizing it, Chicho Osorio had signed his own death sentence. At Fidel's suggestion, he agreed to accompany us to the garrison in order to surprise the soldiers and prove to them they were badly prepared and were neglecting their duties.

As we neared the garrison, with Chicho Osorio as guide, I still wasn't so sure he had not become wise to our trick. But he kept on going, completely unaware, for he was so drunk he could not think straight. When he crossed the river to get near the garrison, Fidel told Osorio that military rules called for the prisoner to be tied up. The man did not resist and he went on, this time unwittingly as a real prisoner. He explained to us that the only guards were posted at the entrance of the barracks under construction and at the house of another one of the overseers, named Honorio. Osorio guided us to a place near the barracks, near the road to El Macío. Comrade Luis Crespo, today a commander, went ahead to scout around and returned saying that the overseer's report was accurate. Crespo had seen the barracks and the pinpoints of light made by the guards' cigarettes.

We were just about ready to approach the garrison when we had to pull back into the woods to let three soldiers on horseback go by. The men were driving a prisoner on foot like a mule. They passed very close to me, and I remember the peasant saying: "I'm just like one of you" and the answer by one of the men whom we later identified as Corporal Bassols: "Shut up and keep going or I'll use the whip on you!" At the time we thought that the peasant would be out of danger by not being in the garrison and would escape our bullets when we attacked. But the following day when the soldiers heard of the attack they murdered him at El Macío.

We had twenty-two weapons ready for the attack. It was a crucial moment because we were short of ammunition. The army garrison had to be taken at all costs, for a failure would have meant expending all our ammunition, leaving us practically defenseless. Lt. Julio Díaz—who later died heroically at the battle of El Uvero—Camilo Cienfuegos, Benítez, and Calixto Morales, armed with semiautomatic rifles, were to surround the palm-thatched house on the right side. Fidel, Universo Sánchez, Luis Crespo, Calixto García, [Manuel] Fajardo—today a commander with the same last name as our physician Piti Fajardo, killed in

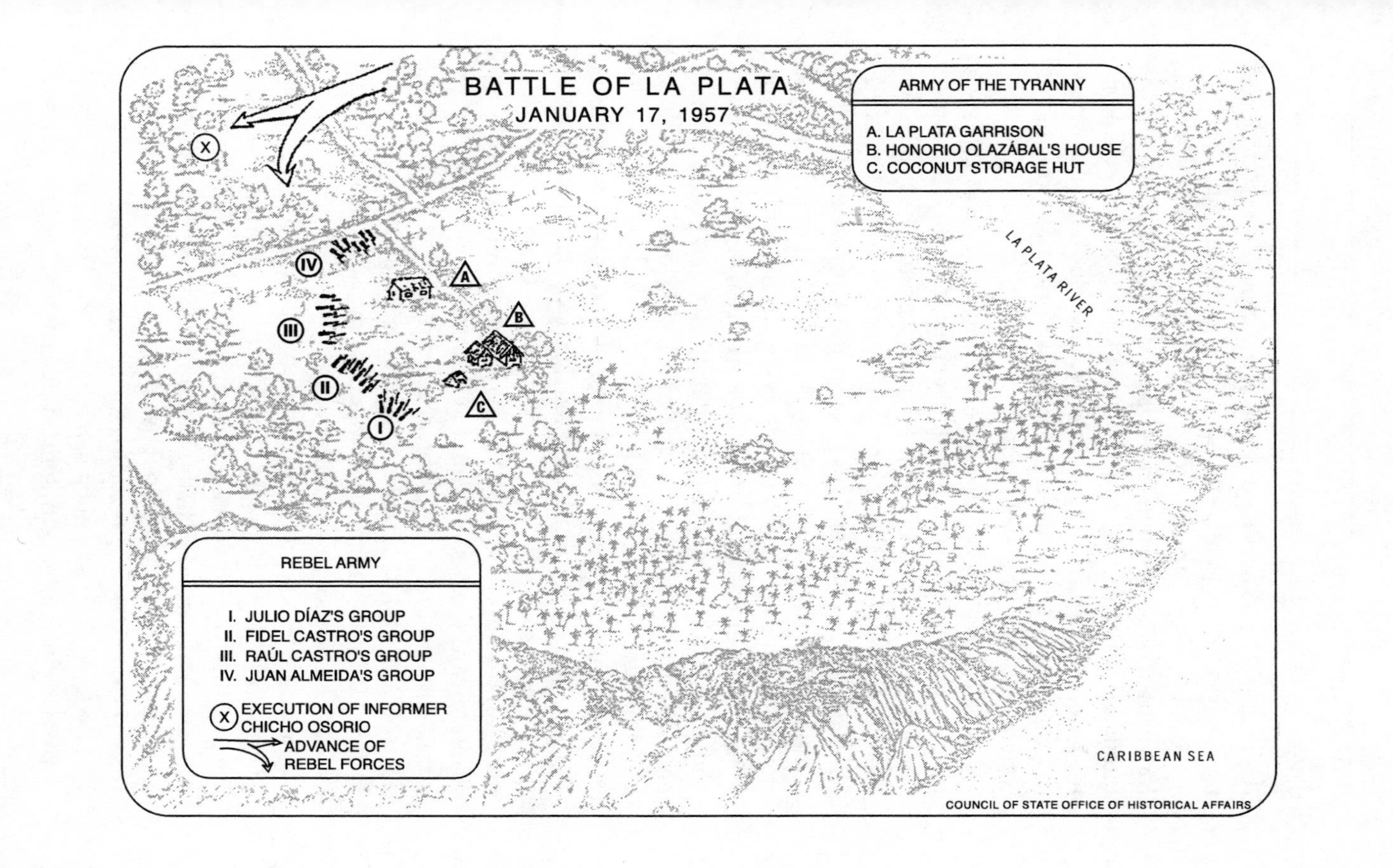
BATTLE OF LA PLATA
JANUARY 17, 1957
ARMY OF THE TYRANNY
A. LA PLATA GARRISON
B. HONORIO OLAZÁBAL'S HOUSE
C. COCONUT STORAGE HUT
LA PLATA RIVER
A
B
C
I
II
III
IV
X
REBEL ARMY
I. JULIO DÍAZ'S GROUP
II. FIDEL CASTRO'S GROUP
III. RAÚL CASTRO'S GROUP
IV. JUAN ALMEIDA'S GROUP
X EXECUTION OF INFORMER CHICHO OSORIO
ADVANCE OF REBEL FORCES
CARIBBEAN SEA
COUNCIL OF STATE OFFICE OF HISTORICAL AFFAIRS

the Escambray—and I would attack the center. The squads led by Raúl and Almeida would attack the garrison from the left.

We approached to within forty meters of the enemy positions. By the light of a full moon, Fidel opened the hostilities with two bursts of machine gun fire and all available rifles joined in. Immediately we demanded the enemy's surrender, but without any response. Murderer-informer Chicho Osorio was executed as soon as the shooting broke out.

The attack had begun at 2:40 A.M., and the guards put up a much stiffer resistance than we had expected. A sergeant, armed with an M-1, opened up with a burst every time we called on them to surrender. We were given orders to use our old Brazilian-type hand grenades. Luis Crespo and I threw ours but they did not go off; Raúl Castro threw a stick of dynamite with the same negative result. It became necessary to get close to the houses and set them on fire even at the risk of our own lives. Universo Sánchez made a futile attempt and Camilo Cienfuegos also failed. Finally, Luis Crespo and I got close to one of the buildings and set it on fire. The light from the blaze allowed us to see that it was simply a place for storing coconuts, but the soldiers had been intimidated and gave up the fight. One of them, trying to escape, ran smack into Luis Crespo's rifle; Luis shot him in the chest, took the man's rifle, and we continued firing toward the house. Camilo Cienfuegos, sheltered behind a tree, fired on the fleeing sergeant and ran out of ammunition. The soldiers, almost defenseless, were being cut to pieces by our bullets. Camilo Cienfuegos was first into the house, where shouts of surrender were being heard.

Quickly we took stock of our booty: eight Springfields, one Thompson submachine gun, and about one thousand rounds; we had fired approximately five hundred rounds. In addition, we now had cartridge belts, fuel, knives, clothing, and some food. Casualties: they suffered two dead, five wounded. We took three prisoners. Some, including the informer-overseer Honorio, had fled. On our side, not a scratch.

We withdrew after setting fire to the soldiers' quarters and after tending the wounded, leaving them in the care of the prisoners. Three of them were seriously wounded, and we were told after the final victory that they died. One of the captured soldiers later joined the forces under Cmdr. Raúl Castro, was promoted to lieutenant, and died in an airplane accident following the war.[2]

Our attitude toward the wounded was in open contrast to that of Batista's army. Not only did they kill our wounded men; they abandoned their own. This difference made a great impact on the enemy over time, and it was a factor in our victory. Fidel gave orders that the prisoners be given all the medicines to take care of the wounded. I was pained at this decision because, as a physician, I felt the need to save all available medicine and drugs for our own men. We freed all the civilians, and at 4:30 on the morning of January 17 we started for Palma Mocha, arriving there at dawn and seeking out the most inaccessible zones of the Sierra Maestra.

A most pitiful scene awaited us: the day before, an army corporal and one of the overseers had warned all the families living in the area that the air force was going to bomb the entire zone, and the exodus toward the coast had begun. No one knew of our presence in the area, so it was evidently a maneuver on the part of the foremen and the Rural Guards to take the land and belongings away from the peasants. But their lie had coincided with our attack and now became a reality. Terror was rampant among the peasants, and it was impossible for us to stop their flight.

La Plata was the first victorious battle of the Rebel Army. This battle and the one following it were the only times that we had more weapons than men. Peasants were not yet ready to join in the struggle, and communication with the bases in the city was practically nonexistent.

PUBLISHED IN VERDE OLIVO, MARCH 12, 1961

2. Víctor Manuel Maché.

JANUARY 1957

The battle of Arroyo del Infierno

THE ARROYO DEL INFIERNO is a narrow brook flowing into the Palma Mocha river. Walking along it, away from the Palma Mocha, and mounting the slopes of the bordering hills, we reached a small circular clearing where we found two peasant huts. Here we pitched camp, although we naturally did not stay in the huts.

Fidel was convinced that the army would come after us and would locate our approximate position. With this in mind, he planned an ambush to trap some enemy soldiers. To this end he posted the men.

Fidel watched our lines closely, and checked and rechecked our defenses. At that time contour lines were marked very irregularly every five meters up the hill. On the morning of January 19 we were reviewing the troops when there was an accident that could have had serious consequences. As a trophy from the battle of La Plata, I had taken a corporal's helmet, and wore it with great pride. But when I went to inspect the troops, walking through the open woods, the forward outpost heard us coming from afar and saw the group headed by someone wearing a helmet. Fortunately at that moment they were cleaning their weapons, and only Camilo Cienfuegos's rifle was working. He opened fire on us and immediately realized his mistake. His first shot missed and then his automatic rifle jammed, preventing him from firing further. This incident was symptomatic of the state of high tension that prevailed as we waited for the relief that the battle would bring. At such times, even those with nerves of steel feel a certain gentle trembling of the knees, and each man longs for the arrival of that luminous moment of battle. None of us was particularly eager to fight, however; we did so out of necessity.

At dawn on January 22 we heard a few isolated shots from the direction of the Palma Mocha river, and this forced us to maintain even stricter discipline in our lines, to be more cautious, and to await the now imminent appearance of the enemy.

Believing the soldiers to be nearby, we cooked neither breakfast nor lunch. Some time before, Crespo and I had found a hen's nest and we rationed the eggs, leaving one, as is customary, so the hen would continue to lay. That day, because of the shots we had heard during the night, Crespo decided we should eat the last egg, and we did so. At noon we saw a human figure in one of the huts. At first we thought that one of our comrades had disobeyed the order not to go near the houses. But it turned out to be one of the dictatorship's soldiers.

Then about six others appeared; some of them soon left, and three remained in view. We saw that the soldier on guard looked around, picked a few weeds, put them behind his ears in an attempt at camouflage, and sat calmly in the shade, his face, clearly visible through the telescopic sight, showing no apprehension. Fidel's opening shot shattered him; he managed only to give a shout, something like "Oh, mother!" and fell over dead. The crossfire spread and the soldier's two companions also fell. Suddenly I noticed that in the closer hut another soldier was trying to hide from our fire. Only his legs were visible from my higher position, since the roof of the hut covered his body. My first shot missed, but the second one caught him full in the chest and he fell, leaving his rifle stuck in the ground by the bayonet. Covered by Crespo, I reached the house where I saw the body, and took his bullets, his rifle, and a few other belongings. The bullet had struck him in the middle of the chest, probably piercing his heart, and death had been instantaneous; he already

BATTLE OF ARROYO DEL INFIERNO

JANUARY 22, 1957

1. FIDEL CASTRO'S GROUP
2. RAÚL CASTRO'S GROUP
3. JUAN ALMEIDA'S GROUP
4. GUILLERMO GARCÍA'S GROUP
5. DANIEL MOTOLÁ'S GROUP
6. JULIO DÍAZ'S GROUP
7. EFIGENIO AMEIJEIRAS'S GROUP

PEASANT HUTS

A. BETO CINTRAS
B. DELFÍN TORRES

ARMY OF THE TYRANNY

1
2
3
4
5
6
7
A
B

COUNCIL OF STATE OFFICE OF HISTORICAL AFFAIRS

showed the first signs of rigor mortis, perhaps because of the exhaustion of his last day's march.

The battle was extraordinarily fierce. Soon, our plan successfully executed, we all withdrew.

On taking inventory we found that we had spent approximately nine hundred bullets and had retrieved seventy from a full cartridge case. We also acquired a rifle, a Garand, which was given to Cmdr. Efigenio Ameijeiras, who used it during a good part of the war. We counted four enemy dead, but months later, on capturing an informer, we learned that actually five had fallen. It was not a total victory, but neither was it a Pyrrhic victory. We had matched our forces against the army in a new situation, and we had passed the test.

This raised our spirits greatly, and enabled us to continue the whole day clambering toward the most inaccessible places in order to escape pursuit by larger enemy forces. In this way, we reached the other side of the mountain. We were walking parallel to Batista's troops, who also withdrew, both groups having crossed the same mountain peaks to reach the other side. For two days our troops and those of the enemy marched almost side by side without realizing it; once we slept in a hut barely separated from another one housing the enemy by a small river like the La Plata and by a couple of bends in the road. The lieutenant commanding the enemy patrol was [Ángel] Sánchez Mosquera, whose name had become infamous throughout the Sierra Maestra in the wake of his pillaging. It is worth mentioning that the shots we had heard several hours before the battle had killed a peasant of Haitian descent who had refused to lead the troops to our hideout. If they had not committed this murder they would not have found us waiting for them.

We were once again overburdened: many of us carried two rifles. Under these circumstances it was not easy to walk, but clearly morale was different from what it had been after the disaster of Alegría de Pío. A few days earlier we had defeated a smaller group, entrenched in a garrison; now we had defeated a column on the march, superior in numbers to our forces. We were able to see in real life the importance of this type of warfare, of wiping out the enemy's forward units. For without a vanguard detachment, an army is paralyzed.

PUBLISHED IN VERDE OLIVO, MARCH 26, 1961

JANUARY- FEBRUARY 1957

Air attack

AFTER THE VICTORY over Sánchez Mosquera's forces, we had walked along the banks of the La Plata river. Later, crossing the Magdalena river, we had returned to the already familiar region of Caracas. But the atmosphere there was now different: the first time we were hidden in the same hill and all the people supported us; now Casillas's troops had passed through, sowing terror throughout the region. The peasants had gone, leaving only their empty huts and a few animals, which we killed and ate. Experience had taught us that it was not safe to live in the houses, so after spending the night in one of the more isolated huts, we returned to the woods and pitched our camp beside a small waterfall almost at the top of Caracas hill.

Manuel Fajardo came to me and asked if it were possible that we would lose the war. My reply, quite aside from the euphoria of victory, was always the same: the war would unquestionably be won. He explained that he had asked me because Morán had claimed it was no longer possible to win the war, that we were lost, and he had urged Fajardo to abandon the campaign. I reported this to Fidel, who told me that Morán had already let Fidel know that he was covertly testing the morale of the troops. We agreed that this was not the best system, and Fidel made a short speech urging greater discipline and explaining the dangers that might arise if it were disregarded. He also announced the three crimes punishable by death: insubordination, desertion, and defeatism.

Our situation was not a happy one in those days. The consolidation of the column had been completed. It still lacked the spirit forged in battle and was without a clear political consciousness. One comrade would leave us today, another the day after; some requested assignments in the city that were often much more dangerous but which meant an escape from the rugged conditions in the countryside. Nevertheless, our campaign continued on its course. Morán displayed indefatigable activity looking for food and making contacts with the peasants of the region.

Such were our spirits on the morning of January 30. Eutimio Guerra, the traitor, had asked permission to visit his sick mother and Fidel had granted it, also giving him some money for the trip. According to Eutimio, the trip would last several weeks. We had not yet understood a series of incidents that were later clearly explained by this man's subsequent behavior. When he rejoined the troop, Eutimio said that he had almost reached Palma Mocha when he learned that the government forces were on our trail. He had tried to warn us, he said, but he found only the corpses of the soldiers in the house belonging to Delfín [Torres], one of the peasants on whose land the battle of Arroyo del Infierno had been fought. Eutimio said he had followed our path across the Sierra until he finally found us. What had actually happened was that he had been captured and was now working as an enemy agent; he had been bribed with money and a military rank in exchange for murdering Fidel.

As part of this plan, Eutimio had left the camp the previous day, and on the morning of January 30, after a cold night, just as we were getting up, we heard the roar of planes that we could not locate exactly since we were in the brush. Our field kitchen was about two hundred meters below us near a small spring, where the forward unit was stationed. Suddenly we heard the dive of a bomber, the rattle of machine gun fire, and then the bombs. At the time our experience was very limited, and we seemed to hear shots from all sides. Fifty-caliber bullets explode when they hit the ground, and what we heard was the firing of machine guns from the air. As the bullets hit near us, however, they gave the impression of coming from the woods. Because of this we thought we were being attacked by ground troops.

I was instructed to wait for the forward detachment and to collect some of the belongings we had abandoned during the air attack. I was to meet the rest of the troop at Cueva del Humo. I was accompanied by Chao, the veteran of the Spanish civil war. For a while we waited for some of the missing men but found no one. We followed the column's tracks, which were none too clear, carrying heavy loads. We came to a clearing and decided to rest. After a while, we heard sounds and saw movement. The column's tracks were also being followed by Guillermo García (today a commander) and Sergio Acuña, both from the forward detachment. After some deliberation, Guillermo García and I returned to the camp to see what was happening since we no longer heard any noise: the planes had disappeared. We beheld a desolate spectacle: with a strange precision that fortunately was not repeated during the war, the field kitchen had been attacked. The hearth had been smashed to pieces by machine gun fire, and a bomb had exploded precisely in the middle of the forward detachment's camp, but naturally there was no one there now. Morán and another comrade had gone to scout, and Morán returned alone, announcing that he had seen the planes from afar, that there were five of them, and that there were no ground troops in the vicinity. The five of us, carrying heavy loads, continued walking past the sad spectacle of the burned-out homes of our old friends. The only living things remaining were a cat that meowed at us pitifully and a pig, which came out grunting on hearing us pass. We had heard of Cueva del Humo but did not know exactly where it was. Thus we spent the night in uncertainty, waiting to see our comrades but fearing that we would meet the enemy instead.

On January 31 we took our positions on the top of a hill overlooking some cultivated fields. In what we thought was Cueva del Humo we made various scouting forays without finding anything. Sergio, one of the five, thought he saw two men in baseball caps, but he was slow in telling us and we could not catch up with them. We went out with Guillermo to scout the bottom of the valley near the banks of the Ají where a friend of Guillermo's gave us something to eat, but all the people were very frightened. The friend told us that Ciro Frías's entire stock of merchandise had been taken by the guards and burned; the mules had been requisitioned and the herdsman killed. Ciro Frías's store was then burned down and his wife taken prisoner. The men who had passed in the morning were under the orders of Major Casillas, who had slept somewhere near the house.

On February 1 we stayed in our little camp, practically in the open, resting from the exhausting march of the previous day. At eleven o'clock in the morning we heard gunfire on the other side of the hill and soon, much closer to us, we heard the heartrending cries of someone begging for help. With this, Sergio Acuña's nerves apparently snapped. Silently, he left his cartridge belt and rifle, and deserted the guard post he was assigned to. I noted in my field diary that he had taken with him a palm leaf hat, a can of condensed milk, and three sausages; at the time we were very sorry about the can of milk and the sausages. A few hours later we heard a noise and we prepared to defend ourselves, not knowing whether the deserter had betrayed us or not. But Crescencio appeared with a large column of almost all our men, and also some new people from Manzanillo led by Roberto Pesant. Missing from our forces were the deserter Sergio Acuña, in addition to Calixto Morales, Calixto García, and Manuel Acuña; also missing was a new recruit who had been lost on this first day during the crossfire.[1]

Once again we descended to the valley of the Ají, and on the way some of the supplies from Manzanillo were distributed, including a surgical kit for me and changes of clothes for everyone. We felt especially moved to get the new set of clothing, which sported initials embroidered by the girls of Manzanillo. The next day, February 2, two months after the landing of the

1. Evangelista Mendoza.

Granma, we were a reunited, homogeneous group; ten more men from Manzanillo had joined us and we felt stronger and in better spirits than ever. We had many discussions on how the surprise attack and the air attack had come about, and we all agreed that our cooking by day and the smoke from the fire had guided the planes to our camp. For many months and perhaps for the duration of the war, the memories of that surprise attack weighed on the spirit of the troop. Right to the end, fires were not built in the open air during the day, for we always feared some unfortunate consequence.

We would have found it impossible to believe, and I think it did not enter anyone's mind, that Eutimio Guerra, the traitor and informer, had been in the observation plane, pointing out to Casillas the place where we were. But that is what happened. His mother's illness had been a pretext to leave us and look for the murderer Casillas.

For some time thereafter Eutimio played an important adverse role in the development of our war of liberation.

PUBLISHED IN VERDE OLIVO, APRIL 16, 1961

FEBRUARY 1957

Surprise attack at Altos de Espinosa

AFTER THE SURPRISE AIR ATTACK recounted in the last chapter, we abandoned Caracas hill and attempted to return to familiar regions where we could establish direct contact with Manzanillo, receive more help from the outside, and better follow the situation in the rest of the country.

For this reason, we crossed the Ají and returned through territories familiar to all of us, until we reached the house of old Mendoza.[1] We had to cut our way with machetes along the edge of the hills, through paths unwalked by men for a very long time, and our progress was very slow. We spent the night on one of those hills, practically without eating. I still remember, as if it were one of the great banquets of my life, when Crespo arrived with a can containing four pork sausages, a result of his earlier frugality, saying that they were for his friends. Crespo, Fidel, and I, along with a fourth man enjoyed that meager ration as if it were a sumptuous feast. The march continued until we reached the house, to the right of Caracas, where old Mendoza was to prepare us something to eat. Despite his fear, his peasant loyalty led him to welcome us each time we passed through there; he was responding to the commitments of a friendship with Crescencio Pérez or some of the other peasants in the troop.

The march was particularly painful for me, for I was suffer-

1. Eligio Mendoza.

ing from an attack of malaria. It was Crespo and that unforgettable comrade Julio Zenón Acosta who helped me through that anguished march. On reaching a hamlet we never slept indoors; but my poor health and that of the famous Morán, who always found an excuse to get sick, made it necessary for us to sleep under a roof while the rest of the troops kept watch in the vicinity, coming to the house only to eat.

We were forced to reduce the size of the troop, for there was a group of men with very low morale, and one or two seriously wounded; among the latter were the present minister of the interior, Ramiro Valdés, and Ignacio Pérez, a son of Crescencio, who later died heroically with the rank of captain. Ramirito had been badly wounded in the knee, the same knee that had already been hit at the Moncada garrison, so we were forced to leave him behind. A few other boys left us, a fact that was a net gain for the troop. I remember one of them had an attack of nerves, there in the solitude of the mountains and the guerrilla camp. He began to shout that he had been promised a camp with abundant food and antiaircraft defenses, but instead the planes were hounding him and he had neither permanent quarters, nor food, nor even water to drink. This was more or less the same impression that all new guerrillas had of campaign life. Afterward, those who stayed and passed the first tests grew accustomed to dirt, to lack of water, food, shelter, and security, and to a life where the only things one could rely on were a rifle and the cohesion and resistance of the small guerrilla nucleus.

Ciro Frías arrived with some recent recruits, bringing news that today makes us smile, but at the time filled us with confusion: news that Díaz Tamayo was on the verge of switching allegiance and "making a deal" with the revolutionary forces;[2] news that Faustino had been able to collect many thousands of pesos. In short, the word was that sabotage was spreading throughout the country and chaos was approaching for the

2. Brigadier General Martín Díaz Tamayo was military head of Batista's troops in the entire province of Oriente.

government. In addition, we heard a sad piece of news, but with an important lesson in it. Sergio Acuña, who had deserted several days before, had gone to the home of some relatives. There, he began to brag to his cousins about his deeds as a guerrilla; a certain Pedro Herrera overheard and denounced him to the Rural Guard. The infamous Corporal Roselló arrived (he has since been brought to justice by the people), tortured him, shot him four times, and apparently hanged him. This clearly showed our men the value of unity and the uselessness of attempting on one's own to flee the collective destiny. But it also made it necessary for us to change locations, for presumably the boy might have talked before being murdered, and he knew we were at the house of Florentino [Enamorado].

There was a curious incident at the time and it was only later, putting two and two together, that things became clear to us: Eutimio Guerra told us that he had dreamed about Sergio Acuña's death, and furthermore, that it was Corporal Roselló who killed him. This sparked a long philosophical discussion about whether or not prediction of things to come was possible through dreams. It was part of my daily task to explain things of a cultural or political nature to the men, and I clearly stated that this was not possible, that it could be due to some great coincidence, that we had all believed that Sergio Acuña might end that way, and that Roselló was the man who was at that time devastating the region, etc. Furthermore, Universo Sánchez gave the key by saying that Eutimio was a "storyteller," that someone had told him about it the previous day when he had left the camp to go get fifty cans of milk and a military lantern.

One of the men who insisted most strongly on the theory of illumination was a forty-five-year-old peasant whom I have already mentioned: Julio Zenón Acosta. He was my first pupil in the Sierra. I was teaching him to read and write, and every time we stopped I would teach him a few letters; we were at the stage of learning the vowels. With great determination, looking to the years ahead rather than the ones behind, Julio Zenón had set himself the task of becoming literate. Perhaps his example may be useful to many peasants today, his fellow peasants from the area during the war, or to those who know his story. For Julio Zenón Acosta was another of our great supporters at that time. He was a tireless worker, familiar with the area, always ready to help a comrade in trouble, or a comrade from the city who did not yet have sufficient stamina to get out of tight spots. It was he who brought water from distant water holes, who could make a quick fire, who could find dry kindling even on a rainy day. He was, in fact, our jack-of-all-trades.

One night, shortly before Eutimio's treachery became known, he complained that he did not have a blanket and asked Fidel to lend him one. It was very cold in the hills in February. Fidel answered that both of them would be cold if he gave Eutimio his blanket. He suggested that they sleep under the same blanket and Fidel's two coats. So Eutimio Guerra spent the whole night next to Fidel; he had on him a .45 pistol that Casillas had given him to kill Fidel, and a pair of grenades to protect his retreat from the hilltop. He asked Universo Sánchez and me (the two of us at that time always stayed close to Fidel) about those on guard duty. He said: "I'm very interested in our guards; we have to always be careful." We explained that three men were posted nearby; we ourselves, veterans of the *Granma* and Fidel's trusted men, relieved each other through the night to protect him personally. Thus, Eutimio spent the night beside the revolution's leader, holding his life at the point of a gun, awaiting the chance to assassinate him. But he could not bring himself to do it. That night the fate of the Cuban revolution depended, in large measure, on the uncharted and complex twists of a man's mind, on the balance of courage and fear, of terror and perhaps pangs of conscience, on a traitor's lust for power and wealth. Luckily for us, Eutimio's inhibitions were stronger, and the following day arrived without incident.

We had left Florentino's house and were camped in a dry stream bed in a ravine. Ciro Frías had gone to his home, which was relatively near, and had brought back some hens and some other food, so that the long night of rain with virtually no shelter was compensated in the morning by hot soup and other food. Somebody brought the news that Eutimio had been by there too. Eutimio came and went, for he was trusted by everyone, and he had found us at Florentino's house and explained that after he had left to see his sick mother, he had seen what had happened at Caracas and had followed after us to see what else happened. He also explained that his mother was now well. He was showing signs of extraordinary boldness. We were in a place called Altos de Espinosa, very close to a chain of hills—El Lomón, Loma del Burro, Caracas—that the planes strafed constantly. With the gravity of an oracle, Eutimio said: "Today they will strafe the Loma del Burro." The planes did strafe the Loma del Burro, and Eutimio jumped for joy, exulting in his keen prediction.

On February 9, 1957, Ciro Frías and Luis Crespo left as usual to scout for food, and all was quiet. At ten in the morning a peasant boy named Labrada, a recent recruit, captured someone nearby. He turned out to be a relative of Crescencio and an employee in the store of Celestino [León], where Casillas's soldiers were stationed. He informed us that there were 140 soldiers in the house; in fact, from our position we could see them in the distance atop a barren hill. Furthermore, the prisoner said he had talked with Eutimio and had been told that the following day the area would be bombed. Casillas's troops had moved, but he could not say in what direction they were going. Fidel became suspicious; at last Eutimio's strange behavior had come to our attention and speculations began.

At 1:30 P.M. Fidel decided to leave the area and we climbed to the top of the hill, where we waited for our scouts. Soon Ciro Frías and Luis Crespo arrived; they had seen nothing unusual. We were talking about this when Ciro Redondo thought he saw a shadow moving. He called for silence and cocked his rifle. At that moment we heard a shot and then a burst of fire. At once the air was full of shots and explosions provoked by the attack, which was concentrated on our previous camp. The new camp emptied rapidly; later I found out that Julio Zenón Acosta had died on the hilltop. That uneducated and illiterate peasant who had understood the enormous tasks the revolution would face after its victory, and who was learning the alphabet to prepare himself for this, would never finish that task. The rest of us ran. I had to leave behind my knapsack—my pride and joy—full of medicines and some reserve rations, books, and blankets. I did manage to snatch up a blanket I had taken from the Batista army as a trophy from La Plata, and ran.

Soon I met up with a group of our men: Almeida, Julito Díaz, Universo Sánchez, Camilo Cienfuegos, Guillermo García, Ciro Frías, Motolá, Pesant, Emilio Labrada, and Yayo [Reyes]. We followed a winding path trying to escape the shots, unaware of the fate of our other comrades. We heard isolated explosions behind us; we were easy to follow since the speed of our flight made it impossible to erase our tracks. At 5:15 P.M., by my watch, we reached a craggy spot where the forest ended; after vacillating a while we decided it was better to wait there for nightfall, for if we crossed the clearing in daylight we would be spotted. If the enemy had followed our tracks, we were well placed to defend ourselves. However, the enemy did not appear and we were able to continue on our way, guided uncertainly by Ciro Frías, who knew the region vaguely. It had been suggested that we divide into two patrols in order to ease the march and leave fewer tracks. But Almeida and I were opposed to this because we wanted to preserve the unity of the group. We recognized where we were, at a place called Limones, and after a few hesitations—for some of the men wanted to move on—Almeida, who led the group by virtue of his captain's rank,[3] ordered us to continue to El Lomón, which Fidel had designated as our meeting place. Some of the men argued that El Lomón was a place known to Eutimio and that therefore the army would be there waiting for us. Of course we no longer had any doubt

3. The Rebel Army included three officer ranks: lieutenant, captain, and commander. For an explanation of the development of the command structure and order of battle of the Rebel Army, see page 459.

that Eutimio was a traitor, but Almeida's decision was to comply with Fidel's order.

After three days of separation, on February 12 we met up with Fidel near El Lomón, in a place called La Derecha de la Caridad. There it was confirmed for us that Eutimio Guerra was a traitor, and we heard the whole story. It began after the battle of La Plata, when he was captured by Casillas and, instead of being killed, was offered a certain amount for Fidel's life; we learned that it was he who had revealed our position in Caracas and that he had also given the order to attack the Loma del Burro, since that place had been on our itinerary (we had changed our plan at the last minute). He had also organized the attack on the small hollow in which we were sheltered in the Cañ n del Arroyo, from which we saved ourselves with only one casualty because of the opportune retreat that Fidel ordered. We also had confirmation of the death of Julio Acosta; at least one Rural Guard was dead, and there were also a few wounded. I must confess that my rifle caused neither the death nor the wounds, for I did nothing more than beat a speedy "strategic retreat."

Now we twelve (minus Labrada who had disappeared) were once again reunited with the rest of the group: Raúl, Ameijeiras, Ciro Redondo, Manuel Fajardo, [Juan Francisco] Echevarría, Morán, and Fidel, a total of eighteen men. This was the "Reunified Revolutionary Army" on February 12, 1957. Some of our comrades had been scattered, some raw recruits had abandoned us, and there was the desertion of a veteran of the *Granma* named Armando Rodríguez, who carried a Thompson submachine gun. Toward the end, he had such a terrified and anguished face whenever he heard shots in the distance that we termed that expression the "hunted look." Each time a man evidenced the face of a terrified animal, possessed by the same terror that our ex-comrade had shown in the days before Altos de Espinosa, we immediately predicted an unfortunate outcome, for the "hunted look" was incompatible with guerrilla life. In this case our man with the "hunted look" had "shifted into third," as we said using our new guerrilla slang, and his gun turned up much later at the house of a peasant miles away. His legs had performed impressively.

PUBLISHED IN VERDE OLIVO, JUNE 25, 1961

FEBRUARY 1957

Death of a traitor

After this small army was reunited, we decided to leave the region of El Lomón and move on to new ground. On the way, we continued making contacts with peasants in the area and laying the necessary groundwork for our subsistence. At the same time, we were leaving the Sierra Maestra and heading toward the plains, to places where we were to meet the people from the organization in the cities.

We passed through a village called La Montería, and afterward camped in a small thicket near a little stream, on the property of a man named Epifanio Díaz, whose sons fought in the revolution.[1]

We were moving in order to establish closer ties with the July 26 Movement, since our nomadic and clandestine life made any exchange between the two parts of the Movement impossible. Practically speaking, we were two separate groups, with different strategies and tactics. The deep rift that in later months would endanger the unity of the Movement had not yet appeared, but we could already see that our concepts were different.[2]

It was there on that farm that we met with the Movement's

1. Enrique and Miguel Díaz.
2. The July 26 Movement had two wings at the time, known as the *Sierra* (mountains) and *Llano*. Although Llano means "plains," the term referred to the urban areas, where the July 26 Movement maintained an underground organization. Throughout this period leaders of the two groupings

most important figures in the cities; among them were three women known today to all the people of Cuba: Vilma Espín, now the president of the Federation of Cuban Women and the wife of Raúl; Haydée Santamaría, president of Casa de las Américas and the wife of Armando Hart; and Celia Sánchez, our beloved comrade throughout the entire struggle, who later joined the guerrillas for the duration of the war. Another person who arrived was Faustino Pérez, an old acquaintance of ours, a comrade from the *Granma.* He had gone to carry out some missions in the city and came to report to us, later returning to continue his work in the cities. (A little later he was taken prisoner.)

We also met Armando Hart, and I had my only opportunity to meet that great leader from Santiago, Frank País.

Frank País was one of those men who command respect from the first meeting; he looked more or less as he appears in the photographs we see today, but his eyes had extraordinary depth.

It is difficult today to speak of a dead comrade whom I met only once and whose history belongs to the people. I can only say that his eyes immediately revealed a man possessed by a cause, who believed in it, and that he was clearly a man of superior character. Today he is called "the unforgettable Frank País"; for me, who saw him only once, he truly is unforgettable. Frank is another of the many comrades who, had their lives not been cut short, would today be dedicating themselves to the common task of the socialist revolution. His loss is part of the heavy price that the people paid to gain their liberation.

Frank gave us a quiet lesson in order and discipline, cleaning our dirty rifles, counting bullets and packing them so that they would not be lost. From that day on, I made a decision to take better care of my gun (and I carried through with this, although I cannot say I was ever a model of meticulousness).

But that same thicket was also the scene of other events. For

---

debated questions of strategy. Guevara discusses these in more detail in the chapters "One Year of Armed Struggle" and "A Decisive Meeting."

the first time we were visited by a journalist, and a foreign journalist at that—the famous Matthews. He brought with him only a small box camera with which he took the pictures that were later so widely distributed and so hotly disputed in the stupid statements of a Batista minister.[3] The interpreter on that occasion was Javier Pazos, who later joined the guerrillas and remained for some time.

Matthews, according to what Fidel told me (I was not present at the interview), asked concrete questions, none of them tricky, and he appeared to sympathize with the revolution. I remember that Fidel said, in answer to a question, that yes, he was anti-imperialist, and he objected to the delivery of arms to Batista, insisting that these would not be used for intercontinental defense but only to oppress the people.

The visit by Matthews was naturally very brief. As soon as he left we were ready to move on. We were advised to redouble our guard, however, since Eutimio was in the area; Almeida was immediately ordered to find him and take him prisoner. The patrol was made up of Julito Díaz, Ciro Frías, Camilo Cienfuegos, and Efigenio Ameijeiras. It was Ciro Frías who easily overcame Eutimio, and he was brought to us. We found on him a .45 pistol, three grenades, and a safe-conduct pass from Casillas. Once captured with this incriminating evidence on him, he could not doubt his fate. He fell on his knees before Fidel and asked simply that we kill him. He said he knew he deserved death. At that moment he seemed to have aged; on his temple were a good many gray hairs we had never noticed before.

The moment was one of extraordinary tension. Fidel up-

3. Herbert L. Matthews, a senior correspondent for the *New York Times*, interviewed Castro in the Sierra Maestra on February 17, 1957. The publication of the interview days later made a sharp impact within Cuba and internationally. Batista's defense minister Santiago Verdeja claimed the article was "a chapter in a fantastic novel," and that "at no time did the said correspondent have an interview" with Castro. The *Times* replied by running a photo of Matthews with Castro, reprinted in the photo section of this volume.

braided him harshly for his betrayal, and Eutimio wanted only to be shot, for he recognized his guilt. All of us who were witnesses will never forget the moment when Ciro Frías, a close friend of his, began to speak. He reminded Eutimio of everything he had done for him, of the little favors he and his brother had done for Eutimio's family, and of how Eutimio had betrayed them, first by causing the death of Ciro's brother—whom Eutimio had denounced to the army several days before—and then by trying to wipe out the whole group. It was a long and moving speech, which Eutimio listened to in silence, his head bent. We asked him if he wanted anything, and he answered yes, that he wanted the revolution, or rather us, to take care of his children.

The revolution has kept this promise. Eutimio Guerra's name reappears today in this book, but it has already been forgotten, perhaps even by his children. They now have a new name and are attending one of our many new schools; they receive the same treatment as all the sons and daughters of the people, and are preparing themselves for a better life. But one day they will have to know that their father was executed by the revolutionary power because of his treachery. It is also just that they be told how their father—a peasant who had allowed himself to be tempted by corruption and had tried to commit a grave crime, moved by the desire for glory and wealth—nevertheless recognized his error, and had not even hinted at a desire for clemency, which he knew he did not deserve. Finally, they should also know that in his last moments he remembered his children and asked that they be treated well.

Just then a heavy storm broke and the sky darkened; in the midst of a deluge, the sky crossed by lightning and the noise of thunder, as one of these strokes of lightning burst and was followed closely by a thunderbolt, Eutimio Guerra's life was ended. Even those comrades standing near him did not hear the shot.

The following day, as we were burying him, there was a small incident I remember. Manuel Fajardo wanted to put a cross on his grave, and I refused to let him because such evidence of the execution was very dangerous for the owners of the property where we were camped. So he cut a small cross into the trunk of a nearby tree. And this is the sign that marks the grave of the traitor.

Morán left us at that time; he knew how little we thought of him by then, and we all considered him a potential deserter. (He had earlier disappeared for two or three days on the pretext of looking for Eutimio and had got lost in the forest.)

As we were preparing to leave, a shot sounded and we found Morán with a bullet in his leg. The men who were nearest had many heated discussions at the time. Some said that the shot was accidental, while others insisted he shot himself in order to stay behind.

Morán's subsequent history—his treachery and his death at the hands of revolutionaries in Guantánamo—would seem to establish that he shot himself intentionally.

When we left, Frank País agreed to send a group of men during the first days of the following month, March. They were to join us at the house of Epifanio Díaz in the vicinity of El Jíbaro.

PUBLISHED IN VERDE OLIVO, JULY 9, 1961

FEBRUARY– MARCH 1957

Bitter days

THE DAYS FOLLOWING OUR DEPARTURE from Epifanio Díaz's house were for me personally the most painful days of the war. These notes have attempted to give an idea of what the first part of our revolutionary struggle was like for all the combatants. If in this section, more than any other, I must refer to my personal participation, it is because it is connected to later episodes and it is not possible to separate the two without losing the continuity of the narrative.

After leaving Epifanio's house, our revolutionary group consisted of seventeen men from the original army, as well as three new comrades: Gil, Sotolongo, and Raúl Díaz. These three comrades had arrived on the *Granma;* they had been hiding for some time near Manzanillo and, hearing of our presence, had decided to join us. Their stories were the same as all of ours; they had been able to evade the Rural Guards by seeking refuge in the house of one peasant after another, had reached Manzanillo, and had hidden there. Now they joined their fate to that of the whole column. In that period, as can be seen, it was very difficult to enlarge our army; a few new men came, but others left. The physical conditions of the struggle were very hard, but the spiritual conditions were even more so, and we lived with the feeling of being continually under siege.

In those days we were walking slowly in no fixed direction, hiding in small thickets in a region where the foliage had been consumed by livestock, leaving only remnants of vegetation. One night we heard on Fidel's small radio that a comrade from the *Granma* who had left with Crescencio Pérez had been captured. We already knew about this from Eutimio's confession, but the news had not yet been officially given; now at least we knew he was alive. Prisoners did not always emerge alive from an interrogation by Batista's army. Every now and then, from different directions, we heard machine gun fire; the Rural Guards were shooting into the wooded areas. Although the enemy troops would expend considerable ammunition, they rarely entered these areas.

In my field diary I noted, on February 22, that I had the first symptoms of what might become a serious asthma attack, for I was without my antiasthmatic medicine. The date of the new rendezvous was March 5, so we were forced to wait for a few days.

In that period, as I said, we moved very slowly, without a fixed route, marking time until March 5, the day when Frank País was to send us a group of men with arms. We had already decided that we first had to strengthen the firepower of our small front before increasing it in numbers, and therefore all available arms in Santiago were to be sent up to the Sierra Maestra.

One day, dawn found us by the side of a small stream where there was almost no vegetation. We spent a precarious day in that spot, in a valley near Las Mercedes, which I believe was called La Majagua (names are now a little vague in my memory). We arrived by night at the house of old Emiliano,[1] another of the many peasants who in those days were frightened each time they saw us but who nevertheless valiantly risked their lives for us, and thus contributed to the development of the revolution. It was the rainy season in the Sierra and each night we were soaked, which is why we went into homes of peasants despite the danger, for the area was crawling with soldiers.

My asthma was so bad that I could not move very well, and

1. Emiliano Leyva.

we had to sleep in a little coffee grove near a peasant's home where we regrouped our forces. On the day I am talking about, February 27 or 28, censorship in the country had been lifted, and the radio gave continuous news of everything that had happened during the past months. They spoke of terrorist acts and of the Matthews interview with Fidel; it was then that the minister of defense made his famous statement that the Matthews interview was a lie and challenged him to publish the photos.

Hermes was a peasant, the son of old Emiliano, and it was he who helped us with meals and showed us the route we should take. But on the morning of February 28 he did not appear as he usually did, and Fidel ordered us to evacuate the spot immediately and post ourselves elsewhere, overlooking the roads, for we did not know what would happen. At about four in the afternoon, Luis Crespo and Universo Sánchez were watching the roads and the latter saw a large troop of soldiers coming along the road from Las Vegas, preparing to occupy the crest. We had to run fast to the edge of the hill and cross to the other side before the troops blocked our path; it was not difficult since we had seen them in time. The mortars and machine guns were beginning to sound from where we had just left, which proved that the Batista army knew of our presence there. Everybody else was able to reach the peak easily and go over it; but for me it was a tremendous chore. I made it to the top, but with such an attack of asthma that, for all practical purposes, each step was difficult. I remember how much Crespo helped me when I could go no further and was asking to be left behind. In the special way of speaking used by our troops, he said to me: "You Argentine son of a — ! You'll walk or I'll hit you with my rifle butt!" Besides saying this, he virtually carried both me and my pack, as we slogged over the hill through a heavy downpour.

We thus reached a small hut, learning that we were in a place called Purgatorio. There Fidel passed himself off as Major [Armando] González of Batista's army, who was searching for the insurgents. The owner of the house, coldly polite, offered us his house and waited on us. But there was also a friend from a neighboring hut who was an extraordinary toady. Because of my physical state I could not fully enjoy the delicious dialogue between Fidel in the role of Major González of Batista's army and the peasant who gave him advice and wondered why that boy, Fidel Castro, was in the hills fighting.

We had to reach some decision, because it was impossible for me to continue. When the indiscreet neighbor had left, Fidel told the host who he really was. The man immediately embraced him, saying he was a supporter of the Orthodox Party, who had always followed [Eduardo] Chibás, and that he was at our service. At that moment we had to send the man to Manzanillo to establish contact, or at least to bring back medicines, and I had to be left near the house without even his wife knowing I was there.

The last man to join our group, a man of doubtful repute but great strength, was assigned to stay with me. Fidel, in a generous move, gave me a Johnson repeater, one of the treasures of our group. We all pretended to leave in the same direction, and after a few steps my companion (whom we called "Teacher"[2]) and I disappeared into the forest to reach our hiding place. That day the radio reported that Matthews had been interviewed by telephone and had announced that the famous photographs would be published. Díaz Tamayo had countered that this was impossible since Matthews could not have crossed the army lines surrounding the guerrillas. Armando Hart was in prison, accused of being the second in command of the Movement. The date was February 28.

The peasant carried out his assignment and brought me a good amount of adrenaline. Then came ten of the most bitter days of the struggle in the Sierra: walking along, supporting myself on trees and leaning on the barrel of my rifle, accompanied by a frightened combatant who trembled each time we heard shots and who had an attack of nerves each time my asthma made me cough in some dangerous spot. It took us ten long days to

2. Luis Barreras.

reach Epifanio's house once again, when normally it was little more than a day's trip. The date agreed upon for the rendezvous was March 5, but it was impossible for us to arrive by then. Because of the soldiers in the region and our slow movement, we did not arrive at the friendly home of Epifanio Díaz until March 11.

The inhabitants of the house informed us of all that had happened. Fidel's group of eighteen men had split up due to an error, when they thought they were going to be attacked by the army in a place called Altos de Meriño; twelve men had gone on with Fidel and six with Ciro Frías. Later, Ciro Frías's group had fallen into an ambush, but they all came out of it unscathed and met up again nearby. One of them, Yayo, who came back without his rifle, had passed by Epifanio Díaz's house going toward Manzanillo; from him we learned everything. The troops who Frank was to send were ready, although he himself was in prison in Santiago. We met with the troop's leader; he was Jorge Sotús and carried the rank of captain. He had been unable to come on the fifth, for information about the new group had gotten around and the roads were heavily guarded. We made all the necessary arrangements for the speedy arrival of the fifty or so new recruits.

PUBLISHED IN VERDE OLIVO, JULY 23, 1961

MARCH 1957

Reinforcements

ON MARCH 13, as we awaited the new revolutionary troop, we heard on the radio of an attempt made on Batista's life, and they gave the names of some of the people killed.[1] First there was José Antonio Echeverría, the student leader; then there were others, like Menelao Mora. People who were not involved in the attempt also died. The following day we learned that Pelayo Cuervo Navarro, a fighter from the Orthodox Party who had always maintained a firm position against Batista, had been assassinated and his body left in the aristocratic residential section of the Country Club known as El Laguito. It is worth noting that, paradoxically, the murderers of Pelayo Cuervo Navarro and the sons of the dead man joined together in the unsuccessful invasion of Playa Girón sent to "liberate" Cuba from "Communist ignominy."

Despite the veil of censorship, some details of this memorable though unsuccessful attempt on Batista's life came through. Personally, I had not known the student leader, but I had met his friends in Mexico, when the July 26 Movement and the Stu-

1. On March 13, 1957, more than fifty fighters from the student-based Revolutionary Directorate conducted an unsuccessful attack on the Presidential Palace, in an attempt to kill Batista. Simultaneously, José Antonio Echeverría led a smaller group of Directorate combatants in seizing one of Havana's main radio stations. Some three dozen revolutionaries were killed in these attacks, including Echeverría.

dent Directorate had agreed to joint action. These were Cmdr. Faure Chomón (today ambassador to the USSR), Fructuoso Rodríguez, and Joe Westbrook, all of whom participated in the attempt on Batista's life.

The men had almost penetrated to the third floor where the dictator was. What could have been a successful blow, however, turned into a massacre of all those unable to get out of the trap that the Presidential Palace had become.

The arrival of our reinforcements was scheduled for March 15. We waited many hours at the agreed-upon place, in a canyon where the river bends and where it was easy to wait in hiding; but no one arrived. Later they explained to us that there had been some problems. Subsequently they arrived, at dawn on March 16. The men were so tired they could hardly walk the few steps to the wooded area, where they rested until daybreak. They came in trucks owned by a rice farmer from the area who, frightened by the implications of his act, went into exile in Costa Rica. He later returned, transformed into a hero, aboard a plane bringing some weapons from that country; his name was Hubert Matos.

The reinforcements consisted of about fifty men, only thirty of whom were armed. They brought two automatic rifles, one Madsen and one Johnson. After a few months of living in the Sierra, we had become veterans, and we saw in the new troop all the defects that those who had landed on the *Granma* had had: lack of discipline, inability to adjust to major difficulties, lack of decision, incapacity to adapt to this life. The group of fifty was led by Capt. Jorge Sotús and was divided into five squads of ten men, each of whose leaders were lieutenants; they had been given these ranks by the Movement in the Llano, and these still awaited ratification. The squad leaders were a comrade named Domínguez, who I believe was killed in Pino del Agua a little while later; René Ramos Latour, an organizer of the urban militias, who died heroically in battle during the last days of the dictatorship's final offensive; "Pedrín" Sotto, our old friend from the *Granma*, who finally managed to join us and was also killed in battle and posthumously promoted to commander by Raúl Castro on the "Frank País" Second Eastern Front;[2] also, Comrade Pena, a student from Santiago who reached the rank of commander and took his own life after the revolution; finally, Lieutenant Ermus, the only group leader to survive the two years of the war.

Of all the problems that the new troop had, difficulty in marching was one of the greatest. Their leader, Jorge Sotús, was one of the worst, and he constantly lagged behind, setting a bad example for the men. I had been ordered to take charge of the troop, but when I mentioned this to Sotús he told me that he had orders to turn the men over to Fidel, and that he could not turn them over to anyone else as long as he continued as the leader, etc., etc. In that period I still had a complex about being a foreigner, and I did not want to take extreme measures, although I noticed a great uneasiness among the troops. After several very short marches, which took an extremely long time because of the men's poor preparation, we reached a place at La Derecha where we were to wait for Fidel Castro. With me there was the small group of men who had been separated from Fidel earlier: Manuel Fajardo, Guillermo García, Juventino [Alarcón], Pesant, the three Sotomayor brothers,[3] and Ciro Frías.

In those days the enormous difference between the two groups was easily noticeable: ours was disciplined, compact, inured to warfare; that of the novices was still suffering the sickness of the first days: they were not used to eating only once a day, and if the ration did not taste good they would not eat it. The novices had their packs full of useless items, and if the packs were too heavy they would rather, for example, give up a can of condensed milk than a towel (a crime for a guerrilla). We took advantage of this by collecting all the cans and food they left behind. After we were installed in La Derecha the situation became

2. See the section on the evolution of the Rebel Army's fronts and columns beginning on page 459.
3. José and Marciano Arias Sotomayor and their cousin Ángel Emoncerrat.

very tense because of constant friction between Jorge Sotús, a man of authoritarian spirit who could not get on with the men, and the troops in general. We had to take special precautions, and René Ramos, whose nom de guerre was Daniel, was put in charge of the machine gun squad at the mouth of our refuge so that we had a guarantee that nothing would happen.

Some time later, Jorge Sotús was sent on a special mission to Miami. There he betrayed the revolution by aligning himself with Felipe Pazos, whose boundless ambition for power made him forget his commitments and nominate himself provisional president in a cooked-up intrigue in which the State Department played an important role.

Over time Captain Sotús showed signs of wanting to redeem himself, and Raúl Castro gave him the opportunity, which the revolution has denied no one. However, he began to conspire against the revolutionary government and was sentenced to twenty years in prison, escaping thanks to the complicity of one of his guards who fled with him to the ideal haven for *gusanos:*[4] the United States.

At the time of our story, however, we tried to help him as much as possible, to smooth his disagreements with the new comrades, and to explain to him the necessity for discipline. Guillermo García went to fetch Fidel from the Caracas region, while I made a little trip to pick up Ramiro Valdés, who had more or less recovered from the wound in his leg. On the night of March 24, Fidel arrived; it was impressive to watch his arrival with the twelve comrades who at that time stuck firmly by his side. There was a notable difference between the bearded men, with their packs made of any available material and tied with whatever could be found, and the new soldiers with clean-shaven faces, clean uniforms, and pretty knapsacks. I explained to Fidel the problems we had encountered, and a small council was set up to decide on future plans. It was composed of Fidel himself,

4. *Gusano,* meaning "worm," is a term popularly used in Cuba to refer to counterrevolutionaries.

Raúl, Almeida, Jorge Sotús, Ciro Frías, Guillermo García, Camilo Cienfuegos, Manuel Fajardo, and myself. Fidel criticized my attitude in not exercising the authority that had been conferred on me, and leaving it in the hands of the recently arrived Sotús, against whom there was no personal animosity but whose attitude, in Fidel's opinion, should not have been tolerated. New platoons were also organized, pooling all the troops together to then form three groups under the command of Capts. Raúl Castro, Juan Almeida, and Jorge Sotús; Camilo Cienfuegos would lead the forward detachment and Efigenio Ameijeiras the rear guard. I was general staff physician, and Universo Sánchez functioned as general staff squad leader.

Our troop reached a new level with these additional men, and we also had acquired two more automatic rifles. These weapons, although of doubtful efficiency since they were old and badly worn, nevertheless helped to strengthen our force. We discussed what we could immediately do; it was my opinion that we should attack the first possible enemy post in order to temper the new men in battle. But Fidel and all the other members of the council thought it better to march for some time so they could get used to the rigors of life in the woods and the mountains, and to long marches over steep hills. So we decided to move toward the east and walk as much as possible, seeking the opportunity to attack some group of soldiers after having some elementary practical lessons in guerrilla warfare.

The troop prepared itself enthusiastically and left to fulfill its tasks. Its blood-baptism was to be the battle of El Uvero.

PUBLISHED IN VERDE OLIVO, AUGUST 13, 1961

MARCH–APRIL 1957

Toughening up the troops

MARCH AND APRIL 1957 were months of restructuring and apprenticeship for the rebel troops. After being reinforced at La Derecha, our army consisted of about eighty men and was organized as follows:

The forward detachment, headed by Camilo, had four men. The next platoon was led by Raúl Castro and had three lieutenants, Julito Díaz, Ramiro Valdés, and Nano Díaz, each with a squad. (The two comrades named Díaz, both of whom died heroically in El Uvero, were not related. One of them was from Santiago, where the Díaz Brothers Refinery is honored with that name in memory of Nano and his brother, who fell in Santiago de Cuba. The other one, Julito, a comrade from Artemisa, was a veteran of the Moncada and the *Granma*.)

With Capt. Jorge Sotús were Lts. Ciro Frías (later killed on the Frank País Front), Guillermo García (today head of the Western Army), and René Ramos Latour (killed after attaining the rank of commander in the Sierra Maestra). Then came the general staff, or command post, which was made up of Fidel as commander in chief, Ciro Redondo, Manuel Fajardo (today a commander), Crespo (commander), Universo Sánchez (commander), and myself as doctor.

The platoon that customarily followed in line was that of then-captain Almeida, whose lieutenants were Ermus, Guillermo Domínguez (killed at Pino del Agua), and Peña. Efigenio Ameijeiras, a lieutenant, and three men made up the rear guard.

Given the size of our group, the men began to cook by squad. Food, medicine, and ammunition were distributed separately by squad. In almost all the squads, and certainly in all the platoons, there were veterans who showed the new men how to cook, how to get the most out of the food; they also taught them how to pack their knapsacks, and how best to march through the Sierra.

The road between La Derecha, El Lomón, and El Uvero can be covered in a few hours by car, but for us it meant months of slow and cautious walking, all the while pursuing our principal mission of preparing the men for combat and for life later on. It was thus that we again passed through Altos de Espinosa, where we veterans formed an honor guard around the grave of Julio Zenón, who had been killed there some time before. There I found a piece of my blanket, tangled in the brambles as a reminder of my speedy "strategic retreat." I put it in my pack, firmly resolving never again to lose any more equipment in that manner.

I was assigned a new recruit, Paulino, as an assistant to carry the medical supplies.[1] This eased my task a little so that I could attend to the men's medical needs for a few minutes each day after our long marches. We again passed by Caracas hill, where we had had such a disagreeable encounter with enemy planes, thanks to Guerra's betrayal. There we found one of the extra rifles that one of our men had left behind during the retreat in order to move more easily. By now we no longer had any extra weapons; on the contrary, we were short. We had entered a new phase. There had been a qualitative change; now there was a whole area that the enemy avoided for fear of meeting us, although it's also true that we showed little interest in encountering them either.

The political situation in those days was full of opportunist maneuvers. The well-known voices of Pardo Llada, Conte

1. Paulino Fonseca.

Agüero, and other vultures of that ilk specialized in demagogic outbursts calling for harmony and peace, and timidly criticizing the government. The government had spoken of peace; the new prime minister, [Andrés] Rivero Agüero, indicated that if necessary he would go to the Sierra Maestra to bring peace to the countryside. Nevertheless, a few days later Batista stated that it was no longer necessary to speak to Fidel or the insurgents, that Fidel Castro was not in the Sierra, and that, therefore, there was no reason to talk with "a bunch of outlaws."

In this way the Batista group showed its willingness to continue the fight, the only thing on which both sides agreed, for it was also our intent to continue the fight at any price. In those days a new chief of operations was named: Colonel Barreras, well known for embezzling army ration funds. He later calmly watched the destruction of the Batista entity from Caracas, Venezuela, where he was military attaché.

At that time we had with us some engaging characters, who were helpful as propagandists for our movement in the United States. Two of them in particular brought us a few problems as well. There were three North American boys who had left their parents at the naval base at Guantánamo[2] and joined our fight. Two of them never heard a shot in the Sierra, and, exhausted by the climate and the great many privations, they left, taken back by the journalist Bob Taber. The third one participated in the battle of El Uvero, and later he too left, sick but having fought in a battle. The boys were not politically prepared for a revolution and were simply satisfying their thirst for adventure in our company for a few months. We were sorry, but also glad, to see them go. I personally was especially pleased, for in my capacity as doctor it fell on my shoulders to frequently take care of

2. A reference to the U.S. naval base at Guantánamo on the southeastern part of the island, set up shortly after the U.S. military occupation of Cuba in 1898. Since 1959 it has been held against the demand of the Cuban government that it be returned.

The three recruits were Charles Ryan, Victor Buehlman, and Michael Garvey.

them because they could not stand the rigors of our life.

During that same period, the government took some journalists up several thousand meters in a military plane to prove to them that there was no one in the Sierra Maestra. It was a strange operation, which did not convince anybody; it also demonstrated the manner in which the Batista government deceived public opinion with the help of Conte Agüero and the like, men disguised as revolutionaries who lied to the people on a daily basis.

During those trying days, I finally obtained a canvas hammock. A hammock is a precious belonging, which I had not received before because of the rigorous guerrilla axiom by which canvas hammocks had to be given only to those men who had already made hammocks of sacking. This was done to combat laziness. Anyone could make himself a hammock of sacking, and having done so he had the right to the next canvas one that came along. I was unable to use a hammock made of sacking, however, because of my allergies: the lint greatly affected me, and I was forced to sleep on the ground. Since I did not have a hammock of sacking, I was not entitled to a canvas one. Such small details were part of the everyday annoyances every guerrilla faced. But Fidel noticed, broke the rule, and awarded me a hammock. I shall always remember that it was on the banks of the La Plata, in the last foothills before reaching Palma Mocha, and one day after eating our first horse.

The horse was more than a luxury meal; it was also a kind of trial by fire, testing the men's capacity to adapt. The peasants in our group were indignant, and they refused to eat their ration of horsemeat; some of them considered Manuel Fajardo a virtual murderer, for he was the man chosen to slaughter the animal since he had been a butcher in peacetime.

This first horse belonged to a peasant named Popa, from the other side of the La Plata. Popa must now know how to read, and if he sees the magazine *Verde Olivo* he will remember that night when three sinister-looking rebels banged on the door of his hut, unjustly mistaking him for an informer, and took from him that tired old horse, with large harness sores on its back. This animal was to be our ration hours later, and its meat would constitute an exquisite feast for some. But it was also a test for the prejudiced stomachs of the peasants, who believed they were committing an act of cannibalism as they chewed up man's old friend.

PUBLISHED IN VERDE OLIVO, OCTOBER 1, 1961

APRIL 1957

A famous interview

IN MID-APRIL 1957 we returned with our army in training to the region of Palma Mocha, in the vicinity of the Turquino mountain. During that period our most valuable men for the struggle in the mountains were those of peasant origin.

Guillermo García and Ciro Frías, with patrols of peasants, came and went from place to place in the Sierra, bringing news, scouting, getting food; in fact, they constituted the real mobile vanguard of our column. In those days, we were once again in the region of Arroyo del Infierno, the site of one of our battles. The peasants who came to greet us filled us in on the tragic details of that attack: who had led the guards directly to our camp, who had died there. In fact the peasants, skillful in the art of the grapevine, gave us full information on the entire life of the region.

Fidel, who did not have a radio at that point, asked to borrow one from a local peasant, who lent him his, and thus through a large radio carried in a soldier's knapsack we were able to hear the news direct from Havana. They were once again speaking more freely on the radio because of the reestablishment of so-called guarantees.[1]

Guillermo García, dressed in the uniform of an army corpo-

1. On April 15 a forty-five-day suspension of civil guarantees, which included press censorship, expired. The government measure had been imposed March 2, three days after an earlier forty-five-day suspension of rights had been lifted.

ral, accompanied by two comrades disguised as army soldiers, went to look for the informer who had led the army to us. They brought him back the following day "on the orders of the colonel." The man had come innocently, but when he saw the ragged army he knew what awaited him. With great cynicism he told us everything about his relations with the army and how he had told "that bastard Casillas" that he would be perfectly willing to take the army to where we were and capture us, for he had spied on us; but they did not listen to him.

Some days later, on one of the hills nearby, the informer was executed and buried. Around the same time we received a message from Celia announcing that she would be coming with two North American journalists to interview Fidel, under the pretext of seeing the three North American boys. She also sent some money collected from sympathizers of the Movement.

It was decided that Lalo Sardiñas would bring the North Americans through the region of Estrada Palma since, as an ex-merchant in the region, he knew it well. We were devoting our time to making contact with peasants who could serve as links and who could maintain permanent encampments as centers of contact with the whole region, which was growing in size. Thus we located houses that we used as supply centers for our troops, and there we installed warehouses from which we drew supplies according to our needs. These places also served as rest stops for the fast human stagecoaches who moved along the edge of the Sierra Maestra from one place to another carrying messages and news.

These messengers showed an extraordinary capacity for covering very long distances in a short time. As a result, we were constantly fooled by their version of "a half-hour's walk" or "just over there." For the peasants this almost always turned out to be exact, even though their concept of time and distance was quite different from that of a city dweller.

Three days after Lalo Sardiñas left, we heard that six people were coming up through the region of Santo Domingo; there were two women, two "gringos" (the journalists), and two others who nobody knew. However, we also received some contradictory news to the effect that the Rural Guards, having learned of their presence from an informer, had surrounded the house where they were. In the Sierra news travels with remarkable speed, but it also gets distorted. Camilo left with a platoon with orders to free Celia Sánchez, who we knew was part of the group, and the North Americans at all costs. They arrived safe and sound, however. The false alarm was due to troop movements provoked by a denunciation, which in those days was easy to produce among backward peasants.

On April 23 the journalist Bob Taber and a photographer arrived at our camp. With them came comrades Celia Sánchez and Haydée Santamaría and the men sent by the urban Movement: Marcos or "Nicaragua"— Commander [Carlos] Iglesias—today governor of Las Villas and in those days in charge of armed actions in Santiago; and Marcelo Fernández, coordinator of the Movement and currently vice president of the National Bank, who acted as interpreter.

The days went according to schedule, as we tried to show the North Americans our strength and to evade their more indiscreet questions. We did not know anything about these journalists. They nevertheless interviewed the three boys, who answered all the questions very well, showing the new spirit they had developed in that primitive life among us, despite the difficulties of adjusting to it and not having anything in common with us.

We were also joined in those days by one of the most likable and best-loved figures of our revolutionary war, "Vaquerito." Together with another comrade, Vaquerito found us one day and said that he had spent over a month looking for us. He told us he was from Morón in Camagüey. As always in such cases, we subjected him to interrogation and gave him the rudiments of a political orientation, a task that frequently fell to me. Vaquerito did not have a political idea in his head, nor did he seem to be anything other than a happy, healthy boy, who saw all of this as a marvelous adventure. He came barefoot and Celia lent him an extra pair of shoes, which were made of leather and were the type worn in Mexico; this was the only pair that fit him, since his feet were so small. With the new shoes and a great big palm leaf hat, Vaquerito looked like a Mexican cowboy or *vaquero,* which is how he got his name.

As is well known, Vaquerito did not see the end of the revolutionary struggle, for as head of the Suicide Squad of Column no. 8, he died one day before the capture of Santa Clara. We all remember his extraordinary gaiety, his continual joviality, and the strange and novel manner he had of confronting danger. Vaquerito was an amazing liar; I wonder if he ever had a conversation where he did not so adorn the truth that it was practically unrecognizable. But in his activities as a messenger in the early days, and later as a soldier or as head of the Suicide Squad, Vaquerito demonstrated that for him reality and fantasy had no exact boundaries, and the same feats that his agile mind invented he was able to carry out on the battlefield. His extreme bravery had become legend by the time our epic war was over, which he did not live to see.

Sometime after he joined us, I decided to question Vaquerito about his life. It was after one of the nightly reading sessions we had in the column. Vaquerito began to tell us about himself, and we began surreptitiously calculating his age, pencil in hand. When he finished, after many sparkling anecdotes, we asked him how old he was. Vaquerito at that time was a little over twenty, but adding up all his deeds and the jobs he had held, it worked out that he had begun to work five years before he was born.

Comrade Nicaragua brought news of more weapons in Santiago, remnants of the assault on the Presidential Palace. There were ten automatic rifles, eleven Johnson rifles, and six short carbines, he reported. There were a few more, but plans were under way to open another front in the region of the Miranda sugar mill. Fidel opposed this idea and only allowed a few arms for this second front, giving orders that all possible weapons be brought up to reinforce us. We continued the march, withdrawing from the uncomfortable company of some Rural Guards who were marauding nearby. But first we decided to climb the Turquino peak. Ascending Cuba's highest mountain had an almost mystical significance for us. In any case, we were already quite near the top.

The entire column climbed to the Turquino peak, and up there we finished the interview with Bob Taber. He was preparing a film that was later televised in the United States, at a time when we were not feared so much. (One example of this came from a peasant who joined us, who said that Casillas had offered him three hundred pesos and a pregnant cow if he would kill Fidel.) The North Americans were not the only ones who were wrong about the price of our highest commander.

According to an altimeter we had, the Turquino mountain was 1,850 meters above sea level. I note this as an incidental point, for we never tested the instrument; but at sea level it worked well, and this figure differs substantially from that given in official texts.

Since an army company was on our heels, Guillermo was sent with a group of comrades as snipers. Because of my asthmatic condition, which obliged me to walk at the end of the column and did not permit any special efforts, I was relieved of the Thompson submachine gun I was carrying. About three days passed before I got it back. These were some of the tensest days in the Sierra for me, for I was unarmed while there was the daily possibility of encounters with the enemy.

During those days of May 1957, two of the North American boys left the column with Bob Taber, who had finished his story, and they reached Guantánamo safe and sound. We continued our slow march along the crest of the Maestra and its slopes. We were making contacts, exploring new regions, and spreading the revolutionary flame and the legend of our troop of *barbudos* [bearded ones] across the Sierra. The new spirit was communicated far and wide. Peasants came to greet us with less fear, and we in turn had more trust in them. Our relative strength had increased considerably, and we felt more secure against any surprise attack by the Batista army. In general, we were becoming closer friends of the peasants.

PUBLISHED IN VERDE OLIVO, OCTOBER 15, 1961

MAY 1957

On the march

THE FIRST TWO WEEKS OF MAY were days of continual marching toward our objective. At the beginning of the month, we were on a hill along the crest of the Sierra Maestra close to the Turquino; we were crossing regions that later were the scenes of many events of the revolution. We passed through Santa Ana and El Hombrito; later on, at Pico Verde, we found Escudero's house and we continued until we reached the Loma del Burro. We were moving eastward, looking for the weapons that were supposed to be sent from Santiago and would be hidden in the region of the Loma del Burro, close to Oro de Guisa. One night during this two-week journey, while going to carry out a private necessity, I confused the paths and was lost for three days until I found the troops again at a spot called El Hombrito. At that time I realized that we were each carrying on our backs everything necessary for individual survival: salt, cooking oil, canned foods, canned milk, everything required for sleeping, making a fire, and cooking, and also a compass, on which I had relied very heavily until then.

Finding myself lost, the next morning I took out the compass and, guiding myself with it, I continued for a day and a half until I realized that I was even more lost. I approached a peasant hut and the people directed me to the rebel encampment. Later we would realize that in such rugged territory as the Sierra Maestra a compass can only give a general orientation, never a definite course; one has either to be led by guides or to know the area oneself, as we later knew it when I was operating in that same region.

I was very moved by the warm reception that greeted me when I rejoined the column. When I arrived they had just held a people's trial in which three informers were tried, and one of them, named Nápoles, was condemned to death. Camilo chaired that tribunal.

During those days I had to perform my duties as doctor, and in each little village or hamlet I set up my consulting station. It was monotonous, for I had few medicines to offer and the clinical cases in the Sierra were all more or less the same: prematurely aged and toothless women, children with distended bellies, parasitism, rickets, general vitamin deficiency—these were the marks of the Sierra Maestra.[1] Even today they continue, but in much smaller proportion. The children of those mothers of the Sierra have gone to study at the Camilo Cienfuegos School City; they are grown up and healthy and are different boys and girls from the first undernourished inhabitants of our pioneer School City.[2]

I remember that a little girl was watching the consultations that I gave to the women of the region. They came in with an almost religious air to find out the cause of their sufferings. When her mother arrived, the little girl, after attentively watching several previous examinations in the little hut that served as my clinic, chattered gaily: "Mommy, this doctor says the same thing to everybody."

1. Average life expectancy in Cuba during the late 1950s was estimated to be between 55 and 62 years, with infant mortality at 60 per 1,000 live births. Health conditions in rural areas such as the Sierra Maestra were even worse. In 1957, 14 percent of rural workers had suffered from tuberculosis; 13 percent from typhoid fever; 31 percent from malaria; and 36 percent from intestinal parasites. By the mid-1990s average life expectancy in Cuba had reached over 75 years, with infant mortality dropping to under 10 per 1,000 live births, and with an extensive network of health care in both rural and urban areas.
2. The Camilo Cienfuegos School City was the first boarding school built in the Sierra Maestra after the revolution, with a capacity of five thousand children from all parts of the Sierra.

And it was absolutely true; my knowledge was good for little else. But in addition, they all had the same clinical traits, and without knowing it they each told the same heartrending story. What would have happened if the doctor had diagnosed the strange tiredness that the young mother of several children suffered when she carried a pail of water up from the creek to the house as being due simply to too much work on too poor and meager a diet? Her exhaustion is something inexplicable to her, since all her life the woman has taken the same pails of water to the same place, and only now does she feel tired. The people in the Sierra grow like wild flowers, untended and without care, and they wear themselves out rapidly, working without reward. There, during those consultations, we began to feel in our flesh and blood the need for a definitive change in the life of the people. The idea of agrarian reform became clear, and oneness with the people ceased being theory and was converted into a fundamental part of our being.

The guerrillas and the peasantry began to merge into a single mass, without our being able to say at what precise moment on the long revolutionary road this happened, nor at which moment the words became profoundly real and we became a part of the peasantry. In my own case, at least, those consultations with the peasants of the Sierra converted my spontaneous and somewhat lyrical resolve into something of a different nature, more real. Those suffering and loyal inhabitants of the Sierra Maestra have never suspected the role they played in forging our revolutionary ideas.

It was there that Guillermo García was promoted to captain and took charge of all the peasants who joined the column. Perhaps Comrade Guillermo does not remember the date: it is noted in my diary as May 6, 1957.

The following day, Haydée Santamaría left with precise instructions from Fidel, to make the necessary contacts. But a day later we got the news of the arrest of Nicaragua—Commander Iglesias, who was in charge of bringing us the weapons. This was quite disconcerting for us, as we could not imagine what we would do now to get them; nevertheless, we decided to continue walking in the same direction.

We reached a place near Pino del Agua, a small ravine with an abandoned lumber yard on the very edge of the Sierra Maestra; there were also two uninhabited peasant huts. Near a road, one of our patrols captured an army corporal. This individual was well known for his crimes going back to the time of Machado. For this reason some of our troops proposed that he be executed, but Fidel refused; we simply left him guarded by the new recruits who did not yet have rifles. He was warned that any attempt to escape would cost him his life.

Most of us continued on our way to see if the weapons had arrived at the agreed spot, and if so, to transport them. It was a long hike, although with less weight, since our full knapsacks had been left in the camp where the prisoner was. The march, however, was fruitless: the equipment had not arrived, which we naturally attributed to the arrest of Nicaragua. We were able to purchase a substantial amount of food at a store, so we returned to camp with a different, although welcome, load.

We were returning slowly by the same road, exhausted, moving along the crests of the Sierra Maestra and crossing the open spaces carefully. Suddenly we heard shots ahead of us. We were worried because one of our men had gone on ahead in order to reach the camp as soon as possible; he was Guillermo Domínguez, a lieutenant of our troop and one of the men who had arrived with the reinforcements from Santiago. We prepared for all contingencies while we sent out some scouts. After a reasonable length of time, the scouts appeared accompanied by Comrade Fiallo, a new recruit who belonged to Crescencio's group and had joined the guerrillas during our absence. He had come from our camp and explained that there was a dead body on the road, and that there had been an encounter with the enemy, who had retreated in the direction of Pino del Agua where there was a larger detachment.

We advanced cautiously, and came upon the body, which I recognized. It was Guillermo Domínguez; he was naked from the waist up and had a bullet hole in the left elbow, and a bayonet wound in the left upper chest; his head was literally shattered by a shot, apparently from his own shotgun. Some buckshot pellets remained as evidence in the lacerated flesh of our unfortunate comrade.

We were able to reconstruct the facts by analyzing various data: the enemy soldiers were apparently scouting for their friend, the corporal we had captured. They had heard Domínguez coming toward them, walking without much concern, for he had traveled the same path the day before. They had taken him prisoner; but some of Crescencio's men were coming to meet us from the other direction. On surprising the soldiers from the rear, Crescencio's men fired and the soldiers retreated, murdering our comrade Domínguez before fleeing.

Pino del Agua is the site of a sawmill in the middle of the Sierra, and the path the guards took is an old crossroad for transporting lumber. We had to follow this trail for a hundred meters, in order to reach our narrow path. Our comrade had not taken the most elementary precautions in this case, and was unlucky enough to bump into the soldiers. His bitter fate served us as an example for the future.

PUBLISHED IN VERDE OLIVO, DECEMBER 24, 1961

MAY 1957

The weapons arrive

IN A REGION OF THE SIERRA MAESTRA near the sawmill at Pino del Agua, we killed the magnificent horse that the imprisoned corporal had been riding. The animal was useless to us in such craggy terrain, and we were low on food. (As an aside, while eating his fill of horsemeat stew, the prisoner, unaware of the source of his meal, kept lauding the animal and stressing that it had been loaned to him by a friend. He gave us the name and address so that we would be sure to return it.) In any case, our customary diet was such that we could not afford to disdain fresh meat, whether from a horse or any other animal.

That day on the radio we heard news of the sentencing of our comrades from the *Granma*.[1] In addition, we learned that a magistrate had cast his personal vote against the sentence. The magistrate's name was Urrutia, and his honorable gesture later brought him nomination as provisional president of the republic. In and of itself, the vote of a magistrate was no more than a worthy gesture—which it clearly was at that time—but it had more serious consequences later on: it led to the appointment of a bad president, a man incapable of understanding the revo-

1. Twenty-one captured *Granma* expeditionaries were tried and convicted in May 1957 by a three-judge panel in Santiago de Cuba. Manuel Urrutia, one of the judges, voted against the conviction. For a list of the *Granma* expeditionaries and what happened to them after the landing, see pages 424–25.

lutionary process, incapable of absorbing the profound character of a revolution that was not made for his backward mentality. His character and his reluctance to say where he really stood brought many conflicts. Things came to a head in the days surrounding the celebration of the first July 26 after the revolution, when he resigned as president in the face of unanimous rejection by the people.

On one of those days a contact from Santiago arrived. His name was Andrés, and he had precise information about the weapons: they were safe and would be moved in the next few days. A delivery point was fixed in the region of a coastal sawmill operated by the Babún brothers. The arms would be delivered with the full knowledge of these men, who felt they could do a lucrative business by involving themselves in the revolution. (Subsequent developments divided the family, and three of the Babún sons have the dubious distinction of being among the *gusanos* captured at Girón.)

It is curious to note how in that period many people tried to use the revolution for their own ends by doing small favors for us in order to reap rewards from the new government later on. In this case the Babún brothers hoped to obtain a free hand in the commercial exploitation of the forests, all the while pitilessly evicting the peasants, thereby increasing the size of their landed estates.

It was around that time that we were joined by a North American journalist, of the same mold as the Babún family. He was Hungarian by birth, and his name was Andrew St. George. At first he showed only one of his faces, the better one, which was simply that of a Yankee journalist. In addition to that he was an FBI agent. Since I was the only person in the column who spoke French (in those days nobody spoke English), I was chosen to take care of him. Quite frankly, he did not seem to me as dangerous as he turned out to be in our second interview, when he was already showing himself openly as an agent. We were walking on the edge of Pino del Agua toward the source of the Peladero river. These were rugged areas and we all carried heavy packs. The Peladero river has a tributary, the Arroyo del Indio. Here we spent a couple of days, getting food and moving the arms we had received. We passed through a few peasant settlements and established a kind of extralegal revolutionary state, leaving sympathizers who were to inform us of anything that happened and to tell us of the enemy's movements. But we always lived in the forests; only occasionally, at night, did we unexpectedly come across a group of houses and then some of us slept in them. But the majority always slept under the protection of the mountains, and during the day all of us were on guard, protected by a roof of trees.

Our worst enemy at that time of year was the *macagüera,* a species of horsefly given that name because it hatches and lays its eggs in the Macagua tree. At a certain time of year it reproduces prolifically in the mountains. The *macagüera* bites exposed areas of the body, and as we scratched, given all the dirt on our bodies, the bites easily became infected and caused abscesses of varying sizes. The uncovered parts of our legs, our wrists, and our necks always bore proof of the presence of the *macagüera.*

Finally, on May 18, we received news of the weapons and also an approximate inventory. This news became immediately known and caused great excitement in the camp, for all the fighters wanted better weapons. Everyone had the secret hope of acquiring something, either by directly getting one of the new weapons, or else having those getting the new weapons pass their old ones down to them. We also heard that the film made by Bob Taber in the Sierra Maestra had been shown in the United States with great success. This news cheered everyone except Andrew St. George, who, in addition to being an FBI agent, had his petty journalist's pride and felt cheated. The next day he left by yacht from the Babún estate for Santiago de Cuba.

That day, besides learning where the weapons were, we also found out that one of our men had deserted. Since everyone at the camp knew of the arrival of the weapons, this was especially dangerous. Patrols were sent to look for him. They returned with the news that he had managed to take a boat to Santiago. We assumed it was to inform the authorities, although later it came out that the desertion was simply brought about by the man's physical and moral inability to endure the hardships of our life. In any case, we had to double our precautions. Our struggle against the lack of physical, ideological, and moral preparation among the combatants was a daily one; the results were not always encouraging. The weaker men often asked permission to leave for the most petty of reasons, and if they were refused, the same thing would happen as in this case. It should not be forgotten that desertion was punishable by death directly upon capture.

That night the weapons arrived. For us it was the most marvelous spectacle in the world: the instruments of death were on exhibit before the covetous eyes of all the combatants. Three tripod machine guns, three machine guns, three Madsen light machine guns, nine M-1 carbines, ten Johnson automatic rifles, and a total of six thousand rounds of ammunition were delivered. Although the M-1 carbines had only forty-five rounds apiece, they were highly prized weapons and were distributed according to the merits earned by the fighters and their length of time in the Sierra. One of the M-1s was given to Ramiro Valdés (today a commander), and two went to the forward detachment, which Camilo headed. The other four were to be used to cover the tripod machine guns. One of the machine guns went to Capt. Jorge Sotús's platoon, another to Almeida's, and the third to the general staff (I had the responsibility for operating it). The tripods were distributed as follows: one for Raúl, another for Guillermo García, and the third for Crescencio Pérez. In this way, I made my debut as a full-time combatant, for until then I had been a part-time combatant and my main responsibility had been as the troop's doctor. I had entered a new stage.

I shall always remember the moment I was given the machine gun. It was old and of poor quality, but to me it was a real acquisition. Four men were assigned to assist me with this weapon. These four combatants have subsequently followed very different paths: two of them were the Beatón brothers, Pupo and

Manolo, executed by the revolution after they murdered Cmdr. Cristino Naranjo and took up arms in the Oriente mountains, until a peasant captured them. Another was a boy of fifteen who was almost always the one to carry the enormously heavy equipment for the machine gun. His name was Joel Iglesias, and today he is president of the Association of Rebel Youth and a commander in the Rebel Army. The fourth man, today a lieutenant, was named Oñate, but we gave him the affectionate nickname of Cantinflas.

The arrival of the weapons did not mean an end to our odyssey, aimed at instilling greater ideological and combat strength in the troop. A few days later, on May 23, Fidel ordered new discharges, among them an entire squad. Our force was reduced to 127 men, the majority of them armed, and about eighty well-armed.

Out of the entire squad that was dismissed—which included its leader—there remained only one man, called Crucito, who later became one of our best-loved fighters. Crucito was a natural poet, and he had long contests with the city poet, Calixto Morales, a *Granma* veteran. Morales had nicknamed himself "the nightingale of the plains," to which Crucito in his peasant ballads always answered with a refrain, directed in mock derision at Calixto: "You old buzzard of the Sierra."

This magnificent comrade had set down the entire history of the revolution in ballads, which he composed at every rest stop while puffing on his pipe. Since there was very little paper in the Sierra, he would compose the ballads and consign them to memory, so that none of them remained when a bullet put an end to his life in the battle of Pino del Agua.

In the area of the lumber facilities we received the invaluable help of Enrique López, an old childhood acquaintance of Fidel and Raúl, who at the time was employed by the Babúns and served as a supply contact. He also made it possible for us to move through the entire area without danger. This region was full of roads used by army trucks; several times we prepared ambushes aimed at capturing some trucks, but we were never able to do so. Perhaps this contributed to the success of the approaching operation, which was to have one of the greatest psychological impacts of any in the history of the war: the battle of El Uvero.

On May 25, we heard the news that an expeditionary force led by Calixto Sánchez had arrived aboard the boat *Corynthia* and had landed at Mayarí; a few days later we were to learn of the disastrous result of this expedition: Prío sent his men to die without ever bothering to accompany them.[2] The news of this landing showed us the absolute necessity for diverting the enemy forces in order to give those men a chance to reach some place where they could reorganize and begin their actions. We did all this out of solidarity with the other group, without even knowing its social composition or its true goals.

At this point we had an interesting discussion, involving principally Fidel and me. I was of the opinion that we ought not lose the opportunity of capturing a truck and that we should devote ourselves specifically to ambushing them on the roads where they passed by carelessly. But Fidel was already planning the action at El Uvero. He felt that it would be much more important and would bring us a more resounding success if we captured the army post at El Uvero. It would have a tremendous moral impact and would become known throughout the country. This would not be the case with the capture of a truck, which could be reported as a highway accident with a few killed and injured; and although people might suspect the truth, our effective fighting presence in the Sierra would never be known. This

2. On May 24 twenty-seven combatants landed on the coast of northern Oriente. The expedition had been organized by the military wing of the Authentic Party led by Carlos Prío. Sixteen expeditionaries were quickly captured and executed, including the group's leader Calixto Sánchez. One of the expeditionaries, Fernando Virelles, made his way to the Sierra Maestra and joined the Rebel Army. Since being ousted by Batista's 1952 coup, Prío had used the Authentic military organization as a vehicle to pressure Batista to make a deal, as well as to check the growth of the July 26 Movement and other revolutionary currents.

did not mean that we would totally reject the idea of capturing a truck, under optimum conditions, but we should not make this the focal point of our activities.

Today, several years after that discussion (which at the time did not convince me) I must recognize that Fidel's judgment was correct. It would have been much less productive for us to carry out an isolated action against one of the patrols that traveled in the trucks. At that period, our eagerness to fight always led us impatiently to adopt drastic attitudes; perhaps we could not yet see the more distant objectives. In any case, we began the final preparations for the battle of El Uvero.

PUBLISHED IN VERDE OLIVO, JANUARY 7, 1962

MAY 1957

The battle of El Uvero

HAVING DECIDED ON THE POINT OF ATTACK, we then had to work out exactly the form it would take; we had to solve such important problems as ascertaining the number of soldiers present, the number of guard posts, the type of communications they used, the access roads, the civilian population and its distribution, and so forth. In all of this we were magnificently served by Comrade [Gilberto] Cardero, today a commander in the Rebel Army, who was, I believe, the son-in-law of the lumber company's manager.

We assumed that the army had more or less exact data on our presence in the area, since we had captured two informers who carried army identification documents and confessed to being sent by Casillas to ascertain our position and our customary meeting places. The spectacle of the two men begging for mercy was truly repugnant, but at the same time poignant. The laws of war, however, could not be ignored in those difficult times, and both spies were executed the following day.

That same day, May 27, the general staff met together with all the officers. Fidel announced there would be combat within the next forty-eight hours, and he ordered us to have the men and equipment ready to move out. We were not given details at that point.

Cardero would be the guide, for he knew the post of El Uvero like the back of his hand: its entrances and exits, as well as its access roads. That night we moved out; it was a long march of some sixteen kilometers, but all downhill on roads that had been specially constructed by the Babún Company to reach its sawmill. However, it took us about eight hours, for we were slowed by the extra precautions we had to take, especially as we approached the danger zone. Finally we were given the orders of attack, which were very simple: we were to take the guard posts and riddle the wooden barracks with bullets.

We knew that the garrison had no major defenses apart from some logs scattered in the immediate vicinity. Its strong points were the guard posts, each with three or four soldiers and strategically placed around the outside of the garrison. Overlooking the barracks was a hill from which our general staff would direct the battle. We were to approach the building through the thickets and station ourselves a few meters away. We were carefully instructed not to fire on the outlying buildings since they sheltered women and children, including the manager's wife, who knew about the attack but preferred to stay there in order to avoid suspicion later. As we left to occupy our attack positions, we were most of all concerned about the civilians.

The garrison of El Uvero was located on the edge of the sea, so that to surround it we needed only to attack from three sides.

One guard post overlooked the road along the coast from Peladero, which we also used in part; the platoons led by Jorge Sotús and Guillermo García were sent to attack it. Almeida was to take charge of eliminating a guard post facing the mountain, more or less to the north. Fidel would be on the hill overlooking the garrison, and Raúl's platoon would advance from the front. I was assigned an intermediate post with my automatic rifle and my assistants. Camilo and Ameijeiras were to advance from the front, actually between my position and Raúl's. But they miscalculated since it was dark, and began shooting from my left instead of my right. Crescencio Pérez's platoon was to advance along the road to Chivirico and hold back whatever army reinforcements were sent.

We expected the element of surprise to make the battle quite

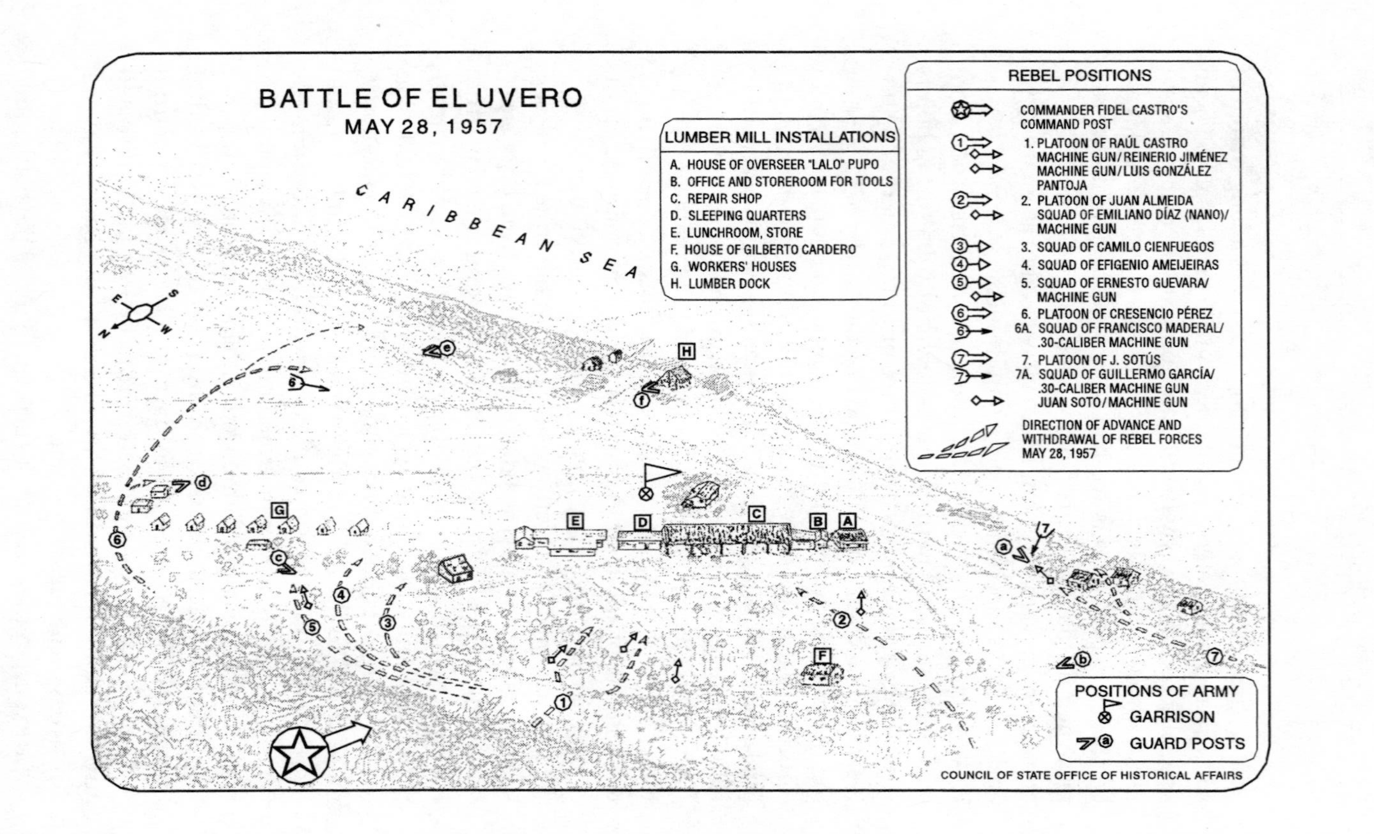

BATTLE OF EL UVERO
MAY 28, 1957
CARIBBEAN SEA
LUMBER MILL INSTALLATIONS
A. HOUSE OF OVERSEER "LALO" PUPO
B. OFFICE AND STOREROOM FOR TOOLS
C. REPAIR SHOP
D. SLEEPING QUARTERS
E. LUNCHROOM, STORE
F. HOUSE OF GILBERTO CARDERO
G. WORKERS' HOUSES
H. LUMBER DOCK
REBEL POSITIONS
COMMANDER FIDEL CASTRO'S COMMAND POST
1. PLATOON OF RAÚL CASTRO
MACHINE GUN/REINERIO JIMÉNEZ
MACHINE GUN/LUIS GONZÁLEZ PANTOJA
2. PLATOON OF JUAN ALMEIDA
SQUAD OF EMILIANO DÍAZ (NANO)/ MACHINE GUN
3. SQUAD OF CAMILO CIENFUEGOS
4. SQUAD OF EFIGENIO AMEIJEIRAS
5. SQUAD OF ERNESTO GUEVARA/ MACHINE GUN
6. PLATOON OF CRESENCIO PÉREZ
6A. SQUAD OF FRANCISCO MADERAL/ .30-CALIBER MACHINE GUN
7. PLATOON OF J. SOTÚS
7A. SQUAD OF GUILLERMO GARCÍA/ .30-CALIBER MACHINE GUN
JUAN SOTO/MACHINE GUN
DIRECTION OF ADVANCE AND WITHDRAWAL OF REBEL FORCES MAY 28, 1957
POSITIONS OF ARMY
GARRISON
GUARD POSTS
COUNCIL OF STATE OFFICE OF HISTORICAL AFFAIRS

short. The minutes passed, however, and we were not able to position our men in the manner we had foreseen. Our guides, Cardero and another from the region named Eligio Mendoza, brought whatever news there was. We could see that dawn was approaching before we would be in position to surprise the soldiers as initially planned. Jorge Sotús advised us that he was not at his assigned position but that it was too late now to move. When Fidel opened fire with his telescopic rifle, we were able to locate the garrison from the answering shots that began in a matter of seconds. I was on a small elevation and had a perfect view of the garrison; but I was very far from it, so my men and I advanced to find better positions.

Everyone was advancing. Almeida moved toward the post defending the entrance to the little barracks in his area. To my left I could see Camilo wearing his beret with a handkerchief over the back of his neck like a French Foreign Legion hat, except his sported the Movement insignias. We advanced cautiously amid the general exchange of fire.

The small squad was joined by men who had been separated from their own units; a comrade from Pilón called "Bomba"—Comrade Mario Leal—and [Manuel] Acuña joined what already constituted a small combat unit. The resistance had become intense, and we arrived at a flat open space where we were forced to advance with infinite precautions, for the enemy fired continuously and accurately. From my position, barely fifty or sixty meters from the enemy outpost, I saw two soldiers run out of the trench in front of us, and I fired at both of them, but they hid in the outbuildings and these were sacred to us. We continued advancing, although there was now nothing more than a narrow, totally open strip of land between us and the enemy, whose bullets whistled dangerously near. At that moment, in the midst of the battle, I heard a groan near me, and then some shouts. I thought it must be a wounded enemy soldier, and I dragged myself forward, shouting to him to surrender. It turned out to be Comrade Leal, who was wounded in the head. I hastily examined him and found that both entrance and exit wounds were in the parietal region. Leal was losing consciousness, and the limbs on one side of his body—I don't remember which—were becoming paralyzed. The only bandage I had on hand was a piece of paper, which I put on the wounds. Soon thereafter, Joel Iglesias went to watch over him, while we continued the attack. Then Acuña too was wounded. No longer advancing, we continued firing at the well-placed trench in front of us, which answered our fire. We were just mustering our courage, and mustering our energies for an assault on the warehouse to end the resistance, when the garrison surrendered.

This description has taken only a few minutes to tell, but the actual battle lasted about two hours and forty-five minutes from the first shot until the garrison surrendered. At my left, some of the men from the forward detachment, Víctor Mora and three others, I seem to recall, captured the last soldiers putting up resistance. From the trench emerged a soldier holding his gun above his head. From all sides came shouts of surrender. We advanced rapidly on the barracks, and we heard one last rattle of machine gun fire, which I later found out had killed Lt. Nano Díaz.

We reached the outbuilding where we made prisoners of the two soldiers who had escaped my shots, and also the post doctor and his adjutant. The doctor was a quiet, gray-haired man, whose subsequent fate I'm unaware of; I do not know whether he is part of the revolution today. A strange thing happened with this man. My knowledge of medicine had never been very extensive; the number of wounded was enormous and my vocation at that moment was not centered on health care. When I brought the wounded to the army doctor, however, he asked me how old I was and when I had finished my training. I explained that it had been some years ago, and then he said frankly: "Look, son, you'd better take charge of all this because I've just graduated and have had very little experience." What with his lack of experience and his natural fright on finding himself a prisoner, he had forgotten all his medical training. So once more I had to change from soldier to doctor, which in fact involved little more than washing my hands.

After the battle, which was one of the bloodiest of the revolutionary war, we pooled our experiences, and I can now give a more general picture of the action than what I have related up to now in describing my personal participation. The battle proceeded more or less as follows: When Fidel's shot gave the signal to open fire, everyone began to advance on their given objectives. The army responded with intense fire, in many cases against the hill from which our leader directed the battle. A few minutes after the action began, Julito Díaz died at Fidel's side when he was hit in the head by a bullet. The minutes passed and the fierce resistance continued; we were unable to press on toward our goal. The most important task in the center was Almeida's: he was in charge of eliminating the guard post at all costs in order to open the way for his troops and those of Raúl, who were attacking the garrison head-on.

The men later recounted how Eligio Mendoza, the guide, had picked up his rifle and flung himself into the battle. A superstitious man, he had a "saint" who protected him, and when he was told to be careful, he answered contemptuously that his "saint" would defend him from anything; a few minutes later he fell, hit by a bullet that literally shattered his body.

The well-entrenched enemy troops drove us back, causing several casualties. It was very difficult to advance through the central area; from the position along the road to Peladero, Jorge Sotús attempted to flank the position with an adjutant nicknamed "Policeman,"[1] but the latter was immediately killed by the enemy and Sotús had to throw himself into the sea to avoid being killed also. From that moment on he was practically erased from the battle. Other members of his platoon attempted to advance, but they too were forced back. A peasant named Vega, I believe, was killed; Manals was wounded in the lung; Quique Escalona received wounds in the arm, buttocks, and hand. The enemy post, well protected by a wooden palisade, fired auto-

1. Francisco Soto.

matic and semiautomatic rifles, devastating our small troop.

Almeida ordered a final assault in which he would attempt by any means to eliminate the enemy resistance he faced; Silleros, Maceo, Hermes Leyva, Pena, and Almeida himself were wounded (the latter in the shoulder and left leg), and Comrade Moll was killed. Nevertheless, this push forward overcame the guard post, and a path to the barracks was opened. From the other side, Guillermo García's accurate machine gun shots had wiped out three of the defenders; the fourth came running out and was killed in flight. Raúl, with his platoon divided in two, advanced rapidly on the garrison. It was the action of Captains García and Almeida that decided the battle; each one destroyed the assigned guard post and made the final assault possible. Another individual who deserves special mention is Luis Crespo, who came down from the general staff position to participate in the assault.

Enemy resistance was crumbling. A white handkerchief had been shown and we reached the barracks. At that moment someone, probably one of our men, fired again and from the barracks came a burst of fire that took Nano Díaz through the head. Up to that point, Nano's machine gun had wrought havoc on the enemy. Crescencio's platoon hardly participated in the battle, because his machine gun had jammed; so he guarded the road from Chivirico. There he stopped some fleeing soldiers. The battle had lasted two hours and forty-five minutes, and no civilian had been wounded, despite the great number of shots fired.

When we took inventory of the battle we found the following situation: On our side at that point there were six dead: Moll, Nano Díaz, Vega, "Policeman," Julito Díaz, and Eligio Mendoza. Gravely wounded were Leal and Silleros. The others wounded, with varying degrees of seriousness, were Maceo in the shoulder, Hermes Leyva with a surface wound on the chest, Almeida in the left arm and left leg, Quique Escalona in the right arm and hand, Manals in the lung, Pena in the knee, Manuel Acuña in the right arm. In all, 15 comrades had been put out of action.

The enemy had 19 wounded, 14 dead, another 14 prisoners, and 6 escapees, which made a total of 53 men, under the command of a second lieutenant who had shown the white flag when he was wounded.

If one considers that we had about 80 men and they had 53, for a total of 133 men, of whom 38—that is to say more than a quarter—were put out of action in a little over two and a half hours of fighting, one can see what kind of battle it was. It was an assault by men who had advanced bare-chested against an enemy protected by very poor defenses. Great courage was shown on both sides. For us this was the victory that marked our coming of age. From this battle on, our morale grew tremendously; our decisiveness and our hopes for triumph increased also. Although the months that followed were difficult ones, we were already in possession of the secret of victory. This action at El Uvero sealed the fate of all the small garrisons situated far from major clusters of enemy forces, and they were all closed down soon after.

One of the first shots of the battle hit the telephone lines, cutting communication with Santiago. Only a couple of small planes flew over the battlefield, but the air force did not send reconnaissance planes until hours later, when we were already high in the mountains. We have been told that, apart from the fourteen dead soldiers, three of the five parrots that the guards had in the barracks were killed. One has only to consider the small size of this bird to get a picture of what kind of attack the building underwent.

My return to the medical profession had a few poignant moments. My first patient was Comrade Silleros. A bullet had split open his right arm and, after piercing a lung, had apparently embedded itself in his spine, paralyzing both legs. His condition was critical, and I was only able to give him a sedative and bind his chest tightly so that he could breathe more easily. We tried to save him in the only way possible at that time: we took the fourteen prisoners with us and left our two wounded men, Leal and Silleros, with the enemy, having received the doctor's word of honor that they would be cared for. When I told this to Silleros, mouthing the usual words of comfort, he answered me with a sad smile that said more than any words could have, expressing his conviction that it was all over for him. We knew this too, and I was tempted at that moment to place a farewell kiss on his forehead. But such an action on my part would have signified to him a death sentence, and duty told me that I must not further spoil his last minutes by confirming something he already knew. I said goodbye, as affectionately as possible and with great pain, to the two combatants who remained in the hands of the enemy. They cried out that they would prefer to die among their own troop; but we also had the duty to fight to the end for their lives. There they remained, bound together with the nineteen wounded Batista soldiers who had also been cared for as well as conditions allowed. Our two comrades were decently treated by the enemy army, but Silleros did not reach Santiago. Leal survived his wound, was imprisoned on the Isle of Pines for the rest of the war, and today still bears the indelible marks of that important episode in our revolutionary war.

In one of Babún's trucks we hauled the largest possible quantity of every kind of equipment, especially medical. We left last, heading toward our hideout in the mountains, which we reached in time to care for the wounded and take leave of the dead, who were buried by a bend in the road. We realized there would now be an intense pursuit, and we decided that those men who could walk ought to move on quickly, leaving the wounded behind in my care. Enrique López would undertake to furnish me with transportation for the wounded, a hiding place, some assistants, and all the necessary contacts through whom we could receive medicines and give proper medical treatment to the men.

Almost no one slept that night, as we heard from each man about their individual feats and what they saw during the battle. Out of curiosity I noted down all the enemy soldiers supposedly killed during the battle, and it turned out there were more enemy corpses than there had been enemy soldiers. The feats of each man had grown in his own imagination. This kind of experience taught us that all facts must be validated by several persons; being exaggeratedly careful, we even demanded physical proof, such as items taken from a fallen soldier, before we accepted an enemy casualty. Preoccupation with the truth was always a central theme in reports from the Rebel Army, and we attempted to imbue our men with a profound respect for truth and a feeling of how necessary it was to place truth above any transitory advantage.

In the morning, we watched the victorious troop leave us, bidding farewell sadly. My aides Joel Iglesias and Oñate stayed with me, as well as a guide named Sinecio Torres and Vilo Acuña, today a commander, who stayed to be with his wounded uncle.

PUBLISHED IN VERDE OLIVO, FEBRUARY 4, 1962

MAY–JUNE 1957

Caring for the wounded

THE DAY AFTER THE BATTLE OF EL UVERO, planes circled overhead beginning at dawn. Our farewells to the departing column were over, and we devoted ourselves to erasing the traces of our entry into the forest. We were a mere hundred meters from a truck road and we waited for Enrique López and the trucks that would take us to our hideout.

Of the wounded, Almeida, Pena, and Quique Escalona were unable to walk; I had to urge Manals not to walk either because of the wound in his lung; Manuel Acuña, Hermes Leyva, and Maceo could all walk on their own. To protect, nurse, and transport them were Vilo Acuña, the guide Sinecio Torres, Joel Iglesias, Alejandro Oñate, and myself. The morning was well advanced when a messenger came to tell us that Enrique López could not help us because his daughter was ill and he had to leave for Santiago; he left word for us saying he would send us some volunteers to help. We're still waiting for them today.

The situation was difficult, for Quique Escalona's wounds were infected, and I could not determine exactly how serious Manals's wound was. We scouted the nearby roads and found no enemy soldiers, so we decided to move the wounded to a peasant hut three or four kilometers away. It was abandoned, but the owner had left behind a number of chickens.

On the first day two workers from the sawmill helped us with the grueling job of carrying the wounded in hammocks. At dawn the next day, after eating well and finishing off quite a few chickens, we quickly left the place, since we had stayed there a whole day immediately after the attack, practically at the very spot, close to highways on which soldiers could arrive. The place was at the end of one of those roads constructed by the Babún Company to reach deeper into the forest. With the few available men, we began a short but difficult trek down to the Arroyo del Indio. Then we climbed a narrow path to a small shack where a peasant named Israel lived with his wife and brother-in-law. It was exceedingly difficult moving our wounded comrades over such rugged terrain, but we did it. The peasant couple even gave us their own double bed for the wounded to sleep in.

We put in hiding some of the weapons that were in poor condition and a variety of less important war booty that we were unable to carry, for the weight of the wounded increased with each step. Evidence of our presence always remained in some peasant hut, in the form of some object we had forgotten. Because of this and since we had the time, we decided to return to the previous spot and erase all traces, since our security depended on it. At the same time Sinecio left to find some friends of his in the region of Peladero.

A short time later Acuña and Joel Iglesias told me they had heard strange voices on the other slope. We really thought that the hour had come to do battle under the most difficult circumstances, for our obligation was to defend to the death the precious burden of wounded men with which we had been entrusted. We advanced so that the encounter would take place as far as possible from the hut. Some prints of bare feet on the path—which seemed very odd—indicated that the intruders had taken the same trail. Approaching warily, we heard an unconcerned conversation among several persons; with my Thompson submachine gun loaded and the assistance of Vilo and Joel, I took the speakers by surprise. They turned out to be the prisoners from El Uvero whom Fidel had freed and who were simply looking for a way out of the forest. Some of them were barefoot; an old corporal, almost unconscious, hoarsely expressed his admiration for us and our familiarity with the woods. They were without a guide and had only a safe-conduct pass signed by Fidel. Taking advantage of the impression our surprise appearance had made on them, we warned them not to enter the forest again for any reason.

They were all from the city and were not used to the hardships of the mountains and how to cope with them. We took them to the clearing where the hut in which we had eaten the chickens was located and showed them the way to the coast, but not without reminding them once more that the area from the forest inward belonged to us, and that our patrol—for we looked like a simple patrol—would immediately notify the forces of that sector of any foreign presence. Despite all this, we felt it prudent to move on as soon as possible.

We spent that night in the hospitable little hut, but at dawn we moved into the forest, first asking the owners of the house to find some chickens for the wounded. We spent the whole day waiting for the husband and wife, but they did not return. Later on we learned they had been captured in the little house and that the next day the enemy soldiers had used them as guides and had passed by our camp of the day before.

We kept a careful watch and no one could have surprised us, but the outcome of a battle under those conditions was not difficult to foresee. As night approached, Sinecio arrived with three volunteers: an old man named Feliciano, and two men who would later become members of the Rebel Army. These were [Teodoro] Bandera, killed in the battle of El Jigüe with the rank of lieutenant, and Israel Pardo, the oldest of a family of fighters, who currently holds the rank of captain. These comrades helped us to move the wounded speedily to a peasant house on the other side of the danger zone, while Sinecio and I waited almost until nightfall for the peasant couple bringing the food. Naturally, they were unable to come because they were already prisoners. Suspecting a betrayal, we too decided to leave the new house early the next day. Our frugal meal consisted of some root vegetables picked in the vicinity of the house.

Afterward, a tremendous downpour made it difficult to reach the Pardo house, but we finally got there close to nightfall. The short distance of four kilometers had been covered in twelve hours, in other words at three hours per kilometer.

At that time Sinecio Torres was practically the savior of the small group, for he knew the roads and the people of the region and he helped us in everything. It was he who two days later arranged for Manals to get to Santiago to be treated; we were also preparing to send Quique Escalona, whose wounds were infected. In those days contradictory news would arrive, sometimes telling us that Celia Sánchez was in prison, other times that she had been killed. Rumors also circulated to the effect that an army patrol had taken Hermes Cardero prisoner. We did not know whether or not to believe these often hair-raising news items. Celia, for example, was our only known and secure contact. Her arrest would mean complete isolation for us. Fortunately the news about Celia was not true, although Hermes Cardero had indeed been captured, but he miraculously stayed alive while passing through the dungeons of the tyranny.

On the banks of the Peladero river lived David [Gómez], the overseer of a large landed estate. He cooperated greatly with us. Once David killed a cow for us, and we had to go out and get it. The animal had been slaughtered on the river bank and cut into pieces; we had to move the meat by night. I sent the first group with Israel Pardo in front, and then the second led by Bandera. Bandera was quite undisciplined, and he did not follow the orders. He let the others carry the full weight of the carcass, so that it took all night to move it. A small troop was now being formed under my command, since Almeida was wounded. Conscious of my responsibility, I told Bandera that he was no longer a combatant, but was now merely a sympathizer, unless he changed his attitude. He really did change; he was never a model combatant when it came to discipline, but he was one of those enterprising and broad-minded men, simple and ingenuous, whose eyes were opened to reality through the shock of the revolution. He had been cultivating his small, isolated parcel of land in the mountains, and he had a true passion for trees and for agriculture. He lived in a small shack with two little pigs, each with its own name, and a little dog. One day he showed me a picture of his two children who lived with his estranged wife in Santiago. He explained that some day, when the revolution triumphed, he would be able to go someplace where he could really grow something, not like that inhospitable piece of land virtually hanging from the mountaintop.

I spoke to him of cooperatives, and he did not understand very well. He wanted to work the land on his own, by his own efforts; nevertheless, little by little, I was convincing him that it was better to work it collectively, that machinery could also increase his own productivity. Unquestionably Bandera would today have been a vanguard fighter in the area of agricultural production; there in the Sierra he improved his reading and writing and was preparing for the future. He was a diligent peasant who understood the value of contributing with his own efforts to writing a page of history.

I had a long conversation with the overseer David, who asked me for a list of all the important things we needed, for he was going to Santiago and would pick them up there. He was a typical overseer, loyal to his boss, contemptuous of the peasants, racist. But when the army took him prisoner and tortured him barbarically on learning of his relations with us, his first concern on returning was to convince us—who thought he was dead—that he had not talked. I do not know if David is in Cuba today, or if he followed his old bosses whose land was confiscated by the revolution. In those days, however, he was a man who felt the need for a change, although he never imagined that the change would also reach him and his world. The revolution has been built on many sincere efforts on the part of simple men. Our mission is to develop the goodness and nobility in each one, to convert every man into a revolutionary—from those like David who do not understand well, to those like Bandera who died without seeing the dawn. The revolution was also made by blind and unrewarded sacrifices. Those of us who today see its accomplishments have the obligation to remember those who fell by the wayside, and to work for a future where there will be fewer stragglers.

PUBLISHED IN VERDE OLIVO, APRIL 29, 1962

JUNE 1957

Return journey

We spent the entire month of June 1957 nursing the men wounded during the attack on El Uvero and organizing the small troop that would be returning with us to Fidel's column.

Contacts with the outside world were made through the overseer David, whose advice and opportune information, as well as the food he brought us, greatly alleviated our situation. In those first days we did not have the invaluable help of Pancho Tamayo, a man who was murdered by the Beatón brothers after the war. Pancho Tamayo, an old peasant from the area, got in touch with us later and also served as a contact.

Sinecio began showing signs of a loss of revolutionary morale; he got drunk on the Movement's money and committed indiscretions. He also neglected to carry out the orders he received and, after one of his binges, he brought us eleven new recruits, all of them unarmed. We generally tried to prevent the enlistment of unarmed men. Nevertheless, new people joined the young guerrilla force by every means and under all conditions, and the peasants, knowing where we were, often brought us new volunteers. No fewer than forty persons passed through the ranks of our small column, but desertions were continual, sometimes with our consent, other times without it, so the troop never had more than twenty-five to thirty members at any one time.

My asthma had gotten somewhat worse, and the shortage of medicine immobilized me almost as much as the wounded. I was able to relieve the illness somewhat by smoking dried *clarín* leaves, a local remedy, until medicine from civilization arrived. This helped me restore my health in preparation for our leaving. But departure was delayed several days. Finally we organized a patrol to round up all the weapons we had left behind as unusable after the attack on El Uvero, which would be added to the guerrilla arsenal.

Under the new conditions, all those old weapons, including a .30-caliber machine gun, were potential treasures, with all their defects, and we spent a whole night looking for them. We finally fixed the departure date for June 24. Our army at the time was made up of 26 men: 5 recuperating wounded, 5 helpers, 10 recruits from Bayamo, 4 recruits from the vicinity, and 2 others who just showed up on their own. The march was organized with Vilo Acuña heading the forward detachment; next, what could be called the general staff, which I led, since Almeida, recovering from the wound to his thigh, had enough work just walking; finally, there were two small squads led by Maceo and Pena.

Pena was a lieutenant at that time. Maceo and Vilo were soldiers, and Almeida, as captain, held the highest rank. We did not leave on June 24 because of a few problems. For one thing, it was announced that one of the guides was arriving with a new recruit, and we had to wait for them. Then we heard that the guide was coming with a new supply of medicines and food. Old Tamayo came and went constantly, bringing news and some supplies of canned food and clothing. At one point we had to find a cave in which to leave some food, because our contacts in Santiago had finally come through and David brought us an important shipment that was impossible to transport, since we were traveling with convalescents and raw recruits.

On June 26 I made my debut as an oral surgeon, although in the Sierra I was given the more modest title of "toothpuller." My first victim was Israel Pardo, today a captain, who came out of it pretty well. The second was Joel Iglesias; all I would have needed to remove his canine tooth was a stick of dynamite, and in fact he saw the end of the war with the tooth still in place since my efforts had been fruitless. On top of the meagerness of my skill, we had a scarcity of anesthetics, so I frequently resorted to "psychological anesthesia"— a few harsh insults when the patient complained too much about the goings-on in his mouth.

Even the thought of long marches caused some of the men to leave us, but new ones replaced them. Tamayo brought us a group of four men. Among them was Félix Mendoza, who came with a rifle. He explained that army troops had surprised him and his companion, and while the other man was being arrested, he had thrown himself over a cliff and escaped unscathed. We later learned that the "army" was a patrol of ours led by Lalo Sardiñas, who had met up with his companion who had since joined Fidel's troop. We were also joined by Evelio Saborit, today a commander in the Rebel Army.

With the arrival of Félix Mendoza and his men, we were now thirty-six in number, but the following day three left, then we were joined by two others, and we numbered thirty-five in all. Nevertheless, when the march started, our numbers diminished once again. We were climbing the slopes of Peladero, making very little progress each day.

The radio informed us of generalized violence throughout the island. On July 1 we heard the news of the death of Josué País, Frank's brother, along with other comrades, killed in the ongoing battle being waged in Santiago. Despite the short daily marches our troops were feeling demoralized and some of the new recruits asked to leave in order to "carry out more useful missions in the city." On the way down La Botella hill we passed the house of Benito Mora, who entertained us in his humble living quarters, which clung to the steep rocks of that part of the Sierra.

Shortly before arriving at Mora's house, I assembled the small troop, telling them that moments of great danger were approaching, that the enemy was close by, that we would probably have to pass many days without food, walking twenty-four hours a day. I urged whoever did not feel up to it to say so now; some of the men had the frankness to express their fears and they left. There was another man, named Chicho [Fernández], spokesman for a small group, who swore they would all follow us until death, in a tone of extraordinary conviction and determination. Imagine our surprise when, after passing Benito Mora's house and camping in a small valley for the night, this same group communicated to us its desire to leave the guerrillas. We agreed to this, and jokingly baptized the place "the Valley of Death," for Chicho's tremendous determination and that of his friends had lasted only up to that point. The name for that little stream of water stuck until we left the Sierra.

We were now twenty-eight men, but on leaving the next day, we were joined by two new recruits; they were ex-soldiers who came to fight for freedom in the Sierra. They were Gilberto Capote and Nicolás. Bringing them was Arístides Guerra, another of the local contacts who later became an invaluable asset to our column and who we nicknamed the "King of Grub." During the entire war, the King of Grub did us innumerable services, and these were often more dangerous than actually fighting the enemy, such as moving mule teams from Bayamo to our zone of operations.

As we continued our short daily journeys, we tried to familiarize the recruits with their weapons. We assigned the two ex-soldiers to teach them how to handle a rifle, how to load and unload, dry-run shooting, and so forth. This went so poorly that no sooner had the lessons begun than one of the instructors fired a shot; we had to remove him from that job, and we eyed him suspiciously, although the consternation on his face was such that it would have taken a great acting talent to simulate it. The two ex-soldiers could not withstand the march and they left again with Arístides, but Gilberto Capote returned to us later, dying heroically at Pino del Agua, with the rank of lieutenant.

We left the place we were camped at, the house of Polo Torres at La Mesa, which later became one of our centers of operations. We were now being guided by a peasant named Tuto Almeida. Our aim was to reach the Nevada and then head to where Fidel was, crossing over the northern slopes of the Turquino mountain. We were walking in that direction when we saw in the distance two peasants who tried to flee when we approached. We ran after them, and they turned out to be two black girls with the last name Moya. They were Adventists whose religious beliefs made them against violence of any kind; nevertheless, they gave us their full support then and for the duration of the war.

We ate heartily and rested there, but when we passed through Mar Verde (we had to in order to reach the Nevada), we found out there were army troops throughout the entire region. After a brief deliberation of our small general staff with the guides, we decided to fall back and go directly across the Turquino, a rougher route but less dangerous under the circumstances.

On our small transistor radio we heard disquieting news; it was reported that heavy battles were being fought in the region of Estrada Palma, and that Raúl was very badly wounded. (Today, with the passage of time, I cannot say whether we heard this over our radio, or over "Radio Bemba."[1]) We did not know whether to believe this or not, for we had learned to mistrust all such reports. But we tried to hurry our march in order to reach Fidel as soon as possible. We walked through the night, spending part of it in the house of a lone peasant, called Vizcaíno because of his Basque origins. He lived on the foothills of the Turquino, all alone in a small peasant hut, and his only friends were a few Marxist books, which he kept carefully hidden in a small hole beneath a stone, far from his house. He proudly spoke of his Marxist adherence, which few people in the area knew about. Vizcaíno showed us which path to follow, and we continued our slow march.

Sinecio was getting further and further from his own area, and for a simple peasant like him, now practically an outlaw, this situation brought him anguish. One fine day, during a halt in the march, while a recruit named Cuervo was on guard with his Remington, Sinecio Torres joined him at the post with another rifle. When I heard of this, about a half hour later, I went to find them, for I did not trust Sinecio very much, and rifles were rather

1. A Cuban expression meaning "rumor mill" or "grapevine."

precious at that time. Both of them had already deserted. Bandera and Israel Pardo went after them, aware that the fugitives were armed with heavy weapons while they themselves had only revolvers. They did not meet up with the deserters.

It was very difficult to maintain troop morale. We were short of weapons and lacked direct contact with the commander of the revolution; we were practically feeling our way, inexperienced and surrounded by enemies who loomed as giants in our imagination and in the tales of the peasants. The reluctance of the recruits from the cities, and their unfamiliarity with the thousand and one difficulties of the Sierra, was provoking continual crises in the morale of our group. There was an attempted desertion led by an individual called "El Mexicano," who had reached the rank of captain and today is in Miami as a traitor to the revolution.

I found out about this from Comrade Hermes Leyva, the cousin of Joel Iglesias. I called a meeting to resolve the question. El Mexicano swore on the graves of all his ancestors that even when he had thought of leaving, it was not with the aim of deserting the struggle; he had meant only to form a small guerrilla band that would assault and kill informers, for there was not enough action in our ranks. The truth is that he really did want to devote himself to killing informers, but for their money, a typical banditlike action. In a subsequent battle, at El Hombrito, Hermes was our only casualty, and there was suspicion that El Mexicano might have been the one who killed him, since Hermes had reported him earlier. No one could ever prove this, however.

El Mexicano remained in the column, giving his word as a man and as a revolutionary, etc., etc., that he would not leave or attempt to leave, nor would he incite anyone else to do so.

After short but difficult marches, we reached the region of Palma Mocha, on the western slope of the Turquino, near Las Cuevas. The peasants received us very well, and we established direct contact with them through my new profession as "toothpuller," which I exercised with great enthusiasm.

We ate and restored our strength to continue rapidly to the familiar regions of Palma Mocha and El Infierno. We arrived on

June 15. There we were informed by Emilio Carrera, a local peasant, that Lalo Sardiñas and his men had set up an ambush nearby. He was concerned about this, for in case of an attack on an enemy patrol, his house would be endangered.

On June 16 the small new column met the platoon from Fidel's column led by Lalo Sardiñas, who told us why he had felt it necessary to join the revolution. He had been a merchant who used to bring us supplies from the city; but he had been taken by surprise and had to kill a man, leading him on the road to joining the guerrillas. Lalo had received instructions to wait there for the arrival of the advance unit of Sánchez Mosquera's enemy column. We learned that once again the obstinate Sánchez Mosquera had penetrated the region of the Palma Mocha river and was almost surrounded by Fidel's column, but had managed to elude them by crossing the Turquino on forced marches, reaching the other side of the mountain.

We already knew of the proximity of the troops; a few days before, on reaching a peasant hut, we had seen the trenches the soldiers had occupied until the previous day. We did not suspect that this apparent proof of a sustained offensive against us was in reality a sign of the repressive column's retreat, marking a qualitative change in operations in the Sierra. We now had sufficient strength to surround the enemy and force him, under threat of annihilation, to flee.

The enemy understood this lesson well and made only sporadic incursions into the Sierra. But one of the most tenacious, aggressive, and bloody enemy officers was Sánchez Mosquera, who rose from a simple lieutenant in 1957 to colonel, a rank that was awarded him after the final defeat in the army's general offensive in June of the following year. His career was meteoric in terms of rank and fruitful in terms of personal enrichment, for he robbed the peasants mercilessly each time he and his troops penetrated the maze of the Sierra Maestra.

PUBLISHED IN VERDE OLIVO, JUNE 10, 1962

JULY 1957

A betrayal in the making

IT WAS A PLEASURE to look at our troop again: close to two hundred men, well disciplined, with increased morale, and with some new weapons. The qualitative change already mentioned before was now quite evident in the Sierra Maestra. There was a true liberated territory, and precautionary measures were not as necessary. There was a certain amount of freedom to carry on conversations at night while resting in our hammocks. We were allowed to visit the villages of the people in the Sierra, developing closer ties with them. It was also a real joy to see the welcome given us by our old comrades.

Felipe Pazos and Raúl Chibás[1] were the big celebrities of those days, although they had two totally different personalities. Raúl Chibás lived solely off the reputation of his brother[2]—who had been a real symbol of an era in Cuba—but he had none of his brother's virtues; he was neither expressive nor wise nor even intelligent. Only his absolute mediocrity allowed him to be a unique and symbolic figure in the Orthodox Party. He spoke very little, and he wanted to get out of the Sierra at once.

Felipe Pazos had a personality of his own. He had the pres-

1. Bourgeois opposition figures who made a brief visit to the Sierra Maestra.
2. Eduardo Chibás was the founder and leader of the opposition Cuban People's (Orthodox) Party. He shot himself in 1951 during a radio broadcast as a public protest against government corruption and died several days later.

tige of a great economist and the reputation of being an honest person, won by not stealing from the public treasury while president of the National Bank under Prío Socarrás's regime, a regime marked by gross larceny and embezzlement. How magnificent, one might think, to remain unpolluted throughout those years. A great merit, perhaps, for a functionary who pursued his administrative career, indifferent to the country's grave problems. But how can anyone imagine a revolutionary who does not speak out daily against the inconceivable abuses rampant at the time? Felipe Pazos skillfully managed to keep his mouth shut, and following Batista's coup he left the post of president of the National Bank, adorned with a great reputation for honesty, intelligence, and talent as an economist. Petulantly, he expected to come to the Sierra and take over. This pint-sized Machiavelli thought he was destined to control the country's future. It is possible he had already hatched the idea of betraying the movement; perhaps that came later. But his conduct was never entirely honest.

Basing himself on the joint declaration[3] that we will analyze below, Pazos appointed himself representative of the July 26 Movement in Miami, and he was about to be designated provisional president of the republic. In this way, Prío was assured that he had a man he could trust in the leadership of the provisional government.

We did not have much time to talk in those days, but Fidel told me about his efforts to make the document a really militant one that would lay the basis for a declaration of principles. This was a difficult task in face of those two Stone Age mentalities immune to the call of the people's struggle.

Fundamentally, the manifesto issued "the slogan of a great civic revolutionary front comprising all opposition political parties, all civic institutions, and all revolutionary forces."

3. The Manifesto of the Sierra Maestra was issued July 12, 1957, by Fidel Castro, Felipe Pazos, and Raúl Chibás and published in the July 28 issue of *Bohemia*. Extensive excerpts from the Sierra Manifesto can be found in Marta Harnecker, *Fidel Castro's Political Strategy: From Moncada to Victory* (New York: Pathfinder, 1987), pp. 49–52.

It made a series of proposals: the "formation of a civic revolutionary front in a common front of struggle"; the appointment of "an individual to head the provisional government." It contained an explicit declaration that the front would neither call for nor accept intervention by another nation in Cuba's internal affairs and "would not accept any sort of military junta as a provisional government of the republic." The document expressed the determination to remove the army from politics entirely and guarantee the nonpolitical nature of the armed forces. It declared that elections would be held within one year.

The program, which was to serve as a basis for a provisional government, proclaimed freedom for all political prisoners, civilian and military; absolute guarantee of freedom of the press and radio, with all individual and political rights to be guaranteed by the constitution; appointment of provisional mayors in all municipalities, after consultation with the civic institutions of the locality; suppression of all forms of government corruption and adoption of measures designed to enhance the efficiency of all state bodies; establishment of a civil service, democratization of trade union politics, promoting free elections in all trade unions and industrywide union federations; immediate launching of an all-out drive against illiteracy and for civic education, stressing the rights and duties of the citizen in relation to society and the homeland; "putting in place the foundations for an agrarian reform designed to distribute unused land and transform into owners all the cane growers who rent their land and all the sharecroppers, tenant farmers, and squatters who work small plots of land owned either by the state or private persons, after payment of compensation to the former owners"; adoption of a healthy fiscal policy to safeguard our currency's stability and aimed at investing the nation's credit in productive works; acceleration of the industrialization process and creation of new jobs.

In addition, there were two points of special emphasis: "First: the need to appoint, at this time, the person who will preside over the provisional government of the republic, to show to the entire world that the Cuban people can unite behind a call for freedom, and support the person who, for his impartiality, integrity, capabilities, and decency, can personify such a call. There are more than enough able men in Cuba who can preside over the republic." (Naturally, Felipe Pazos at least, one of the signers, knew in his heart of hearts that there were not "more than enough men"; there was only one and it was he.)

"Second: that this person shall be appointed by all the civic, and therefore nonpolitical, institutions, whose support would free the provisional president from any commitments to any party, thus ensuring absolutely clean and impartial elections."

The document also stated: "It is not necessary to come to the Sierra for discussions. We can have representatives in Havana, Mexico, or wherever necessary."

Fidel had pressed for more explicit statements regarding the agrarian reform, but it was very difficult to crash through the monolithic front of the two cavemen. "Putting in place the foundations for an agrarian reform designed to distribute unused land"— that was precisely the kind of policy that the *Diario de la Marina* might agree with. To top it off, there was the part reading: "after payment of compensation to the former owners."

The revolution did not carry out some of the commitments as originally stated. We must emphasize that it was our enemies who broke the tacit pact expressed in the manifesto, when they refused to acknowledge the authority of the Rebel Army and made an attempt to shackle the future revolutionary government.

We were not satisfied with the agreement, but it was necessary; at the time it was progressive. It could not last beyond the moment when it would represent a brake on the revolution's development. But we were ready to comply with it. By their treachery, the enemy helped us to break uncomfortable bonds and show the people what these individuals' true intentions were.

We knew that this was a minimum program, a program that limited our efforts, but we also had to recognize that it was impossible to impose our will from the Sierra Maestra. For a long period of time, we would have to depend upon a whole series of "friends" who were trying, in order to advance their own macabre maneuvers, to use our military strength and the great trust that the people already felt in Fidel Castro. Above all they wanted to maintain imperialist domination of Cuba, through its comprador bourgeoisie closely linked with their masters to the north.

The manifesto had its positive sides: it mentioned the Sierra Maestra and stated explicitly: "Let no one be deceived by government propaganda about the situation in the Sierra. The Sierra Maestra is already an indestructible bulwark of freedom, which has taken root in the hearts of our countrymen, and it is here that we will know how to do justice to the faith and the confidence of our people." The words "we will know how" meant that Fidel Castro knew how. The other two proved incapable of following the development of the struggle in the Sierra Maestra, even as spectators; they came down immediately. One of them, Chibás, was surprised and roughed up by Batista's police. Both of them afterward went to the United States.

It was a well-planned coup: a group of the most distinguished representatives of the Cuban oligarchy arrived in the Sierra Maestra "in defense of freedom," signed a joint declaration with the guerrilla chief isolated in the wilds of the Sierra, and left with full freedom to play their trump card in Miami. What they failed to take into account was that political coups always depend on the opponent's strength, in this case, the weapons in the hands of the people. Quick action by our leader, who had full confidence in the guerrilla army, prevented the betrayal's success. Months later, when the results of the Miami Pact became known, Fidel's fiery reply paralyzed the enemy. We were accused of being divisive and of trying to impose our will from the Sierra. But they had to change their tactics and prepare a new trap: the Caracas Pact.[4]

4. For more on the Miami Pact and the text of Castro's denunciation, see the chapter "One Year of Armed Struggle."

The Caracas Pact, broadcast over Radio Rebelde on July 20, 1958, was signed by many of the same bourgeois forces that had backed the Miami Pact in November 1957; unlike the Miami Pact, however, it was also signed by Fidel Castro on behalf of the July 26 Movement and Rebel Army. The

The Sierra Manifesto, dated July 12, 1957, was published in the newspapers at the time. To us, this declaration was simply a brief pause along the road. Our main task—to defeat the oppressor's army on the battlefield—had to go on. A new column was being organized then, with me in charge, and I became a captain. There were other promotions; Ramiro Valdés was promoted to captain and his platoon joined my column. Ciro Redondo, too, was promoted to captain, and was to lead another platoon. The column was made up of three platoons. The first one, the forward unit, was led by Lalo Sardiñas, who was also the detachment's second-in-command. Ramiro Valdés and Ciro Redondo led the other two platoons. This column, which was called the "Dispossessed Peasants," was made up of close to seventy-five men, heterogeneously dressed and armed; nonetheless, I was very proud of them. A few nights later, I was to feel even prouder, closer to the revolution, if that were possible, more anxious to prove that my officer's insignia was well deserved.

We wrote a letter of congratulations and appreciation to "Carlos"— the underground name of Frank País, who was living his final days. It was signed by all the officers of the guerrilla army who knew how to write. (Many of the Sierra peasants were not very skilled in this art, and were already an important component of the guerrillas.) The list of signatures was done in two columns, and as we wrote down our ranks in the second column, when my turn came, Fidel said simply: "Put down commander." Thus, in a most informal manner, almost in passing, I was promoted to commander of the second column of the guerrilla army, which would later become known as Column no. 4.

The letter, written in a peasant's house, was the guerrilla fight-

---

Caracas Pact called for a popular armed insurrection to establish a provisional government, thereby making clear its opposition to a military junta imposed by an officers' coup. It also called for an end to U.S. support for Batista, reflecting the shift in the relationship of forces within the opposition since the time of the earlier document. Excerpts can be found in Harnecker, *Fidel Castro's Political Strategy*, pp. 56–59.

ers' warm message to their brother in the city, who was fighting so heroically in Santiago itself to obtain supplies for us and lessen the enemy's pressure.

There is a bit of vanity hiding somewhere within every one of us. It made me feel like the proudest man on earth that day. My insignia, a small star, was given to me by Celia. The award was accompanied by a gift: one of the wristwatches ordered from Manzanillo. With my recently formed column, my first task was to set a trap for Sánchez Mosquera, but he was the wiliest of all the Batista henchmen and had already left the area.

We had to do something to justify the semi-independent life we were to lead in what was to be our new zone, the region of El Hombrito where we were headed, so we began to plan a series of great deeds.

We had to prepare to celebrate with dignity the glorious date of July 26 that was approaching, and Fidel gave me free rein to do whatever I could, as long as it was done prudently. At the final meeting we met a new doctor who had joined the guerrillas: Sergio del Valle, now head of the general staff of our revolutionary army. At that time he practiced his profession as the conditions of the Sierra allowed.

We needed to prove that we were still alive, since we had received a few setbacks on the plains. Weapons from the Miranda sugar mill that were to be used to open another front had been seized by the police, and several valuable leaders, among them Faustino Pérez, had been captured. Fidel had opposed dividing our forces but had given in at the insistence of the Llano comrades. The correctness of Fidel's view was demonstrated, and from then on we devoted ourselves to strengthening the Sierra Maestra as the first step toward the expansion of the guerrilla army.

PUBLISHED IN VERDE OLIVO, AUGUST 5, 1962

AUGUST 1957

The attack on Bueycito

OUR NEW INDEPENDENCE brought with it new problems. It now became necessary to establish rigid discipline, to organize commands, and to establish some form of general staff in order to assure success in battles to come. This was not an easy task given the men's lack of discipline.

No sooner had the detachment been formed than one of our dearest comrades left us, Lieutenant Maceo. He went to Santiago on a mission, and we would never see him again, for he died there in the struggle.

We also made a few promotions: William Rodríguez became a lieutenant, as did Raúl Castro Mercader. By this measure we were trying to give shape to our small guerrilla force. One morning we were greeted by the unpleasant news that a man had deserted with his rifle, a .22-caliber weapon, which was precious in the deplorable conditions of that period. The deserter was known as Chino Wong; he was from the forward detachment, and he had most likely gone to his community in the foothills of the Sierra Maestra. Two men were sent after him, but we lost hope when Israel Pardo and Bandera returned after a fruitless search for other deserters. Israel, because of his familiarity with the terrain and his great physical resilience, was assigned to carry out special functions at my side.

We began to formulate a very ambitious plan, which consisted of first attacking Estrada Palma during the night and then going to the nearby villages of Yara and Veguitas to capture the small garrisons there, and then return to the mountains by the same path. In this way we could take three garrisons in a single assault, counting on the element of surprise. We had some target practice, using bullets sparingly, and we found that all our weapons were good, except for the Madsen machine gun, which was very old and dirty. In a short note to Fidel we outlined our plan and asked for his approval or rejection. We did not receive an answer, but on July 27 we learned over the radio of the attack on Estrada Palma by two hundred men led by Raúl Castro, according to the official report.

The magazine *Bohemia,* in its only uncensored issue put out at that time, published a report on the damage inflicted by our troops at Estrada Palma, where the old barracks was burned down; it also mentioned Fidel Castro, Celia Sánchez, and an entire roster of revolutionaries who had come down from the mountains. Truth was mixed with myth, as happens in these cases, and the journalists were unable to disentangle them. In reality, the attack was made not by two hundred men but by many fewer, and it was led by Cmdr. Guillermo García (a captain in those days). There was no real combat, since [Col. Pedro] Barreras had retreated shortly before, fearing logically that there would be heavy attacks on July 26 and perhaps unsure of his position. The Estrada Palma operation was merely an expedition. The following day the army's troops gave chase to our guerrillas, and in the area near San Lorenzo, I believe, one of our men was captured, having fallen asleep (such were our organizational weaknesses at the time). After hearing this news, we decided to move rapidly to attack some other garrison in the days immediately following July 26, and to continue maintaining an atmosphere befitting an insurrection.

As we ascended the Maestra, one of the two men who had gone to look for the deserter caught up with us, near a place called La Jeringa. He told us that the other man sent on the mission had confided that he was an intimate friend of Chino Wong and could not betray him. He invited our comrade to desert and indicated that he himself was not returning to the guerrillas. The comrade ordered him to halt, but the new deserter continued walking, so the comrade shot and killed him.

I gathered the entire troop together on the hill facing the spot where this grim event had taken place. I explained to our guerrillas what they were going to see and what it meant. I explained once again why desertion was punishable by death and why anyone who betrayed the revolution must be condemned. We passed silently, in single file, before the body of the man who had tried to abandon his post. Many of the men had never seen death before and were perhaps moved more by personal feelings for the dead man and by political weakness natural at that period than by any disloyalty to the revolution. These were difficult times, and we used this man as an example. It is not important to give the men's names here; we will say only that the dead man was a poor young peasant from the vicinity.

We now passed through some familiar territory. On July 30 Lalo Sardiñas made contact with an old friend, a merchant in the mining region named Armando Oliver. We made an appointment in a house near the California region and there we met with him and Jorge Abich. We spoke of our intention to attack Minas and Bueycito. It was risky to put this secret in the hands of other people, but Lalo Sardiñas knew and trusted them.

Armando informed us that Casillas came to the vicinity on Sundays, because in line with the inveterate habit of the army officers, he had a girlfriend there. Nevertheless, we preferred to attack quickly before our presence was known, rather than trust our luck to capture this officer who was notorious for his crimes. We agreed that on the following night, July 31, we would start the attack. Armando Oliver would take charge of getting us trucks, guides, and a miner who would blow up the bridges linking the Bueycito road with that of the highway connecting Manzanillo and Bayamo. The following day, at two in the afternoon, we began our march. We spent a couple of hours getting to the crest of the Maestra, where we hid all our packs, continuing with only our field equipment. We had to march a long time, and we passed a row of houses, in one of which a party was going on. We called all the people together and "laid down the law," making clear we would hold them responsible if our presence were discovered. We hurried on. Naturally, the danger of these encounters was not very great, since there was no telephone or any means of communication in the Sierra Maestra in those days, and an informer would have had to run on ahead of us.

We reached the house of Comrade Santiesteban, who placed a pickup truck at our disposal; we also had two other trucks that Armando Oliver had sent us. Thus, with the entire troop in the trucks (Lalo Sardiñas's squad in the first, Ramirito's and mine in the second, and Ciro with his platoon in the third), we reached the village of Las Minas in less than three hours. In Las Minas the army had relaxed its vigilance, so the main task was to make sure no one moved toward Bueycito. The rear guard squad, under the command of Lt. Vilo Acuña, today a commander in our Rebel Army, remained here, and we continued on with the rest of the men to the outskirts of Bueycito.

At the entrance to the village, we stopped a coal truck and sent it on ahead with one of our men to see if there were army guards on watch, for sometimes at the entrance to Bueycito an army post inspected everything coming from the Sierra. But there was no one; all the guards were sleeping happily.

Our plan was simple, although a bit pretentious. Lalo Sardiñas would attack the west side of the garrison; Ramiro and his platoon would surround it; Ciro, with the machine gun belonging to the command post squadron, would be ready to attack from the front; and Armando Oliver would arrive casually by car, suddenly shining the headlights on the guards. At that moment, Ramiro's men would invade the barracks, taking everyone prisoner; at the same time, precautions had to be taken to capture all the guards who were sleeping in their own houses. The squad commanded by Lieutenant Noda (who died later in the attack on Pino del Agua) was charged with detaining all vehicles on the highway until firing began, and William was sent to blow up the bridge connecting Bueycito with the Central Highway, to slow up the enemy forces.

The plan could not be carried out: it was too difficult for inexperienced men unfamiliar with the terrain. Ramiro lost part of his platoon in the darkness and arrived somewhat late; the car never left; at one point some dogs barked loudly as we were putting our troops into position.

As I was walking along the main street of the village, a man came out of a house. I shouted, "Halt! Who goes there?" The man, thinking I was a soldier, identified himself: "The Rural Guard!" When I aimed my gun at him, he jumped back into the house, slamming the door, and from inside I could hear the sound of falling tables and chairs and breaking glass as he ran to the back of the house. The two of us had what amounted to a tacit agreement: I would not shoot, since the important thing was to take the garrison, and he did not shout a warning to his companions.

We continued advancing, and were putting the last men in position when the barracks sentry moved forward, curious about the barking dogs and probably about the noise of my encounter with the soldier. We came face to face with each other, only a few meters apart. My Thompson was aimed and he had a Garand. Israel Pardo was with me. I shouted, "Halt!" and the man made a movement. That was enough for me: I pulled the trigger with the intention of shooting him in the chest, but nothing happened and I was left defenseless. Israel Pardo fired, but his defective .22 rifle did not discharge either. I don't really know how Israel came out of this alive. I only remember what I did under the hail of bullets from the soldier's Garand: I ran with a speed I have never matched since, and in full flight turned the corner and landed in the cross street. There I put my submachine gun back into firing order. However, the soldier had unwittingly given the signal to attack, since his was the first shot our men heard. On hearing firing from all sides, the soldier, terrified, hid behind a column, where we found him at the end of the short battle a few minutes later. While Israel went to make contact, the shooting stopped, and we received news of the surrender. Ramirito's men, when they heard the first shots, had moved in and attacked the garrison from the rear, firing through a wooden door.

There were twelve enemy troops in the garrison, six of whom were wounded. We had suffered one dead: Pedro Rivero, a recent recruit, who was shot in the chest. Three of our men had slight wounds. We set fire to the garrison, after removing everything that could be useful to us, and we left in the trucks, taking with us as prisoners the post sergeant and an informer named Oran.

The villagers along the way offered us cold beer and soft drinks, for it was daylight now. The small wooden bridge near the Central Highway had been blown up. As we passed in the last truck, we blew up another small wooden bridge over a creek. The miner who did it was brought to us by Oliver as a new member of the troop, and he was a valuable acquisition; his name was Cristino Naranjo. He later became a commander and was murdered in the days following the triumph of the revolution.

We continued on and reached Las Minas. We stopped there to hold a small meeting. In a rather theatrical scene, a member of the Abich family, a shopkeeper in the area, asked us, in the name of the people, to free the sergeant and the informer. We explained that we were holding them prisoner only to guarantee that there would be no reprisals among the population. But Abich was so insistent that we agreed to free them. So the two prisoners were released and the people's safety assured. As we headed for the Sierra we buried our dead comrade in the town cemetery. Only a few reconnaissance planes passed high overhead. To make sure we were not spotted, we stopped in a small grocery store along the road, where we attended to the three wounded men: one had a surface wound in the shoulder but it had torn the flesh, so the treatment was somewhat difficult; the other had a slight wound in the hand from a small-caliber weapon; and the third had a bump on his head. This he had gotten when the mules in the barracks, frightened by the shooting or wounded in the crossfire, had begun to kick wildly; at one point, according to the man, the animals had dislodged a piece of plaster, which had fallen on his head.

At Alto de California, we left the trucks and distributed the new weapons. Although my participation in the battle had been minimal and not in the least heroic (the few shots fired my way were aimed at the posterior part of my anatomy), I was awarded a Browning machine gun, the jewel of the garrison, replacing my old Thompson, which never fired at the right moment. The best weapons were divided up and given to the best fighters, and we dismissed those who had acted poorly, including the "wet ones," a group of men who had fallen into the river while fleeing the first shots. Among those who performed well we can cite Capt. Ramiro Valdés, who led the attack, and Lt. Raúl Castro Mercader, who together with his men played a decisive role in the small battle.

When we reached the hills again, we learned that a state of siege had been declared and censorship established. We also learned of a great loss to the revolution—the murder of Frank País in the streets of Santiago. With his death one of the purest and most glorious lives of the Cuban revolution was snuffed out; the people of Santiago, Havana, and all of Cuba took to the streets in the spontaneous August strike. The government's semicensorship became total censorship, and we entered a new period characterized by the silence of the pseudo-oppositionist chatterboxes and by the savage murders committed by Batista's thugs throughout Cuba, which spread the war to the entire country.

In Frank País we lost one of our most valiant fighters. But the reaction to his murder demonstrated that new forces were joining the struggle and the fighting spirit of the people was growing.

PUBLISHED IN VERDE OLIVO, AUGUST 26, 1962

AUGUST 1957

The battle of El Hombrito

THE COLUMN WAS ONLY A MONTH OLD, and we were already restless in our sedentary life in the Sierra Maestra. We were in the valley called El Hombrito [the little man], so named because from the plains one could see a pair of gigantic slabs of rock, one on top of the other, on the peak, resembling the figure of a small man.

The men were still very green and we had to prepare them before they faced more difficult situations. But the exigencies of our revolutionary war compelled us to be ready for combat at any moment. We were obliged to attack any enemy columns invading that part of the Sierra Maestra, which by then was becoming Free Territory of Cuba.

During the night of August 29 a peasant informed us that a large troop of soldiers was preparing to ascend the Sierra Maestra, precisely along the road to El Hombrito, which ends at the valley or continues on to Altos de Conrado. We were wary of false information, so I took the man hostage and ordered him to tell the truth, threatening him with dire punishment if he were lying. He swore and reswore that it was true and that the soldiers were already at the farm of Julio Zapatero, a couple of kilometers from the Maestra.

That night we moved into position. Lalo Sardiñas's platoon was to occupy the eastern flank in a small grove of dry ferns and open fire on the column when it stopped. Ramiro Valdés, leading those men with less firepower, was to be on the western flank in order to carry out an "acoustical attack," so as to spread alarm. Although they were lightly armed, their position was less dangerous, since the soldiers would have had to cross a deep ravine to reach them.

The footpath on which the enemy would be coming bordered the hill on the side where Lalo was concealed. Ciro would attack them from the side. I, with a small column of the best-armed men, would open hostilities by firing the first shot. The best squad was led by Lt. Raúl Mercader, of Ramiro's platoon; they were to be used as shock troops to gather the fruits of victory. The plan was very simple: when the enemy reached a small bend in the road, turning almost ninety degrees around a boulder, I was to let ten or twelve of the enemy pass and then shoot the last one, in order to separate those men from the rest. Then the others would be rapidly annihilated by my men; Raúl Mercader's squad would advance; the weapons of the dead would be taken; and we would retreat at once, protected by the fire of the rear guard led by Lt. Vilo Acuña.

At dawn I was in a coffee grove, the position assigned to Ramiro Valdés. We were watching Julio Zapatero's house, situated below on the slope of the mountain. As the sun rose we saw men coming in and out, going through normal wake-up routines. After a while some of them put on their helmets, demonstrating the truth of our peasant's information. All of our men were ready in their combat positions.

I went to my post, and we watched the first men of the column climbing laboriously. The wait was interminable, and my fingers played on the trigger of my new weapon, the Browning machine gun, ready to fire it in combat for the first time. Finally word came that they were approaching, and we heard their unworried voices and their noisy shouts. The first one passed, then the second, then the third. Unfortunately they were walking very far apart from each other, and I calculated that we would not have enough time for the dozen to pass as planned. As I counted the sixth, I heard a shout from up front, and one of

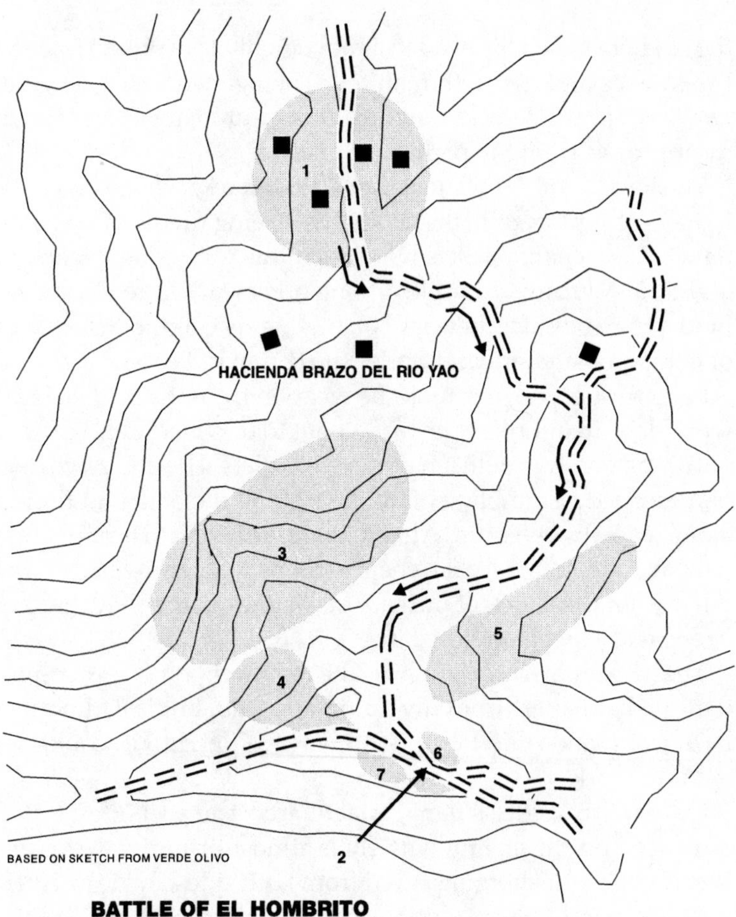

BATTLE OF EL HOMBRITO
AUGUST 29, 1957

1 SETTLEMENT WHERE SOLDIERS WERE CAMPED
2 SHOOTING BEGINS
3 RAMIRO VALDÉS'S PLATOON
4 CIRO REDONDO'S PLATOON
5 LALO SARDIÑAS'S PLATOON
6 RAÚL CASTRO MERCADER'S SQUAD; CHE GUEVARA'S LOCATION
7 VILO ACUÑA'S SQUAD
■ HOUSES

the soldiers raised his head in a movement of surprise. I opened fire at once and the sixth man fell. Then generalized firing began, and, at the second burst from my automatic, the six men disappeared from the path.

I ordered Raúl Mercader's squad to attack, while some volunteers also moved in; the enemy was being fired on from both flanks. Lieutenant Orestes [Guerra] of the forward detachment and Raúl Mercader himself, among others, advanced; from behind a large boulder they fired on the enemy column, which was of company strength and under the command of Major Merob Sosa. Rodolfo Vázquez took the weapon from the soldier I had wounded. To our regret he turned out to be a medic and carried only a .45 revolver with ten or twelve bullets. The other five men had escaped, scrambling off to the right of the path and fleeing along a nearby river bed. After a while we began to hear the first bazooka shots fired by the enemy troops, now recovered somewhat from the shock of our surprise attack, since they had not expected to meet any resistance.

The Maxim machine gun was the only weapon of any weight that we had, apart from my automatic rifle. But it had not yet been fired, and Julio Pérez, who was assigned to it, could not get it to work.

On Ramiro Valdés's flank, Israel Pardo and Joel Iglesias had advanced on the enemy with their almost primitive weapons. Meanwhile, our shotguns, fired from both sides, made an infernal racket and increased the enemy's confusion. I ordered the two lateral platoons to retreat, and when they began to move, we too began our retreat, leaving the rear guard in charge of maintaining fire until all of Lalo Sardiñas's platoon had passed, since we anticipated a second line of resistance.

As we withdrew, Vilo Acuña, having accomplished his mission, returned, announcing the death of Hermes Leyva, cousin of Joel Iglesias. In the course of our withdrawal we came upon a platoon sent by Fidel, whom I had notified of the imminence of a clash with superior enemy forces. Capt. Ignacio Pérez was leading the group. We retreated about a thousand meters from the spot of the battle and planned a new ambush. The soldiers arrived at the small plateau where the battle had taken place. Before our very eyes, they burned Hermes Leyva's body, in that way taking their vengeance. In our impotent rage, we were limited to long-range firing, which they answered with bazookas.

It was then that I found out that the soldier who had provoked my hasty shot with his shout had simply yelled, "This is a piece of cake!" He must have been referring to the fact that he was reaching the peak of the hill. This battle proved to us how poorly prepared our troop was, unable to fire accurately at a moving enemy line at such close range. (There could not have been more than ten or twenty meters between the head of the enemy column and our positions.) Notwithstanding, it was a great triumph for us, for we had completely stopped Merob Sosa's column, which retreated at nightfall, and we had won a small victory over them. We had the minimal compensation of winning one small weapon, but it cost us the life of a valiant fighter. All this we had accomplished with a handful of weapons against an entire company—140 men at least—all of them well armed for modern warfare, who had used bazookas and perhaps even mortars against our positions, although their shots had been as wild and haphazard as ours.

After this battle there were some promotions: Alfonso Zayas was named lieutenant for his valiant behavior, and there were some others I cannot remember. That night, or the following day, after the soldiers had retreated, we had a conversation with Fidel in which he joyfully told us how they had attacked the Batista forces in the region of Las Cuevas, and I learned also of the deaths of some brave comrades in that fight: Juventino Alarcón, from Manzanillo, one of the first to join the guerrilla unit; Pastor [Palomares]; Yayo Castillo; and [Rigoberto] Oliva, son of a lieutenant in Batista's army, a magnificent fighter and a magnificent young man, as were all of them.

The battle won by Fidel was much more important than our own, since it involved not an ambush but an attack on a defended encampment. Although they did not destroy the enemy forces, they had inflicted many casualties, and the soldiers retreated from that position of ours the next day. One of the heroes of the day was Pilón,[1] a brave combatant of ours who was black. It is said that he arrived at a peasant's hut where he saw "a pile of strange tubes with boxes next to them," which turned out to be bazookas abandoned by the enemy. But none of us—much less Félix (Pilón)—knew anything about this weapon except its name. He left them there and later withdrew, suffering from a leg wound. Thus we lost the opportunity of acquiring these weapons, which are so effective in attacks on small enemy fortifications.

There were new repercussions from our battle; a day or two later we learned that an army communiqué had spoken of five or six dead; later we learned that, in addition to our comrade whose body they had committed outrages against, there were four or five murdered peasants for us to mourn. The sinister Merob Sosa had assumed they were responsible for the ambush because they had not reported our troops' presence in the area. I remember their names: Abigaíl, Calixto, Pablito Lebón, of Haitian descent, and Gonzalo González. All of them were completely innocent—or at least partially so, for they knew of our presence and sympathized with our cause, as did all the peasantry—but they had been totally unaware of the maneuver we were preparing. Knowing the methods employed by the heads of Batista's army, we concealed our intentions from the peasants; if one of them happened to pass an area where an ambush was being prepared, we held him until it was over. The unfortunate peasants were murdered by Sosa's men in their homes, which were then set on fire.

This battle showed us how easy it was, under specific circumstances, to attack enemy columns on the march. Furthermore, we became convinced of the tactical correctness of always aiming at the front of the approaching troops, in an attempt to kill the first one or the first few. In this way the rest of their troops

1. Félix Lugones.

would refuse to advance, thus immobilizing the enemy force. Little by little this tactic was being crystallized, and it finally became so systematic that the enemy literally stopped entering the Sierra Maestra, and there were scandals involving soldiers who refused to march in the forward spot. At that point, however, there had not yet been enough battles for this to become the reality.

Now reunited with Fidel, we were able to talk about our modest feats, which nonetheless were impressive because of the great disproportion of forces existing between our poorly armed soldiers and the very well armed forces of repression.

This battle more or less marked the moment of the government troops' definitive withdrawal from the Sierra. Thereafter they only entered rarely, in feats of daring by Sánchez Mosquera, the bravest, the most murderous, and one of the most thieving of all of Batista's military chieftains.

PUBLISHED IN VERDE OLIVO, NOVEMBER 18, 1962

SEPTEMBER 1957

The first battle of Pino del Agua

AFTER MEETING UP WITH FIDEL on August 29 we marched for several days, sometimes together, sometimes separately, with the aim of reaching the Pino del Agua sawmill together. Our information was that there were either no enemy forces at Pino del Agua, or at the very most only a small garrison.

Fidel's plan was as follows: if there were a small garrison, to capture it; if not, to show our presence there and then he would continue, with his troop, in the direction of the Chivirico sector, while we would wait in ambush for the Batista army. In such circumstances, we knew, the army always came right away, to make a show of strength and thereby counteract the revolutionary impact of our presence on the minds of the peasants.

In the days leading up to the battle of Pino del Agua, during the march from Dos Brazos del Guayabo to the battle site, various incidents occurred, whose principal actors were to play a role in the subsequent history of the revolution.

One of these events was the desertion of two peasants from the vicinity. These were Manolo and Pupo Beatón, who had joined the guerrilla ranks shortly before El Uvero and fought in that battle; now they were abandoning our camp. These two individuals were subsequently readmitted, and Fidel pardoned their betrayal. But they never managed to rise above their seminomadic and banditlike behavior. For personal reasons, Manolo murdered Cristino Naranjo after the revolution's triumph. He succeeded in escaping from La Cabaña fortress where he had been confined and organized a small guerrilla force in the very region where he had fought alongside us in the Sierra Maestra. There he committed more crimes, such as the murder of Pancho Tamayo, a brave comrade who had joined us during the first days of the revolution. Eventually a group of peasants captured Manolo and his brother Pupo; both of them were shot in Santiago.

There was also another painful incident. A comrade named Roberto Rodríguez was disarmed for insubordination. He was very undisciplined, and the lieutenant of his squad took away his weapon, exercising a disciplinary right. Roberto got hold of a comrade's revolver and committed suicide. We had a small disagreement on the subject; I was opposed to rendering him military honors, whereas the men thought that he should be added to the list of their dead. I argued that committing suicide under such conditions should be repudiated, whatever good qualities the man might have possessed. After a few stirrings of insubordination by some of the men, we wound up holding a wake, without rendering him honors.

One or two days earlier he had told me a part of his story. He was clearly a boy of excessive sensitivity, who was making great efforts to adapt himself to guerrilla life and to discipline, all of which went counter to his physical weakness and his instinctive rebelliousness.

Two days later we sent a small detachment to Minas de Bueycito to make a show of force there, since it was September 4.[1] The little group was commanded by Capt. Ciro Redondo, who

1. On September 4, 1933, a group of junior army officers that included Sgt. Fulgencio Batista overthrew a government picked by U.S. ambassador Sumner Welles. That event gave a new impulse to the revolutionary upsurge that had toppled the dictatorship of Gerardo Machado earlier in the year. By early 1934, however, Batista—by then army chief of staff—had begun to suppress the anti-imperialist forces led by Antonio Guiteras, in the process consolidating his position as Cuba's strongman. Batista held power until 1944. Following the 1952 coup, Batista claimed the mantle of September 4 as a source of legitimacy for his regime.

brought us a prisoner named Leonardo Baró. This individual was to play an important role in the ranks of the counterrevolution. He remained our prisoner for a good while, and one day told me a heartrending story of his mother's illness. I took him at his word. I tried in passing to convince him to make a political demonstration. I proposed that he take a bus, see his mother in Havana, and then demand asylum in an embassy, proclaiming his unwillingness to fight against us any more and denouncing the Batista regime. He would not agree, alleging that he could not denounce the regime for which his brothers were fighting, and we agreed that he should limit himself, in asking asylum, to declaring he did not want to fight any more.

We sent him off with four comrades. They had precise instructions not to allow him to see anyone on the way, since he was well acquainted with the names of a good many peasants who had visited us at our camp. Furthermore, the comrades were told to make the trip on foot, as far as the outskirts of Bayamo, where they were to leave him and return by another route.

These men did not obey their orders. They allowed themselves to be seen by many people; they even held a meeting at which Baró was present, as a liberated prisoner and an alleged sympathizer. Then they traveled to Bayamo by jeep. On the way they were intercepted by Batista's troops, and the four comrades were murdered. We never knew for sure if Baró had participated in this crime or not. What we do know is that he immediately installed himself at Minas de Bueycito and put himself under the orders of the killer Sánchez Mosquera. Then he began to identify, among those who came to do their marketing, the peasants who had been in contact with our guerrilla group.

My error cost the people of Cuba countless victims.

Several days after the triumph of the revolution, Baró was captured and executed.

Soon after the incident, we went down to San Pablo de Yao, where we were welcomed with open arms. We occupied the hamlet peacefully for several hours (there were no enemy troops) and began to make contacts, meeting many people from the area.

We loaded up all available items in trucks provided us by the merchants who sold us supplies on credit (during that period we paid with vouchers). It was then that we met our great comrade Lidia Doce, who later—until her death in Havana—was in charge of the column's various contact tasks with the outside.[2]

The job of bringing the goods from Yao was very difficult. The road that ascends from San Pablo de Yao to Pico Verde, past the Cristina mine, is very steep, and only trucks with four-wheel drive, not too heavily loaded, can make the climb. Ours broke down en route, and the supplies had to be reloaded onto the backs of mules and men.

Those days also witnessed a series of separations for a variety of reasons. One comrade, a good fighter, was expelled for drunkenness while on guard duty during the expedition to Yao, having thus endangered the entire column. Another, Jorge Sotús, left his post as squad chief and went to Miami on a mission for Fidel. In reality, Sotús never was able to adapt to the Sierra, and his men disliked him because of his despotic nature. His career had many ups and downs. In Miami his attitude was a vacillating one, if not traitorous. He rejoined the ranks of our army, was pardoned, and his past errors forgiven. During the Huber Matos days he betrayed us and was sentenced to twenty years' imprisonment. Aided by a jailer, he escaped and fled to Miami. He was killed while making final preparations for a pirate raid on Cuban territory, apparently electrocuted in an accident.

Among the other comrades who left us at that time was Marcelo Fernández, coordinator of the July 26 Movement in the cities. He was returning to work in his area of responsibility after having spent a considerable amount of time in the Sierra Maestra.

After these incidents we resumed our march, reaching Pino del Agua on September 10. Pino del Agua is a hamlet built around a sawmill along the crest of the Sierra Maestra. During that period it was managed by a Spaniard. There was a handful of workers, but not one enemy soldier. We occupied the hamlet that night,

2. For more on Lidia Doce, see the chapter "Lidia and Clodomira."

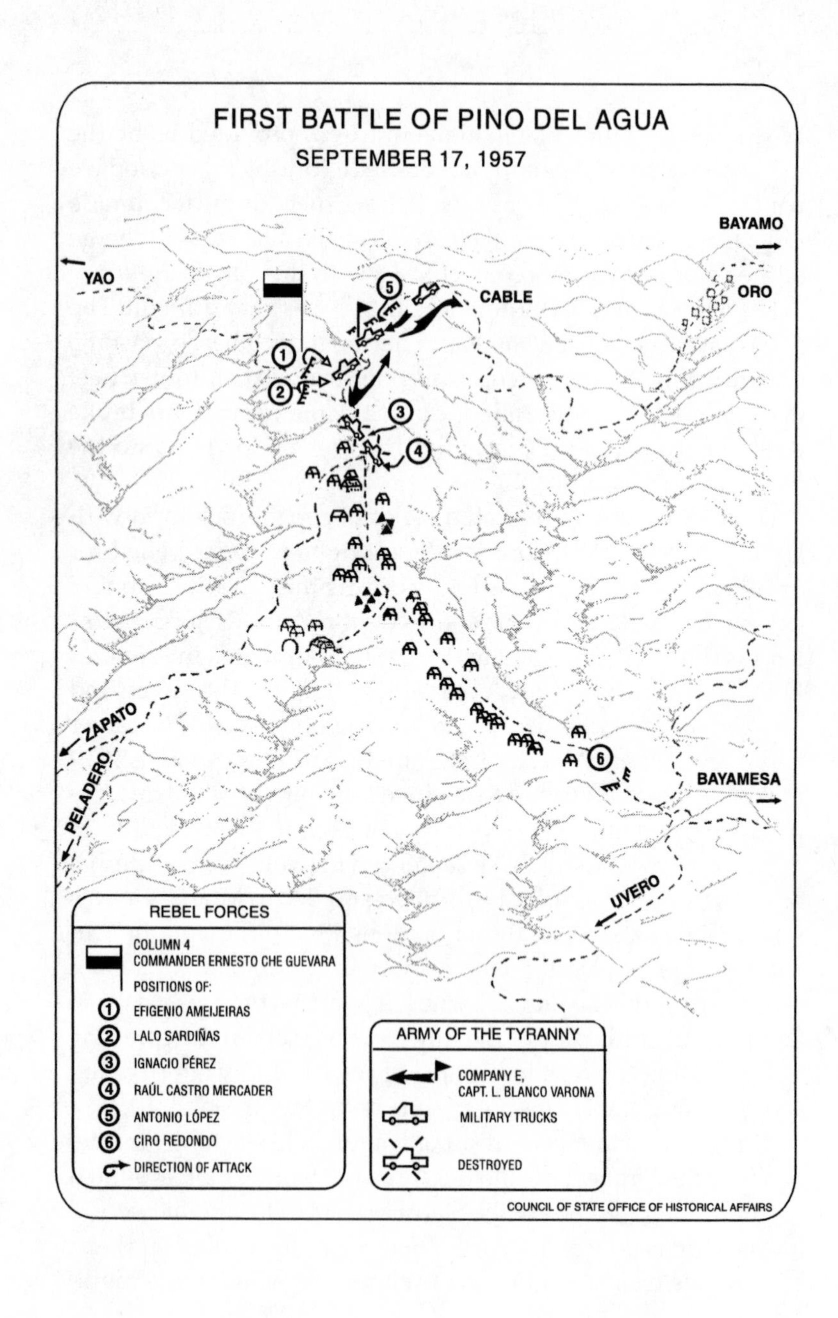
FIRST BATTLE OF PINO DEL AGUA
SEPTEMBER 17, 1957
BAYAMO
YAO
CABLE
ORO
ZAPATO
PELADERO
BAYAMESA
UVERO
REBEL FORCES
COLUMN 4
COMMANDER ERNESTO CHE GUEVARA
POSITIONS OF:
1 EFIGENIO AMEIJEIRAS
2 LALO SARDIÑAS
3 IGNACIO PÉREZ
4 RAÚL CASTRO MERCADER
5 ANTONIO LÓPEZ
6 CIRO REDONDO
DIRECTION OF ATTACK
ARMY OF THE TYRANNY
COMPANY E,
CAPT. L. BLANCO VARONA
MILITARY TRUCKS
DESTROYED
COUNCIL OF STATE OFFICE OF HISTORICAL AFFAIRS

and Fidel disclosed his itinerary to the villagers, calculating that someone among them would pass the information on to the army.

We engaged in a small diversionary maneuver: while Fidel's column continued its march toward Santiago in full view of all, we made a detour during the night and laid an ambush for the enemy. In charge of essential supplies—assuming the enemy did not take too long to arrive—was, as always, old Tamayo, who lived in the vicinity, at a place called Cuevas de Peladero.

We distributed the men in such a way that all roads would be under surveillance. We extended our surveillance to the road from Yao to Pico Verde, several leagues[3] from Pino del Agua, and to another more direct trail, not passable by truck, that went up to the Maestra. The group at Pico Verde was very small, armed with hunting rifles, and charged with giving the alarm if need be. This road was a good line of retreat, and we counted on using it after the action. Efigenio Ameijeiras remained in charge of keeping watch over one of the access roads along the rear, which also came from the Pico Verde sector. Lalo Sardiñas and his squad remained in the zone of El Zapato, guarding several lumber roads that end at the banks of the Peladero river. But that was a superfluous precaution, since in order to reach these roads, the enemy would have had to make a very long march through the Sierra, and it was not their custom to march in columns through the mountains. Ciro Redondo and his platoon were assigned to defend the access way coming from Siberia. That is the region that joins El Uvero and Pino del Agua, two sawmills connected by a road that passes by the spot chosen for Ciro on the edge of the Maestra.

Our forces were distributed along the side of the road going uphill from Guisa, in a forest on the cliff. Our aim was to surprise the trucks and concentrate our fire on the spot where they would likely be coming from. The spot chosen permitted us to see the trucks coming from a great distance. The plan was simple: we would fire on them from both sides, immobilizing the first

3. One league in Cuba is roughly 2.6 miles (4.24 kilometers).

truck at a bend in the road, and firing on all the following ones in order to halt them. If the element of surprise could be maintained, we thought we could capture three or four vehicles. The platoon assigned to the action had the best weapons and was reinforced by some of Capt. Raúl Castro Mercader's men.

We spent about seven days in ambush, waiting patiently, before the troops arrived. I was at the small command post, where food was being prepared for the men on ambush. Suddenly I was informed that the enemy was approaching. Since at that spot the slopes are very steep, we heard the hum of the motors even before we saw anything, as the trucks clambered up the rugged terrain.

Our forces prepared for battle. At the main spot we placed the men under the command of Capt. Ignacio Pérez, whose job was to stop the first truck. Along the flanks were the others who were to fire on the other vehicles. Twenty minutes before the battle, a torrential downpour fell, normal in the Sierra, soaking us to the bone. Meanwhile, the enemy soldiers were advancing, more concerned with the rain than with the possibility of an attack. The man charged with opening hostilities fired his Thompson submachine gun, but under the circumstances, hit no one. The fusillade became general, and the soldiers in the first truck, more frightened and surprised than hurt by our attack, leaped onto the road and disappeared behind the cliff. In the process, they killed one of our great fighters, José de la Cruz, known as "Crucito," the poet of our column.

Some strange things happened in this battle. An enemy soldier took refuge under the truck at the bend in the road and would not show his head to anyone. A minute or two later I arrived at the scene. Many of our people were retreating, obeying what they mistakenly thought was an order—a frequent accident in the midst of battle. Arquímides Fonseca was wounded in the hand while retrieving a submachine gun abandoned by its gunner. I had to give orders for everyone to return to his combat post and asked Lalo Sardiñas and Efigenio Ameijeiras to concentrate their forces with us.

A fighter named Tatín was on the road. As I walked down it he said to me, defiance in his voice: "He's there, under the truck! Let's go! Let's go! We'll see who's a real man and who's not!" I summoned up my courage, deeply offended by his implication that I was reluctant. When we tried to approach the anonymous enemy combatant firing on us from beneath the truck, however, we had to acknowledge that the price for demonstrating our manliness would be very great indeed. Neither my accuser nor I passed the test. The soldier dragged himself away with his submachine gun and was saved from being killed or falling prisoner.

There were five army trucks transporting one company. The squad led by Lt. Antonio López carried out fully its orders not to allow anyone to pass after the opening of hostilities. Nevertheless, some of the soldiers, putting up fierce resistance, impeded our advance. Lalo Sardiñas and Efigenio Ameijeiras arrived with their reinforcements; they advanced on the trucks and eliminated all resistance. Some of the soldiers fled in disarray down the road; others fled in the two trucks they had managed to save, abandoning all the other equipment and ammunition.

Through Gilberto Cardero, we received information concerning the enemy's forces and some of their plans. This comrade had been taken prisoner during a reconnaissance mission in another area. He had remained captive for a certain time, and the enemy had brought him along so that he would poison Fidel. The idea was for him to empty the contents of a vial in Fidel's food. When he heard the shots, Cardero threw himself out of the truck, like all the soldiers, but instead of fleeing the fusillade, he reported to us at once and rejoined our ranks, telling of his odyssey.

In capturing the first truck, we found two dead and one wounded soldier, who was still going through the motions of fighting as he lay dying. One of our fighters finished him off without giving the man an opportunity to surrender—which he was unable to do, being only half-conscious. The combatant responsible for this barbaric act had seen his family wiped out by Batista's army. I reproached him violently, unaware that my remarks were overheard by another wounded soldier, concealed and motionless under some tarpaulins on the truck bed. Emboldened by my words and by the apology of our comrade, the enemy soldier made his presence known and begged us not to kill him. He had a fractured leg and remained at the side of the road while the battle went on elsewhere. Every time a fighter passed near him he would shout, "Don't kill me! Don't kill me! Che says not to kill prisoners!" When the battle was over, we transported him to the sawmill and gave him first aid.

As for the other trucks, we had inflicted only a few casualties, but a large number of weapons remained in our possession. The final results of the battle: one Browning automatic rifle; five Garands; one tripod machine gun and its ammunition; and another Garand, which Efigenio Ameijeiras's troop made off with. Efigenio, who belonged to Fidel's column, judged his platoon's participation in the battle to have been decisive, so he felt they had a right to some of the captured weapons. But Fidel had put this detachment under my orders precisely so they would help us capture weapons. Therefore, ignoring their protestations, I divided the trophies among the men of my column, except for the Garand that had already been appropriated.

The Browning was given to Antonio López, lieutenant of one of the squads that had performed best. The Garands went to Lt. Joel Iglesias, Virelles (a member of the *Corynthia* expedition, who had joined our troops), Oñate, and two others whose names I do not remember. We then proceeded to set the three captured trucks on fire, since we were unable to transport them.

While we were assembling our troops, some planes passed overhead, advised of our attack. Several bursts of gunfire from our direction sufficed to drive them away.

Mingolo, one of the Pardo brothers,[4] had been sent to warn Fidel of the soldiers' approach, I seem to recall; but we decided to send another messenger to tell him the results of our battle. He was accompanied by Cardero, to recount his adventure. We

4. Benjamín Pardo Guerra.

sent word to Ciro to withdraw from his position since the battle was over. Mongo Martínez carried that message.

After a few minutes we heard gunfire. A group of our men, armed with hunting rifles, had discovered a soldier who was advancing surreptitiously. They ordered him to halt; when he ignored the command, they fired. The man fled, abandoning his gun. They brought us a Springfield as evidence of their triumph. We were concerned that there were still dispersed soldiers in the region, but the gun was added to our tally.

Two or three days later Mongo Martínez returned. He announced that some enemy soldiers had taken him by surprise, firing on him with hunting rifles, and that he was forced to flee because he was wounded. His face was literally covered with marks from a gunshot wound. This was the source of the Springfield that our comrades had seized from the enemy! The result had been that this wounded comrade, believing the soldiers to be very near, had taken a crossroad and got lost in the woods, without having let Ciro Redondo know about our battle or the order to withdraw. The next day Ciro, who had heard echoes of the battle, sent a messenger to us, and the order was conveyed to him.

While the B-26s were flying low over the sawmill in search of victims, we were calmly having our breakfast. Installed in various parts of the building, we drank hot chocolate brought to us by the mistress of the house—who was not exactly cheered by the sight of the B-26s passing back and forth, almost grazing the roof. The planes finally left, and we, utterly relaxed, were about to leave when we saw on the road from Siberia (which Ciro had been watching a few hours earlier) four trucks, full of soldiers. This was another group going in the opposite direction to meet up with the first one. It might have been possible to set a similar trap, but it was already too late; a good number of our men had fallen back to safer positions. We fired in the air twice, our signal of retreat, and left quietly.

This battle had important repercussions, for the news of it spread throughout Cuba. The enemy toll was three dead and one wounded, in addition to one prisoner, captured by Efigenio's platoon the next day during a final combing of the zone. It was Corporal Alejandro, who remained with us as our cook until the end of the war. Crucito was buried at the site of our battle. Our entire troop was greatly saddened, having lost in him a great comrade and its peasant bard. Crucito used to carry on fierce poetic duels with Calixto Morales, whom he called "the old buzzard of the Sierra," as against himself, "the nightingale of the Maestra."

Distinguishing themselves in this battle were Lt. Efigenio Ameijeiras, Capt. Lalo Sardiñas, Capt. Víctor Mora, Lt. Antonio López and his squad, Dermidio Escalona, and Arquímides Fonseca. The latter was then put in charge of the tripod machine gun, which he was to use after his hand healed from a bullet wound. On our side we had one dead, one light wound, some contusions, some scratches, and Monguito's powder burns.

We withdrew from Pino del Agua by various routes, heading toward the region of Pico Verde. There we would reorganize ourselves while waiting for the arrival of Fidel, who had already learned of the clash.

Analysis of the battle showed that, although a political and military victory, it nonetheless revealed our enormous shortcomings. The factor of surprise should have been exploited to the hilt, virtually wiping out the occupants of the first three trucks. Furthermore, after hostilities had begun, a false order to retreat had been circulated, leading the men to lose control and cooling their fighting ardor. A lack of decisiveness was evident in seizing the vehicles, which were defended by a small number of soldiers. In addition, by spending the night at the sawmill we exposed ourselves unnecessarily. And the final withdrawal was carried out in great disorder. All this proved the imperative necessity of improving combat preparations and discipline among our troop, a task to which we devoted ourselves in the days to come.

PUBLISHED IN VERDE OLIVO, MARCH 17, 1963

OCTOBER 1957

An unpleasant incident

AFTER THE BATTLE OF PINO DEL AGUA, we set about to improve the organizational structure of our guerrilla force, strengthened at that point by several of Fidel's units. Our goal was to increase its usefulness and effectiveness in combat.

Lieutenant López's squad, which had distinguished itself at Pino del Agua, and whose members were all very serious young men, was chosen to act as a disciplinary commission. Its responsibilities would be surveillance and overseeing established norms of vigilance, general discipline, keeping the camp clean, and revolutionary morale. But its life was brief; it was dissolved under tragic circumstances a few days after its creation.

About this time, in the vicinity of the hill called La Botella, in a little camp that we ordinarily used as a way station, we executed a man named Cuervo, who had deserted with his rifle two months before. What became of his gun we never found out. But we did know of his activities: using the pretext of fighting for the revolutionary cause and executing spies, he simply victimized an entire section of the population of the Sierra, perhaps in collusion with the army.

In view of his status as a deserter, the trial was speedy, then proceeding to his physical elimination. The execution of antisocial individuals who took advantage of the prevailing atmosphere in the area to commit crimes was, unfortunately, not infrequent in the Sierra Maestra.

We learned that Fidel had completed his tour of the Sonador region, after going to Chivirico, and on his return trip he was in our area. Consequently, we decided to march toward the Peladero in an attempt to join up with him as rapidly as possible.

At that time there was a merchant in the coastal area, Juan Balansa, whose ties with the dictatorship and the large landholders were known, although he had never shown any active hostility toward our guerrillas. Nevertheless, Juan Balansa had a mule, celebrated in the vicinity for its staying power, and as a kind of war tax, we made off with it. With the mule, we arrived at Pinalito, near the Peladero river. On reaching its banks, we had to descend the steep cliffs. We were faced with the alternative of slaughtering the beast and carrying the pieces of meat, abandoning it in enemy territory, or trying to have it go as far as it could. We opted for the latter solution, since carrying the meat would have been very difficult.

The mule made its way downward, decisively and surefooted, in places where we had to crawl along, clinging to vines, or hanging on as best we could to rocky protuberances, through places where even our little mascot—a puppy dog—refused to walk, waiting to be picked up and carried. The mule gave an extraordinary display of acrobatic talent.

It continued its exploits by crossing the Peladero river in a place full of boulders, by a series of spectacular leaps from rock to rock. This is what won the animal its right to live. Later, it was mine to ride, my first regular mount, until the day it fell into the hands of Sánchez Mosquera, during one of our numerous encounters with him in the Sierra.

On the banks of the Peladero river there occurred the unpleasant incident that led to the abolition of the disciplinary commission. The commission was continually meeting resistance to its work from a group of comrades not reconciled to the establishment of disciplinary standards, compelling the commission to take drastic measures.

Members of one of the rear guard squads played a tasteless practical joke on the members of the commission. According to the jokers, there was a very serious matter requiring the commission to come right away. It turned out to be some manure the comrades had left to make fun of them. Because of the incident, various members of the group were arrested, among them Humberto Rodríguez, of sad repute due to his penchant for playing the role of executioner whenever we found ourselves faced with the painful duty of executing a malefactor. After the revolution triumphed, Rodríguez, with another rebel soldier as his accomplice, murdered a prisoner; they subsequently escaped from La Cabaña prison.

Two or three comrades were imprisoned along with Humberto. Under guerrilla conditions, "prison" did not mean much. But when the crime was serious enough, a prisoner guilty of a lack of discipline would be deprived of food for a day or two. This was indeed a punishment that struck home.

Two days after the incident, while the principal participants were still prisoners, it was announced that Fidel was in the vicinity, in the region called El Zapato. I went there to welcome and talk with him. Just a few minutes into our meeting, Ramiro Valdés came to us bringing news: Lalo Sardiñas, in an impulsive act of punishment toward an undisciplined comrade, had held his pistol to the man's head as if to shoot him. The gun went off unintentionally and the man was killed on the spot. There were stirrings of a riot among the troops. I wasted no time in getting back to the camp and putting Lalo under guard. Hostility against him was rife. The men were demanding a summary trial and execution.

We began to take statements and look for evidence. Opinions were divided: some of the men stated point-blank that it was premeditated murder. Others said it was an accident. Independently of this question, it was expressly forbidden within the guerrilla unit to inflict corporal punishment on a comrade, and this was not Lalo Sardiñas's first offense.

The situation was of the greatest delicacy. Comrade Sardiñas had always been a very brave combatant, a strict defender of discipline, and a man with a great spirit of sacrifice. Those who were fiercely demanding the death penalty, on the other hand, were far from the best of the group. There were a number of factors to take into account, in particular the struggle to impose discipline.

The witnesses' declarations went on into the night. Fidel came to our camp. He was opposed to applying the death penalty but did not deem it wise to make a decision of this nature without consulting all the fighters. The next stage of the trial called for Fidel and me to defend the accused, who observed the deliberations concerning his fate impassively, without showing the slightest trace of fear. After a series of impulsive speeches demanding his death, it was my turn to take the floor and ask people to reflect deeply on this problem. I tried to explain that the comrade's death had to be ascribed to the conditions of the struggle, to the very fact that we were at war, and that it was after all the dictator Batista who was guilty. My words, however, were not convincing to this hostile audience.

It was already into the night; we had lit several pine torches and some candles so as to continue the discussion. Fidel then spoke, for a full hour. He explained why, in his opinion, Sardiñas should not be executed. He enumerated all our faults, our lack of discipline, the other errors we committed daily, the weaknesses resulting from this. And he explained that, in the end, this reprehensible act had been committed in defense of the concept of discipline and that we should keep that fact in mind. As he spoke, illuminated by the light of the torches, standing tall against a background of shrubs, his voice had a deeply moving effect, and many of the men were clearly convinced by our leader's opinion. His enormous powers of persuasion were put to the test that night.

Fidel's eloquence, however, could not put an end to all opposition. It was decided that two alternative sanctions should be put to a vote: immediate death by shooting, or demotion and the punishment this would entail. Owing to the inflamed passions, a number of factors went into the vote, in which a man's life was at stake. We had to suspend proceedings because some were voting twice, and excited argumentation was fast distorting the terms of the solution. Once more the two alternatives up for a vote were explained, and everybody was asked to clearly make his decision known.

I was put in charge of tallying the votes, in a little notebook. Lalo was beloved by many among us. We recognized his guilt, but we wanted his life to be spared, for he was a valuable cadre of the revolution. I recall that Oniria,[1] a young woman who had joined our column, then not much older than a girl, asked in an anguished voice if she too could vote in her capacity as a combatant. She was permitted to do so, and after all had cast their votes, we began to count the ballots.

I recorded the results of this strange vote on little squares of paper, similar to those used in medical laboratories. It was extremely close. After the last hesitations, here is how opinion was divided among the 146 guerrillas who voted: 70 declared themselves in favor of the death penalty; 76 for another type of punishment. Lalo was saved.

But that was not the end of it. The next day a group of men unreconciled to the majority decision announced they had decided to leave the guerrilla unit. This group included elements of very poor quality, but there were also some valuable men. Paradoxically, Lt. Antonio López, head of the disciplinary commission, and various members of his squad were dissatisfied and left the Rebel Army. I remember several names: someone named Curro, Pardo Jiménez (who had participated in the struggle despite being a nephew of a Batista minister). I don't know what happened to these comrades. Leaving with them were also the three Cañizares brothers, whose fate was less than heroic: one of them died at Playa Girón and another was taken prisoner there after participating in the attempted mercenary invasion. These men, who had not respected the majority and abandoned the struggle, subsequently put themselves at the service of the enemy, and it was as traitors that they returned to fight on our soil.

1. Oniria Gutiérrez.

Our revolutionary war was already beginning to acquire new characteristics. The consciousness of the leaders and the combatants was being deepened. We were beginning to feel in our flesh and blood the need for an agrarian reform and for profound and integral changes in the social structure that had to be carried out in order to cleanse the country. But this deepening consciousness among the best and the most numerous part of our fighters provoked clashes with those elements who had joined the struggle solely out of a lust for adventure, or perhaps not only for laurels but for material gain as well.

A certain number of other malcontents withdrew. I do not remember most of their names. There is one that comes to mind, however, an individual named Roberto, who subsequently spun out an interminable tale, full of lies, which Conte Agüero, opening himself up to ridicule, published in *Bohemia*. Lalo Sardiñas was demoted and sentenced to win his rehabilitation by fighting the enemy as a simple soldier as part of a small platoon. One of our lieutenants, Joaquín de la Rosa, Lalo's uncle, decided to accompany him. As a replacement for Captain Sardiñas, Fidel gave me one of his best fighters: Camilo Cienfuegos, who became captain of our column's forward detachment.

It was necessary for us to head out immediately. Our mission was to neutralize a group of bandits who, cloaking themselves under the banner of our revolution, were committing their crimes in the region where we had begun our struggle, as well as in the region close to Caracas and El Lomón. Camilo's first mission in our column was to advance rapidly and capture all those elements, who would then be put on trial.

PUBLISHED IN VERDE OLIVO, APRIL 28, 1963

OCTOBER 1957

The struggle against banditry

CONDITIONS IN THE SIERRA were now permitting us to live freely in a quite vast territory. The army rarely occupied any of it; in many places, they never even bothered to set foot. But we did not have a system of government that was either extensive enough or sufficiently organized to stop the bands of marauders who, under the pretext of revolutionary activities, indulged in looting and banditry and a host of other offenses.

Moreover, political conditions in the Sierra were still quite unsettled. The political development of the inhabitants was still very superficial, and the presence of a threatening enemy army made it very difficult to overcome these weaknesses.

Once again, the enemy tightened its vise. There were various signs indicating a new advance on the Sierra. This created nervousness among the inhabitants of the district. The least resolute among them were already looking for a way to save themselves from the dreaded invasion by Batista's assassins. Sánchez Mosquera was camped in the hamlet of Minas de Bueycito, and it was becoming evident that a new incursion was in the making.

As for us, during those days of October 1957, we were in the valley of El Hombrito, laying the groundwork for a liberated territory. We were establishing the first rudiments of industrial activity in the Sierra—an oven for baking bread was set up at that time. In this same sector of El Hombrito there was an encampment that served as a sort of halfway house for the guerrilla forces. Groups of young men who had arrived to join up with us were placed under the authority of trusted peasants.

The leader of the group was named Arístidio. He had been a member of our column until a few days before the battle of El Uvero. But he did not participate in it because he had fallen and fractured a rib. He later showed little desire to continue as a member of the guerrilla unit.

Arístidio was a typical example of a peasant who joined the ranks of the revolution without having any clear understanding of its significance. In sizing up the situation, he decided there were more advantages in waiting to see which way the wind would blow. He sold his revolver for a few pesos and began to repeat to anyone who would listen that he was not crazy enough to allow himself to be quietly caught at home, after the guerrillas left, and that he would make contact with the army. His declarations were brought to my attention from a number of sources. These were difficult moments for the revolution. In my capacity as chief of the sector, we conducted a very summary investigation, and Arístidio was executed.

Today we may ask ourselves whether he was really guilty enough to deserve death, and if it might not have been possible to save a life that could have been put to use by the revolution in its constructive phase. War is harsh, and at a time when the enemy was intensifying its aggressiveness, one could not tolerate even the suspicion of treason. It might have been possible to spare him months earlier, when the guerrilla movement was much weaker, or months later, when we were far stronger. But Arístidio had the bad luck that his weaknesses as a revolutionary combatant emerged at the precise moment when we were sufficiently strong to drastically punish an offense such as his, but not strong enough to punish him in a different way, since we had no jail or any other type of confinement.

Leaving the region for a time, our forces set out in the direction of Los Cocos along the Magdalena river, where we were to join up with Fidel and capture a gang, led by Chino Chang, that was ravaging the Caracas region. Camilo, who had gone ahead with the forward detachment, had already taken a certain number of prisoners before we arrived at that region, where we stayed for about ten days. It was there in a peasant hut that Chino Chang was tried and condemned to death. He was leader of a band that had tortured and murdered peasants, sowing terror in the district, all the while usurping the name and stealing the possessions of the revolution. Along with Chang another peasant was condemned to death who, while boasting of his authority as a "messenger" for the Rebel Army, raped an adolescent. We also tried a good number of members of the gang, consisting of youths from the cities and a few peasants seduced by the prospect of a wild, carefree, and comfortable life dangled before them by Chang.

Most were acquitted. With three, however, we decided to stage a symbolic lesson.

First we executed Chino Chang and the peasant rapist. They were tied to a tree in the forest, both of them calm. The peasant died without a blindfold, his eyes facing the guns, shouting "Long live the revolution!" Chang met death with absolute serenity but asked for the last rites to be administered by Father Sardiñas,[1] who was at that moment far from the camp. Since we were unable to grant this request, Chang said he wanted it known he had asked for a priest, as if this public testimony would serve as an extenuating circumstance in the hereafter.

It was then that we conducted the symbolic execution of the three youths. They had been deeply involved in Chang's outrages, but Fidel felt they should be given another chance. We blindfolded them and subjected them to the anguish of a simulated firing squad. After shots were fired in the air, the boys realized they were still very much alive. One of them threw himself on me and, in a spontaneous gesture of joy and gratitude, gave me a big noisy kiss, as if I were his father.

1. Guillermo Sardiñas, a Catholic priest who had joined the Rebel Army in June 1957, eventually rising to the rank of commander.

These events were witnessed by Andrew St. George, the CIA agent. His reportage was published in *Look* magazine and won him a prize in the United States for the most sensational story of the year.

Today, in retrospect, this device, practiced for the first time in the Sierra, might seem barbaric. At that time, however, no other form of punishment for those men was possible. True, they did not quite deserve death, but they had on their record a number of serious offenses. All three joined the Rebel Army. I later heard reports of the brilliant performance of two of them throughout the entire insurrectionary stage; as for the third, he stayed in my column for a long time. Whenever the conversation with other soldiers touched on various episodes of the war, if he found a comrade who questioned any of his stories, he always said emphatically: "No one can accuse me of being afraid of death, and Che is my witness."

Two or three days later, we captured another group. Their execution was especially painful. Among them was a peasant named Dionisio [Oliva] and his brother-in-law Juan Lebrigio, two of the very first who aided our guerrilla troop. Dionisio, who had helped unmask the traitor Eutimio Guerra, and who had assisted us during one of the most difficult moments of the revolution, had later grossly abused our confidence, as had his brother-in-law. They had appropriated for their own personal use all the provisions that the urban organizations had sent us; they had set up several camps where they indiscriminately slaughtered the cattle. Once on this path, they descended as far as committing murder.

At that time in the Sierra, a man's wealth was measured essentially by the number of women he had. Dionisio, faithful to custom and taking himself for a potentate, had, by virtue of the powers conferred on him by the revolution, taken over three houses, with a woman and a substantial food supply in each. In the course of his trial, Fidel indignantly reproached him concerning his treason to the revolution and his immoral conduct in supporting the women with the people's money. Dionisio replied, with a good measure of peasant artlessness, that it was not three but two, since one of the three was his legitimate wife (which was true).

Together with them we also executed two of Masferrer's spies, who had been caught red-handed and confessed, as well as a boy named Echevarría, who had been assigned to special missions in the Movement. The Echevarría family had furnished several fighters to the Rebel Army (one of the brothers had been in the *Granma* expedition). But this boy, after having formed a little troop while waiting for our arrival, succumbed to who-knows-what temptation and began to organize armed assaults in guerrilla territory.

The case of Echevarría was poignant. He recognized his errors but did not want to die by execution. He begged us to let him die in the next battle; he swore that he would seek death there, but he did not want to dishonor his family. Condemned to death by the tribunal, Echevarría (whom we had nicknamed "Squinty") wrote a long, moving letter to his mother, explaining the justice of his punishment and asking her to remain faithful to the revolution.

The last of the executed was a colorful character called "Teacher," who was my sole company during some difficult hours when I had wandered through the mountains, sick. He soon left the guerrillas, using some illness as a pretext, and dedicated himself to a life of immoralities. Culminating his exploits, he passed himself off as me in my capacity as doctor, attempting to rape a peasant girl who had sought medical treatment from him.

They all died proclaiming their commitment to the revolution, except for Masferrer's two spies. I was not present at the scene, but I'm told that when Father Sardiñas, present this time, approached one of the condemned to offer the last rites, the man answered: "Look, Father, see if anyone else needs you; I don't really believe in that stuff."

With such men as these the revolution was being made. Rebels at the beginning against all injustice, they soon became lone rebels accustomed to satisfying their own personal needs, with no conception of a struggle to change the social order. Whenever the revolution relaxed its vigilance on their acts for even a minute, they fell into errors that, with astonishing ease, led them into crime.

Dionisio and Juanito Lebrigio were no worse than other occasional delinquents who the revolution spared and who today can be found even in the ranks of our army. But that moment called for an iron fist. We were obliged to inflict exemplary punishment in order to curb all violations of discipline and to eliminate the seeds of anarchy, which sprang up in areas lacking a stable government.

Echevarría, taking it a step further, could have become a hero of the revolution, a distinguished fighter like his two brothers, officers of the Rebel Army. But he had the bad luck to commit an offense in that particular epoch, and he had to pay with his life. I hesitated to name him in these pages, but his attitude in the face of death was so upright, so revolutionary, so firm, and he recognized so clearly the justice of his punishment, that his death, it seemed to us, did not denigrate him. Rather, it served as an example, tragic though it was, but valuable, in that it helped others to understand the need to keep our revolution pure, uncontaminated by acts of banditry that were the heritage of Batista's men.

During these trials a case was argued for the first time by a lawyer who had taken refuge in the Sierra after various disputes with Llano leaders of the July 26 Movement. He became minister of agriculture after the revolution, until the very moment when the agrarian reform law was signed (by others, since he did not wish to commit himself to it). His name was [Humberto] Sorí Marín.

After we had performed the painful duty of establishing peace and moral order in all the territory over which the Rebel Army was moving to exercise administrative control, we headed back toward El Hombrito. Our column was divided into three platoons. The forward detachment was led by Camilo Cienfuegos and four lieutenants: Orestes [Guerra] (now a commander, who was point man), Boldo,[2] Leyva, and Noda. The second platoon was under the command of Capt. Raúl Castro Mercader, whose lieutenants were Alfonso Zayas, Orlando Pupo, and Paco Cabrera. Ramiro Valdés was in charge of our command unit, with Joel Iglesias as his lieutenant. Joel, not yet sixteen years old, was in command of men over thirty, whom he addressed respectfully as *usted* when giving orders; they addressed him as *tú*, but obeyed his orders with discipline.[3] The rear guard platoon was led by Ciro Redondo, with lieutenants Vilo Acuña, Félix Reyes, William Rodríguez, and Carlos Mas.

Toward the end of October 1957 we reestablished ourselves at El Hombrito. We then began efforts to establish a region firmly defended by our army. With the aid of two students recently arrived from Havana—one studying engineering, the other veterinary medicine—we began to lay plans for a miniature hydroelectric station, which we were trying to construct at the El Hombrito river. We also laid out plans to publish our *mambí* newspaper, *El Cubano Libre*.[4] An old but nonetheless precious mimeograph machine had been brought up from the city. With its aid we printed the first issues of the paper, whose editors and printers were the two students Geonel Rodríguez and Ricardito Medina.

Thus it was that we began to organize our life at this sedentary stage. We did so thanks to the generosity of the nearby residents, particularly our good friend "Old Lady Chana" as we all called her.[5] We proceeded then to build an oven for baking bread

2. Mauro LaRosa.
3. *Tú* and *usted* are, respectively, the familiar and the formal forms of address in Spanish meaning "you." Tú is commonly used among family and friends, as well as to teenagers and children.
4. *Mambí* was the name given to fighters against Spanish colonial rule in Cuba's wars of independence of 1868–78 and 1895–98. *El Cubano Libre* had been the name of the newspaper published by the independence fighters in those wars.
5. Ponciana Pérez.

in an old abandoned hut, so that enemy planes would not notice any new construction. We also had an immense July 26 Movement flag made, bearing the inscription: "Happy 1958!" We planted it on the highest plateau of El Hombrito, so that it would be seen from afar, as far as Minas de Bueycito. Meanwhile we traveled through the sector, establishing a real authority. At the same time we were preparing to face the imminent incursion by Sánchez Mosquera, constructing fortifications along the most likely points of access.

PUBLISHED IN VERDE OLIVO, JUNE 9, 1963

NOVEMBER 1957

The murdered puppy

FOR ALL THE HARSHNESS OF CONDITIONS in the Sierra Maestra, the day was superb. We were hiking through Agua Revés, one of the steepest and most intricate valleys in the Turquino basin, patiently following Sánchez Mosquera's troops. The relentless killer had left a trail of burned-out farms, sadness, and despair throughout the entire region. But his trail led him, by necessity, to ascend along one of the two or three points of the Sierra where we knew Camilo would be: either the Nevada ridge, or the area we called the "Ridge of the Crippled," now known as the "Ridge of the Dead."

Camilo had left hurriedly with about a dozen men, part of his forward detachment, and this small number had to be divided up in three different places to stop a column of over a hundred soldiers. My mission was to attack Sánchez Mosquera from behind and surround him. Our fundamental aim was encirclement; we therefore followed him patiently, over a considerable distance, past the painful trail of burning peasant houses, set aflame by the enemy's rear guard. The enemy troops were far away, but we could hear their shouts. We did not know how many of them there were. Our column's march was a difficult one, along the slopes, while the enemy advanced through the center of a narrow valley.

Everything would have been perfect had it not been for our new mascot, a little hunting dog only a few weeks old. Despite repeated commands by Félix [Mendoza] for the animal to return to our center of operations—a house where the cooks were staying—the puppy continued to trail behind the column. In that part of the Sierra Maestra, crossing over the slopes is extremely difficult due to the lack of paths. We went through a difficult patch of felled trees covered over by newly grown foliage, and passage became extremely arduous. We were bounding through tree trunks and bushes trying not to lose touch with our guests.

Our small column marched silently along. Not even the sound of a broken twig intruded upon the usual noises of the forest. Suddenly the silence was broken by the disconsolate, nervous barking of the little dog. It had remained behind and was barking desperately, calling on its masters to help it through the difficult patch. Someone picked up the animal, and we continued on again. However, as we rested in the middle of a creekbed with a lookout keeping watch on the enemy's movements, the little dog once again began to howl hysterically. Comforting words no longer had any effect; the animal, afraid we would leave it behind, barked desperately.

I remember my emphatic order: "Félix, that dog must stop its howling once and for all. You're in charge; strangle it. There will be no more barking." Félix looked at me with eyes that said nothing. He and the little dog were in the center of all the troops. Very slowly he took out a rope, wrapped it around the animal's neck, and began to tighten it. The cute little movements of the dog's tail suddenly became convulsive, before gradually dying out, accompanied by a steady moan that escaped from its throat, despite the firm grip. I don't know how long it took for the end to come, but to all of us it seemed like forever. With one last nervous twitch, the puppy stopped moving. There it lay, sprawled out, its little head spread over the twigs.

We continued the march without even a word about the incident. Sánchez Mosquera's troops had moved ahead of us somewhat, and within moments, shots were heard. We quickly descended the slopes, amid the difficult terrain, searching for the best path to reach the rear guard. We knew that Camilo had attacked. It took us a considerable amount of time to reach the last house before the ascent; we were taking many precautions as we walked, thinking we would confront the enemy at any moment. The exchange of fire had been intense, but it did not last long. We all waited tensely. The last house was also abandoned. The soldiers had left no traces. Two scouts climbed the "Ridge of the Crippled" and soon returned with the news: "There is a grave up above. We dug it up and found an enemy soldier buried." They also brought the identity papers of the victim, found in his shirt pocket. There had been a clash with one dead. The dead was theirs, but nothing more was known.

We returned slowly, discouraged. Two scouting parties came upon a large number of footprints along both sides of the ridge of the Maestra, but nothing else. We made the return trip slowly, this time through the valley.

We arrived during the night at a house, also vacant. It was in the settlement of Mar Verde, and there we were able to rest. Soon a pig was cooked along with some yucca, and we ate. Someone sang a tune on a guitar, since the peasant houses had been hastily abandoned with all their belongings still inside.

I don't know whether it was the sentimental tune, or the darkness of night, or just plain exhaustion. What happened, though, is that Félix, while eating seated on the floor, dropped a bone, and a house dog came out meekly and grabbed it up. Félix patted its head, and the dog looked at him. Félix returned the glance, and then he and I exchanged a guilty look. Suddenly everyone fell silent. An imperceptible stirring came over us, as the dog's meek yet roguish gaze seemed to contain a hint of reproach. There in our presence, although observing us through the eyes of another dog, was the murdered puppy.

PUBLISHED IN HUMANISMO, NOVEMBER 1959–FEBRUARY 1960

NOVEMBER 1957

The battle of Mar Verde

SHORTLY BEFORE DAWN, at 5:00 or 5:30 in the morning, I awoke after a restful sleep, with a sixth sense developed in military life, although dulled that day by fatigue and by the comfort of a peasant's bed in the settlement of Mar Verde. We calmly made breakfast while awaiting news from the numerous messengers who had been sent out to make contact with the guerrilla squads.

The sun had barely begun to shine when one of the few peasants remaining in the area came with a strange and alarming piece of news. He had seen soldiers looking for hens and eggs in a house no more than half a kilometer away. I immediately sent him to find out everything he could about the soldiers; to make contact with them and find out how many there were. The peasant was not eager to carry out his mission fully. He returned, however, with news that a large group of soldiers was camped in the house belonging to Reyes, one or two kilometers up the Nevada mountain. It could be none other than Sánchez Mosquera.

We then had to rapidly organize how to do battle. Our goal was to surround them at a suitable point and then annihilate them.

I had to first consider what his future plans might be. He had two possible routes: Number one, he could take the path along the Nevada, heading in the other direction. This would be an exhausting trek, passing through Santa Ana to reach California,

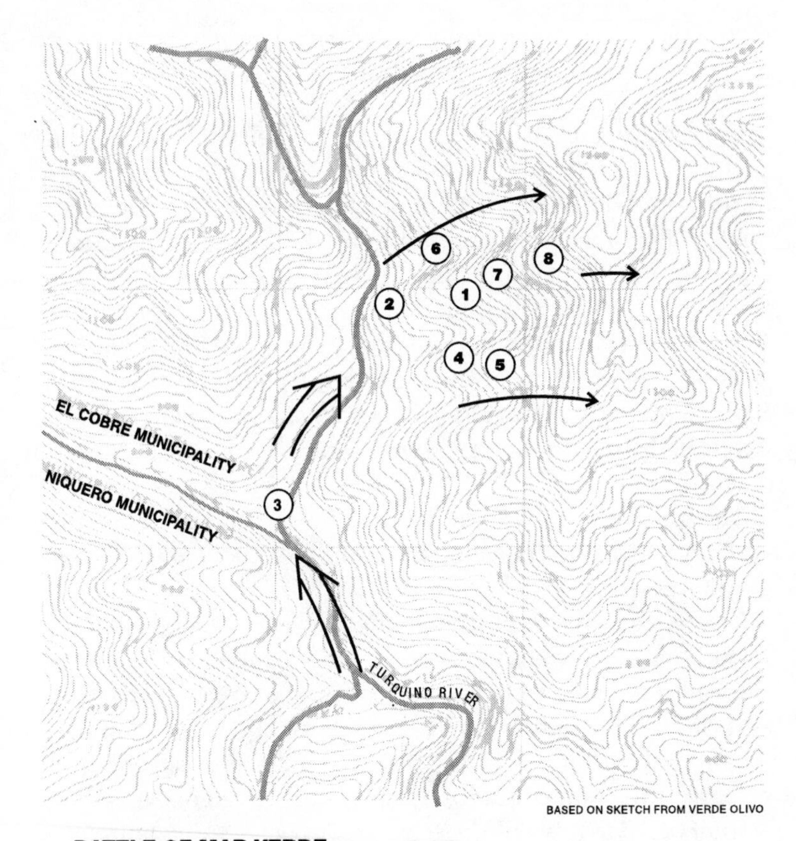

BATTLE OF MAR VERDE
NOVEMBER 29, 1957

1 SÁNCHEZ MOSQUERA'S APPROXIMATE POSITION
2 FIRST AMBUSH SITE (CHE GUEVARA)
3 EISLER LEYVA'S SQUAD
4 RAÚL CASTRO MERCADER'S PLATOON
5 ALFONSO ZAYAS'S POSITION
6 VILO ACUÑA AND ENRIQUE NODA'S SQUADS
7 SPOT WHERE CIRO REDONDO DIED
8 CAMILO CIENFUEGOS'S FORCES
→ LINE OF REBELS' RETREAT
⇒ ROUTE OF ENEMY REINFORCEMENTS

and from there to Minas de Bueycito. Alternately—and what seemed most logical, both because of the shortness of the trip and the possibilities it entailed for him—Sánchez Mosquera could follow the opposite route along the Turquino river, arriving at the small village of Ocujal, which is at the very foot of the Turquino mountain. Owing to my uncertainty, it was necessary for us to rapidly reinforce both positions, to prevent them from breaking out of the encirclement. If they decided to take the high road across the Nevada, there would be no possibility for us to confront them with adequate forces, unless Camilo had followed them.

The previous day Camilo had clashed with them near Altos de Conrado, but at the moment we did not know where he was stationed.

Messengers were rapidly arriving, however. Our reserve force in El Hombrito was mobilized in the Nevada region and the cemetery, in order to take positions above Sánchez Mosquera and close off his route. Camilo had arrived and was in that zone. An order was sent instructing them not to let themselves be seen or engage in combat until they heard the first shots, unless the soldiers tried to leave through the area they were defending. The squads of lieutenants Noda and Vilo Acuña were sent to the west. Capt. Raúl Castro Mercader closed the circle to the east. My small squad, with some reinforcements, was in charge of conducting the ambush in the event they tried to descend toward the sea—which we considered likely.

In the early hours of the morning, with the circle already complete, the alarm was sounded. We could see the point man of the enemy's forward detachment advancing along the main road that followed the small stream emptying into the Turquino river. The spot chosen to begin the battle, in the event they arrived along my side, was flanked by a line of hilly pastureland that enabled our troops to keep hidden on one side. But they were not to attack or make observations until the battle began. This was to occur at one side of the road; on the other was a patch of trees, with a mango tree at the end; that was where I was posted.

It was my job to fire on the soldiers at point-blank range; one or two meters ahead of me was Joel Iglesias and other comrades. The position was ideal for killing the first ones, but it did not enable us to continue the fight; we thought the enemy troops would immediately retreat to look for better positions, at which time we would be able to abandon the ambush.

We heard the soldiers passing almost right in front of us; in the pasture the others had seen that there were only three men, but they were unable to alert us in time. During those days my only weapon was a Luger pistol, and I felt nervous over the fate of the two or three comrades who were closer to the enemy than I was. For that reason I hurried the first shot too much and missed. As happens at such times, the firing immediately became generalized, and an attack was launched against the house where the bulk of Sánchez Mosquera's forces were stationed.

Then in the very midst of the ambush, an eerie moment of silence occurred. As we went to gather the dead after the initial exchange, there was no one on the main road. Alongside the road was a thicket, and a dug-out hollow in the Tibisí, through which the enemy soldiers had slipped away. We immediately began a search to surround them, since no more soldiers had appeared.

While we were searching, Joel Iglesias, followed by Rodolfo Vázquez and Geonel Rodríguez, entered the same path the soldiers had taken, through the trail of brush. I heard his voice calling on them to surrender and assuring the prisoners' lives. Suddenly a rapid burst of fire could be heard, and I was informed that Joel was seriously wounded. All things considered, Joel's fate was extraordinary. Three Garand rifles had opened fire on him at point-blank range: his rifle was hit by two bullets, and its butt was destroyed. Another shot burned his hand, another hit his cheek, two went through his arm, two went through his leg, and other shots grazed him. He was covered in blood but his wounds were nevertheless relatively light. We immediately retrieved him and sent him in a hammock to the field hospital for medical attention.

Before concentrating on the battle in general, we had to continue looking for the three soldiers. Soon Silva's voice was heard, shouting, "There they are!" and pointing out the place with a burst from his 12-gauge shotgun. We soon heard the soldiers calling out to surrender. We thus obtained three Garands with their corresponding prisoners; one of our good combatants was wounded. That, for the moment, was the tally.

We sent the prisoners along the same road as our wounded man and were then able to concentrate on organizing the battle. Through interrogating the prisoners, we learned that Sánchez Mosquera had between eighty and a hundred men. It was not possible to know whether or not the figure was accurate, but those were the prisoners' statements. The soldiers were in a well-defended position and had automatic weapons, light arms, and an abundant supply of ammunition.

We understood that it was best to avoid frontal combat, with such doubtful prospects, since we had approximately the same number of combatants, but with inferior weapons, and Sánchez Mosquera was in a well-defended, entrenched position. We decided to pursue them in such a way as to obstruct their movement until nightfall, when we would begin our attack.

A few hours later, however, news arrived that enemy reinforcements commanded by Captain Sierra were ascending the mountain from the direction of the sea. We immediately organized two patrols with instructions to stop them: one of them, led by William Rodríguez, was to attack them at the region of Dos Brazos del Turquino. The other patrol, commanded by Lieutenant Leyva, was to await reinforcements and attack as soon as they reached the top of a mountain only two kilometers from the battle site, at a very favorable position for us, where we would annihilate their forward detachment. I was personally in charge of preparations at this spot, leaving other comrades in charge of preparing the other ambushes.

The entire front was calm, and only occasionally did we fire at the zinc roof of the house where the soldiers were stationed, to keep them in check. At midafternoon, however, a prolonged exchange of fire was heard at the top of the position. Later I learned the sad news: Ciro Redondo, trying to attack the enemy lines, had been killed and his body lost, although his weapons were rescued by Camilo. On our side we also began to hear shots announcing the arrival of the enemy troops. Moments later, intense fire began, and our defenses along the southern part were overwhelmed by the reinforcements that had reached Sánchez Mosquera.

We were forced to retreat. Once again the killer was saved. We issued the pertinent orders to effect an orderly retreat, and we left, walking slowly. We reached the Guayabo stream, and later, the valley of El Hombrito, our most secure refuge.

After we arrived there and heard the results of all the actions, it was possible to piece together what had happened: According to the accounts of the combatants, a number of enemy soldiers were killed, although it was not possible to verify this. The defenders of the extreme south position, under the command of Lieutenant [Eisler] Leyva, stated the same thing. However, a number of knapsacks being stored at the position of our combatants in the southern zone were lost. One of these combatants, named Alberto, had been sent in the morning to take the prisoners; upon returning he decided to catch some sleep there instead of continuing the battle, and the enemy troops took him by surprise while sleeping, together with all the knapsacks. Later we learned he was murdered in the region of El Hombrito.

Our wounded were Roberto Fajardo; Joel Pardo, from the battle the day before with Sánchez Mosquera; a combatant named Reyes, who later died with the rank of captain; Javier Pazos; and Joel Iglesias. Killed was Ciro Redondo. There was a great deal of sadness. In addition to our regret at not being able to take advantage of the victory against Sánchez Mosquera, there was the loss of our great comrade Ciro Redondo.

I then sent a letter to Fidel proposing his posthumous promotion, and shortly afterward the rank was conferred. News of this was published in our newspaper *El Cubano Libre.*

The battle, and Ciro Redondo's death, occurred on November 29, 1957.

Shortly before withdrawing, a bullet hit the trunk of a tree a few centimeters from my head, and Geonel Rodríguez scolded me for not ducking. Later on Geonel reasoned, perhaps with a touch of mathematical speculation learned through his engineering training, that he had a greater chance than I did of surviving to the end of the revolution, since he never risked his life unnecessarily. And it was true, Geonel Rodríguez—who had his baptism of fire in that battle—never risked his life unnecessarily. He was always an exemplary combatant, owing to his courage, decisiveness, and intelligence. But it was he who did not live to see the end of the revolutionary war. A few months later he died during the army's great offensive against our positions.

That night we slept at the Guayabo. It was necessary to prepare everything to prevent any surprises and to reach El Hombrito without having to fight our way there. That was our fundamental task at the moment.

PUBLISHED IN VERDE OLIVO, SEPTEMBER 8, 1963

DECEMBER 1957

Altos de Conrado

THE DAYS FOLLOWING THE BATTLE of Mar Verde were ones of intense activity. We knew very well that our forces did not yet have sufficient fighting capacity to engage in continuous combat, to encircle the enemy effectively, or to resist frontal attacks. For this reason we redoubled our defense measures in the valley of El Hombrito. This valley is a few kilometers from Mar Verde; to reach it one must take the road that goes up to Santa Ana and crosses the Guayabo, a little mountain stream. One can also reach it, however, by going along the Guayabo river to the south, past La Botella hill, or by taking the road from Minas del Frío.

We made sure that all these points of access were well defended. It was also necessary to establish a constant watch to avoid having the enemy swoop down and surprise us by moving their troops directly through the mountains.

The bulk of our excess supplies had been sent to the area of La Mesa, at the house of Polo Torres. We had also taken our wounded there, among them Joel Iglesias, the only one unable to walk, because of the wounds to his leg.

Sánchez Mosquera's troops were stationed at Santa Ana, and there were other enemy troops who had taken the California road, toward an unknown destination.

Four or five days after the Mar Verde encounter, the combat alert sounded. Sánchez Mosquera's troops were advancing by the most logical route, the one that goes directly from Santa Ana to El Hombrito. We immediately warned our men on ambush, and checked the land mines. These first mines manufactured by us had a rudimentary firing system: it consisted of a spring and a spike that, when released and thrust forward by the spring, struck the detonator. However, they had not worked during the ambush at Mar Verde, and this time they functioned no better.

A few moments later, the noise of firing reached our command post. We were advised that since the mines had not gone off and the enemy had arrived in force, our men had retreated, although not without first inflicting enemy casualties. Their first victim, according to the description we were given, was a big fat sergeant armed with a .45 revolver, who led a mounted column. Lt. Enrique Noda and another fighter, El Mexicano, fired at him at close range with their Garands, and their descriptions of the man coincided. They also spoke of other casualties, but the fact remained that Sánchez Mosquera's troops had routed our defenses.

(Weeks later, a peasant by the name of Brito came to thank me for our generosity; he had been forced by the enemy to take a position at the head of the column, and he had clearly seen our boys "pretend to take aim and shoot at him." This same peasant told me there had been no casualties on that occasion, but there had been some at Altos de Conrado.)

The spot we were occupying was so difficult to defend with our few forces that we had not bothered to dig trenches worthy of the name; we had only the old defenses, put up to prevent access from Minas de Bueycito. Furthermore, as the enemy advanced along the road, they endangered all our ambushes, so we ordered them lifted and we retreated. No one remained in the area but a few families, determined to courageously resist the army's outrages, or perhaps to make secret contact with them.

Slowly we fell back along the road leading to Altos de Conrado [Conrado's heights], which is nothing more than a small hillock atop the Sierra Maestra, on whose heights lived a peasant named Conrado. This comrade was a member of the Popular Socialist

Party, and had been in contact with us from the beginning, rendering many valuable services. He had evacuated his family, and his house was isolated. The spot was perfect for an ambush. There were only three narrow paths leading to it, which wound through the dense vegetation of the hills, and was thus very easy to defend. The rest of it was defended by jagged cliffs and steep slopes, extremely difficult to climb.

At one spot where there was a small depression, the road widens. There we made preparations to resist Sánchez Mosquera's attack. On the first day we had placed two bombs, with their fuses, in the hearth of the little hut. The trap was very simple: if we withdrew, the enemy would probably move into the house and use the hearth. Covered completely by the ashes lay the two bombs; we calculated that the heat of the fire or a live coal would light the fuses, setting off an explosion that would surely leave a number of victims. But this, of course, would be useful only later; first, we would have to engage in battle at Altos de Conrado.

We stayed there for three days, waiting patiently, with round-the-clock watches. At that altitude, and at that time of year, nights are very cold and damp. And to be honest, we were not yet trained or accustomed to the hardships of spending an entire night in the open, in battle position.

With the mimeograph machine used to print our newspaper *El Cubano Libre* (the first issue of which had appeared a few days earlier), we produced a leaflet directed at the Batista soldiers. Our intention was to post these on the trees along the road they would be taking.

On the morning of December 8, from the heights of our boulder, we heard the troop beginning its ascent; it wound along the road, arriving about two hundred meters below us. We sent someone to post the leaflets, and Comrade Luis Olazábal did so. We heard the enemy troops having a violent argument, in the midst of which I clearly heard (since I was on watch along the wall) the shouts of someone who was apparently an officer giving an order: "By my balls, you're going in front!" And the soldier, or whoever it was, angrily saying no. The argument ceased and the troop began moving.

We could see the column advancing, in small groups, hidden among the trees. After observing them for a while, I began to question the advisability of revealing our ambush to them by means of the leaflets. I finally ordered Luis to go back down and remove them. He had only a few seconds to do so, for the first soldiers were coming rapidly up the hill.

Battle arrangements were very simple: we assumed that when the enemy arrived in the open, a single man would come into view, at some distance from his companions. That man, at least, had to be killed. Camilo was waiting for him, hidden behind a large mastic tree; at the moment when the soldier passed him, looking attentively ahead, Camilo would fire his machine gun at him, at less than a meter's distance. The sharpshooters whom we had concealed in the brush on both flanks would then open fire. Lieutenant Ibrahín [Sotomayor] and someone else, at the edge of the road, some ten meters from Camilo, were to cover him by firing from the front, so that no one could approach his position after he killed the point man.

My post was some twenty meters away, off to the side behind a tree trunk which protected half of me. My gun was pointed directly at the approach to the path along which the soldiers were coming. There were several of us who at first were unable to look, for we were in an exposed position and would have been visible. We were supposed to wait for Camilo to open fire. I sneaked a glance, violating the order that I myself had given. I could at that moment sense the tension prior to combat. I saw the first soldier appear. He looked around suspiciously and advanced slowly. In truth, everything smelled of an ambush—with its untypical landscape, the little clearing and the spring in the midst of the forest's luxuriant vegetation. The trees, some cut down, others standing and charred by fire, gave an impression of desolation. I hid my head, waiting for the battle to begin. There was the crack of gunfire and then shooting became generalized. I learned later that it was not Camilo who had fired but Ibrahín, who had been unnerved by the waiting. He had fired ahead of time, and this was instantly followed by general fire, although in reality we could see very little from any vantage point. Our isolated shots, all of which should have been lethal, and the firing by the soldiers, in wasteful bursts, joined but did not mingle. We could recognize from each noise which of the two facing armies was shooting. Several minutes later (five or six), we heard overhead the first whistles of mortar shells or bazookas; but their trajectory was too long and they exploded well behind us.

Suddenly I felt a disagreeable sensation, similar to a burn or the tingling of numbness. I had been shot in the left foot, which had not been protected by the tree trunk. I had just fired my rifle (I had chosen one with a telescopic sight, to improve my aim); at the moment I was hit, I heard some men moving rapidly in my direction making a great noise as they pushed the tree branches aside. My rifle was of no further use to me, since I had just discharged it; and my pistol had fallen from my hand when I threw myself to the ground. It was underneath me, but I could not lift myself up since I was directly exposed to enemy fire. With desperate quickness, I rolled over and succeeded in grabbing the pistol; at that very moment I saw one of our men, the one we called Cantinflas, coming toward me. On top of the nerve-racking moments and the pain from my wound, I suddenly had poor Cantinflas on my hands telling me he was withdrawing because his gun was jammed. I snatched his Garand from him and examined it, while he crouched near me. The only thing wrong was that the clip was slightly tilted. I handed it back to him, in working order, along with a razor-sharp diagnosis: "You are an imbecile!" Cantinflas, whose real name was Oñate, took the gun and threw himself into the fray. Leaving the protection of the tree trunk, he hastened to empty his Garand, in a demonstration of courage. He could not finish, however, because he was hit by a bullet, which penetrated his left arm and came out through his shoulder blade, after following a curious trajectory. Now we were both wounded, with little chance of retreating under the rain of bullets. There was nothing to do but crawl toward the tree trunks, then slip around them, wounded though we were, and not knowing where the rest of our group was. Little by little we did so, but Cantinflas fainted. In spite of the pain, I was able to move more freely, and I arrived where the others were, to ask them for help.

We knew there were deaths in the enemy ranks, but not the exact number. After rescuing the wounded (the two of us), we set off toward the house of Polo Torres two or three kilometers downhill. After the first moment of euphoria and the excitement of combat wore off, I began to feel the pain more sharply, making it difficult to walk. At last, halfway there, I mounted a horse and thus arrived at our makeshift hospital. Cantinflas, meanwhile, was carried off on our field stretcher—a hammock.

The gunfire had ceased, and we assumed the enemy had taken Altos de Conrado. We sent out sentries to slow their advance, along a little stream in a place we had christened "Pata de la Mesa," [table leg]; at the same time we organized the withdrawal of the peasants and their families. I sent a long letter to Fidel describing the events.

I sent the column commanded by Ramiro Valdés to link up with Fidel. There was a certain air of defeat and fear among our troop, and I wanted to stay there with a minimum of men so as to preserve a maximum of mobility for our defense. Camilo remained at the head of the small defense group.

The day after the battle, owing to the apparent calm, we sent Liens, one of our best scouts, to find out what the enemy was doing. We then learned they had completely withdrawn from the sector. Liens went as far as Conrado's house but saw no trace of the soldiers. He even brought us, as proof of his search, one of the bombs we had hidden inside.

In reviewing our weapons, we noticed that Comrade Guile Pardo's[1] gun was missing. He had swapped his gun for another, and in retreating he had taken only the second, leaving the first

1. Ramón Pardo Guerra.

at his battle position. That was one of the most serious crimes one could commit. He was given a categorical order: he had to go out equipped only with small arms to retrieve the gun from the hands of the enemy, or else bring back another. Crestfallen, Guile left to carry out his mission, but he returned several hours later, grinning, with his own gun in his hands. The mystery was eventually cleared up: the army had never advanced from the spot where they dug in to resist our attack. Each of them had retreated along their own side, so that not a living soul had reached our comrade's post. The gun had been caught in a downpour, nothing more.

This point of advance made by the army was, for a good while, its furthest penetration in the Sierra. In this particular sector, it was their deepest penetration. A trail of burned-down huts—typical of Sánchez Mosquera's passing—was all that remained of El Hombrito and other villages. Our oven had been painstakingly destroyed; in the midst of the smoking ruins we found nothing but some cats and a pig; they had escaped the destructive fury of the invading army only to wind up in our mouths. A day or two after the battle Machadito, the present minister of public health,[2] operated on me with a razor and extracted an M-1 rifle bullet. From that time on, my recovery was rapid.

Sánchez Mosquera had carried off everything he could, from sacks of coffee to furniture, which his soldiers had to carry. We had the impression that it would be a long time before he would make another incursion into the Sierra.

It then became necessary to prepare the political conditions of the area and to begin once more to organize our basic industrial center, which would no longer be at El Hombrito but further back, in the same area of La Mesa.

PUBLISHED IN VERDE OLIVO, OCTOBER 6, 1963

2. José Machado Ventura.

War and the peasant population

LIVING IN A CONTINUAL STATE OF WAR creates a new state of mind in the popular consciousness in order to adapt to this new phenomenon. The individual must undergo a long and painful process of adaptation to enable him to withstand the bitter experience that threatens his tranquillity. The Sierra Maestra and other newly liberated zones had to undergo this bitter experience.

The situation of the peasants in the rugged mountain zones was nothing less than frightful. The peasant, having migrated from afar with a yearning for freedom, had put all his efforts into squeezing out an existence from the newly cleared land. Through a thousand and one sacrifices he had coaxed the coffee plants to grow on the craggy slopes where creating anything new entails sacrifice. All this he did by his own sweat, responding to the age-old yearning of man to possess his own plot of land, working with infinite love this hostile crag, which he treated as part of his very self.

Suddenly, when the coffee plants were beginning to blossom with the fruit that represented his hope, the lands were claimed by a new owner. It might be a foreign company, a local land-grabber, or some other speculator taking advantage of peasant indebtedness. The political bosses and local army chieftains worked for the company or the land-grabber, jailing or murdering any peasant who was unduly rebellious against these arbitrary acts.

Such was the panorama of defeat and desolation that we found, paralleling our own defeat at Alegría de Pío, the product of our inexperience (our only reverse in this long campaign, our bloody baptism of fire). The peasantry recognized those lean men whose beards, now legendary, were beginning to flourish, as companions in misfortune, fresh victims of the repressive forces, and gave us their spontaneous and disinterested aid, without expecting anything in return from the vanquished rebels.

Days passed and our small troop of now seasoned soldiers sustained the victories of La Plata and Palma Mocha. The regime responded with all its brutality, including the mass murder of peasants. Terror was unleashed on the rustic valleys of the Sierra Maestra, and the peasants withdrew their aid. A barrier of mutual mistrust loomed up between the peasants and the guerrillas, the former out of fear of reprisals, the latter out of fear of betrayal by the weak-willed. Our policy, nevertheless, was a just and understanding one, and the peasant population began once more to return to our cause.

The dictatorship, in its desperation and criminality, ordered the resettlement of thousands of peasant families from the Sierra Maestra to the cities.

The strongest and most resolute men, including almost all the youth, preferred liberty and war to slavery and the city. Long caravans of women, children, and old people took to the roads, leaving their birthplaces, going down to the plains, where they huddled in the outskirts of the cities. For the second time Cuba experienced the most criminal page of its history: resettlement. The first to order it was Weyler, the bloody general of colonial Spain;[1] now it was being ordered by Fulgencio Batista, the worst traitor and assassin known to Latin America.

Hunger, misery, illness, epidemics, and death decimated the

1. Gen. Valeriano Weyler was Spain's governor of Cuba in 1896 during the independence war. He ordered the forced resettlement of much of the rural population in concentration camp–type conditions.

peasants resettled by the tyranny. Children died for lack of medical attention and food, when a few steps away the resources existed that could have saved their lives. The indignant protest of the Cuban people, international scandal, and the dictatorship's inability to defeat the rebels compelled the tyrant to suspend the resettlement of peasant families from the Sierra Maestra. And once again they returned to the land of their birth, miserable, sick, and decimated. Earlier they had experienced bombings by the dictatorship, the burning of their huts, mass murder; now they experienced the inhumanity and barbarism of a regime that treated them worse than colonial Spain treated the Cubans in the war of independence. Batista had surpassed Weyler.

Peasants returned with an unbreakable will to struggle until death or victory, as rebels until death or freedom.

Our little guerrilla band, of city extraction, began to don palm leaf hats. The people lost their fear and decided to join the struggle and proceed resolutely along the road to their redemption. In this change, our policy toward the peasantry and our military victories came together as one, and already we were revealed to be an unbeatable force in the Sierra Maestra.

Faced by the choice, all the peasants chose the path of revolution. The change of mental attitude, of which we have already spoken, now revealed itself fully. The war was a fact—painful, yes, but transitory, a situation within which the individual had to adapt himself in order to survive. Once the peasants understood this, they began to make the efforts necessary to confront the adverse circumstances that would come.

The peasants returned to their abandoned plots of land. They stopped the slaughter of their animals, saving them for worse times to come. They became used to the savage strafings, and each family built its own shelter. They accustomed themselves to periodic flights from the battle zones, with family, cattle, and household goods, leaving only their huts to the enemy, which displayed its hatred by burning them to the ground. They got used to rebuilding on the smoking ruins of their old dwellings, uncomplaining but with concentrated hatred and the will to conquer.

When the distribution of cattle began as a measure to fight the dictatorship's food blockade,[2] the peasants tended their animals with loving care and worked in groups, establishing what were in effect cooperatives in their efforts to move the cattle to a safe place, giving over all their pastureland and their mules to the common effort.

It is a new miracle of the revolution that—under the imperative of war—the staunchest individualist, who zealously protected the boundaries of his property and his own rights, joined the great common effort of the struggle. But there is an even greater miracle: the rediscovery by the Cuban peasant of his own happiness, within the liberated zones. Whoever witnessed the apprehensive murmurs with which our forces were formerly received in each peasant household notes with pride the carefree clamor, the happy, hearty laughter of the new Sierra inhabitant. That is a reflection of the self-confidence that the awareness of his own strength gave to the inhabitant of our liberated area. That is our future task: for the Cuban people to regain the concept of their own strength, and to achieve absolute assurance that their individual rights, guaranteed by the constitution, are their dearest treasure. Even more than the pealing of bells, it will be the return of the old, happy laughter, of carefree security, lost by the Cuban people, which will signify liberation.

PUBLISHED IN LUNES DE REVOLUCIÓN, JULY 26, 1959

2. Responding to the government's blockade of food supplies to the Sierra Maestra, in April 1958 Fidel Castro ordered the Rebel Army to requisition cattle herds from large landed estates surrounding the Sierra Maestra. Ten thousand head of cattle were brought up to the mountains and distributed to the peasants for meat and dairy consumption.

DECEMBER 1957

One year of armed struggle

By the beginning of 1958 we had been fighting for more than a year. A brief recapitulation is necessary—of our military, organizational, and political situation, and of our progress.

Concerning the military aspect, let us recall that our troops had disembarked on December 2, 1956, at Las Coloradas beach. Three days later we were taken by surprise and routed at Alegría de Pío. We regrouped ourselves at the end of the month and began small-scale actions, appropriate to our strength, at La Plata, a small garrison on the banks of the La Plata river, on the southern coast of Oriente.

During this period, beginning with the disembarkation and the rapid defeat at Alegría de Pío until the battle of El Uvero, our troop was composed of a single guerrilla group led by Fidel Castro and was characterized by constant movement. We could call this the nomadic phase.

Between December 2 and May 28, the date of the battle of El Uvero, we slowly established links with the city. During this period, these relations were characterized by a lack of understanding on the part of the leadership of the July 26 Movement in the cities of our importance as the vanguard of the revolution and of Fidel's stature as the leader of the revolution.

At that point, two distinct opinions began to crystallize regarding the tactics to be followed. These corresponded to two distinct concepts of strategy, which were thereafter known as the *Sierra* and the *Llano*. Our discussions and our internal conflicts were quite sharp. Nevertheless, the fundamental concerns of this phase were survival and the establishment of a guerrilla base.

The process occurring among the peasantry has already been analyzed many times. Immediately after the Alegría de Pío disaster there was a warm sentiment of comradeship and spontaneous support for our defeated troop. After our regroupment and the first clashes, simultaneously with repressive actions by the Batista army, there was terror among the peasants and coldness toward our forces. The fundamental problem was that if they saw us, they had to denounce us; because if the army learned of our presence through other sources, they were lost. Denouncing us did violence to their own conscience; moreover, it still put them in danger, since revolutionary justice was swift.

In spite of a terrorized or at least a neutralized and insecure peasantry, which in general chose to avoid this serious dilemma by leaving the Sierra, our army was entrenching itself more and more, taking control of the terrain and achieving absolute control of a region of the Sierra Maestra extending beyond the Turquino mountain in the east and toward the Caracas Peak in the west. Little by little, as the peasants came to recognize the invincibility of the guerrillas and the long duration of the struggle, they began responding more logically, joining our army as fighters. From that moment on, not only did they join our ranks but they provided supportive action. After that the guerrilla army was strongly entrenched in the countryside, especially since it is usual for peasants to have relatives throughout the zone. This is what we call "having the guerrillas don palm leaf hats."

The column was strengthened not only through aid given by peasants and by individual volunteers but also by the forces sent from the National Directorate and by the Oriente Provincial Committee [of the July 26 Movement], which had considerable autonomy. In the period between the disembarkation and El Uvero, a column arrived consisting of some fifty men divided into five platoons, each combatant with a weapon, although the weapons were of different types and only thirty were of good quality. The battles of La Plata and Arroyo del Infierno took place before this group joined us. We had been taken by surprise at Altos de Espinosa, losing one of our men there; the same thing almost happened in the Gaviro region, after a traitor in our ranks, who had been given the mission of killing Fidel, led the army to us three times.

The bitter experiences of these surprises and our arduous life in the mountains were tempering us as veterans. The new troop received its baptism of fire at the battle of El Uvero. This action was of great importance because it marked the moment in which we carried out a frontal attack in broad daylight against a well-defended post. It was one of the bloodiest events of the war, in terms of the duration of the battle and the number of participants. As a consequence of this clash, the enemy was dislodged from the coastal regions of the Sierra Maestra.

After El Uvero I was put in charge of a small group of wounded men, which grew through the recruitment of new combatants by the ones and twos. Then, when this smaller group reunited with the principal column, I was named head of a second column, called Column no. 4, which was to operate east of the Turquino mountain. It is worth noting that the column led by Fidel himself was to operate primarily to the west of the Turquino, and ours on the other side, as far as we could extend ourselves. There was a certain tactical independence of command, but we were under Fidel's orders and kept in touch with him every week or two by messenger.

This division of forces coincided with the anniversary of July 26, and while the troops of the "José Martí" Column no. 1 made a demonstration of attacking Estrada Palma, we marched rapidly toward Bueycito, a settlement we attacked and captured in our column's first battle. Between that time and January 1958, a rebel territory was consolidated. The army, in order to penetrate this territory, had to concentrate forces and advance in strong columns; preparations were extensive and results were few, since

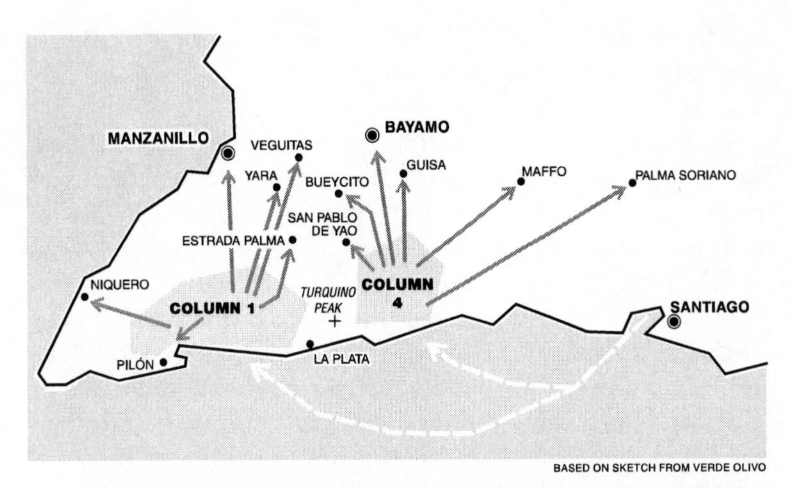

ZONES OF OPERATIONS OF COLUMN NO. 1 COMMANDED BY FIDEL CASTRO AND COLUMN NO. 4 COMMANDED BY CHE GUEVARA, LATE 1957 TO EARLY 1958. TOWNS THEY ORGANIZED TO OBTAIN SUPPLIES FROM ARE INDICATED WITH ARROWS.

they lacked mobility. Various enemy columns were encircled and others decimated, or at least stopped. Our knowledge of the area and our capacity for maneuver increased, and we entered the sedentary, fixed-encampment period. In the first attack on Pino del Agua we used subtler methods, deceiving the enemy completely, since we were by then familiar with their habits. It was as Fidel had anticipated: a few days after he let himself be seen in the area, a punitive expedition would arrive, and my men would ambush it; meanwhile Fidel would pop up elsewhere.

At the end of the year the enemy troops retreated from the Sierra again, and we remained in control of the territory from the Caracas Peak on the west, to Pino del Agua on the east, and the sea on the south. The army occupied the small villages on the slopes of the Sierra Maestra to the north.

Our zone of operations would expand greatly after Pino del Agua was attacked for the second time by our entire troop under the personal command of Fidel. Two new columns were formed, the "Frank País" column commanded by Raúl, and Almeida's column. Both had come out of Column no. 1, commanded by Fidel, which was a steady supplier of these offshoots, created for the purpose of establishing our forces in distant territories.

This was a period of consolidation for our army, in which we had insufficient forces to attack the enemy's fortified and relatively easily defended positions, while they did not advance on us. This situation lasted until the second battle of Pino del Agua on February 16, 1958.

On our side we had suffered the deaths of the *Granma* martyrs, all of them deeply felt but especially those of Ñico López and Juan Manuel Márquez. There were other combatants of great standing, because of their daring behavior and moral qualities, who lost their lives during this first year. Among them we can mention Nano and Julio Díaz, not brothers—the latter a veteran of the Moncada—both of them killed in the battle of El Uvero; Ciro Redondo, killed at Mar Verde; Captain [Juan] Soto, who met his death in the battle of San Lorenzo. In the cities, among the many martyrs of our struggle, we must highlight the death of Frank País, which was the greatest loss to the revolution until that time.

To the list of military feats in the Sierra Maestra must be added the work carried out by the Llano forces in the cities. There were groups fighting against the Batista regime in all the principal towns of the country, but the two focal points of the struggle were Havana and Santiago. In the former, the July 26 Movement tried without success to institute a series of armed actions that gave evidence of constant signs of life. Santiago, on the other hand, was becoming a front line trench in the long battle against the Batista dictatorship, linked geographically with the Sierra Maestra.

A total connection between the Llano and the Sierra was always lacking, due to two fundamental factors: the geographical isolation of the Sierra, and the tactical and strategic differences between the two groups of the July 26 Movement. This latter situation stemmed from differing social and political conceptions. The Sierra was isolated because of natural conditions and also because the army's cordon was sometimes extremely difficult to pass through.

In this brief sketch of the country's struggle during the course of the year, we must mention the activities, generally fruitless and culminating in unfortunate results, of other groups of fighters.

On March 13, 1957, the Student Directorate attacked the Presidential Palace in an attempt to execute Batista. In that action a select handful of fighters were killed, headed by the president of the Federation of University Students—a great fighter, a true symbol of our young people, José Antonio Echeverría, "Manzanita" [little apple].

A few months later, in May, a landing was attempted. It had probably been betrayed even before setting sail from Miami, since it was financed by the traitor Prío. It resulted in a virtual massacre of all its participants. This was the *Corynthia* expedition, led by Calixto Sánchez, who was killed together with almost all his comrades. The author of the crime was Cowley, the murderer from northern Oriente, who was later executed by members of our Movement.[1]

Fighting groups were established in the Escambray mountains, some of them led by the July 26 Movement and others by the Student Directorate. The latter group was originally led by a member of the Directorate who betrayed first his organization and then the revolution itself—[Eloy] Gutiérrez Menoyo, today in exile. The fighters loyal to the Directorate formed a separate column that was later led by Commander [Faure] Chomón; the others set up the Second National Front of the Escambray.

Small nuclei were formed in the Cristal and Baracoa mountains.[2] These were sometimes half guerrillas and half cattle rus-

1. Col. Fermín Cowley, head of the military district of Holguín, directed the Christmas 1956 murder of twenty-two government opponents, and the May 1957 murder of captured combatants of the *Corynthia*. He was killed by July 26 Movement members November 23, 1957.
2. Part of the Sagua-Baracoa chain of mountains in eastern Oriente province. See map on page 461.

tlers; Raúl had to clean them out when his Column no. 6 entered the area.

Another incident in the armed struggle of that period was the uprising at the Cienfuegos naval base on September 5, 1957, led by Lieutenant [Dionisio] San Román, who was murdered when the revolt failed. The Cienfuegos base was not supposed to rise alone, nor was this a spontaneous action. It was part of a large underground movement inside the armed forces, led by a group of so-called pure military men, untainted by the crimes of the dictatorship. As can be seen clearly today, this group was penetrated by U.S. imperialism. For some obscure reason the uprising was postponed to a later date, but the Cienfuegos naval base did not receive the order in time and, unable to stop the uprising, decided to go through with it. At first they were in control, but they committed the tragic mistake of not heading for the Escambray mountains, only a few minutes away from Cienfuegos, at a time when they controlled the entire city and had the means to do so rapidly and form a solid front in the mountains.

National and local leaders of the July 26 Movement participated in this action. So did the people; at least they shared in the enthusiasm that led to the revolt, and some of them took up arms. This may have created moral obligations on the part of the uprising's leaders, tying them even closer to the conquered city; but the course of events followed a line characteristic of this type of revolt, which history has seen before and will see again. Obviously an important role was played by the underestimation of guerrilla struggle on the part of academy-trained officers, by their lack of confidence in the guerrilla movement as an expression of the people's struggle. Thus it was that the conspirators, probably assuming that without the aid of their comrades-in-arms they were lost, decided to carry on a fight to the death within the narrow boundaries of a city, their backs to the sea. Eventually they were virtually annihilated by the superior forces of the enemy, which had mobilized its troops at its convenience and converged on Cienfuegos. The July 26 Movement, participating as an unarmed ally, could not have changed the course of events, even if its leaders had seen the outcome clearly, which they did not. The lesson for the future is: he who has the strength dictates the strategy.

Large-scale killing of civilians, repeated failures, murders committed by the dictatorship in various aspects of the struggle analyzed here—all these factors indicated that guerrilla action on favorable terrain was the best method of popular struggle against a despotic and still-powerful government, the least grievous for the sons of the people. After the guerrilla force was set up, we could count our losses on our fingers—comrades of outstanding courage and tenacity in battle, to be sure. In the cities, on the other hand, it was not only the resolute ones who died, but many of lesser significance to the revolution, and even many who were innocent of any involvement at all. This was due to greater vulnerability in the face of repressive action.

By the end of this first year of struggle, a generalized uprising throughout the country was looming on the horizon. There were acts of sabotage, ranging from those that were well-planned and carried out on a high technical level to trivial terrorist acts arising from individual initiative, leaving a tragic toll of innocent deaths and sacrifices among the best fighters, of no real benefit to the people's cause.

Our military situation was being consolidated and the territory we occupied was extensive. We were in a state of armed truce with Batista; his men did not go up into the Sierra and ours hardly ever went down. The enemy's encirclement was as tight as they could make it, but our troops still managed to evade them.

Organizationally, our guerrilla army had developed sufficiently to have, by the year's end, elementary organization of provisions, certain minimal industrial services, hospitals, and lines of communication.

The guerrilla's problems were very simple: to subsist as an individual he needed a small amount of food, certain indispensable items of clothing and medicine; to subsist as a guerrilla unit, that is, as an armed force in struggle, he needed arms and ammunition; for his political development he needed channels of propaganda. In order to assure these minimal necessities, a communications and information apparatus was required.

In the beginning the small guerrilla units, some twenty men, would eat a meager ration of Sierra vegetables, chicken soup on special occasions; sometimes the peasants provided a pig, for which they were scrupulously paid. As the guerrilla force grew and groups of "pre-guerrillas" were trained, more provisions were needed. The Sierra peasants did not have cattle and generally theirs was a subsistence diet. They depended on the sale of their coffee to buy indispensable manufactured items, such as salt, which could not be found in the Sierra. As an initial step we arranged for certain peasants to plant specific crops—beans, corn, rice, etc.—which we guaranteed to purchase. At the same time, we came to terms with certain merchants in nearby towns for the supplying of foodstuffs and equipment. Mule teams were organized, belonging to the guerrilla forces.

As for medicines, we obtained them in the cities, not always in the quantity or quality we needed; for this reason it was necessary to maintain here too some kind of functioning apparatus for their acquisition.

Obtaining arms from the Llano was difficult. On top of the natural difficulties of geographical isolation there were the arms requirements of the city forces themselves, and their reluctance to turn them over to the guerrilla forces. Fidel was constantly involved in sharp discussions in an effort to get equipment to us. The only substantial shipment we can point to during that first year of struggle, other than what the combatants themselves brought with them when they joined, were the weapons that remained from the attack on the Presidential Palace. These were transported with the cooperation of a large landowner and timber merchant of the zone, Babún, who we have already mentioned in these pages.

Ammunition was very scarce. What we received came in small quantities and was lacking in the necessary variety. Unfortunately, it was impossible for us to manufacture it or even to re-

PHOTOS: BOHEMIA

Top, Santiago's main police station, as it burned November 30, 1956, during uprising organized by July 26 Movement to coincide with scheduled *Granma* landing. Only the exterior walls were left standing.

Repression intensified following the uprising. *Below,* protest in Santiago de Cuba against police murder of 15-year-old William Soler on January 2, 1957. Sign reads, "Stop the murder of our children. Cuban mothers." At front, in light-colored jacket, is Soler's mother.

BOHEMIA

BOHEMIA

GRANMA

COUNCIL OF STATE OFFICE OF HISTORICAL AFFAIRS

Three days after December 2, 1956, *Granma* landing, the 82 expeditionaries were taken by surprise and dispersed at Alegría de Pío in Oriente province. *Facing page, top,* Gen. Martín Díaz Tamayo on his way to direct army operations in Oriente, December 1956. *Middle,* army troops in pursuit following rebel defeat at Alegría de Pío.

Left, U.S. and Cuban military officials, early 1957, in Cuba to discuss increased U.S. aid to Batista. Second from right is Francisco Tabernilla, head of Cuban general staff; next to him, center, is Col. Harold Isaacson, head of U.S. Military Mission in Cuba.

By late December, half of the rebel forces who had not been killed or captured had regrouped and made their way to the Sierra Maestra mountains. Together with initial peasant recruits, they numbered 24 combatants. *Above,* Granma expeditionary leader Fidel Castro (second from right) with, left to right, July 26 Movement leaders Frank País, Faustino Pérez, and Armando Hart, at time of meeting of its National Directorate in Sierra Maestra, February 16, 1957.

This page, top, Frank País (facing camera) during April 1957 trial of accused participants in November 30, 1956, uprising and captured *Granma* expeditionaries. At front left, July 26 Movement cadre Léster Rodríguez.

Bottom, Batista police respond to attack on Presidential Palace by fighters of Revolutionary Directorate, March 13, 1957.

This page, Rebel Army members in Sierra Maestra, May 1957. From left: Guillermo García, Ernesto Che Guevara, Universo Sánchez, Raúl Castro, Fidel Castro, Crescencio Pérez, Jorge Sotús, Juan Almeida.

Bottom, Castro being interviewed by *New York Times* correspondent Herbert Matthews, February 17, 1957. Following a Batista official's claim that the interview was faked and Castro was not in the Sierra, publication of the photo caused a sensation in Cuba.

COUNCIL OF STATE OFFICE OF HISTORICAL AFFAIRS

WIDE WORLD PHOTOS

GRANMA

COUNCIL OF STATE OFFICE OF HISTORICAL AFFAIRS

BOHEMIA

Main photo: Santiago de Cuba, July 31, 1957: funeral march of 60,000 for Frank País, gunned down in cold blood by police the day before. That same day, *above,* U.S. ambassador Earl Smith (foreground right) during visit to Santiago; he is met by women demonstrators calling for end to U.S. support to Batista.

GRANMA

Facing page, bottom: Raúl Chibás (left) and Felipe Pazos (center) meet with Fidel Castro, June 1957, prior to issuing of the Manifesto of the Sierra Maestra. In November Pazos was one of the signers of the Miami Pact, brokered by former Cuban president Carlos Prío; that pact was denounced by July 26 Movement and fell apart.

Left, Prío at his exile home in Florida, August 1955, when he announced he would not return to Cuba for fear of provoking violence.

COUNCIL OF STATE OFFICE OF HISTORICAL AFFAIRS

BOHEMIA

Facing page, top, Fidel Castro, on mule, speaks with peasants in the Sierra, early 1958. *Bottom,* Batista's army routinely rounded up peasants in the Sierra Maestra and frequently executed them.

Above, left, Castro instructs combatant in use of his weapon. *Top right*, Guevara, left, with Rebel Army courier Lidia Doce, later captured and killed by Batista forces. (INSTITUTE OF CUBAN HISTORY) *Bottom right,* boxcars destroyed in Oriente by July 26 Movement's urban underground as part of sabotage campaign.

COUNCIL OF STATE
OFFICE OF
HISTORICAL AFFAIRS

GRANMA

COUNCIL OF STATE OFFICE OF HISTORICAL AFFAIRS

GRANMA

GRANMA

GRANMA

Facing page, top, Rebel Army combatants on the march; Haydée Santamaría, followed by Celia Sánchez and Universo Sánchez. *Bottom,* Rebel Army weapons factory, created by Second Eastern Front, under the command of Raúl Castro.

Above, left, Mimeograph machine and typewriter used for producing the Rebel Army newspaper *El Cubano Libre*, established by Guevara's column in November 1957.

Top right, members of Guevara's column and peasants at El Hombrito camp at end of 1957; Guevara is sitting, with stick; banner reads, "Happy 1958, M-26" (July 26 Movement). (INSTITUTE OF CUBAN HISTORY)

Bottom, right, Batista officials prepare May-July 1958 "encircle and annihilate" offensive, the failure of which set stage for revolutionary victory at end of year. Rolando Masferrer is at center (with hat), flanked by Col. Pedro Barreras (left) and Col. Joaquín Casillas (right). Masferrer was head of the notorious Batista paramilitary squad called the "Tigers."

WIDE WORLD PHOTOS

ELI WEINBERG

As the revolutionary war unfolded in 1956–58, anti-imperialist struggles were on the rise in other parts of the world and the mass mobilizations that eventually toppled Jim Crow segregation in the U.S. South were building.

Top, students in Caracas, Venezuela, protest Latin American tour of U.S. vice president Richard Nixon, May 14, 1958.

Bottom, demonstration in support of Nelson Mandela and other imprisoned leaders of the African National Congress during Treason Trial, South Africa, December 1956.

BETTMANN

Top, Egyptian toilers hail nationalization of largely British- and French-owned Suez Canal, carried out in July 1956. At center, President Gamal Abdel Nasser.

Bottom, Federal troops sent in face of racist violence to protect Black children attempting to desegregate whites-only school in Little Rock, Arkansas, 1957.

INSTITUTE OF CUBAN HISTORY

At the end of August 1958, Rebel Army columns led by Guevara and Camilo Cienfuegos moved westward from the Sierra Maestra to Las Villas province in central Cuba, to expand the revolutionary struggle.

Top, "Ñico López" School for Recruits, established by Guevara at Rebel Army camp at Caballete de Casas in Las Villas. Photo shows assembly of fighters to commemorate anniversary of death of Cuban independence fighter Antonio Maceo, December 7, 1958.

Bottom, leaders of units of July 26 Movement and Revolutionary Directorate, at Directorate's camp at Dos Arroyos in Las Villas. Standing: Jorge Martín, Humberto Castelló, Faure Chomón, René Rodríguez, Rolando Cubela, Guevara, Ramiro Valdés. Kneeling at left, José Moleón, Raúl Nieves. The two organizations signed Pedrero Pact December 1, 1958, agreeing to joint action against Batista regime.

Facing page, top, members of Column 8's Suicide Squad, made up of young fighters who volunteered for most dangerous assignments. Second from left is the unit's leader Capt. Roberto Rodríguez (Vaquerito), who died in combat shortly after photo was taken; third from left is Lt. Leonardo Tamayo, who accompanied Guevara to Bolivia in 1966–67 using nom de guerre Urbano. (GRANMA)

COUNCIL OF STATE OFFICE OF HISTORICAL AFFAIRS

INSTITUTE OF CUBAN HISTORY

Bottom left, Guevara communicating by radio with Rebel forces during Las Villas campaign. With him is rebel combatant Iván Prat.

Bottom right, Camilo Cienfuegos, commander of Column 2, in northern Las Villas.

Top, Raúl Castro addresses congress of peasants organized by Rebel Army's Second Eastern Front, in Soledad, Mayarí Arriba, September 21, 1958. Behind him are Papito Seguera (standing) and Vilma Espín.

Bottom, members of Rebel Army's small air force, late 1958. At far left is pilot Luis Silva Tablada, killed in 1961 defending Cuba against U.S.-backed invasion at Bay of Pigs. Standing second from right, is Efigenio Ameijeiras, second in command of Second Eastern Front.

COUNCIL OF STATE OFFICE OF HISTORICAL AFFAIRS

GRANMA

charge cartridges during this first period, except for bullets for the .38 revolver, which our gunsmith would recharge with a little gunpowder, and some of the .30-06's, which were used only in the single-shot rifles, since they caused the semiautomatics to jam and interfered with their proper functioning.

With regard to the organization of daily life at camp and of communications, we established certain sanitary regulations at this time. During this period the first hospitals were organized, one of them in the region under my command, in a remote, inaccessible place, offering relative security to the wounded, since it was invisible from the air. But since it was in the heart of a dense forest, its dampness made it unhealthy for the wounded and sick. This hospital was organized by Comrade Sergio del Valle, while Doctors Martínez Páez, Vallejo, and Piti Fajardo organized similar hospitals for Fidel's column. However, it was not until the second year of the struggle that our hospitals improved significantly.

The troop's equipment needs, such as cartridge boxes and belts, knapsacks, and shoes, were met by a small leather-goods workshop set up in our zone. (When we turned out the first army cap, I took it to Fidel, bursting with pride. But I quickly became the butt of tremendous laughter, because everyone said it looked like the hat of a *guagüero,* a word I was unfamiliar with at the time.[3] The only one showing me any mercy was a municipal councillor from Manzanillo, who was visiting the camp in order to make arrangements for joining us, and who took it back with him as a souvenir.)

Our most important industrial creation was a small forge and armory, where defective weapons were repaired and where bombs, mines, and the famous M-26 were manufactured. At first the mines were made of tin cans and filled with material from bombs frequently dropped by enemy planes that had not exploded. These mines were very faulty. Furthermore they had a

3. A bus driver. From the word *guagua* (bus), used in the Spanish-speaking Caribbean.

firing pin, which struck the detonator, but it often failed. Later a comrade had the idea of using the whole bomb for larger attacks, removing the detonator and using instead a loaded shotgun; we would pull the trigger from a distance by means of a cord, and this would cause an explosion. Afterward, we perfected the system, making special fuses of metal alloy and electric detonators. These gave better results. Even though we were the first to develop this, it was given real impetus by Fidel; later on, Raúl in his new center of operations created stronger industries than those we had during the first year of war.

To please the smokers among us, we set up a cigar factory; the cigars we made were terrible but, lacking anything better, we found them heavenly.

Our army's butcher shop was supplied with cattle, which we confiscated from informers and large landowners. We shared equitably: one part for the peasant population, one part for our troops.

As for the dissemination of our ideas, first we started a small newspaper, *El Cubano Libre*, in memory of those heroes of the jungle. Three or four issues came out under my directorship; it was later edited by Luis Orlando Rodríguez, and subsequently Carlos Franqui, who gave it new impetus. We had a mimeograph machine brought up to us from the cities, on which the paper was printed.

By the end of the first year of the war and the beginning of the second, we had a small radio transmitter. The first regular broadcasts were made in February 1958; our only listeners were Pelencho, a peasant who lived on the hill facing the station, and Fidel, who was visiting our camp in preparation for the attack on Pino del Agua. He listened to it on our receiver. Little by little the technical quality of the broadcasts improved. It was then taken over by Column no. 1 and by December 1958 had become one of the stations in Cuba with the highest "ratings."[4]

4. Radio Rebelde, created under Guevara's direction, went on the air February 24, 1958.

All these small advances, including some pieces of equipment—such as a winch and some generators, which we laboriously carried up to the Sierra so as to have electric light—were due to our own connections. To cope with our difficulties we had to begin creating a network of communications and information. In this respect Lidia Doce played an important part in my column; Clodomira [Acosta] did so in Fidel's.

Help came in those days not only from the people in the neighboring villages; even the city bourgeoisie contributed a few things to the guerrilla struggle. Our lines of communication reached as far as the towns of Contramaestre, Palma, Bueycito, Minas de Bueycito, Estrada Palma, Yara, Bayamo, Manzanillo, and Guisa. These places served as relay stations. Goods were then carried on muleback along hidden trails in the Sierra up to our positions. At times, those among our men who were in training but were not yet armed went down to the nearest towns, such as Yao or Las Minas, with some of our armed men, or they would go to well-stocked stores in the district, returning to our retreat with supplies on their backs. The only item we never, or almost never, lacked in the Sierra Maestra was coffee. At times we lacked salt, one of the most important foods for survival, whose virtues one becomes aware of only when it is scarce.

When we began to broadcast from our own transmitter, the existence of our troops and their fighting determination became known throughout the republic. At that point our links became more extensive and complex, reaching as far as Havana and Camagüey in the west, where we had important supply centers, and Santiago in the east.

Our information service developed in such a way that the peasants in the zone immediately notified us of the presence, not only of the army, but of any stranger; we were easily able to detain the individual while investigating his activities. In this way we eliminated many army agents and spies who infiltrated the zone for the purpose of checking up on us and our activities.

We began structuring a legal system, but as of then no law of the Sierra had been promulgated.

Such was our organizational situation at the beginning of the last year of the war.

As for the political struggle, it was very complicated and contradictory. The Batista dictatorship was supported by a congress elected by so many frauds that it could count on a comfortable majority to do its bidding.

Certain dissident opinions were allowed expression—when there was no censorship—but spokesmen for and officials of the regime, calling for national unity, spoke with powerful voices, and the networks transmitted their messages throughout the island. The hysterical voice of Otto Meruelo alternated with the pompous buffooneries of Pardo Llada and Conte Agüero. The latter, repeating in print what he said on the air, called on "brother Fidel" to accept coexistence with the Batista regime.

The opposition groups were varied and dissimilar, even though most had as a common denominator the wish to take power (read: public funds) for themselves. This brought in its wake a sordid internal struggle to win that victory. The groups were totally infiltrated by Batista agents who, at key moments, denounced to the government any significant activities. Although these groups were characterized by gangsterism and personal ambition, they also had their martyrs, some of national repute. In effect, Cuban society was in such total disarray that brave and honest men were sacrificing their lives to maintain the comfortable existence of such personages as Prío Socarrás.

The Student Directorate took the path of insurrectional struggle, but their movement was independent of ours and they had their own line. The PSP joined with us in certain concrete actions, but mutual distrust hampered joint action and, fundamentally, the party of the workers did not understand with sufficient clarity the role of the guerrilla force, nor the place of Fidel in our revolutionary struggle.

During a fraternal discussion, I once made an observation to a PSP leader, which he later repeated to others as an accurate characterization of that period: "You are capable of creating cadres who can silently endure the most terrible tortures in jail, but you cannot create cadres who can take a machine gun nest." As I saw it from my guerrilla vantage point, this was a consequence of their strategic conception: a determination to struggle against imperialism and the abuses of the exploiting classes, together with an inability to envision the possibility of taking power. Later, some of their men, of guerrilla spirit, were to join us, but by then the end of the armed struggle was near; therefore its influence on them was slight.

Within our own movement there were two quite clearly defined tendencies, which we have already referred to as the *Sierra* and the *Llano*. Differences over strategic conception separated us. The Sierra was already confident of being able to carry out the guerrilla struggle, to spread it to other places and thus, from the countryside, to encircle the cities held by the dictatorship; and through strangulation and attrition to destroy the entire apparatus of the regime. The Llano took an ostensibly more revolutionary position, that of armed struggle in all the cities and towns, culminating in a general strike that would topple Batista and allow the swift seizure of power.

This position was more revolutionary only in appearance, because in that period the political development of the Llano comrades was incomplete and their conception of a general strike was too narrow. A general strike called the following year without warning, in secrecy, without prior political preparation or mass action, would lead to the defeat of April 9.[5]

These two tendencies were represented in the National Directorate of the Movement, which was changing as the struggle developed. In the preparatory stage, until Fidel left for Mexico, the National Directorate was composed of Fidel, Raúl, Faustino Pérez, Pedro Miret, Ñico López, Armando Hart, Pepe Suárez, Pedro Aguilera, Luis Bonito, Jesús Montané, Melba Hernández, and Haydée Santamaría—if my information is correct, since my personal participation at that time was very limited and docu-

5. For a discussion on the failed general strike of April 9, 1958, see the chapter "A Decisive Meeting."

mentation is scarce. Later, for various reasons of incompatibility, Pepe Suárez, Pedro Aguilera, and Luis Bonito left the body. While we were in Mexico the following people joined the committee: Mario Hidalgo, Aldo Santamaría, Carlos Franqui, Gustavo Arcos, and Frank País.

Of all these comrades named, the only ones to go to the Sierra during the first year and remain there were Fidel and Raúl. Faustino Pérez, a member of the *Granma* expedition, was put in charge of actions in the city. Pedro Miret was jailed a few hours before we were to leave Mexico, and remained there until the following year, when he arrived in Cuba with an arms shipment. Ñico López died only a few days after the landing. Armando Hart was jailed at the end of that year (or early in the next). Jesús Montané was jailed after the *Granma* landing, as was Mario Hidalgo. Melba Hernández and Haydée Santamaría worked in the cities. Aldo Santamaría and Carlos Franqui joined the struggle in the Sierra the following year. Gustavo Arcos remained in Mexico, in charge of political liaison and supplies. Frank País, assigned to head up actions in Santiago, died in July 1957.

Later, the following were to join the leadership body in the Sierra: Celia Sánchez, who remained with us during all of 1958; Vilma Espín, who was working in Santiago and finished the war in Raúl Castro's column; Marcelo Fernández, coordinator of the Movement, who replaced Faustino after the April 9 strike and stayed with us only a few weeks, since his work was in the towns; René Ramos Latour, in charge of organizing the Llano militia, came up to the Sierra after the April 9 defeat and died heroically as a commander, during the second year of the struggle; David Salvador, in charge of the labor movement, on which he left the imprint of his opportunist and divisive actions (he was later to betray the revolution and is now in prison). Some of the Sierra fighters, such as Almeida, were to join the national leadership some time later.

As can be seen, during this stage the Llano comrades constituted the majority. Their political background, which had not been influenced very much by the maturing of the revolution, led them to favor a certain type of "civil" action, and to a kind of resistance to the caudillo they saw in Fidel and to the "militarist" faction represented by us in the Sierra. The differences were already apparent, but they were not yet strong enough to provoke the violent discussions that characterized the second year of the war.

It is important to point out that the fighters against the dictatorship in both the Sierra and the Llano were able to hold opinions on tactics that were at times diametrically opposed, without having this lead to abandoning the insurrectional struggle. Their revolutionary spirit continued to deepen until the moment when—victory in hand, followed by the opening rounds of the struggle against imperialism—they all came together in a powerful party-type organization whose unquestioned leader was Fidel. This group then joined together with the Directorate and the Popular Socialist Party to form our United Party of the Socialist Revolution.[6] In the face of all pressures from outside our movement, and all attempts to divide or infiltrate it, we always presented a common front of struggle. Moreover, even those comrades who saw the Cuban revolution less clearly at the moment we are speaking of were wary of opportunists.

When Felipe Pazos, invoking the name of the July 26 Movement, sought to appropriate for himself and for the most corrupt oligarchic interests of Cuba the positions offered by the Miami Pact,[7]

6. In 1961 the July 26 Movement, Popular Socialist Party, and Revolutionary Directorate united to form the Integrated Revolutionary Organizations. The new organization became the United Party of the Socialist Revolution in 1963, and was renamed the Communist Party of Cuba in October 1965.
7. On November 1, 1957, a "Document of Unity of Cuban Opposition to the Batista Dictatorship" was signed in Miami, including by a number of leading figures in the bourgeois opposition to Batista, such as former president Carlos Prío of the Cuban Revolutionary (Authentic) Party and leaders of the Cuban People's (Orthodox) Party; also signing were representatives of the Revolutionary Directorate, Federation of University Students, and Revolutionary Workers Directorate. In addition, the document bore the signature of Felipe Pazos, one of the three signers of the Sierra Manifesto. The "Miami Pact," which included both a public and secret part, created a "Cuban Liberation Junta" that claimed the right to name a post-Batista pro-

nominating himself for the post of provisional president, the entire Movement was solidly united against this stand and supported the letter that Fidel Castro sent to the organizations involved in the struggle against Batista. Below we reproduce this historic document in its entirety. It is dated December 14, 1957, and was copied out by Celia Sánchez, since during that period there was no other way to print it.[8]

Letter by Fidel Castro to signers of the Miami Pact

Cuba
December 14, 1957

To the leaders of:
The Cuban Revolutionary Party
The Cuban People's Party
The Authentic Organization
The Federation of University Students
The Revolutionary Directorate
The Revolutionary Workers Directorate

A moral, patriotic, and even historic duty compels me to address this letter to you, motivated by events and circumstances that have concerned us deeply these last few weeks, which have also been the busiest and most difficult ones since our arrival in Cuba. For it was on Wednesday, November 20, a day when our forces sustained three battles in the space of only six hours (suggest-

---

visional government. News of the pact did not reach the Sierra Maestra until three weeks later, when it had already been widely circulated internationally.

8. In January 1958 the letter was mimeographed by Guevara's Rebel Army column for public distribution. When press censorship was briefly lifted, the letter was printed in its entirety in the February 2, 1958, issue of *Bohemia*, in a special run of 500,000 copies.

ing the sacrifices and efforts that our men here have made, without the slightest aid from other organizations), that we received in our zone of operations the surprising news and the document containing the public and secret terms of the Unity Pact, said to have been signed in Miami by the July 26 Movement and the organizations I am now addressing. Perhaps it was through an irony of fate that the arrival of this document—at a time when arms are what we need—coincided with the strongest offensive the dictatorship has launched against us.

Under the conditions of struggle we face, communications are difficult. Nevertheless, in the very midst of operations, it was necessary to convene the leaders of our organization to discuss this matter, in which not only the prestige but even the historic justification of the July 26 Movement is at stake.

Our men are fighting an enemy incomparably superior in numbers and in weapons. For an entire year they have sustained themselves with nothing but the dignity with which one fights for a cause he truly loves and the conviction that it is a cause worth dying for. They have tasted the bitterness of being forgotten by other compatriots who, possessing all the means to assist them, have systematically—if not criminally—refused to do so. They have seen, at close range, daily sacrifice in its purest and most selfless form. They have experienced the pain of seeing the best among them fall, not knowing who beside them will perish in new and inevitable holocausts to come, fated not to see the day of triumph they so tenaciously worked for, with no other hope or aspiration than that their sacrifice not be in vain. It is not difficult to understand why the news of a widely and deliberately publicized pact, which commits the Movement to a future course without even the courtesy—not to speak of the elementary obligation—of consulting its leaders and combatants, would provoke the ire and indignation of us all.

Acting in an improper fashion always leads to the worst consequences. This must be borne in mind by those who consider themselves capable of an undertaking as arduous as the overthrow of a tyranny, and the even harder task of successfully reorganizing the country following a revolutionary process.

The July 26 Movement has neither designated nor authorized anyone to enter into such negotiations. Nonetheless, it would not have been opposed to selecting a representative had it been consulted on such an initiative. In that event, it would have given very concrete instructions to its representatives when discussing a matter with such serious consequences to the present and future activities of our organization.

Instead, our information concerning relations with some of these groups was limited to a report by Mr. Léster Rodríguez, our delegate for military matters abroad, with powers limited strictly to such matters. He wrote us the following:

"With respect to Prío and the Directorate, I can report to you that I have held a series of discussions with them for the sole and exclusive purpose of coordinating military plans, up to the formation of a provisional government guaranteed and respected by the three groups. I of course proposed that they accept the Sierra Letter, which specifies that this government should be formed in accordance with the will of the country's civic forces.[9] That led to the first difficulty.

"When the commotion around the general strike occurred,[10] we held an emergency meeting. I proposed that we utilize all the forces at hand right away in an effort to resolve the problem of Cuba once and for all. Prío answered that he lacked sufficient forces to undertake any action with assurance of victory, and that it would be madness to accept my proposal. I answered that he should please let me know when he had everything ready to set sail; then we would be able to discuss possible pacts. In the meantime, he should do me the favor of letting me work on my own account, and that of those whom I represent in the July 26

9. This is a reference to the "Manifesto of the Sierra Maestra," referred to earlier in the chapter "A Betrayal in the Making."

10. A reference to the spontaneous strikes that began in Santiago de Cuba following the murder of Frank País on July 30, 1957. The strikes lasted for almost a week and spread throughout the island, including Havana and other cities.

Movement, with complete independence. In short, we came to no agreement with these gentlemen, nor do I believe it is advisable to do so in the future. For at the moment when Cuba needed it most, they denied having the weapons that have since been seized—and in such amounts that it moves one to indignation."[11]

This report, which speaks for itself, confirmed our suspicion that the rebels could expect no outside help whatsoever.

If the organizations that you represent had deemed it worthwhile to discuss the articles of unity with any members of our Movement, these articles could not have been announced publicly, under any circumstances, as conclusive agreements without the knowledge and approval of the National Directorate of the Movement—and even less so when they fundamentally differed from the points raised by us in the Manifesto of the Sierra Maestra. To function in any other way is simply to make pacts for public relations purposes and to fraudulently invoke the name of our organization.

There is the incredible case of what confronted the National Directorate of our Movement, which functions clandestinely inside Cuba. After receiving the text of the pact, they had decided to reject its public and secret provisions. No sooner had they done so than they learned through underground flyers, and through the foreign press, that the pact had been announced publicly as a signed agreement. They were thus confronted by a fait accompli and were faced with the alternatives of repudiating it as a lie, with all the confusion that would bring, or accepting it, without even being able to express their point of view.

As one can easily imagine, by the time the provisions of the document reached us in the Sierra, it had already been circulating publicly for many days.

Faced with this dilemma, the National Directorate, before proceeding to publicly repudiate the agreements, raised with

11. Prío spent an estimated $5 million accumulating weapons for the Authentic Party's military organization and other anti-Batista organizations. Almost all of these were seized by Batista's police.

you the need for the Junta to incorporate a series of points from the Manifesto of the Sierra Maestra. Meanwhile they convened a meeting in rebel territory in which the views of all its members were weighed and a unanimous decision was adopted, forming the basis of this letter.

Naturally enough, any unity agreement will inevitably be welcomed by national and international public opinion. There are several reasons for this. For one thing, those abroad do not know the real situation of the political and revolutionary forces opposing Batista. Within Cuba, on the other hand, the word "unity" was draped with a certain aura, based on a former relationship of forces that has clearly changed considerably since then; and additionally, because in general it is a positive thing to unite the efforts of everyone, from the most enthusiastic to the most timid.

But what is important for the revolution is not unity in itself, but the principles on which it is based, how it is achieved, and the patriotic intentions motivating it.

Agreeing to a unity whose provisions we have not even discussed; having it signed by persons with no authority to do so; and announcing it publicly without further ado from the comfort of a foreign city, thereby putting the Movement in the situation of facing a public deceived by a fraudulent pact—this is a trick of the lowest sort, which a truly revolutionary organization can have no part in. It is an act of deception to the country and to the world.

Moreover, such a trick is possible only because of the simple fact that the leaders of the other organizations that signed this pact are living in exile, making an imaginary revolution, while the leaders of the July 26 Movement are in Cuba, making a real revolution.

Our letter, however, might not have been necessary, regardless of the very bitter and humiliating procedure attempting to tie the Movement to this pact. Differences over form must never overshadow essentials. We might still have accepted it, despite everything, because of some of the positive ideas raised by the

Junta, and because of the help being offered us, which we genuinely need. The simple fact, however, is that we disagree with a number of its essential points.

No matter how desperate our situation in face of thousands of the dictatorship's troops mobilized to annihilate us, and perhaps with more determination because of it (since nothing is more humiliating than to accept an onerous condition under trying circumstances), we would never accept the sacrifice of certain principles that are fundamental to our conception of the Cuban revolution. These principles are contained in the Manifesto of the Sierra Maestra.

To omit from the unity document the explicit declaration that we reject every form of foreign intervention in the internal affairs of Cuba is a sign of lukewarm patriotism and of cowardice, which must be condemned in and of itself.

Declaring that we are opposed to intervention is not simply asking that there be no intervention in support of the revolution, which would undercut our sovereignty and undermine a principle that affects all the peoples of the Americas. It also means opposing all intervention on the side of the dictatorship by supplying the planes, bombs, tanks, and modern weapons that maintain it in power. No one knows this better than we do, not to mention the peasants of the Sierra, who have suffered it in their own flesh and blood.

In short, ending such intervention means achieving the overthrow of the dictatorship. Are we such cowards that we won't even demand no intervention on the side of Batista? Are we so insincere that we ask in an underhanded way for someone else to pull our chestnuts out of the fire? Are we so halfhearted that we dare not utter a single word on the issue? How then can we call ourselves revolutionaries and subscribe to a unity document with historical pretensions?

The unity document omits the explicit rejection of any kind of military junta as a provisional government of the republic.

The worst thing that could happen to Cuba at the present time would be the replacement of Batista by a military junta, as this would be accompanied by the dangerous illusion that the nation's problems had been resolved by the dictator's absence. There are some politicians of the worst stripe, including accomplices of the March 10 coup now estranged from it (perhaps from being even more ambitious and despotic), who are considering solutions that only enemies of the country's progress would look kindly on.

Experience in Latin America has shown that all military juntas tend toward autocracy. The worst of all evils that has gripped this continent is the implantation of military castes in countries with fewer wars than Switzerland and more generals than Prussia. One of our people's most legitimate aspirations at this crucial hour, when the fate of democracy and the republic will either be saved or ruined for many years to come, is to guard the most precious legacy of our country's liberators: the tradition of civilian rule. This tradition dates back to the emancipation struggle and was broken the day a uniformed junta first took control of the republic—something never attempted by even the most glorious generals of our independence struggle, either in wartime or in peace.

Are we willing to renounce everything we believe in? Are we to omit such an important declaration of principles out of fear of wounding sensibilities? (This is a fear more imagined than real with regard to honest officers who could support us.) Is it so hard to understand that a timely definition of principles might forestall in time the danger of a military junta that would serve no other purpose than perpetuating the civil war?

We do not hesitate to declare that if a military junta replaces Batista, the July 26 Movement will resolutely continue its struggle for liberation. It is preferable to do battle today than to fall into a new and insurmountable abyss tomorrow. Neither military junta nor military puppet government. The slogan should be, "Civilians, govern with decency and honor. Soldiers, go to your barracks." And each and everyone, do your duty!

Or are we to wait for the generals of the March 10 coup, to whom Batista will gladly cede power (when it becomes unsustainable) as the best way to guarantee a transition that does the least damage to his interests and those of his cronies? It is astounding how lack of vision, absence of high ideals, and lack of a genuine desire to struggle can blind Cuban politicians!

If one lacks faith in the people, if one lacks confidence in their great reserves of energy and struggle, then one has no right to interfere with their destiny, distorting and misdirecting it during the most heroic and promising moments of the republic's life. Keep the revolutionary process free of all politicking, all childish ambitions, all lust for personal gain, all attempts to divide up the spoils. Men are dying in Cuba for something better. Let the politicians become revolutionaries, if that is what they so desire; but don't turn the revolution into bastard politics. Our people have shed too much blood and made too many sacrifices to deserve such bitter frustration in the future!

Apart from these two fundamental principles omitted in the unity document, we are in total disagreement with other of its aspects.

Even if we were to accept clause (b) of article 2 of the secret part, regarding the powers of the Junta of Liberation, which states: "To name the president of the republic who will assume this office in the provisional government," we cannot accept clause (c) of the same article, which includes among such powers "to approve or disapprove the cabinet as a whole named by the president of the republic, as well as any changes in its composition in the event of total or partial crisis."

How can one conceive that the president's powers to appoint and replace his collaborators is to be subject to the approval of a body that has no relationship to the powers of state? Inasmuch as this junta is to be composed of representatives of different parties and sectors, and therefore of different interests, is it not clear that such a procedure would convert the naming of the cabinet into divvying up posts as the only way to reach agreement in each case? Is it possible to agree to a stipulation that implies the establishment of two executive powers within the government? There is only one guarantee that all sectors of the country should demand of the provisional government: to limit its mission to a specific minimum program and to display absolute impartiality in presiding over the period of transition to complete constitutional normalcy.

To seek to involve itself in appointing each minister implies an aspiration to control public administration, putting it at the service of political interests. Such an attempt is possible only among parties and organizations lacking mass support, which can survive only within the confines of traditional politicking. Such an approach is sharply counterposed to the high revolutionary and political aims that the July 26 Movement has for the republic.

The very presence of secret agreements that do not deal with matters of organizing the struggle or plans for action, but instead take up questions of keen interest for the nation, such as the structure of the future government—something that must be proclaimed publicly—is in itself unacceptable. Martí said that in a revolution the methods are secret but the goals must always be public.

Another point that is equally unacceptable to the July 26 Movement is secret provision number 8, which states: "The revolutionary forces are to be incorporated, with their weapons, into the regular armed bodies of the republic."

In the first place, what is meant by "revolutionary forces"? Are we to grant a badge of membership to every policeman, sailor, soldier, and everyone else who at the final hour comes forward with a weapon in his hand? Are we to give a uniform and invest authority to those who today have weapons kept in hiding, in order to take them out on the day of triumph? To those who are standing aside while a handful of compatriots battle the entire forces of the tyranny? Are we to leave the door open, in a revolutionary document, to a revival of gangsterism and anarchy, which not very long ago were the shame of the republic?

Our experience in the territory dominated by our forces has taught us that the maintenance of public order is a key question for the country. Events have shown us that as soon as the prevailing order is eliminated, a series of problems are unleashed and crime, if left unchecked, sprouts up all over. It was the timely application of severe measures, with full public blessing, that put an end to the outbreak of banditry. The local residents, accustomed in the past to viewing agents of authority as enemies of the people, offered protection and shelter to those fleeing from the former system of justice. Now, when they see our soldiers as defenders of their interests, the most complete order prevails; and the best guardians of it are the citizens themselves.

Anarchy is the worst enemy of a revolutionary process. To combat it from now on is a fundamental need. Whoever does not understand this has no concern for the fate of the revolution, and those who have not sacrificed for the revolution, logically enough, do not share this concern. The country needs to know that there will be justice, but under the strictest order. Crime will be punished no matter where it comes from.

The July 26 Movement claims for itself the role of maintaining public order and reorganizing the armed forces of the republic.

1. Because it is the only organization that possesses organized and disciplined militias throughout the country, as well as an army in the field, with twenty victories over the enemy.

2. Because our combatants have demonstrated a spirit of chivalry free of all hatred toward the military, invariably respecting the lives of prisoners, tending their wounded, never torturing an adversary, even when they are known to possess important information. And they have maintained this conduct with an unprecedented equanimity.

3. Because the armed forces must be imbued with the spirit of justice and nobility that the July 26 Movement has instilled in its own soldiers.

4. Because the calmness with which we have acted in this struggle is the best guarantee that honorable military men have nothing to fear from the revolution. They will not be held accountable for those whose infamous acts and crimes have disgraced the military uniform.

There still remain certain aspects of the unity document that are difficult to understand. How is it possible to come to an agreement without a clearly defined strategy of struggle? Do the Authentic Party leaders still envision a putsch in the capital? Will they continue to accumulate weapons and more weapons that sooner or later will fall into the hands of the police, instead of giving them to those who are fighting? Have they finally accepted the thesis of the general strike held by the July 26 Movement?

As we see it, there has also been a regrettable underestimation of the military importance of the struggle in Oriente. What is being waged at present in the Sierra Maestra is not guerrilla warfare but a war of columns. Our forces, which are inferior in numbers and weaponry, take maximum advantage of the terrain, maintain permanent vigilance of the enemy, and operate with great speed of movement. It need hardly be said that the moral factor has been of decisive importance to the struggle. The results have been astounding, and some day these will be known in all their details.

The entire population has risen up. If there were enough weapons, our detachments would not have to guard a single zone. The peasants would not allow a single enemy soldier to pass. The defeats of the dictatorship, which obstinately sends large forces, could be disastrous. Anything I could tell you about the courage of the people here would be too little. The dictatorship takes barbaric reprisals. Its mass murder of peasants compares with the massacres perpetrated by the Nazis in any country of Europe. Each defeat it suffers is paid for by the defenseless population. The communiqués issued by the general staff announcing rebel losses are always preceded by a massacre. This has led the people to a state of absolute rebellion. But what is most painful, what makes one's heart bleed, is to think that no one has sent a single rifle to these people. While peasants here see their homes burned and their families murdered, desperately begging for rifles, there are arms hidden away in Cuba that are not being used, not even to eliminate some miserable henchman. It seems they are waiting for these weapons to be captured by the police, or for the tyranny to fall, or for the rebels to be exterminated.

There is nothing less noble than the actions of many compatriots. Even now there is still time to correct this and help those who are fighting. As far as we are concerned, from a personal point of view, this is unimportant. No one should worry that we are motivated by self-interest or pride.

Our fate is sealed; no uncertainty torments us. Either we die here to the last rebel, and a whole generation of Cuban youth will perish in the cities; or we triumph against the most incredible obstacles. For us defeat is impossible. The year of sacrifice and heroism with which our men have resisted can no longer be erased. Our victories are there, and they too cannot be easily erased. Our men, firmer than ever, will fight to the last drop of blood.

The defeat will be for those who denied us all assistance; those who made initial commitments but left us on our own. It will be for those, lacking faith in dignity and ideas, who wasted their time and their prestige in shameful dealings with the despot Trujillo. The defeat will be for those having weapons but who cowardly hid them at the hour of battle. It is they, not we, who deceive themselves.

There is one thing we can state with certainty: had we seen other Cubans battling for freedom, pursued and facing extermination; had we seen them not surrender or back down day after day, we would not have hesitated one minute to join them and die together, if that were necessary. For we are Cubans, and Cubans do not remain passive even when it is to fight for the freedom of any other country of the Americas. Are there Dominicans gathering on a little island to liberate their nation? For each Dominican, ten Cubans arrive. Are Somoza's henchmen invading Costa Rica? Cubans rush there to fight.[12] How is it now that

12. In 1947 Castro and hundreds of others participated in an aborted expedition that was being prepared in Cuba against the dictatorship of Rafael Trujillo in the Dominican Republic. In 1955 a number of Cuban revolutionaries went to Costa Rica following an attack on that country by the Somoza dictatorship in Nicaragua; among them were José Antonio Echeverría and other leaders of the Revolutionary Directorate.

when our own country is waging the fiercest battle for its freedom, there are Cubans in exile, expelled from their homeland by the tyranny, who refuse assistance to Cubans who fight?

To obtain aid, must we bow to impossible demands? Must we offer up the republic as war booty? Must we forsake our ideals and turn this war into a new art of killing fellow human beings, into a useless shedding of blood that does not promise the country any benefit from so much sacrifice?

The leadership of the struggle against the tyranny is, and will continue to be, in Cuba and in the hands of revolutionary fighters. Whoever wants to be considered a leader of the revolution, either now or in the future, must be inside the country directly confronting the responsibilities, risks, and sacrifices that Cuba now demands.

The exile community must assist this struggle, but it would be absurd for it to try to tell us from abroad which mountaintop we should take; which cane field we can burn; which acts of sabotage should be done; or the time, place, or manner to carry out the general strike. That is not just absurd, but ridiculous. Assist us from abroad; raise money among Cuban exiles and émigrés; wage a campaign for the Cuban cause in the press and before public opinion; denounce from over there the crimes we here are suffering. But do not pretend, from Miami, to lead a revolution that is being waged throughout the cities and the countryside of Cuba, amid battles, agitation, sabotage, strikes, and a thousand and one other forms of revolutionary action that are part of the July 26 Movement's strategy of struggle.

As it has stated on more than one occasion, the National Directorate is prepared to hold discussions inside Cuba with the leaders of any opposition organization, to coordinate specific plans, and to carry out concrete deeds deemed useful in overthrowing the tyranny.

The general strike will be carried out through the practical coordination of efforts by the Civic Resistance Movement, the National Workers Front, and any other sector free from political partisanship, and in intimate contact with the July 26 Movement, as the only opposition organization that is waging battle throughout the entire country at the present time.

The workers section of the July 26 Movement is involved in organizing strike committees in every work center and every sector of industry, together with opposition elements from all organizations that are prepared to join the strike and offer moral guarantees that they are going to carry it out. These strike committees will form the National Workers Front, which will be the only representative of the proletariat that the July 26 Movement will recognize as legitimate.[13]

The overthrow of the dictator will bring with it the ouster of the spurious congress; of the leadership of the Confederation of Cuban Workers; and of all the mayors, governors, and other officials who, directly or indirectly, owe their positions to the so-called elections of November 1, 1954, or to the military coup of March 10, 1952. It also involves the immediate release of all political, civil, and military prisoners and detainees, as well as the prosecution of all those complicit with the crimes, the arbitrary acts, and the tyranny itself.

The new government will be guided by the constitution of 1940, will guarantee all rights recognized therein, and will be free of all political partisanship.

The executive branch will assume the legislative functions that the constitution grants to the congress of the republic. It will have as its principal duty to conduct general elections in accordance with the electoral code of 1943 and the constitution of 1940 and to carry out the ten-point minimum program put forward in the Manifesto of the Sierra Maestra.

13. The National Workers Front (FON) was formed in Havana in December 1957 at the initiative of the July 26 Movement and its workers section. It raised a series of demands around wages, jobs, pensions, and union rights, and called for a general strike to help bring down the Batista regime. In November 1958, it was succeeded by the United National Workers Front (FONU), which included trade union cadres belonging to the July 26 Movement, the Popular Socialist Party, the Revolutionary Directorate, and other unionists.

The Supreme Court will be declared dissolved as a result of its incapacity to resolve the situation of lawlessness created by the coup. This does not preclude that some of its current members may be named to the new body, provided they defended constitutional principles or maintained a firm attitude against crime, arbitrary behavior, and abuse during these years of tyranny.

The president of the republic will decide on the manner of constituting the new Supreme Court, which in turn will proceed to reorganize all the courts and autonomous institutions, removing all those whom it considers to have been clearly complicit with the tyranny. Acting impartially it will remand such individuals to trial when appropriate. In each case new officials will be named in accordance with the law.

Political parties will have only one right during the life of the provisional government: the freedom to defend their program before the people, to mobilize and organize citizens within the broad framework of our constitution, and to participate in the general elections that are called.

The Manifesto of the Sierra Maestra raised the need to designate the person called upon to serve as president of the republic. Our Movement expressed its view that this person should be selected by the civic institutions as a whole. Nevertheless, five months have passed and this procedure has still not been carried out. Inasmuch as the question of who will replace the dictator is more urgent than ever, and it is not possible to wait one more day with this question unanswered, the July 26 Movement is giving its own answer. We present to the people the only formula possible to guarantee legality and the fulfillment of the previously agreed-upon articles of unity and of the provisional government itself. That individual should be the distinguished magistrate of the Provincial Court of Oriente, Dr. Manuel Urrutia Lleó. It is not we but his conduct itself that singles him out, and we hope he will not refuse this service to the republic.

The reasons pointing to him are the following:

1. He is the judicial official who most upheld the constitution, when he declared from the bench, during the trial of the *Gran-*

ma expeditionaries, that organizing an armed force against the regime was not a crime but was perfectly legal under both the letter and spirit of the constitution and the law. This gesture by a magistrate has no precedent in the history of our struggles for freedom.

2. His lifelong dedication to the honest administration of justice guarantees that he has sufficient training and character to serve with fairness all legitimate interests at the moment that the tyranny is overthrown by the people's action.

3. No one other than Dr. Manuel Urrutia is as free from all partisanship, since, owing to his judicial responsibilities, he has never belonged to any political grouping. There is no other citizen of his stature, free of all political alignments, who is so identified with the revolutionary cause.

Moreover, owing to his position as magistrate, this formula is the one closest to constitutional procedures.

These are our conditions, the disinterested conditions of an organization whose sacrifices exceed all others but was not even consulted when its name was put on a unity manifesto it does not subscribe to. If they are rejected, then we will continue the struggle on our own, as we have done up to now, with no weapons other than those we take from the enemy in each battle, with no aid other than that given by the suffering people, with no source of sustenance other than our ideas.

For when all is said and done, it is the July 26 Movement alone that has been carrying out actions throughout the entire country. It is the members of the July 26 Movement alone who have spread rebellion from the wild mountains of Oriente to the western provinces of the country. It is the members of the July 26 Movement alone who are carrying out sabotage, the execution of assassins, the burning of cane fields,[14] and other revolu-

14. The July 26 Movement had called for the obstruction of the 1958 sugar harvest through the burning of sugar cane fields belonging to the large landed estates. As Cuba's principal export, sugar was a key source of revenue for the Batista dictatorship.

tionary acts. It is the July 26 Movement alone that has been able to organize workers in revolutionary action throughout the nation. And it is the July 26 Movement alone that has helped organize the Civic Resistance Movement, which today groups together the civic sectors in almost all the localities of Cuba.

Some may interpret these words as arrogance. However, it is also the July 26 Movement alone that has declared it does not want to participate in the provisional government, and it is the one organization that has put all its moral and material power at the service of the ideal citizen to preside over the necessary provisional period.

Let it be understood that we have renounced any quest for bureaucratic posts or participation in the government. But let it also be known once and for all that the membership of the July 26 Movement does not renounce—and will never renounce—orienting and leading the people from clandestinity, from the Sierra Maestra, or from the graves of our dead. And we do not renounce this, because it is not we but an entire generation that has the moral commitment toward the people of Cuba to fundamentally resolve its great problems.

We are prepared, even if alone, to triumph or die. The struggle will never be as difficult as it was when we were only twelve men; when we did not have a people organized and tempered by war throughout the Sierra; when we did not have, as today, a powerful and disciplined organization throughout the country; when we did not possess the formidable mass support demonstrated at the time of the death of our unforgettable Frank País.

To die with dignity does not require company.

Fidel Castro Ruz
Sierra Maestra, December 14, 1957

PUBLISHED IN VERDE OLIVO, JANUARY 5, 1964

JANUARY–FEBRUARY 1958

The second battle of Pino del Agua

BY THE BEGINNING OF 1958 a type of truce had come about between our forces and Batista's troops. Nevertheless the army would issue communiqués reporting eight rebel losses one day, twenty-three the next—of course without suffering any themselves. This was their prevailing technique, above all in the region where my column was operating, in which Sánchez Mosquera devoted himself to imaginary battles against rebel forces, murdering peasants whose corpses added to his service record.

At the end of January censorship was lifted and, for the last time until the war ended, the newspapers printed some news. An air of truce was blowing through government circles. Ramírez León, a Batista legislator, made a more or less spontaneous trip accompanied by a legislator from Manzanillo, Lalo Roca, and a Spanish journalist from *Paris Match,* named Meneses, who conducted a series of interviews in the Sierra.

In the United States, long statements concerning the denunciation of the Miami Pact were being published by the July 26 Committee in Exile, whose president was Mario Llerena and whose treasurer was Raúl Chibás. (These representatives found their work in that part of the world so good for their health that it has apparently become their permanent residence at present. Perhaps they are working at professions similar to what they did during the war of liberation, when they seemed to be honest people.)

The interviews with Meneses, which were published in the magazine *Bohemia,* had repercussions throughout the entire world as well. Within the country there was an interesting polemic between Masferrer and Ramírez León, during those fleeting days when the Havana press published a little news.

Censorship had been lifted in five of the six provinces. In Oriente, constitutional guarantees remained suppressed and censorship continued.

In the middle of January a group of July 26 members, taken prisoner as they were leaving the Sierra, were brought before the press. They included Armando Hart, Javier Pazos, Luis Buch, and a guide named Eulalio Vallejo. This news was of some interest—despite the fact that comrades were taken prisoner every day, and were often murdered—because it gave an indication of the polemic that had already become more or less public between the two parts of the July 26 Movement. In response to a fairly idiotic letter I had sent to Comrade René Ramos Latour, he wrote me a rejoinder. A copy of my letter was circulated, however. Armando Hart wrote me a polemical note and intended to send it to me from the Sierra, where he had gone to see Fidel. However, Fidel believed that this letter would provoke yet another one, until at some point or other the thing could fall into the enemy's hands, which would do us no good. Armando, in disciplined fashion, obeyed the order. But he unintentionally left the note in one of his pockets, and it was on him when he was arrested.[1]

The life of Armando Hart and his comrades hung by a thread during the days they were held incommunicado in prison. The U.S. embassy marshaled its efforts to investigate the source of the dispute. As a result of a whole series of terms expressed in that polemical exchange, the enemy sensed something and perked up its ears.

Independently of this incident, Fidel felt it was important to

1. Contents of Hart's reply, containing references to Guevara's letter, were reported over the radio by Rafael Díaz Balart, a former Batista official.

strike a resounding blow, taking advantage of the fact that censorship had been lifted, and we prepared ourselves for this.

Once again, Pino del Agua was chosen as the spot. We had attacked it once before successfully; from then on Pino del Agua had been occupied by the enemy. Even when the troops did not move about very much, their position on the crest of the Sierra Maestra made wide detours necessary, and passing near the area was always dangerous. The elimination of Pino del Agua as an advance position of the army could thus be of great strategic importance and, given the new press conditions in the country, could have national repercussions.

From the first days in February, feverish preparations and reconnoitering began, conducted chiefly by Roberto Ruiz and Félix Tamayo (both officers in our present army) since they were from the region. Furthermore, we speeded up preparations on our latest weapon, the M-26, also called "sputnik," to which we attributed an exceptional importance. It was a small bomb made of tinplate, which we first launched by means of a complicated apparatus, a kind of catapult made with the lines from an underwater spear gun. Later we perfected it so that we could launch it by means of a rifle and cartridge, which made the device go much farther.

These little bombs made a great deal of noise and were really frightening. Since they had only a tinplate casing, however, their lethal power was tiny, and they inflicted only minor wounds when they exploded close to some enemy soldier. In addition, it was very difficult to time the moment at which the fuse was lit so that the end of the trajectory and the explosion would occur simultaneously. Because of the shock when launched, the fuse was apt to go out, and the little bomb would not explode, falling intact into enemy hands. After the enemy learned how it worked, the fear wore off. In this first battle, though, it had its psychological effect.

We made our preparations with great care, and on February 16 the attack took place. The communiqué published by our army in *El Cubano Libre*—which is reproduced at the end of this chapter—gives a fairly accurate summary of what happened.

The strategic plan was very simple: Fidel, knowing that there was an entire company in the sawmill, doubted that our troops could take the camp; our goal was to attack it, destroy their guard posts, surround it, and wait for their reinforcements, for we knew very well by then that soldiers on the march are much more vulnerable than quartered troops. We established various ambushes, expecting great results from them. At each one we stationed the number of men necessary to deal with the expected enemy strength.

The attack was directed personally by Fidel, whose general staff was on a hill to the north, commanding a clear view of the sawmill. In map no. 2 one can see the battle plan:[2] Camilo was to advance along the road which comes from Uvero, passing through the Bayamesa; his troops, the forward detachment platoon of Column no. 4, were to take the posts, advance as far as the terrain would permit, and hold on. The soldiers' retreat was to be met by Capt. Raúl Castro Mercader's platoon, situated on the edge of the road to Bayamo; in case the enemy tried to reach the Peladero river, Capt. Guillermo García with some twenty-five men were waiting for them.

When firing started, our mortar, which had exactly six shells and was operated by Quiala, was to come into action; then the siege would begin. An ambush led by Lt. Vilo Acuña on the Loma de la Virgen would aim at intercepting the troops coming from Uvero; and farther away, to the north, waiting for the troops who would come from Yao by way of Vega de los Jobos, was Lalo Sardiñas with some lightly armed men.

In this ambush we tested a special type of mine for the first time, with results that were far from encouraging. Comrade Antonio Estévez (later killed during an attack on Bayamo) had contrived a system for exploding undetonated airplane bombs, using a gunshot as detonator. We installed the device, foreseeing that the army would advance through that area, where we

2. See the sketch on the following page.

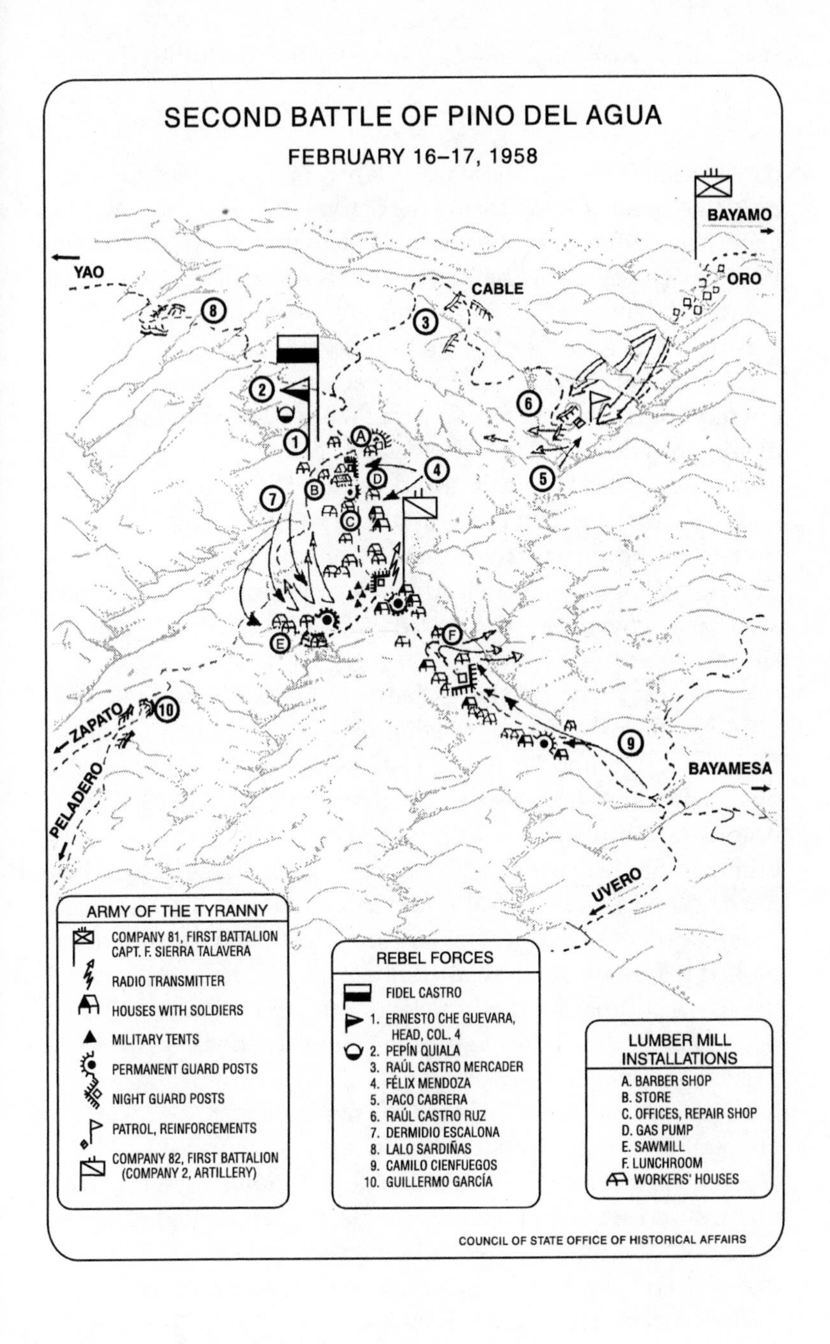
SECOND BATTLE OF PINO DEL AGUA
FEBRUARY 16–17, 1958
BAYAMO
YAO
ORO
CABLE
ZAPATO
PELADERO
BAYAMESA
UVERO
ARMY OF THE TYRANNY
COMPANY 81, FIRST BATTALION
CAPT. F. SIERRA TALAVERA
RADIO TRANSMITTER
HOUSES WITH SOLDIERS
MILITARY TENTS
PERMANENT GUARD POSTS
NIGHT GUARD POSTS
PATROL, REINFORCEMENTS
COMPANY 82, FIRST BATTALION
(COMPANY 2, ARTILLERY)
REBEL FORCES
FIDEL CASTRO
1. ERNESTO CHE GUEVARA, HEAD, COL. 4
2. PEPÍN QUIALA
3. RAÚL CASTRO MERCADER
4. FÉLIX MENDOZA
5. PACO CABRERA
6. RAÚL CASTRO RUZ
7. DERMIDIO ESCALONA
8. LALO SARDIÑAS
9. CAMILO CIENFUEGOS
10. GUILLERMO GARCÍA
LUMBER MILL INSTALLATIONS
A. BARBER SHOP
B. STORE
C. OFFICES, REPAIR SHOP
D. GAS PUMP
E. SAWMILL
F. LUNCHROOM
WORKERS' HOUSES
COUNCIL OF STATE OFFICE OF HISTORICAL AFFAIRS

had so little strength. There was a lamentable mistake: the comrade in charge of announcing the arrival of the enemy, very inexperienced and nervous, gave the signal at the moment a civilian truck was approaching; the mine worked, and the driver became the innocent victim of this new weapon, which, after it was developed further, was to be so effective.

At dawn on February 16 Camilo advanced to take the posts; but our guides had not foreseen that the guards would pull back during the night until they were very close to the camp, so there was quite a delay before the attack began. The men thought they had come to the wrong place, and each step was made very cautiously without realizing what the enemy had done. It took Camilo and his twenty men advancing in single file no less than an hour to cover the five hundred meters between the two positions.

Finally they reached the settlement; the enemy had installed a simple alarm system consisting of some string with tin cans tied to it, at ground level. The cans would rattle when stepped on or when the string was touched. But they had also left some horses grazing, so that when the column's advance guard bumped into the string, this was confused with the noise of the horses. Thus, Camilo was able to get right up close to the soldiers.

On the other side, our vigil was anxiety-ridden because hours passed before the long-awaited attack began. Finally we heard the first shot that marked the beginning of the battle, and we opened with a bombardment—the six mortar shells—that ended very soon, uneventfully.

The enemy had seen or heard the first attackers, and with the burst of gunfire that initiated the battle they wounded Comrade [Ángel] Guevara, who later died in our hospital. In a few minutes Camilo's forces had wiped out the resistance, taking eleven weapons (among them two light machine guns) and three prisoners, in addition to leaving seven or eight dead. But resistance in the barracks was immediately organized, and our attacks were held off.

Lieutenants Noda and Capote and the fighter Raimundo Liens

died one after another while attempting to advance; Camilo was wounded in the thigh; and Virelles had to retreat, abandoning the machine gun he had been manning. Despite his wound, Camilo continued to fire, attempting to rescue the weapon. In the dawn's first light, caught in a hail of fire, he was wounded again, but luckily the bullet that penetrated his abdomen left his body through the side without touching any vital organs. While Camilo was being rescued, with the machine gun lost, another comrade named Luis Macías was wounded and dragged himself through the bushes in the opposite direction from his comrades' line of retreat, and there he died. Some isolated fighters, from positions close to the garrison, were bombarding it with the "sputniks," or M-26s, sowing confusion among the soldiers. Guillermo García could not participate at all in this battle, since the soldiers made no attempt to leave their refuge; as we had foreseen, they immediately radioed for help.

At midmorning the situation was calm throughout the region, but from our command post we heard some shouts that filled us with anxiety, something like: "There goes Camilo's machine gun," followed by a volley. Along with the abandoned tripod machine gun, Camilo had left his hat, which had his name written on the back, and the enemy soldiers were making fun of us. We sensed that something had happened, but throughout the entire day we could not make contact with the troops on the other side. Camilo, attended by Sergio del Valle, refused to retreat, and they remained there awaiting further developments.

Fidel's predictions were coming true: the company led by Captain Sierra sent its forward unit from Oro de Guisa to scout out what was happening at Pino del Agua. Paco Cabrera's entire platoon was waiting for them, some thirty or thirty-five men stationed by the roadside on the hill called El Cable because there was a cable to help vehicles make the difficult climb.

Our squads were posted under the command of Lieutenants Suñol, Álamo, Reyes, and William Rodríguez; Paco Cabrera was also there as leader of the platoon, but the people in charge of holding off the forward units were Paz and Duque, who faced the road. The small enemy force advanced and was completely destroyed: eleven dead, five wounded prisoners who were treated in a house and left there; Second Lieutenant Laferté, who today is one of us, was taken prisoner; twelve rifles were captured, among them two M-1s and a machine gun as well as a Johnson.

One or two soldiers who were able to flee reached Oro de Guisa with the news. On hearing of this, the soldiers in Oro de Guisa must have asked for help. But between Guisa and Oro de Guisa was precisely where Raúl Castro was posted with all his forces, since that was where we had assumed the enemy would arrive to relieve the besieged men at Pino del Agua.

Raúl organized his men so that Félix Pena and the advance unit would close off the road to enemy reinforcements, and then his squad, together with that of Ciro Frías and the one commanded by Raúl, would immediately attack the enemy, while Efigenio would close the encirclement in the rear.

One detail went unnoticed at that moment: two inoffensive and bewildered peasants, who passed all our positions with roosters under their arms, turned out to be soldiers from Oro de Guisa who had been sent to explore the road. They were able to observe our troops' positions, and they reported to their comrades in Guisa. As a result, Raúl had to bear the brunt of the army's offensive, since they knew his position. They attacked him from a height they had taken, and Raúl had to make a long retreat, during which one man, Florentino Quesada, was killed, and another was wounded.

The road from Bayamo, passing through Oro de Guisa, was the only route taken by the army in its attempt to advance. Although Raúl was obliged to retreat, given his disadvantaged position, the enemy troops advanced very slowly along the road and did not appear during the whole day. Map no. 4 shows the approximate maneuver.[3]

That day we suffered constant attack by the army's B-26s,

3. Shown in the upper right-hand corner of the battle sketch on page 293.

which strafed the hills with no greater result than inconveniencing us and obliging us to take certain precautions.

Fidel was euphoric over the battle. At the same time, he was worried about the fate of our comrades, and at various times he took greater risks than he should have. As a result, days later a group of officers and I sent him the letter inserted at the end of the chapter asking him on behalf of the revolution not to risk his life needlessly. This rather infantile letter, which was inspired by the most altruistic motives, did not, I believe, warrant even a reading on his part, and needless to say, he did not pay the slightest attention to it.

That night I insisted that an attack of the type Camilo had carried out was possible, and we could overcome the guards who were posted in Pino del Agua. Fidel was not in favor of the idea, but he finally agreed to try it, sending a force under the command of [Dermidio] Escalona, composed of the platoons led by Ignacio Pérez and Raúl Castro Mercader. The comrades approached and did everything possible to reach the garrison, but they were repelled by heavy fire and retreated without trying to attack again. I asked to be given command of the force, and Fidel granted this, grudgingly.

My idea was to get as close as possible and, with Molotov cocktails made with gasoline from the sawmill itself, set fire to the wooden houses and compel the men to surrender or at least to come pouring out to face our fire. As we approached the battle site and prepared to take positions, I received this short note from Fidel:

"February 16, 1958. CHE: If everything depends on the attack from this side, without support from Camilo and Guillermo, I do not think anything suicidal should be done, because there is a risk of many casualties and failure to achieve the objective. I seriously urge you to be careful. You yourself are not to take part in the fighting: that is a strict order. Take charge of leading the men well; that is the most important thing right now. Fidel."

Furthermore, Almeida, who had brought the message, told me verbally that I could attack on my own responsibility, according to the terms of the note, but that he, Fidel, was not in agreement. The strict order not to enter into combat; the likelihood, if not the certainty, that several fighters would be killed; the uncertainty of taking the garrison; and not knowing the placement of Guillermo's and Camilo's isolated forces—with all this responsibility weighing on my shoulders, it was too much, and crestfallen, I took the same path as my predecessor Escalona.

The following morning, amid continual aerial incursions, the order for a general retreat was given. After a few shots aimed by telescopic sight at the soldiers who were beginning to leave their shelters, we began to retreat along the ridge of the Sierra Maestra.

As can be noted in the official dispatch that we issued at the time, the enemy suffered from 18 to 22 dead, and we captured 33 rifles, 5 machine guns, and abundant ammunition. To the list of casualties must be added the name of Luis Macías, whose fate was not known at the time, and other comrades such as Luis Olazábal and Quiroga, wounded in different actions of the prolonged battle. In the newspaper *El Mundo* of February 19 the following dispatch appeared:

> EL MUNDO, WEDNESDAY FEBRUARY 19, 1958—Loss of 16 Insurgents and 5 Soldiers Is Reported.—Not Known if Guevara Was Wounded.—The army's general staff issued a communiqué at five o'clock yesterday afternoon denying that an important battle with the rebels had taken place at Pino del Agua, south of Bayamo. It was admitted in the official report that "there have been one or two skirmishes between army reconnaissance patrols and groups of insurgents," and also that at the time of the report, "the rebels' casualties rose to sixteen, while the army as a result of the skirmishes had five casualties." As for whether the well-known Argentine communist Che Guevara was wounded, adds the communiqué, this has not been confirmed at present. Concerning the presence of the insurrectional leader at those encounters, nothing has been confirmed, but it is known that he remains hidden in the intricate caves of the Sierra Maestra.

A little later, or perhaps even at that moment, there was the massacre of Oro de Guisa carried out by Sosa Blanco, the assassin who in the first days of January 1959 was to die before a firing squad.

While the dictatorship could confirm only that Fidel "remains hidden in the intricate caves of the Sierra Maestra," the troops under his personal command begged him not to risk his life needlessly, and the enemy army did not climb up to our bases. Some time later Pino del Agua was cleared, and thus we completed the liberation of the western part of the Sierra Maestra.

A few days after this battle, there occurred one of the most important actions of the struggle: Column no. 3, under Commander Almeida, headed toward the region of Santiago, and the "Frank País" Column no. 6, under Cmdr. Raúl Castro Ruz, crossed the eastern plains, penetrated the Mangos de Baraguá, went on to Pinares de Mayarí, and later formed the "Frank País" Second Eastern Front.

Report on battle of Pino del Agua from *El Cubano Libre*

Pino del Agua is a settlement at the summit of the Sierra Maestra, next to the Bayamesa peak. It was defended by the company led by Captain Guerra, which was entrenched and well fortified. It is the army's farthest point of advance in the Sierra Maestra. The objective of the attack was not to capture the sawmill, but to create an encirclement that would force the army to send reinforcements. The situation of the nearest troops was as follows: in San Pablo de Yao was the company of Sánchez Mosquera, some twelve kilometers from the sawmill. In Oro was the company of Captain Sierra, about six kilometers away. Twenty-five kilometers away was Uvero, with a navy garrison. The other locations from which reinforcements were expected were Guisa and Bayamo. Our forces were at each of the roads leading to Pino del Agua from these places, waiting to intercept them.

At 5:30 A.M. on February 16, the attack was begun by forces

of Column no. 4 under the command of Capt. Camilo Cienfuegos. The attack was led in such a violent manner that the posts were taken without difficulty, causing the enemy eight dead, four prisoners, and a number of wounded. At that moment, the enemy's resistance intensified, causing the deaths on our side of Lts. Gilberto Capote and Enrique Noda and of Comrade Raimundo Liens. Comrade Ángel Guevara was badly wounded and died several days later in one of our field hospitals.

The encirclement continued for an entire day. Forces from Oro arrived, a total of sixteen men, for reconnaissance in the direction of Pino del Agua. These forces were taken by surprise and totally annihilated; three wounded prisoners were captured but were left behind in the houses of peasants because of the impossibility of transporting them. The head of the column, 2d Lt. Evelio Laferté, was taken prisoner. Only two men, apparently wounded, were able to escape; the rest were killed in action.

Our forces defending the roads from Yao and Uvero had to remain inactive since these troops did not move from their bases. The column led by Cmdr. Raúl Castro Ruz was forced to engage in combat under very critical circumstances. His men were unable to fire on the enemy, since they were advancing behind a shield of peasant women and children. In this action Comrade Florentino Quesada was killed. The number of losses suffered by the army is not known.

Hours after the withdrawal of Cmdr. Raúl Castro's column, the army advanced on our positions. Remaining there were a group of terrorized and defenseless peasants who had sought refuge in some huts to escape the battle. All the refuge seekers were ordered out and then machine-gunned in cold blood. Thirteen individuals were killed, the majority of them women and children. Those wounded in this "victorious" action by the army were attended to in Bayamo, and they are the ones listed in the first unofficial communiqués on the battle.

Despite the mistiness of the day, during the entire battle, planes strafed positions occupied by our forces, causing no harm. On the middle of February 17, our forces withdrew from

Pino del Agua, ending the action with a new attack on Oro by elements of Column no. 6. The results of this encounter on the enemy's part are not known; our forces suffered no casualties.

The final tally is as follows: the enemy suffered between eighteen and twenty-five dead, a similar number of wounded, and five prisoners. These are 2d Lt. Evelio Laferté; soldiers Erasmo Yera, Francisco Travieso Camacho, Ceferino Adrían Trujillo, and Bernardo San Bartolomé Martínez Carral (the last of whom was wounded). Thirty-three rifles, five machine guns, and a large amount of ammunition was seized. Our troops suffered the casualties mentioned above, plus three men slightly wounded, one of them being Capt. Camilo Cienfuegos.

Not all of the ambitious plans conceived by our general staff were realized, but a total victory over the army was achieved. We dealt a further blow to their already slipping combat morale and demonstrated to the entire nation the growing power of the revolution and of our revolutionary army, which is preparing to come down onto the plains to continue its series of victories.

Sierra Maestra, February 1958

Letter to Fidel Castro

Sierra Maestra, February 19, 1958

Commander
Dr. Fidel Castro
Dear comrade:

As an urgent necessity, and under the pressure of prevailing circumstances, the officers and responsible personnel in our ranks wish to inform you of the concerns of the troops with regard to your participation in combat.

We implore you to abandon the practice you have always had, which unintentionally endangers the success of our armed struggle and, more importantly, your goal of a true revolution.

Please be advised that this is far from being a sectarian effort on our part that seeks to assert anything. Our only unflagging concern, at all times, is the justified affection and esteem, love of country, of our cause, and of our ideas.

We are sure that you—who are free of all forms of self-adulation—understand the responsibility that rests on your shoulders and the dreams and hopes placed in you by the generations of the past, the present, and the future. In light of all this, we beg you to accept this imperative plea, which is somewhat bold, and perhaps demands too much. But we do so for Cuba. For the sake of Cuba, we ask one more sacrifice from you.

Your brothers in struggle and ideas,

Che
J. Almeida
Celia Sánchez
R. Castro Ruz
Ciro Frías
J. Martínez Páez
S. Valle
Machado
Luis Crespo
Félix Pena
Efigenio Ameijeiras
Luis Orlando Rodríguez
Marín
Universo Sánchez
José Quiala
Idelfredo Figueredo Río
Marcos Borrero
Horacio Rodríguez
Calixto García M.
R. Jiménez Lage
Paco Cabrera
Guillermo García
Ignacio Pérez
M. Fajardo
Vitalio Acuña
Ramiro Valdés
Ochoa
Eduardo Sardiñas
Camilo Cienfuegos
Raúl Castro M.
José Sotomayor
Ernesto Casillas
Fernando Virelles Iñiguez
Abelardo Colomé Ibarra
Humberto Rodríguez Díaz
J. Diz
Hermes Cardero
Olvein Botello
F. Villegas
Armando Velis

PUBLISHED IN VERDE OLIVO, JANUARY 19, 1964

APRIL 1958

Interlude

IN THE MONTHS OF APRIL AND JUNE 1958 both a flow and an ebb in the insurrectional wave could be seen.

Beginning in February, after the battle at Pino del Agua, the crest gradually swelled until it threatened to become a tidal wave. The people were rising in insurrection against the dictatorship throughout the country, and particularly in Oriente province. After the failure of the [April 9] general strike called by the July 26 Movement, the wave subsided until it reached its lowest point in June, when the dictatorship's troops more and more tightened their encirclement of Column no. 1.

In the first days of April, Camilo had left the protection of the Sierra going toward the region of the Cauto river, where he would be appointed commander of the "Antonio Maceo" Column no. 2 and would carry out a series of impressive feats in the plains of Oriente. Camilo was the first commander who went down to the plains to fight with the morale and effectiveness of the army of the Sierra, putting the dictatorship in hard straits until several days after the April 9 failure, when he returned to the Sierra Maestra.

Taking advantage of the situation, during the height of the revolutionary wave, a whole series of camps were set up, composed of some people who were yearning to fight and others who were thinking only of keeping their uniforms clean so as to enter Havana in triumph. After April 9, when the dictatorship's counteroffensive began to step up, those groups either disappeared or joined the Sierra forces.

Morale fell so much that the army considered it opportune to offer pardons, and it prepared some leaflets, which it dropped by air in the rebel zones. The leaflets read:

> Compatriots: If, by having gotten yourself involved in insurrectional plots, you are still in the countryside or in the mountains, now you have the opportunity to make amends and return to your family.
>
> The government has issued orders to offer respect for your life and send you home if you lay down your weapons and abide by the law.
>
> Report to the governor of the province, the mayor of your municipality, the friendly congressman, the nearest military, navy, or police post, or to any ecclesiastic authority.
>
> If you are in a rural area, come with your weapon on one shoulder and with your hands up.
>
> If you come forward in an urban zone, leave your weapon hidden in a safe place, so that it may be collected immediately after you report it.
>
> Do so without wasting time because the operations for total pacification will continue with greater intensity in the area where you are.

Later they published photos of people who had turned themselves in, some real, others not. What was clear was that the counterrevolutionary wave was growing. In the end, it would crash against the peaks of the Sierra, but at the end of April and the beginning of May, it was in full ascent.

Our mission, in the first phase of the period we are discussing, was to hold the front occupied by Column no. 4, which extended to the outskirts of the village of Minas de Bueycito. Sánchez Mosquera was quartered there, and our struggle consisted of fleeting clashes without either side risking a decisive battle. At night we would fire our M-26s at them, but they already knew the scant killing power of that weapon and had simply put up a large wire-mesh netting where the TNT charges exploded in their shells of condensed milk cans, causing only a lot of noise.

Our camp was eventually set up about two kilometers from Las Minas, in a place called La Otilia, in the house of a local landowner. From there we kept watch on Sánchez Mosquera's movements, and there were odd skirmishes every day. The henchmen would go out at dawn, burning the peasants' huts, looting all their belongings, and withdrawing before we intervened. At other times, they would attack some of our rifle units scattered through the area, making them flee. Any peasant suspected of an understanding with us was murdered.

I have never been able to find out why Sánchez Mosquera allowed us to be comfortably settled in a house, in a relatively flat area with little vegetation, without calling the enemy air force to attack us. Our guess was that he was not interested in fighting and that he did not want to let the air force see how close the troops were, because he would then have to explain why he did not attack. Nevertheless, there were repeated skirmishes, as I have said, between our forces.

One of those days I left with an aide to see Fidel, who was then located in El Jíbaro. It was a long walk, practically a whole day's journey. After spending a day with Fidel, we left the following day to return to our camp in La Otilia. For some reason that I do not remember, my aide had to stay behind and I had to accept a new guide. Part of the route ran along a roadway, and later we entered farmland covered with rolling pastures. In this last leg of the trip, already near the house, a strange spectacle presented itself by the light of a full moon that clearly illuminated the surroundings: in one of those rolling fields, with scattered palm trees, there appeared a row of dead mules, some with their harnesses on.

When we got down from our horses to examine the first mule and saw the bullet holes, the guide's expression as he looked at me was an image out of a cowboy movie. The hero of the film arrives with his partner and sees a horse killed by an arrow. He says something like, "The Sioux," and makes a special face for the occasion. That's what the man's face was like and perhaps my own as well, although I did not bother to look at myself. A few meters further on was the second, then the third, then the fourth or fifth dead mule. It had been a convoy of supplies for us, captured by one of Sánchez Mosquera's expeditions. I seem to recall that a civilian was also murdered. The guide refused to follow me. He claimed he did not know the terrain and simply got on his mount. We separated amicably.

I had a Beretta, and with it cocked, taking the horse by the reins, I went on into the first coffee field. When I reached the abandoned house, a loud noise startled me to such an extent that I almost fired, but it was only a pig, also frightened by my presence. Slowly, and very cautiously, I covered the few hundred meters left to reach our position, which I found totally abandoned. After much searching, I found a comrade who had stayed behind sleeping in the house.

Universo [Sánchez], who had remained in command of the troops, had ordered the house evacuated, foreseeing some nighttime or dawn attack. As our troops were well spread out defending the place, I lay down to sleep with my lone companion. That whole scene has no significance for me other than the satisfaction I experienced at having overcome fear during a journey that seemed eternal until at last, alone, I reached the command post. That night I felt brave.

But the toughest confrontation with Sánchez Mosquera took place in a very small village or hamlet called Santa Rosa. As always, at dawn we were advised that Sánchez Mosquera was there, and we headed quickly to the place. I had a touch of asthma and therefore was riding a bay horse with whom I had made good friends. The fighting spread out over various places in a fragmented manner. I had to abandon my mount. With the group of men that was with me, we took up positions on a small hill, scattering ourselves at two or three different heights. The enemy was firing some mortars, without very good aim.

For a moment, the shooting got more intense to my right, and I set off to check the positions, but halfway there it also began on my left. I sent my aide off to I-don't-know-where, and I remained alone, between the two extremes of fire. To my left, Sánchez Mosquera's forces, after firing some mortar shells, climbed the hill amid tremendous shouting. Our people, with little experience, managed to fire only one or two isolated shots, and took off running down the hill. Alone, in an open field, I saw soldiers' helmets begin to appear. A henchman began to run down the hill in pursuit of our fighters, who were heading into the coffee fields. I fired my Beretta at him, missed, and immediately several rifles found me and opened fire. I began a zigzagging race, carrying 1,000 bullets in an awesome leather cartridge belt on my shoulders, greeted by the contemptuous shouts of some enemy soldiers. As I got close to the shelter of the trees, my pistol fell. My only insolent gesture of that sad morning was to stop, retrace my steps, pick up the pistol, and take off running, greeted this time by the small dust clouds that the rifle bullets kicked up like darts around me.

When I felt I was out of danger, without knowing about my comrades or the result of the offensive, I stayed resting, barricaded behind a large rock in the middle of the woods. My asthma, mercifully, had let me run a few meters, but it was taking its vengeance and my heart was jumping inside my chest. I heard branches being broken by people approaching, but it was no longer possible to keep fleeing (which was what I really felt like doing). This time it was another comrade of ours, lost, a recruit who had recently joined our troop. His words of consolation were more or less: "Don't worry, commander, I'll die with you." I had no desire to die, although I did feel tempted to say something about his mother. I don't think I did. That day I felt cowardly.

That night we pieced together all the events. A magnificent comrade—Mariño was his last name—had been killed in one of the skirmishes. Other than that the result was very poor for the enemy. The body of a peasant shot through the mouth, murdered who-knows-why, was all that remained in the army's abandoned positions. There, with a small box camera, the Argentine journalist Jorge Ricardo Masetti, who was visiting us in the Sierra for the first time and with whom I would later maintain a deep and lasting friendship, took a photograph of the murdered peasant.

After those battles we withdrew a bit further back from La Otilia, but I was already being replaced as commander of Column no. 4 by Ramiro Valdés, who had been promoted. I left the area, accompanied by a small group of fighters, to take charge of the school for recruits, which was to train the men who would have to make the crossing from Oriente to Las Villas.[1] Moreover, we had to prepare for what was already imminent: the army's offensive. All the following days, at the end of April and early May, were devoted to preparing the points of defense and trying to bring the largest possible quantity of food and medicine up to the hills to be able to resist what we already saw coming: a large-scale offensive.

As a parallel task, we were trying to collect a tax on the sugar plantation owners and cattle ranchers. In those days Remigio Fernández went up to see us; he was a wealthy cattle rancher who offered us the moon and the stars, but he forgot his promises when he reached the plains.

The sugar plantation owners did not give us anything either. But later, when our strength was solid, we got even, although we spent those days of the offensive without the necessary elements for our defense.

A short time later, Camilo was summoned to better protect our small territory, which contained countless riches: a radio station,

1. In April 1958 Guevara helped establish a Rebel Army school for recruits at Minas del Frío in the Sierra Maestra. Participants received military training under the supervision of Evelio Laferté, the lieutenant in Batista's army captured at the second battle of Pino del Agua and who had joined the Rebel Army. Literacy classes and political instruction were part of the curriculum as well. Following the arrival of Column no. 8 in Las Villas in October 1958, Guevara established another school at Caballete de Casa.

hospitals, munitions depots, and, on top of that, an airstrip located among the hills of La Plata, where a light plane could land.

Fidel maintained the principle that what mattered was not the enemy soldiers, but the number of fighters we needed to make a position invulnerable and that this was what we should rely on. That was our tactic, and that's why all our forces were being gathered around the command post to form a compact front. There were not many more than two hundred usable rifles when the anticipated offensive began on May 25, in the midst of a meeting Fidel was having with some peasants, discussing the conditions under which the coffee harvest could be carried out, since the army did not allow day laborers to go up to pick the crop.

He had called together some 350 peasants, who were very interested in resolving their crop problems. Fidel had proposed creating a Sierra currency to pay the workers, to bring the straw and the bags for packing, to set up producer and consumer cooperatives and a supervisory commission. Moreover, he offered the Rebel Army's help for the harvest. Everything was approved, but just as Fidel himself was about to end the meeting, machine gun fire began. The enemy army had clashed with Capt. Ángel Verdecia's men, and its air force was punishing the area.

PUBLISHED IN VERDE OLIVO, AUGUST 23, 1964

MAY 1958

A decisive meeting

THROUGHOUT THE ENTIRE DAY OF MAY 3, 1958, a meeting, practically unknown until now, took place in the Sierra Maestra, in Altos de Mompié. This gathering, nonetheless, was of extraordinary importance in guiding our revolutionary strategy. From the early hours of the day until two o'clock the following morning, the meeting analyzed the consequences of the April 9 failure and why that defeat took place. It also took the necessary measures to reorganize the July 26 Movement and to overcome the weaknesses resulting from the dictatorship's victory.

Although I was not a member of the National Directorate, I was invited to participate in the meeting at the request of Comrades Faustino Pérez and René Ramos Latour (Daniel), whom I had strongly criticized earlier. In addition to those named, also present were Fidel, Vilma Espín (Débora in the underground), Ñico Torres, Luis Buch, Celia Sánchez, Marcelo Fernández (Zoilo at that time), Haydée Santamaría, David Salvador, and Enzo Infante (Bruno), who joined us at midday. The gathering was tense, since it had to judge the actions of the Llano comrades, who in practice had run the affairs of the July 26 Movement up to that moment.

At this meeting decisions were taken that confirmed Fidel's moral authority, his indisputable stature, and the conviction among the majority of revolutionaries present that errors of judgment had been committed. The Llano leadership had underestimated the enemy's strength and subjectively overestimated their own, without taking into account the methods necessary to unleash their forces. But most importantly, the meeting discussed and passed judgment on two conceptions that had clashed with each other throughout the whole previous stage of directing the war. The guerrilla conception would emerge triumphant from that meeting. Fidel's standing and authority were consolidated, and he was named commander in chief of all forces, including the militias—which until then had been under Llano leadership. Fidel was also named general secretary of the July 26 Movement.

There were many heated exchanges as the meeting analyzed each person's participation in the events under discussion. But perhaps the most violent debate was the one with the workers representatives, who were opposed to any participation by the Popular Socialist Party in the organization of the struggle. The analysis of the strike demonstrated that subjectivism and putschist conceptions permeated its preparation and execution. The formidable apparatus that the July 26 Movement seemed to have in its hands, in the form of organized workers cells, fell apart the moment the action took place. The adventurist policy of the workers leaders had failed in the face of an inexorable reality. But they were not the only ones responsible for the defeat. Our opinion was that the largest share of the blame fell on David Salvador, the workers delegate; on Faustino Pérez, who was responsible for Havana; and on the leader of the Llano militias, René Ramos Latour.

Salvador's fault was having held and put into practice his conception of a sectarian strike, in which the other revolutionary movements would be forced to follow our lead. Faustino's error was his lack of perspective in thinking that it would be possible to seize the capital with his militias, without closely examining the forces of reaction inside their principal bastion. Daniel was criticized for the same lack of vision but specifically in relation to the Llano militias, which were organized as parallel troops to ours, but without the training or the combat morale, and without having gone through the rigorous process of selection in the war.

The division between the Sierra and the Llano was a real one. There was a certain objective basis for it, due to the higher level of maturity achieved over the course of the guerrilla struggle by the Sierra representatives and the lower level of maturity of the fighters from the Llano. But there was another extremely important element, something that might be called occupational deformity. The comrades of the Llano had to work in their environment, and little by little they became accustomed to viewing the work methods required under those conditions as the ideal ones and as the only ones possible for the Movement. Moreover, logically enough from a human standpoint, they began to view the Llano as having a greater relative importance than the Sierra.

After the failures in confronting the dictatorship's forces, there now arose only one authoritative leadership, the Sierra, and concretely one single leader, one commander in chief, Fidel Castro. At the end of an exhaustive and often violent discussion, the meeting resolved to relieve Faustino Pérez of his duties, replacing him with [Delio Gómez] Ochoa, and to relieve David Salvador of his responsibilities, replacing him with Ñico Torres. (This last change did not amount to a substantive step forward as far as the conception of the struggle was concerned. For when the meeting raised the need for unity of all working-class forces to prepare the next revolutionary general strike, which would be called from the Sierra, Ñico expressed his readiness to work in a disciplined manner with the "Stalinists," but said that he did not think this would lead to anything. He referred in those terms to the comrades of the Popular Socialist Party.) The third change, regarding Daniel, did not lead to a replacement, since Fidel directly became commander in chief of the Llano's militias.

The meeting also decided to send Haydée Santamaría to Miami as a special agent of the July 26 Movement, putting her in charge of finances in the exile community. In the political sphere, the National Directorate was to be moved to the Sierra Maestra, where Fidel would occupy the post of general secretary. A secretariat of five members was constituted with one person each in charge of finances, political affairs, and workers affairs. I don't remember now who the comrades assigned to these positions were. But everything related to arms shipments—or decisions about arms—and foreign relations would from then on be the responsibility of the general secretary. The three comrades relieved of their duties were to go to the Sierra, where David Salvador would hold a post as workers delegate and Faustino and Daniel would be commanders. The latter was given command of a column that participated actively in the fighting against the army's final offensive, which was about to be unleashed. He died at the head of his troops while attacking a retreating enemy column. His revolutionary career earned him a place in the select list of our martyrs.

Faustino asked for and obtained authorization to return to Havana and take care of a number of the Movement's affairs, to hand over the leadership, and later reintegrate himself into the struggle in the Sierra. This he did, finishing the war in the "José Martí" Column no. 1 commanded by Fidel Castro. Although history must relate the events just as they occurred, it is necessary to make clear the high opinion we always have had of this comrade, who at a given point was our adversary within the Movement. Faustino was always considered an irreproachably honest comrade, and he was daring to the extreme. I was an eyewitness to his fearlessness, the time he set fire to a plane that had brought us weapons from Miami but had been spotted by enemy aircraft and was damaged. Under machine gun fire Faustino carried out the necessary operation to prevent it from falling into the army's hands, setting it alight while the gasoline poured out through the bullet holes. His whole history gives evidence to his revolutionary mettle.

At that meeting other decisions of lesser importance were made, and a whole series of obscure aspects of our reciprocal relations were clarified. We heard a report by Marcelo Fernández on the organization of the Movement in the cities, and he was assigned to prepare another report for the Movement's cells, detailing the results and decisions of the National Directorate's meeting. We also heard a report on the organization of the Civic Resistance Movement, its formation, its methods of work, its components, and how to broaden and strengthen them.

Comrade Buch reported on the Committee in Exile, on Mario Llerena's halfhearted position and his incompatibility with Urrutia. It was decided to ratify Urrutia as our Movement's candidate for president and transfer to him a stipend that until then Llerena had been receiving as the Movement's only full-time cadre in the exile community. In addition, the meeting decided that if Llerena continued his interference, he would be relieved of his position as chairman of the Committee in Exile. There were many problems abroad; in New York, for example, the groups of Barrón, Pérez Vidal, and Pablo Díaz worked separately, and at times clashed or interfered with each other. It was resolved that Fidel would send a letter to the emigrant and exile groups recognizing the Committee in Exile of the July 26 Movement as the sole official body.

The meeting analyzed all the possibilities for support by the Venezuelan government headed at that time by Wolfgang Larrazábal. He had promised to support the Movement, which in fact he did. The only complaint we might have with Larrazábal was that along with a planeload of weapons he sent us the "distinguished" Manuel Urrutia Lleó. But actually it was we ourselves who had made such a deplorable choice.

Other agreements were reached during the meeting. In addition to Haydée Santamaría, who would go to Miami, Luis Buch was to travel to Caracas with precise instructions regarding Urrutia. Carlos Franqui was ordered to the Sierra to take charge of running Radio Rebelde. The contacts would be made by radio via Venezuela, through codes made up by Luis Buch that worked until the end of the war.

As can be appreciated from the decisions emanating from this meeting, it was of the highest importance. Various concrete problems of the Movement were finally clarified. In the first place, the war would be led militarily and politically by Fidel in his dual role as commander in chief of all forces and as general secretary of the organization. The line of the Sierra would be followed, that of direct armed struggle, extending it to other regions and in that way taking control of the country. We did away with various naive illusions about attempted revolutionary general strikes when the situation had not matured sufficiently to bring about such an explosion, and without having laid the necessary groundwork for an event of that magnitude.

In addition the leadership lay in the Sierra, which objectively eliminated some practical decision-making problems that had prevented Fidel from actually exercising the authority he had earned. In fact, this did nothing more than register a reality: the political predominance of the Sierra people, a consequence of their correct point of view and their accurate interpretation of events. The meeting confirmed the correctness of our earlier doubts: we had considered it likely that the Movement's forces would fail in attempting a revolutionary general strike, if carried out in the manner outlined at a meeting prior to April 9.

Certain very important tasks still remained: above all resisting the approaching offensive, since the army's forces were taking up positions in a ring around the revolution's principal bastion, the command post of Column no. 1, led by Fidel. Afterward, the tasks would include the invasion of the plains, the seizure of the central provinces, and finally, the destruction of the regime's entire political-military apparatus. It would take us seven months to complete those tasks in full.

What was most urgent at the time was to strengthen the Sierra front, and to assure that a small bastion could continue speaking to Cuba and sowing the revolutionary seed among our people. It was also important to maintain communications abroad. A few days earlier I had witnessed a radio conversation between Fidel and Justo Carrillo, who represented the Montecristi Group, that is, a group of aspiring military thugs including representatives of imperialism such as Carrillo himself and

Barquín. Justico offered the moon and the stars, but asked that Fidel make a declaration supporting the "pure" military men. Fidel answered that while this was not impossible, it would be difficult for our Movement to understand a call of this nature when our people were falling victim to soldiers of whom it was difficult to distinguish the good from the bad, since they were all lumped together. In short, the declaration was not made. Llerena was also spoken with, I seem to recall, as well as Urrutia. An attempt was made to issue a call for unity and to prevent the breakup of the flimsy grouping of disparate personalities who, from Caracas, were trying to capitalize on the armed movement for their own gain. Nonetheless, they represented our aspirations for international recognition, and we therefore had to tread carefully.

Immediately after the meeting the participants scattered. It was my task to inspect a whole series of zones, trying to create defensive lines with our small forces to resist the army's push. The really strong resistance would begin in the most mountainous areas, from the Caracas mountain, where the small and poorly armed groups of Crescencio Pérez would be located, to the zones of La Botella or La Mesa, where Ramiro Valdés's forces were distributed.

This small territory had to be defended, with not much more than two hundred functioning rifles, when a few days later Batista's army began its "encirclement and annihilation" offensive.

PUBLISHED IN VERDE OLIVO, NOVEMBER 22, 1964

MAY–DECEMBER 1958

From Batista's final offensive to the battle of Santa Clara

APRIL 9 WAS A RESOUNDING DEFEAT that never endangered the regime's stability. Not only that: after that tragic date, the government was able to transfer troops and gradually place them in Oriente province, bringing destruction to the Sierra Maestra. Our defense more and more had to be conducted from within the Sierra Maestra, and the government kept increasing the number of regiments it placed against our positions, until there were 10,000 men. With these forces it began the offensive on May 25 in the village of Las Mercedes, which was our forward position.

There, Batista's army gave proof of its poor combat effectiveness, and we showed our lack of resources; 200 usable rifles to fight against 10,000 weapons of all sorts. It was an enormous disadvantage. Our boys fought bravely for two days, with odds of 10 or 15 against 1; fighting moreover, against mortars, tanks, and aircraft, until the small group was forced to abandon the village. Our force was commanded by Capt. Ángel Verdecia, who one month later would courageously die in action.

By that time, Fidel Castro had received a letter from the traitor Eulogio Cantillo, who, true to his acrobatic politicking, wrote to the rebel leader as the enemy's chief of operations, saying that the offensive would be launched in any case, but asking "The Man" (Fidel) to watch out for himself, awaiting the final result. The offensive, in fact, ran its course, and in two and a half months of hard fighting, the enemy lost over 1,000 men, counting dead, wounded, prisoners, and deserters. They also left 600 weapons in our hands, including a tank, 12 mortars, 12 tripod machine guns, over 20 machine guns, and countless automatic weapons; also, an enormous amount of ammunition and equipment of all sorts, and 450 prisoners, who were handed over to the Red Cross when the campaign ended.

Batista's army came out of that last offensive in the Sierra Maestra with its spine broken, but it had not yet been defeated. The struggle would go on. It was then that the final strategy was established, attacking along three points: Santiago de Cuba, which was put under a flexible siege; Las Villas, where I was to go; and Pinar del Río, at the other end of the island, where Camilo Cienfuegos, who was now commander of the "Antonio Maceo" Column no. 2, was to march in remembrance of the historic invasion by the great leader of 1895, when Maceo crossed the length of Cuban territory with epic feats, culminating in Mantua. Camilo Cienfuegos was not able to fulfill the second part of his program, as the exigencies of the war forced him to remain in Las Villas.

Once the regiments that assaulted the Sierra Maestra had been wiped out, once the front had returned to its normal level, and once our troops had increased their strength and morale, it was decided to begin the march on the central province of Las Villas. My orders were that the main strategic task was to systematically cut off communications between the two ends of the island. I was also ordered to establish relations with all the political groups that might be in the mountains of that region, and I was given broad powers to militarily govern my assigned area.[1]

With those instructions and thinking that we would make the trip in four days, we were to begin our march, by truck, on August 30, 1958, when an unexpected accident upset our plans. That night a pickup truck was to arrive carrying uniforms and gasoline necessary for the vehicles that were ready; simultaneously, a cargo of arms also arrived, by air, at an airstrip near the road. The plane was sighted just as it landed, even though it

1. See the section on the Las Villas campaign, beginning on page 353.

was at night, and the airstrip was systematically bombed from 8:00 P.M. until 5:00 in the morning. At that time we set fire to the plane to prevent it from falling into the enemy's hands and to prevent the enemy from continuing the bombardment during the day, which would have been even worse for us. The enemy troops advanced on the airstrip, intercepting the pickup truck with the gasoline, and we were left on foot.

So it was that we began the march on August 31, without trucks or horses, hoping to find them later on after crossing the highway connecting Manzanillo to Bayamo. In fact, having crossed it we encountered the trucks, but also—on September 1—we were met by a fierce hurricane that made all roads impassable except for the Central Highway, the only paved one in that part of Cuba, forcing us to give up on using vehicles for transportation. From that moment on, we had to go on horseback or on foot. We were loaded down with quite a bit of ammunition, a bazooka with forty shells, and everything necessary for a long march and for rapidly establishing a camp.

One day after another went by, and they were already becoming difficult even though we were in the friendly territory of Oriente: crossing rivers that were overflowing, canals and streams that had become rivers; struggling with difficulty to prevent our ammunition, arms, and shells from getting wet; looking for horses and leaving the tired ones behind; avoiding inhabited areas as we moved away from the eastern province.

We walked though difficult flooded terrain, suffering attacks by swarms of mosquitoes that made the hours of rest unbearable, eating little and poorly, drinking water from swampy rivers or simply from swamps. Each day of travel more and more dragged out and became truly horrible. A week after we had left camp, by the time we crossed the Jobabo river, which marks the border between Oriente and Camagüey provinces, our forces were greatly weakened. This river, like all the previous ones and like those we would cross later, was flooded. We were also feeling the effects of lack of shoes among our troops, many of whom were walking barefoot through the swamps of southern Camagüey.

On the night of September 9, as we were approaching a place known as La Federal, our forward detachment fell into an enemy ambush, and two valuable comrades were killed.[2] But the most regrettable result was being spotted by the enemy forces, who from then on gave us no respite. After a brief clash, the small garrison there surrendered and we took four prisoners. Now we had to march very carefully, since the air force knew our approximate route. Thus, one or two days later, we reached a place known as Laguna Grande, together with Camilo's force, which was much better equipped than ours. This area is remarkable for its extraordinary number of mosquitoes, which made it absolutely impossible for us to rest outdoors without a mosquito net, which some of us did not have.

These were days of fatiguing marches through desolate expanses where there was only water and mud. We were hungry, thirsty, and could hardly move because our legs were as heavy as lead and the weapons were enormously heavy. We continued advancing with better horses that Camilo left for us when his column got on trucks, but we had to abandon them near the Macareño sugar mill. The guides they were supposed to send us did not arrive, and we set out on the adventure.

Our forward unit clashed with an enemy outpost at a place called Cuatro Compañeros, and the exhausting battle began. It was daybreak, and with great effort we managed to gather a large part of our troop in the largest woods in the area. But the army was advancing along its sides, and we had to fight hard to make it possible for some of our men, who had fallen behind, to cross a railroad line, toward the woods. The enemy planes sighted us then, and the B-26s, the C-47s, the big C-3 reconnaissance planes, and the light planes began bombing an area no more than two hundred meters wide. Finally, we withdrew, leaving one of our men killed by a bomb and carrying several wounded, including Captain Silva, who went through the rest of the invasion with a broken shoulder.

2. Marcos Borrero and Dalcio Gutiérrez.

The following day the picture was less discouraging, since many of those who had fallen behind showed up, and we managed to gather the whole troop, except for ten men who would continue on as members of Camilo's column and with him get as far as the northern front of Las Villas province, in Yaguajay.

Despite the difficulties, we were never without the encouragement of the peasants. We always found someone who would serve as a guide, or who would give us the food without which we could not go on. Naturally, it was not the unanimous support of the whole people we had enjoyed in Oriente, but there was always someone who helped us. At times we were reported to the enemy as soon as we crossed a farm, but that was not because of a direct action by the peasants against us. Rather it was because their living conditions made these people slaves of the landowner; fearful of losing their daily subsistence, they would report to their master that we had passed through that region. The latter in turn would take charge of graciously informing the military authorities.

One afternoon we were listening on our field radio to a report by Gen. Francisco Tabernilla Dolz. With all his thuggish bombast, he was announcing that the hordes led by Che Guevara had been destroyed and giving extensive details on the dead, the wounded, names, and all sorts of things, which were the product of the booty they took from our knapsacks after that disastrous encounter with the enemy a few days earlier. All of this was mixed in with false information cooked up by the army high command. This news of our demise produced great merriment among our troop. But pessimism was getting hold of them little by little. Hunger and thirst, weariness, the feeling of impotence against the enemy forces that were increasingly closing in on us, and above all, the terrible foot disease that the peasants call *mazamorra*—which turned each step our soldiers took into an intolerable torment—had made us an army of shadows. It was difficult to advance, very difficult. Our troop's physical condition worsened day by day, and the meals—today yes, tomorrow no, the next day maybe—in no way helped to alleviate the level of misery we were suffering.

We spent the hardest days surrounded in the vicinity of the Baraguá sugar mill in stinking swamps, without a drop of potable water, continuously attacked from the air, without a single horse that could carry the weakest through inhospitable swampland, with our shoes totally demolished by the muddy salt water, full of vegetation that injured our bare feet. Our situation was really disastrous when, with great difficulty, we broke out of the encirclement at Baraguá and reached the famous Júcaro-Morón trail, a historic spot, the scene of bloody fighting between patriots and the Spaniards during the war of independence.

We had no time to recover even a little. Another downpour, bad weather, on top of enemy attacks or reports of their presence, forced us to march on. The troop was increasingly tired and disheartened. When the situation was most tense, however, when insults, pleas, and sharp remarks of all sorts were the only way to get the weary men to advance, a sight far away in the distance lit up their faces and instilled new spirit in the guerrillas. That sight was a blue streak to the west, the blue streak of the Las Villas mountain range, seen by our men for the first time. From that moment on, the same hardships, or similar ones, became much more bearable, and everything seemed easier. We slipped through the last encirclement by swimming across the Júcaro river, which divides the provinces of Camagüey and Las Villas, and it seemed already that a new light was shining on us.

Two days later we were in the heart of the Trinidad–Sancti Spíritus mountain range, safe, ready to begin the next stage of the war. We rested for another two days, because we had to be on our way immediately and prepare ourselves to prevent the elections scheduled for November 3.[3] We had reached the mountain region of Las Villas on October 16. Time was short and the

3. The Batista regime had organized general elections for November 3, in an attempt to provide a legal cover to the dictatorship. The July 26 Movement called for a boycott and organized to obstruct the elections. Amid massive voter abstention, Batista's candidate for president, Andrés Rivero Agüero, was declared elected.

task was enormous. Camilo was doing his part in the north, sowing fear among the dictatorship's men.

Our task, upon arriving for the first time in the Escambray mountains, was well defined: we were to harass the dictatorship's military apparatus, above all its communications. And, as an immediate objective, we were to prevent the elections from taking place. But the task was made difficult because time was short, and because of the disunity among the revolutionary forces, which resulted in internal quarrels that cost us dearly, including in human lives.

Our job was to attack the neighboring towns to prevent the elections, and plans were worked out to do this simultaneously in the cities of Cabaiguán, Fomento, and Sancti Spíritus, in the rich plains of the center of the island. Meanwhile, the small garrison at Güinía de Miranda—in the mountains—surrendered, and later the Banao garrison was attacked with few results. The days prior to November 3, the date of the elections, were extraordinarily busy. Our columns were mobilized in all directions, almost totally preventing voters in those areas from going to the polls. Camilo Cienfuegos's troops in the northern part of the province paralyzed the electoral farce. In general, everything was halted, from the transport of Batista's soldiers to commercial traffic.

In Oriente, there was practically no voting; in Camagüey, the percentage was a bit higher; and in the western region, in spite of everything, mass abstention was clear. This abstention was achieved spontaneously in Las Villas, as there had not been time to synchronize the masses' passive resistance with the guerrillas' activity.

In Oriente successive battles were taking place on the first and second fronts, although also on the third—with the "Antonio Guiteras" Column—which was exerting more and more pressure on Santiago de Cuba, the provincial capital. Except for the seats of the municipalities, the government had nothing left in Oriente.

The situation was also becoming very serious in Las Villas,

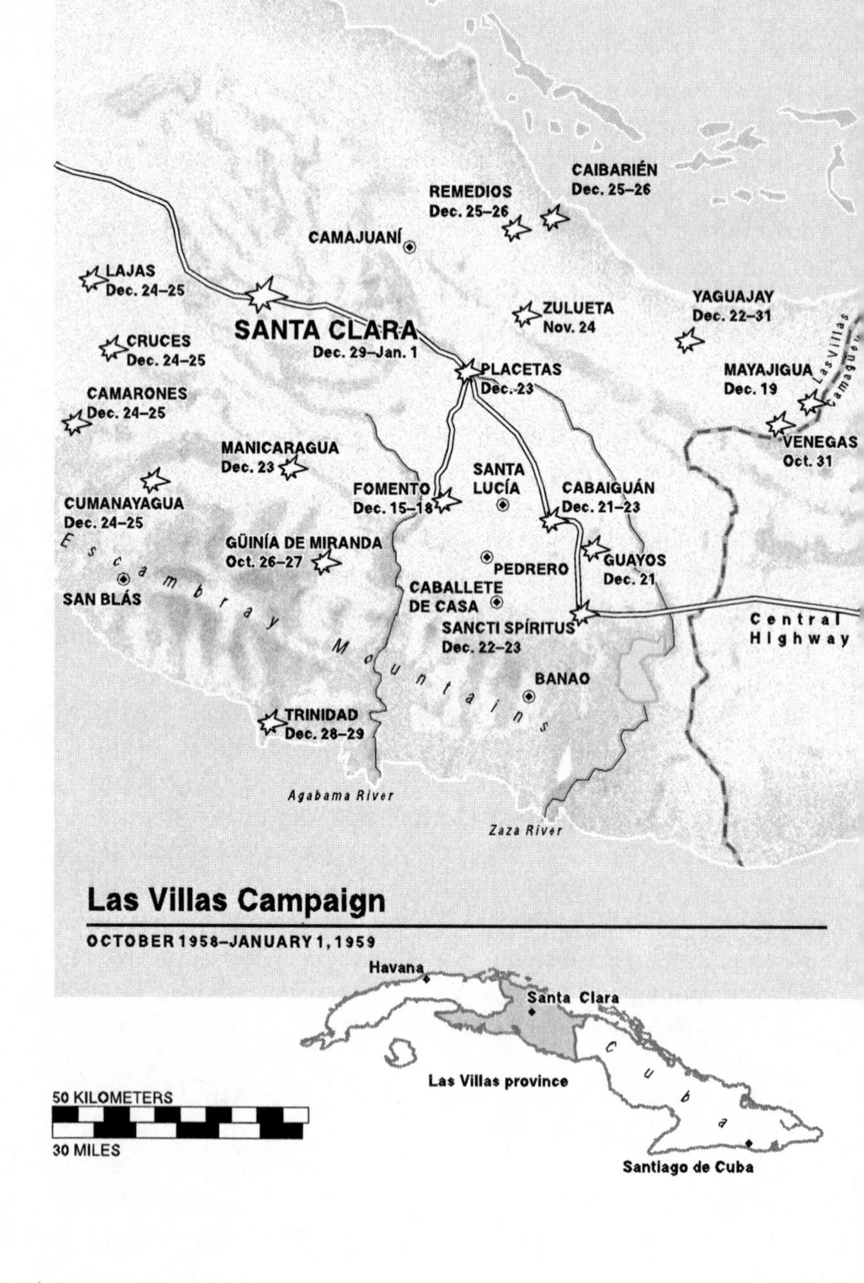

Las Villas Campaign

OCTOBER 1958–JANUARY 1, 1959

with stepped-up attacks on communications routes. Upon arriving, we completely changed the system of struggle in the cities, as we rapidly sent the best militia fighters from the cities to the training camp to receive instruction in sabotage, which proved effective in semiurban areas.

During the months of November and December 1958, we gradually closed the highways. Captain Silva totally blocked the highway from Trinidad to Sancti Spíritus, and the island's Central Highway was seriously damaged when the bridge across the Tuinicú river was dynamited, although it did not completely collapse. The central railroad was cut at several points. In addition, the southern route was cut by the Second Front, and the northern route was closed by Camilo Cienfuegos's troops, leaving the island divided in two. The region most in upheaval, Oriente, received aid from the government only by air and sea, and this too became increasingly uncertain. The symptoms of the enemy's disintegration were increasing.

An extremely intense campaign for revolutionary unity had to be carried out in the Escambray mountains, since a number of groups were operating there: the Second National Front of the Escambray led by Commander Gutiérrez Menoyo; a group organized by the Revolutionary Directorate, led by Cmdrs. Faure Chomón and Rolando Cubela; a smaller group of the Authentic Organization; a group of the Popular Socialist Party, commanded by Félix Torres; and us. In other words, there were five different organizations operating under different commands and in the same province. After laborious talks that I had to have with their respective leaders, we reached a series of agreements, and it was possible to form a more or less common front.

From December 16 onward, the systematic cutting of bridges and all forms of communication had made it very difficult for the dictatorship to defend its forward positions and even those on the Central Highway. Early that morning, the bridge across the Falcón river, on the Central Highway, was destroyed, virtually cutting communications between Havana and the cities to the east of Santa Clara, the capital of Las Villas province. Also, a number of towns—the southernmost being Fomento—were besieged and attacked by our forces. The commander of the city defended his position more or less efficiently for several days. Despite the air force's punishment of our Rebel Army, however, the dictatorship's demoralized troops would not advance overland to support their comrades. Realizing that all resistance was useless, they surrendered, and more than one hundred rifles joined the forces of freedom.

Without giving the enemy any respite, we decided to immediately paralyze the Central Highway, and on December 21 we simultaneously attacked Cabaiguán and Guayos, both on the Central Highway. The latter town surrendered in a few hours, as did Cabaiguán during the following days, with its ninety soldiers. (The surrender of the garrisons was negotiated on the political basis of letting the soldiers go free on condition that they were to leave the liberated territory. Thus, they were given the opportunity to surrender their weapons and to save themselves.) The dictatorship's ineffectiveness was proved once again in Cabaiguán; at no point did it send infantry units to reinforce those under siege.

In the northern region of Las Villas, Camilo Cienfuegos was attacking a number of towns, which he was subduing at the same time that he was closing the circle around Yaguajay, the last bastion of the tyranny's troops. It was under the command of a captain of Chinese ancestry who resisted for eleven days, preventing the movement of the revolutionary troops in the region. At the same time, our troops were already advancing along the Central Highway toward Santa Clara, the provincial capital.

After Cabaiguán had fallen, we attacked Placetas, actively collaborating with the forces of the Revolutionary Directorate. Placetas surrendered after only one day of battle; after taking it, we liberated in rapid succession Remedios and Caibarién on the northern coast, the latter an important port. The panorama was becoming gloomy for the dictatorship, because in addition to the continuous victories scored in Oriente, the Second Front of the Escambray was defeating small garrisons, and Camilo Cienfuegos controlled the north.

When the enemy withdrew from Camajuaní without offering resistance, we were ready to launch the definitive attack on the capital of Las Villas province. Santa Clara is the hub of the island's central plain, with 150,000 inhabitants. It is the center of the railway system and of all communications in the country. It is surrounded by small barren hills, which had previously been taken by the troops of the dictatorship.

At the time of the attack, our forces had considerably increased our fire power, since we had taken several positions and some heavy weapons for which there was no ammunition. We had a bazooka but no shells, and we had to fight against about ten tanks. But we also knew that for us to fight most effectively, we had to reach the city's populous neighborhoods, where tanks are much less effective.

While the troops of the Revolutionary Directorate were taking the Rural Guard's Garrison no. 31, we set about to besiege almost all of Santa Clara's fortified positions. Our fight focused mainly on the defenders of the armored train stationed at the entrance of the road to Camajuaní. These positions were tenaciously defended by the army, which was very well equipped in relation to what we had.

On December 29 we began the struggle. At first the university served as our base of operations. Later we established our command post closer to the city's downtown area. Our men were fighting against troops supported by armored units and would force them to flee, although many paid for their boldness with their lives. The dead and wounded began to fill up the improvised cemeteries and hospitals.

I remember an episode that showed the spirit of our forces in those final days. I had admonished a soldier for sleeping in the midst of battle, and he replied that he had been disarmed for accidentally firing his weapon. I responded with my customary dryness: "Go get yourself another rifle by going to the front line unarmed . . . if you're up to it." In Santa Clara, while I was en-

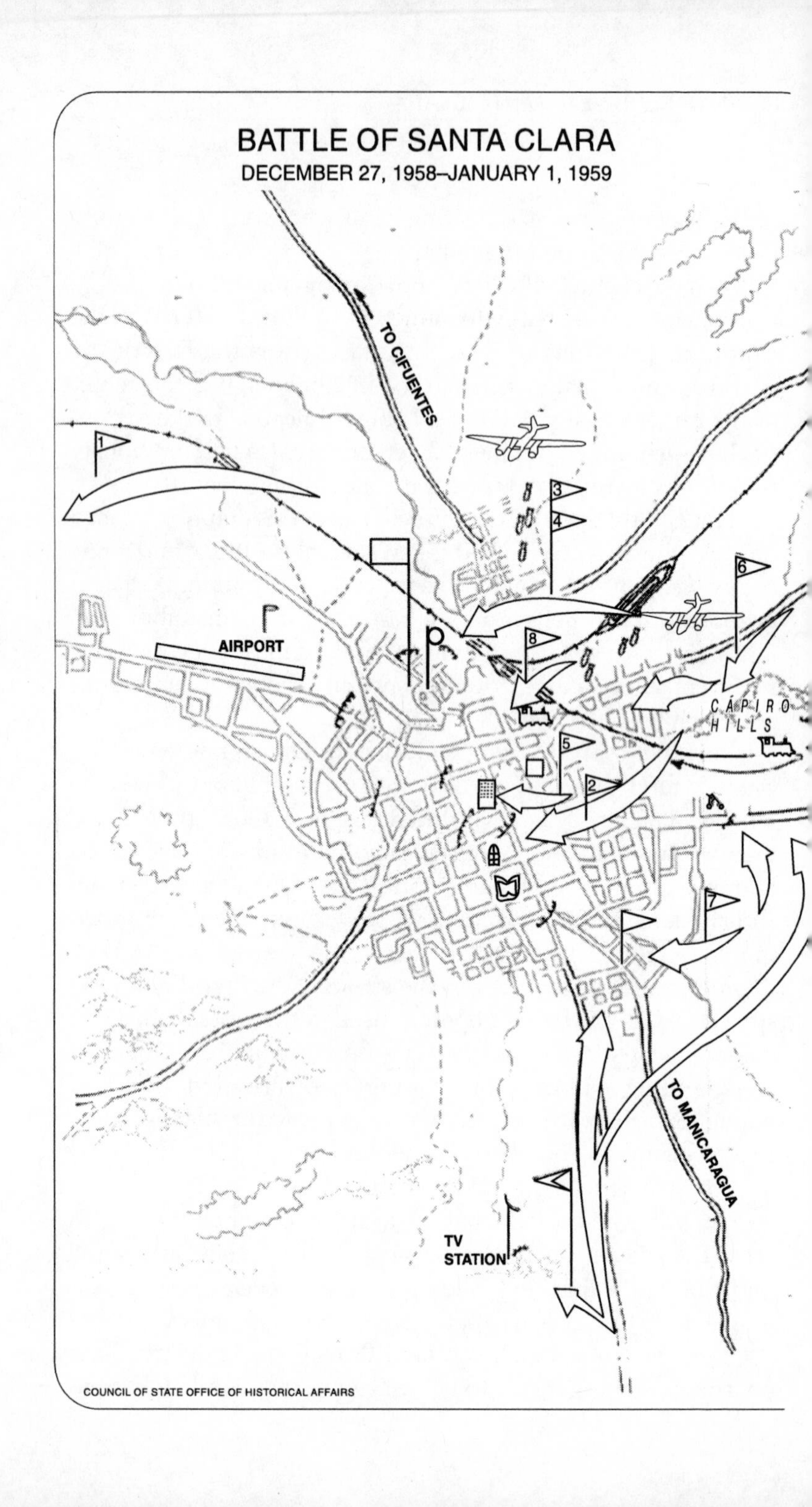
BATTLE OF SANTA CLARA
DECEMBER 27, 1958–JANUARY 1, 1959
TO CIFUENTES
1
3
4
6
8
AIRPORT
CÁPIRO
HILLS
5
2
7
TO MANICARAGUA
TV
STATION
COUNCIL OF STATE OFFICE OF HISTORICAL AFFAIRS

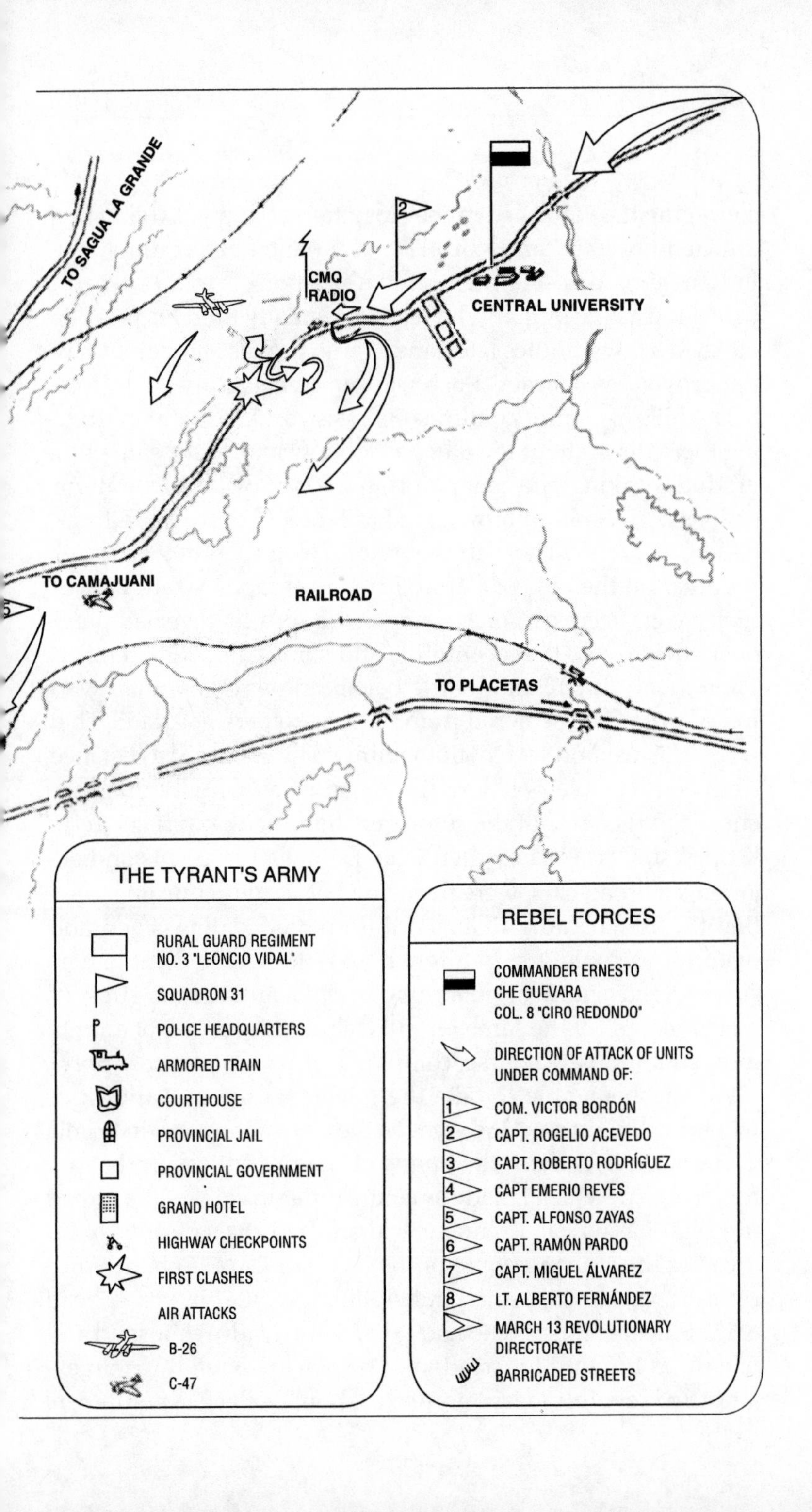

TO SAGUA LA GRANDE
CMQ
RADIO
2
CENTRAL UNIVERSITY
TO CAMAJUANI
RAILROAD
TO PLACETAS
THE TYRANT'S ARMY
RURAL GUARD REGIMENT
NO. 3 "LEONCIO VIDAL"
SQUADRON 31
POLICE HEADQUARTERS
ARMORED TRAIN
COURTHOUSE
PROVINCIAL JAIL
PROVINCIAL GOVERNMENT
GRAND HOTEL
HIGHWAY CHECKPOINTS
FIRST CLASHES
AIR ATTACKS
B-26
C-47
REBEL FORCES
COMMANDER ERNESTO
CHE GUEVARA
COL. 8 "CIRO REDONDO"
DIRECTION OF ATTACK OF UNITS
UNDER COMMAND OF:
1 COM. VICTOR BORDÓN
2 CAPT. ROGELIO ACEVEDO
3 CAPT. ROBERTO RODRÍGUEZ
4 CAPT EMERIO REYES
5 CAPT. ALFONSO ZAYAS
6 CAPT. RAMÓN PARDO
7 CAPT. MIGUEL ÁLVAREZ
8 LT. ALBERTO FERNÁNDEZ
MARCH 13 REVOLUTIONARY
DIRECTORATE
BARRICADED STREETS

couraging the wounded in the Hospital de Sangre, a dying man touched my hand and said, "Do you remember, commander? In Remedios you sent me to find a weapon . . . and I earned it here." It was the fighter who had accidentally fired his weapon. He died a few minutes later, and I think he was content for having proven his courage. Such was our Rebel Army.

The hills of Cápiro continued to resist, and we went on fighting there throughout the day on December 30, at the same time gradually taking different points in the city. By then, communications between downtown Santa Clara and the armored train had been cut off. Those in the train, seeing that they were surrounded on the hills of Cápiro, tried to escape by rail, with all their magnificent cargo. Arriving at the spur that we had previously destroyed, the locomotive and some cars were derailed. Then a very interesting battle began, in which the men were forced out of the armored train by our Molotov cocktails. They were very well protected, but willing to fight only at a distance, from comfortable positions, and against a virtually unarmed enemy, in the style of the colonizers fighting the Indians in the U.S. West. Cornered by men who, from nearby points and adjoining railroad cars, were throwing bottles with burning gasoline, the train became, thanks to the armored plating, a veritable oven for the soldiers. In a few hours, the whole complement surrendered with its twenty-two cars, its antiaircraft guns, its machine guns of the same type, its fabulous quantity of ammunition (fabulous, of course, compared with our meager supply).

We had been able to take the power station and the city's whole northwest side. We went on the air to announce that Santa Clara was virtually in the hands of the revolution. In that announcement, which I made as commander in chief of the armed forces in Las Villas, I remember that I had the sad duty of informing the Cuban people of the death of Capt. Roberto Rodríguez, "Vaquerito," small in height and young in years, head of the Suicide Squad, who had toyed with death a thousand and one times fighting for freedom. The Suicide Squad was an example of revolutionary morale, and only selected volunteers joined it. But whenever a man died—and that happened in every battle—when the new candidate was named, those not chosen would be grief-stricken and even cry. How curious to see those seasoned and noble warriors showing their youth by their tears of despair, because they did not have the honor of being in the front line of combat and death.

Next to fall was the police station, surrendering the tanks that defended it. And in rapid succession Garrison no. 31 surrendered to Commander Cubela, followed in succession by the jail, the courthouse, the provincial government palace, and the Grand Hotel—where snipers had kept firing from the tenth floor almost until the battle ended.

At that moment, only the Leoncio Vidal garrison, the largest fortress in central Cuba, had not surrendered. But by January 1, 1959, there were already signs of growing weakness among the forces defending it. That morning, we sent Captains Nñ ez Jiménez and Rodríguez de la Vega to negotiate the surrender of the garrison.

The news reports were contradictory and extraordinary: Batista had fled that day, leaving the armed forces high command in a shambles. Our two delegates established radio contact with Cantillo, telling him of the surrender offer. But he refused to go along because this constituted an ultimatum, and he had taken over command of the army in strict accordance with instructions from the leader Fidel Castro. We immediately contacted Fidel, telling him the news, but giving our opinion of Cantillo's treacherous attitude, an opinion he absolutely agreed with. (In those decisive hours, Cantillo let all the main figures in Batista's government flee. His attitude was even worse, if one considers that he was an officer who had made contact with us and whom we had trusted as a military man of honor.)

The results that followed are known to everyone: Castro's refusal to recognize Cantillo's authority; Fidel's order to march on the city of Havana; Colonel Barquín's taking over command of the army after leaving the Isle of Pines prison; the seizure of Camp Columbia by Camilo Cienfuegos and of La Cabaña fortress by our Column no. 8; and finally, a number of days later, the installing of Fidel Castro as prime minister of the provisional government. All that belongs to the country's present political history.[4]

We are now in a position in which we are much more than simple factors of one nation. We are now the hope of the unredeemed Americas. All eyes—those of the great oppressors and those of the hopeful—are firmly on us. In great measure, the development of the popular movements in Latin America depends on the future stance that we take, on our capacity to resolve many problems. And every step we take is being observed by the ever-watchful eyes of the big creditor and by the optimistic eyes of our brothers and sisters in Latin America.

With our feet planted firmly on the ground, we are beginning to labor and produce our first revolutionary works, confronting the first difficulties. But what is Cuba's main problem if not the same as of all Latin America, the same as even enormous Brazil with its millions of square kilometers and with its land of marvels that is a whole continent? The one-crop economy. In Cuba, we are slaves to sugarcane, the umbilical cord that binds us to the large northern market. We must diversify our agricultural production, stimulate industry. And we must ensure that our minerals and agricultural products, and—in the near fu-

4. Batista fled Cuba in the early morning hours of January 1, 1959, turning over power to Gen. Eulogio Cantillo. In a nationwide radio address from outside Santiago de Cuba, Castro refused to recognize the new regime and issued a call for a nationwide general strike to begin the following day, which paralyzed the country. In the face of a rebel ultimatum, the army garrison in Santiago de Cuba surrendered in the afternoon of January 1. Meanwhile, Castro ordered the columns led by Guevara and Camilo Cienfuegos to Havana, where they took control of the main army bases on January 2. By the time the main Rebel Army columns arrived in Havana January 8, the revolution had triumphed. Fidel Castro was appointed prime minister on February 16, 1959. A detailed account of these events is contained in Fidel Castro's speech of January 1, 1989, contained in *In Defense of Socialism: Four Speeches on the 30th Anniversary of the Cuban Revolution* (New York: Pathfinder, 1989), pp. 39–58.

ture—our industrial products go to the markets that are best suited for us and by means of our own transport lines.

The government's first great battle will be the agrarian reform, which will be audacious, thorough, but flexible: it will destroy the landed estates in Cuba, although not Cuba's means of production.[5] It will be a battle that will absorb a great part of the strength of the people and the government during the coming years. The land will be given to the peasant free of charge. Landowners who prove that they came by their holdings honestly will be compensated with long-term bonds. But the peasantry will also be given technical assistance; there will be guaranteed markets for the products of the soil. And production will be channeled with a broad national sense of development in conjunction with the great battle for agrarian reform, so that within a short time the infant Cuban industries can compete with the monstrous ones of the countries where capitalism has reached its highest level of development. Simultaneously with the creation of the new domestic market that the agrarian reform will bring about, and the distribution of new products to satisfy a growing market, there will arise the need to export some products and to have the adequate instrument to take them to this or that part of the world. That instrument will be a merchant fleet, which the already approved Maritime Development Law envisages.

With those elementary weapons, we Cubans will begin the struggle for our territory's total freedom. We all know it will not be easy, but we are all aware of the enormous historic responsibility of the July 26 Movement, of the Cuban revolution, of the nation in general, to be an example for all peoples of Latin

5. The agrarian reform law of May 17, 1959, set a limit of 30 *caballerías* (approximately 1,000 acres) on individual landholdings. Implementation of the law resulted in the confiscation of the vast estates in Cuba—many of them owned by U.S. companies. These lands passed into the hands of the new government. The law also granted sharecroppers, tenant farmers, and squatters a deed to the land they tilled. A second agrarian reform in 1963 confiscated the land owned by capitalist farmers in excess of 165 acres.

America, whom we must not disappoint.

Our friends of the indomitable continent can be sure that, if need be, we will struggle no matter what the economic consequence of our acts may be. And if the fight is taken further still, we shall struggle to the last drop of our rebel blood to make this land a sovereign republic, with the true attributes of a nation that is happy, democratic, and fraternal with its brothers and sisters of Latin America.

PUBLISHED IN O CRUZEIRO OF RIO DE JANEIRO, BRAZIL,
JUNE 16, JULY 1, AND JULY 16, 1959

Portraits *of* Revolutionaries

Lidia and Clodomira

I MET LIDIA ABOUT six months after we had begun our revolutionary effort. I was making my debut as commander of Column no. 4, and we were making a lightning raid on the hamlet of San Pablo de Yao, near Bayamo, in the foothills of the Sierra Maestra, in an effort to find provisions. One of the first houses we came to in the village belonged to a family of bakers. Lidia, one of the owners of the bakery, was a woman of about forty-five, whose only son had been a member of our column. From the very first moment she enthusiastically, and with exemplary devotion, joined in the work of the revolution.

When I think of Lidia, I feel something more than just affectionate appreciation for this unblemished revolutionary, for she showed a special devotion to me and preferred working under my orders, regardless of the front to which I might be assigned. On countless occasions Lidia acted as special messenger for me and for the Movement. To Santiago and to Havana she carried the most compromising documents, all of our column's communiqués, and issues of our newspaper, *El Cubano Libre*. To us in the Sierra she brought paper, medicine—in short, whatever we needed and whenever we needed it.

Her unlimited boldness was such that male couriers avoided her. I remember very well the opinion—a mixture of admiration and resentment—of one of them, who told me: "That woman has more b—   than Maceo, but she's going to get us all killed.

The things she does are mad. This is no time for games." Lidia, however, went on crossing enemy lines, again and again.

When I was transferred to the Minas del Frío zone, in Las Vegas de Jibacoa, she followed. This meant leaving the auxiliary camp that she had led for a time; she had done so with spirit and a touch of high-handedness, causing a certain resentment among the Cuban men under her command, who were not accustomed to taking orders from a woman. This camp, located at a place called Cueva between Yao and Bayamo, was the revolution's most forward point. I had to remove her from that command because it was too dangerous a spot. After the enemy had located it, our boys had to leave it under fire many times. I tried to have Lidia transferred from there permanently, but I was only able to do so when she followed me to the new battle front.

Among the anecdotes that reveal Lidia's character, I remember this one: It was the day that Geilín, one of our best fighters—a mere boy from Cárdenas—was killed. He was stationed at Lidia's forward camp at the time. Returning to it after a mission, Lidia observed the soldiers advancing stealthily toward the post, undoubtedly the result of some informer's tip. Lidia's reaction was immediate. She took out her small .32 revolver to fire a couple of warning shots in the air. Friendly hands stopped her in time, however, since the results would have cost the lives of all of them. Meanwhile, the soldiers advanced and surprised our sentry post. Guillermo Geilín defended himself bravely until, twice wounded and knowing what would happen to him if he were taken alive by these thugs, he committed suicide. The enemy soldiers advanced, burned everything that would burn, and left.

The following day I met Lidia. Her expression revealed the greatest despair over the death of the young fighter, as well as indignation toward the person who prevented her from sounding the alarm. "Me, they would have killed," she said, "but the boy would have been saved. Me, I'm already old; he wasn't even twenty." She returned to this subject again and again. At times there seemed to be a kind of boasting in her constant expressions of contempt for death. But the missions entrusted to her were carried out to perfection.

Lidia knew how fond I was of puppies, and she was always promising to bring one from Havana, a promise not easy to keep. During the days of the army's great offensive, Lidia carried out her missions to the letter. She went up and down the Sierra, coming and going with the most urgent documents; she was our connection with the outside world. She was accompanied by another fighter of the same caliber who I knew only by name—a name known and revered by virtually the entire Rebel Army: Clodomira. Lidia and Clodomira had already become inseparable comrades-in-danger; they came and went constantly, always together.

I had asked Lidia to contact me as soon as I arrived in Las Villas, after the invasion, since she was to be our principal means of communication with Havana and with the general command in the Sierra Maestra. I arrived and soon found a letter from her in which she announced that she had a puppy for me, and would bring it on her next trip.

That was the trip that Lidia and Clodomira never made. Soon after, I learned that it was the weakness of a man—a hundred times inferior as a fighter, as a revolutionary, and as a human being—that had permitted the enemy to spot the group that included Lidia and Clodomira. Our comrades defended themselves to the death. Lidia was wounded when she was captured. Their bodies have disappeared. Lidia and Clodomira are sleeping their last sleep, no doubt side by side, as they were when they fought during the last days of the battle for freedom.

Someday, perhaps, their remains will be found, perhaps in some lonely field in that enormous cemetery that the island became.

But within the Rebel Army, among those who fought and sacrificed in those anguished days, the memory will live forever of the women who, by the risks they took daily, made communications with the rest of the island possible. Among all of us—those who were part of the First Front, and me personally—Lidia occupies a favored place. That is why I offer today these reminiscences in homage to her—a modest flower laid on the mass grave that this once happy island became.

PUBLISHED IN HUMANISMO, APRIL 1959

El Patojo

A FEW DAYS AGO a wire service dispatch brought news of the death of some Guatemalan patriots, among them Julio Roberto Cáceres Valle.

In this difficult profession of revolutionary, in the midst of class struggles that are convulsing the entire continent, death is a frequent accident. But the death of a friend, a comrade during difficult hours, and a sharer in dreams of better times, is always painful for the person who receives the news, and Julio Roberto was a great friend. He was short and frail; for that reason we called him "El Patojo," a Guatemalan term meaning "Shorty" or "Kid."

El Patojo had witnessed the birth of our revolutionary effort while in Mexico and had volunteered to join us. Fidel, however, did not want to bring any more foreigners into that struggle for national liberation in which I had the honor to participate.

A few days after the revolution triumphed, El Patojo sold his few belongings and, with only a small suitcase, appeared before me in Cuba. He worked in various branches of public administration, and became the first head of personnel of the Department of Industrialization of INRA [National Institute of Agrarian Reform]. But he was never happy with his work. El Patojo was looking for something different; he was seeking the liberation of his own country. The revolution had changed him profoundly, as it had all of us. The bewildered boy who had left

Guatemala without fully understanding the defeat had now become a fully conscious revolutionary.

The first time we met was on a train, fleeing Guatemala, a couple of months after the fall of Arbenz. We were going to Tapachula, from where we could reach Mexico City. El Patojo was several years younger than I, but we immediately formed a lasting friendship. Together we made the trip from Chiapas to Mexico City; together we faced the same problems—we were both penniless, defeated, and forced to earn a living in an indifferent if not hostile environment.

El Patojo had no money and I only a few pesos; I bought a camera and together we undertook the illegal job[1] of taking pictures of people in the city parks. Our partner was a Mexican who had a small darkroom where we developed the film. We got to know all of Mexico City, walking from one end to another, delivering the bad photographs we had taken. We battled with all kinds of clients, trying to convince them that the little boy in the photo was really very cute and it was really a great bargain to pay a Mexican peso for such a marvel. Thus we ate for several months. Little by little we were getting by, and the contingencies of revolutionary life separated us. I have already said that Fidel did not want to bring him to Cuba, not because of any shortcomings of his, but to avoid turning our army into a mosaic of nationalities.

El Patojo continued on, working as a journalist, studying physics at the University of Mexico, abandoning his studies and then returning to them, without ever getting very far ahead. He earned his living in various places, at various jobs, never asking for anything. I still do not know whether that sensitive and serious boy was overly timid, or too proud to recognize his weaknesses and his personal problems to approach a friend for help. El Patojo was an introvert, highly intelligent, broadly cultured, sensitive. He matured steadily and in his last days put

1. As undocumented workers, they did not have government permission to work.

his great sensibilities at the service of his people. By then he belonged to the Guatemalan Labor [Communist] Party and had disciplined himself through work—he was developing into a fine revolutionary cadre. Little remained of his earlier hypersensitivity. Revolution purifies men, it improves and develops them, just as the experienced farmer corrects the deficiencies of his crops and strengthens their good qualities.

After he came to Cuba we almost always lived in the same house, as was fitting for two old friends. But we no longer maintained the early intimacy in this new life, and I only suspected El Patojo's intentions when I occasionally saw him earnestly studying one of the native Indian languages of his country. One day he told me he was leaving, that the time had come for him to do his duty.

El Patojo had no military training; he simply felt that duty called. He was going to his country to fight, arms in hand, to reproduce somehow our guerrilla struggle. It was then that we had one of our few long talks. I limited myself to recommending strongly three things: constant movement, constant wariness, and constant vigilance. Movement—never stay put; never spend two nights in the same place; never stop moving from one place to another. Wariness—at the beginning, be wary even of your own shadow, of friendly peasants, of informants, of guides, of contacts; be wary of everything until you hold a liberated zone. Vigilance—constant guard duty, constant reconnaissance; establishment of a camp in a safe place and, above all, never sleep beneath a roof, never sleep in a house where you could be surrounded. This was the synthesis of our guerrilla experience; it was the only thing—along with a warm handshake—that I could give to my friend. Could I advise him not to do it? With what right? We had undertaken something at a time when it was believed it couldn't be done, and now he knew it was possible.

El Patojo left, and with time the news of his death came. At first we hoped there had been a confusion of names, that there had been some mistake, but unfortunately his body had been identified by his own mother; there is no doubt he is dead. And not only he, but a group of comrades with him, all of them as brave, as selfless, as intelligent perhaps as he, but not known to me personally.

Once more there is the bitter taste of defeat and the unanswered question: Why did he not learn from the experience of others? Why did those men not heed more carefully the simple advice given them? There is the urgent investigation into how it came about, how El Patojo died. We still do not know exactly what happened, but we do know that the region was poorly chosen, that the men were not physically prepared, they were not sufficiently wary, and, of course, they were not sufficiently vigilant. The repressive army took them by surprise, killed a few, dispersed the rest, then returned to pursue them and virtually annihilated them. They took some prisoners; others, like El Patojo, died in battle. After being dispersed, the guerrillas were probably hunted down, as we had been after Alegría de Pío.

Once again youthful blood has fertilized the fields of the Americas to make freedom possible. Another battle has been lost; we must make time to weep for our fallen comrades while we sharpen our machetes. From the valuable and unfortunate experience of the cherished dead, we must firmly resolve not to repeat their errors, to avenge the death of each one of them with many victorious battles, and to achieve definitive liberation.

When El Patojo left Cuba, he told me he was leaving nothing behind, nor did he leave any messages; he had few clothes or personal belongings to worry about. Old mutual friends in Mexico, however, brought me some poems he had written and left there in a notebook. They are the last verses of a revolutionary; they are, in addition, a love song to the revolution, to the homeland, and to a woman. To that woman whom El Patojo knew and loved in Cuba, are addressed these final verses, this injunction:

Take this, it is only my heart
Hold it in your hand
And when the dawn arrives,
Open your hand
And let the sun warm it. . . .

El Patojo's heart has remained among us, in the hands of his beloved and in the grateful hands of an entire people, waiting to be warmed beneath the sun of a new day that will surely dawn for Guatemala and for all America. Today, in the Ministry of Industry, where he left many friends, there is a small school of statistics named in his memory: "Julio Roberto Cáceres Valle." Later, when Guatemala is free, his cherished name will surely be given to a school, a factory, a hospital, to any place where people fight and work to build a new society.

PUBLISHED IN VERDE OLIVO, AUGUST 19, 1962

Camilo

MEMORY IS A WAY OF REVIVING the past, of recalling the dead. To remember Camilo is to recall the past or the dead, and yet Camilo is a living part of the Cuban revolution, immortal by his very nature. I would simply like to give our comrades of the Rebel Army an idea of who this invincible guerrilla fighter was. I am able to do so since we were always together, from the sad hours of the first setback at Alegría de Pío on. And it is my duty to do so, because, more than a comrade in arms, in joys, and in victories, Camilo was in truth a brother.

I never got to know him in Mexico, as he joined us at the last minute. He had come from the United States without any previous recommendation, and there were doubts about him—and everyone else for that matter—in those risky days. He came on the *Granma,* as just one among the eighty-two who crossed the sea, at the mercy of the elements, to bring something new to the Americas.

I was introduced to Camilo before actually meeting him, through some words of his that became a symbol. It was at the moment of the disaster at Alegría de Pío. I was wounded, sprawled out in a clearing, and by my side was a comrade covered with blood who was firing his last rounds, ready to die fighting. I heard someone cry weakly: "We're lost. We must surrender." Then from somewhere came a forceful voice that seemed to me the voice of the people: "Nobody surrenders here! Hell no!"

Things happened, our lives were saved—mine thanks to the efforts of Comrade Almeida—and five of us wandered around the steep cliffs near Cabo Cruz. One clear, moonlit night we came upon three other comrades sleeping peacefully, without any fear of the soldiers. We jumped them, believing they were enemies. Nothing happened, but the incident served later as the material for a joke among us: the fact that I was among those who had caught them by surprise, and it was I who had to raise the white flag so that they would not shoot us, mistaking us for Batista's men.

The eight of us continued on. Camilo was hungry and wanted to eat; he didn't care what or where, he simply wanted to eat. This led to some serious disagreements with Camilo, because he continually wanted to approach peasant huts to ask for food. Twice, for having followed the advice of "the eaters," we nearly fell into the hands of the army that had killed dozens of our comrades. On the ninth day the "gluttonous" part of our group won out, and we approached a peasant hut, ate, and all got sick. And among the sickest was, naturally, Camilo, who like a hungry lion had gulped down an entire kid.

During that period I was more a medic than a combatant. I put Camilo on a special diet and ordered him to stay behind in the hut, where he would be guarded and receive proper attention. That trouble passed, and we were together again, and the days turned into weeks and months during which many comrades fell along the way. Camilo was showing his mettle, earning the rank of lieutenant of the forward detachment in our one and only beloved column, which would later be called the "José Martí" Column no. 1, under Fidel's personal command. Almeida and Raúl were captains; Camilo, lieutenant of the forward detachment; Efigenio Ameijeiras, lieutenant of the rear guard; Ramiro Valdés, lieutenant in one of Raúl's platoons; and Calixto, soldier in another platoon. In short, all our forces were born there, and I was the group's lieutenant medic. Later, following the battle of Uvero, I was given the rank of captain, and, a few days later, that of commander leading a column. Life went on, and one day Camilo was made captain of the column I commanded, Column no. 4. We bore that number to deceive the enemy, since it was actually only the second. And it was here that Camilo began his new career of exploits. With untiring effort and extraordinary zeal, he hunted down enemy soldiers time and again. Once he killed a soldier in the enemy's advance squad at such close range that he caught the man's rifle before it even hit the ground. Another time he planned to let the first of the enemy soldiers go by until they were level with our troop, and then open fire from the side. The ambush never materialized, because someone in our group got nervous and began firing before the enemy got close enough. By then Camilo had become "Camilo, Lord of the Vanguard," a complete guerrilla fighter who asserted himself through his own colorful way of fighting.

I recall my anxiety during the second attack on Pino del Agua, when Fidel ordered me to stay with him and gave Camilo the responsibility of attacking one of the enemy's flanks. The idea was simple. Camilo was to attack and take one end of the enemy camp and then lay siege. But when the hurricane of fire began, he and his men took the sentry post and continued advancing, entering the village, killing or taking prisoner every soldier in their path. The town was taken house by house until finally the enemy organized its resistance and the barrage of lead began to take its toll among our ranks. Valuable comrades, among them Noda and Capote, lost their lives there.

An enemy machine gunner advanced with his men, but at one point he found himself in the midst of a veritable storm of gunfire. With his assistants killed, the soldier dropped the gun and fled. It was already daybreak; the attack had begun at night. Camilo hurled himself at the machine gun to seize and defend it, and was shot twice. One bullet pierced his left thigh and another went through his abdomen. He got out of there, and his comrades carried him. We were two kilometers away, with the enemy between us. We could hear machine gun bursts and the enemy shouting: "There goes Camilo's gun!" "That's Camilo firing!" and cheers for Batista. We all thought Camilo had been killed. Later we praised his luck that the bullet had entered and left his abdomen without hitting his intestines or any vital organ.[1]

Later came the tragic days of April 9, and Camilo, the trailblazer, went on to create his legend on the Oriente plains, striking terror in the hearts of the enemy forces mobilized in the Bayamo region. Once he was surrounded by six hundred soldiers, with only twenty men, and he resisted an entire day against the enemy's advance that included two tanks. At night they made a spectacular escape.

Then came the offensive, and in the face of imminent danger and the concentration of forces, Camilo was called back, as he was the man Fidel trusted to leave in his place when he went to a specific front.

Later came the marvelous story of the invasion and his chain of victories on the plains of Las Villas—a difficult feat, as the terrain afforded little natural protection. His actions were magnificent for their audacity, and at the same time one could already see Camilo's political sense, his decisions on revolutionary questions, his strength, and his faith in the people.

Camilo was happy, witty, and loved to joke. I remember that in the Sierra a peasant—one of our great, magnificent, anonymous heroes—had received a nickname from Camilo, who accompanied it with a disdainful look. One day the peasant came to see me as head of the column, complaining that he shouldn't be insulted and that he was no "ventriloquist." As I did not understand, I went to speak with Camilo to get an explanation of the man's strange behavior. It turned out that Camilo had looked at the man with a scornful air and called him a ventriloquist, and since the peasant didn't know what the word meant, he was terribly offended.

Camilo had a little alcohol burner, and he used to cook cats

1. For more on this incident, see the chapter "The Second Battle of Pino del Agua."

and offer them as a delicacy to new recruits who joined us. It was one of the many tests of the Sierra, and more than one failed this preliminary "examination" when he refused to eat the cat. Camilo was a man of anecdotes, a thousand anecdotes. They came naturally, in passing. His appreciation of people and his easygoing nature were a part of his personality. These qualities, which today we sometimes forget or overlook, stamped his character and were present in all his actions, something precious that few men can attain. It is true, as Fidel has said, that he had no great amount of "book learning," but he had the natural intelligence of the people, who had chosen him from among thousands to place him in that privileged place earned by his audacity, his perseverance, his intelligence, and his devotion. Camilo was devoted and loyal to two things, and with the same results: he had unlimited personal loyalty toward Fidel, and he was loyal and devoted to the people. The people and Fidel march as one, and Camilo's devotion was projected toward them both as one.

Who killed Camilo?[2] Who physically eliminated the man who lives on in the people? Such men do not die so long as the people do not authorize it. The enemy killed him; they killed him because they wanted him to die, because there are no completely safe airplanes, because pilots are not able to acquire all the necessary experience, because he was overloaded with work and had to be in Havana as quickly as possible. He was killed by his personal characteristics. Camilo did not measure danger. He utilized it as a game, he played with it, he courted it, he attracted it, handled it, and with his guerrilla's mentality, a mere cloud could not detain or derail him from the line he was following. It happened at a time when everyone knew him, admired and loved him; it could have happened before, and then his story would have been simply that of a guerrilla captain.

There will be many Camilos, as Fidel said. And, I might add,

2. Camilo Cienfuegos was killed October 28, 1959, when a plane he was traveling in disappeared over the sea during a trip from Camagüey to Havana.

there have been many Camilos—Camilos who died before completing their magnificent cycle that he managed to complete so as to enter the pages of history. Camilo and the other Camilos—the ones who never made it this far and those yet to come—they are the measure of the people's strength; they are the highest expression of what can be achieved by a nation fighting to defend its purest ideals and with complete faith in the fulfillment of its noblest goals.

There is too much to be said to allow me to put his essence into a lifeless mold, which would be equivalent to killing him. It is better to leave it like this, in general descriptive terms, without spelling out in black and white his socioeconomic ideas, which were not precisely defined. But we must always bear in mind that there was never a man—not even before the revolution—comparable to Camilo: a complete revolutionary, a man of the people, an artist of the revolution, sprung from the heart of the Cuban nation. His mind was incapable of the slightest slackening or deception.

Camilo the guerrilla is a permanent object of daily remembrance; he is the one who did this or that, something by Camilo; he who left his exact and indelible imprint on the Cuban revolution, who is present among those who fell before the triumph and those heroes yet to come. In his constant and eternal rebirth, Camilo is the image of the people.

THIS ARTICLE, WRITTEN ORIGINALLY FOR VERDE OLIVO IN 1964, WAS PUT ASIDE BY GUEVARA. IT WAS PUBLISHED POSTHUMOUSLY IN GRANMA, OCTOBER 25, 1967.

The Las Villas Campaign

September-December 1958

Introductory note

The events of the last six months of the revolutionary war are touched upon only briefly in the preceding pages. As recounted in the introduction, Episodes of the Cuban Revolutionary War *was originally written as a series of articles for the magazine* Verde Olivo, *beginning in early 1961 and ending in November 1964. The chapter, "From Batista's Final Offensive to the Battle of Santa Clara," covering the final months of the war, was written for the Brazilian magazine* O Cruzeiro *in early 1959, two years before Guevara began writing his series. We are including here several documents expanding on events described in that chapter.*

The letters, reports, and documents in this section were written in the midst of the Las Villas campaign itself, between the end of August 1958 and the revolution's victory on January 1, 1959. The final article, "A Sin of the Revolution," was written by Guevara in 1961.

AUGUST 21, 1958

Military order

Cmdr. Ernesto Guevara is assigned the mission of leading a rebel column from the Sierra Maestra to Las Villas province, and to operate in that territory in accordance with the strategic plan of the Rebel Army. Column no. 8, which is given this objective, will bear the name of Ciro Redondo, in honor of the heroic rebel captain killed in action and posthumously promoted to commander.

The "Ciro Redondo" Column no. 8 will leave from Las Mercedes between August 24 and 30.

Cmdr. Ernesto Guevara is named head of all rebel units of the July 26 Movement operating in Las Villas province, in both rural and urban areas. He is granted powers to raise and disburse war funds, in accordance with our military policies; apply the penal code and agrarian laws of the Rebel Army in the territory in which his forces operate; coordinate operations, plans, administrative matters, and military organization with other revolutionary forces operating in that province, who are to be invited to join in a single army corp to strengthen and unify the military forces of the revolution; to organize local combat units and designate officers of the Rebel Army up to the rank of column commander.

The strategic objective of Column no. 8 will be to attack the enemy constantly in the central territory of Cuba, to intercept and totally paralyze enemy troop movements from west to east, and to carry out other actions that are ordered.

Fidel Castro
Commander in chief

SEPTEMBER–OCTOBER 1958

En route to Las Villas

REPORTS TO FIDEL CASTRO

September 3, 1958

Fidel, I am writing you from the open plains, with no aircraft and relatively few mosquitoes, and without eating, due solely to the rapid pace of our march. I will give you a brief account.

We left during the night on August 31 with four horses, since it was impossible to leave in trucks because Magadan took all the gasoline and an ambush was feared in Jibacoa. We passed through the area without incident, since it had been abandoned by the soldiers. But we were unable to continue for more than a couple of leagues, sleeping in a little wooded area on the other side of the highway. I recommend establishing a permanent platoon in Jibacoa, which will permit supplies to be sent from that area, which up to now has been closely watched.

On September 1 we passed the highway and took three cars that broke down with alarming frequency. We reached a spot called Cayo Redondo, where we spent a day as the hurricane approached. The soldiers came near, numbering forty, but they withdrew without a battle. We continued on with the trucks, aided by four tractors. Progress became impossible, however, and we had to abandon them the following day, September 2, and continue on foot with a few horses, reaching the banks of the Cauto river, which was impassable at night owing to rising water. We spent eight hours during the daytime making the crossing, and at night we reached the house of the "Colonel," to follow the route we had planned.[1] We are without horses but can obtain more along the way, and I intend to arrive at the assigned

1. The "Colonel" was Arcadio Peláez, a collaborator of the Rebel Army; the nickname had been given him by Camilo Cienfuegos.

zone of operations with everyone in the saddle. It is not possible to calculate exactly the amount of time I will be delayed owing to the numerous inconveniences along these devilish trails.

I will try to continue sending you reports along the way, creating an efficient mail system, and reporting to you on the people we meet. In this region I recommend only two people up to now: Pepín Magadan, who has his weaknesses but is surprisingly effective; he could be put in charge of obtaining supplies and money; and Concepción Rivero, who is a very serious man, as can be seen.

That's all for now. I send an embrace to a far-off world that is barely visible from here in the distance.

September 8, 1958
1:50 a.m.

After exhausting nighttime marches, I am finally writing to you from Camagüey. There are no immediate prospects of speeding up the march, which averages three to four leagues a day, with some of the troops on horseback, without saddles. Camilo is in the vicinity, and we are waiting for him here, at the Bartles rice plantation, but he did not arrive. The plains are formidable. There are not as many mosquitoes. We have not seen even a single soldier, and the planes seem like inoffensive doves. Radio Rebelde can be heard with great difficulty through Venezuela.

Everything indicates that the enemy does not want to fight, nor do we. I confess that I'm scared of a retreat with 150 inexperienced recruits in these unknown parts, although an armed guerrilla unit of 30 men could work wonders in this zone, and revolutionize it. In passing through I laid the basis for a rice workers union in Leonero. I also spoke to the owners about the tax, but it went nowhere. It's not that I capitulated to the bosses, but it seems to me the quota is excessive. I told them this could be discussed, and I left it for the next one who comes. One per-

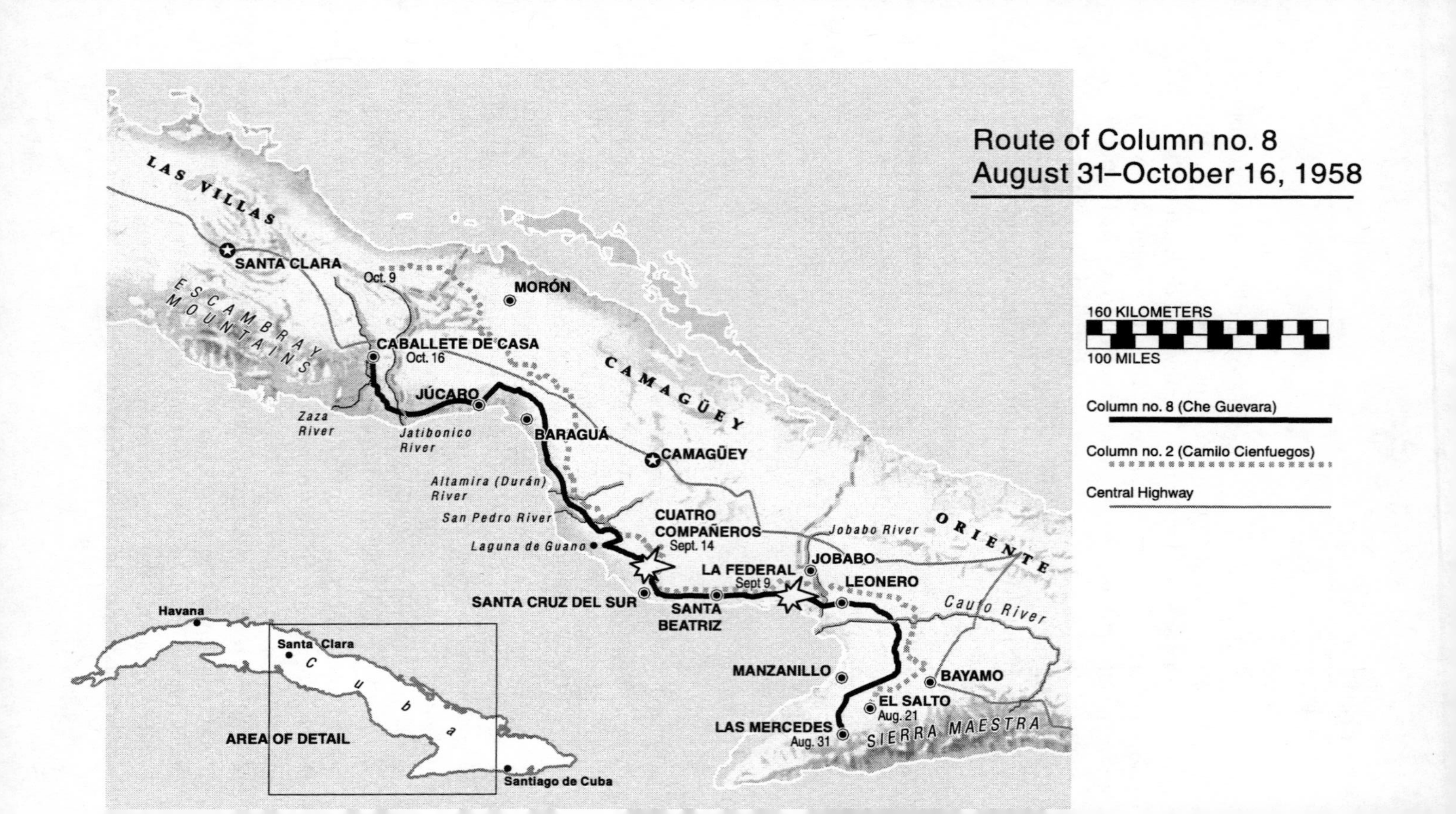
Route of Column no. 8
August 31–October 16, 1958
160 KILOMETERS
100 MILES
Column no. 8 (Che Guevara)
Column no. 2 (Camilo Cienfuegos)
Central Highway
LAS VILLAS
SANTA CLARA
Oct. 9
ESCAMBRAY MOUNTAINS
MORÓN
CABALLETE DE CASA
Oct. 16
CAMAGÜEY
JÚCARO
Zaza River
Jatibonico River
BARAGUÁ
CAMAGÜEY
Altamira (Durán) River
San Pedro River
Laguna de Guano
CUATRO COMPAÑEROS
Sept. 14
Jobabo River
ORIENTE
JOBABO
LA FEDERAL
Sept 9
LEONERO
SANTA CRUZ DEL SUR
SANTA BEATRIZ
Cauto River
MANZANILLO
BAYAMO
EL SALTO
Aug. 21
LAS MERCEDES
Aug. 31
SIERRA MAESTRA
Havana
Santa Clara
Cuba
AREA OF DETAIL
Santiago de Cuba

son with a social consciousness could work wonders in this area, and there is plenty of vegetation to hide in.

With regard to my future route I can tell you nothing, since I myself do not know. It depends more on special circumstances and chance, as we are now waiting for some trucks to see if we can free ourselves of the horses, which were perfect for the pre-airplane days that Maceo lived in, but are very visible from the air. If it were not for the horses, we would be able to move by day in peace.

Mud and water are everywhere, and the Fidel-like speeches I've had to make so we can arrive with the shells in good condition are straight out of the movies. We have had to swim across a number of streams and it was horrible. But the troops are conducting themselves well, even though the punishment squad is growing fast and promises to be the largest one in the column. The next report will be transmitted over the airwaves, if possible, from the city of Camagüey.

That's all, except to repeat the fraternal embrace to those in the Sierra, which can no longer be seen.

September 13, 1958
9:50 p.m.

After several uneven marches, I am writing you still from the middle of Camagüey, where today we are about to cross through the most dangerous part—or one of the two most dangerous parts—of the journey. Camilo crossed last night with a number of technical difficulties but no military problems.

Since the last report I sent you, we have been through some unpleasant things. Owing to a lack of guides, we fell into an ambush at the farm of Remigio Fernández in La Federal in which Marcos Borrero, a captain, was killed. We overcame the eight soldiers, killing three and taking four prisoners, whom we kept with us until finding an opportunity to release them; one escaped and blew the whistle. About sixty soldiers arrived, and on the advice of Camilo, who was nearby, we retreated with minimal combat, but we lost another man, Dalcio Gutiérrez, of the Sierra. Herman [Mark] was wounded slightly in the leg, and Enriquito Acevedo was wounded somewhat seriously in both arms. Those

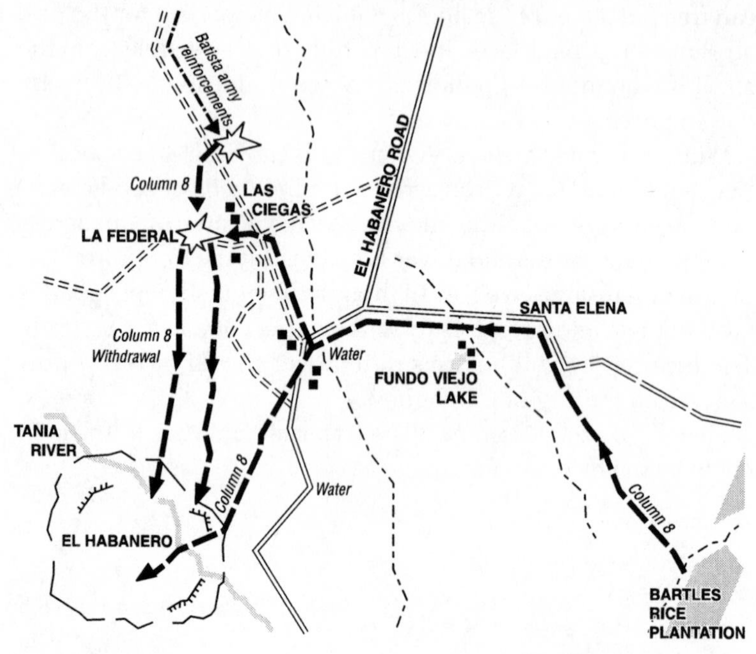

BATTLE OF LA FEDERAL
SEPTEMBER 9, 1958

distinguishing themselves in the action were Acevedo himself, Capt. Ángel Frías, and Lt. Roberto Rodríguez, "Vaquerito."

Later on they tried again to advance and we took a truck by surprise, but with only four of our men in the ambush, causing them at least two casualties. We withdrew to La Federal and rapidly left, taking Enrique to be treated. The following day the B-26s came to strafe. Camilo was able to follow more quickly, and we are waiting for the results of the trucks that I ordered to be fetched.

Some very strange things are going on here, which indicates it would be worthwhile for an experienced and "tough" leader to immediately come to these parts. On no account should more than thirty armed men come, but he could collect here anything at all he needs. It would be worthwhile to operate in the region of Naboas, where the climate is very good owing to the spoils from the Francisco sugar mill. There is solid vegetation as far as Santa Cruz, and from Santa Beatriz, sufficient for this number of men. They should take up what the leadership in Camagüey is doing, since they are making promises to induct everybody, and we are being inundated by unarmed men asking to enlist. I investigated the matter of the crazy guy, and it turns out the man has a terrible case of war psychosis.

There are many other questions I would like to raise with you, but I have run out of time and must leave. They say there are many enemy troops along the way, but by the time this report arrives, you will have found this out by other means.

March to the Escambray

September 13.[2] On that night I sent you the last report reviewing the dangers we were facing. The contacts from the July 26 Movement assured us that the guides would arrive, which did not happen. Faced with this situation, I resolved to continue in any case with an improvised guide. The end result was that we arrived at dawn at a post at Cuatro Compañeros.

The appropriate precautions could not all be taken, and although we suffered no losses, a state of confusion was created. Being completely unfamiliar with the area, we marched toward a wooded area that could be seen in the early morning light, but to get there we had to cross a railway line that the

2. This and the following five entries were written in late October, after the column had reached the Escambray mountains in Las Villas. Each report recounts the events beginning with the date listed.

guards were advancing toward in two different directions. It was necessary to engage in combat to permit the men furthest behind to get through. Captain Silva was wounded, but he has continued on with exemplary stoicism in front of his men, despite having suffered a fracture in his right shoulder joint. We had to continue fighting over the railroad line in an area no more than two hundred meters long, slowing the enemy

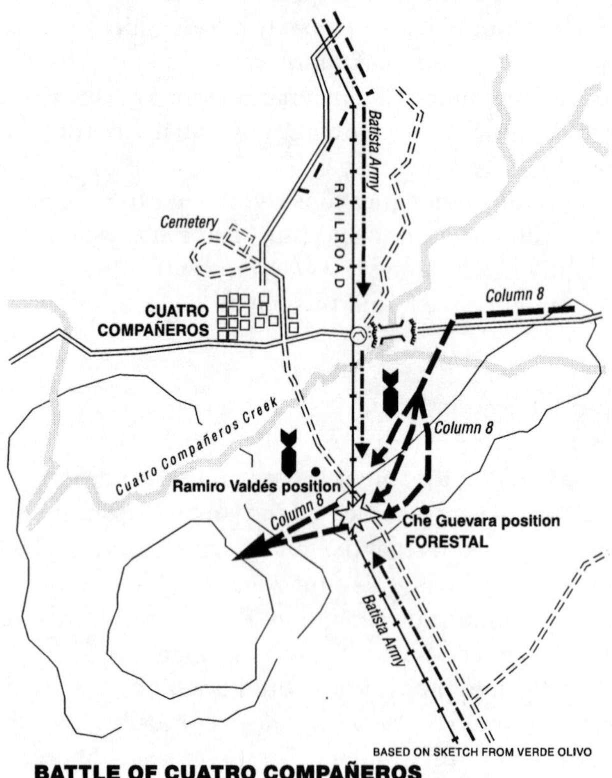

BATTLE OF CUATRO COMPAÑEROS
SEPTEMBER 14, 1958

advance, since we did not have enough men. This situation lasted two and a half hours. At 9:30 in the morning I gave the order to withdraw, having lost Comrade Juan [Hernández], whose right leg was destroyed by a 100-lb. bomb, and there were others wounded. These were all the result of forty-five minutes of bombing and strafing by two B-26s, two C-47s, and two low-flying light planes.

In the subsequent days, the men were reorganized. We finally learned that ten men who had been dispersed were now in Camilo's column, and there was only one man missing, nicknamed Morenito,[3] whose first and last names I will include at the end.

Without permitting ourselves a single day's rest, we then passed through Remedios, a rice plantation, Cadenas, some unimportant spots, and Laguna de Guano. All this was done without a guide, at times making use of a peasant, and at times guiding ourselves by compass. The social consciousness of the Camagüayan peasantry is minimal, and we had to face the consequences of numerous informers.

September 20. On that day we heard over the radio Tabernilla's report about Che Guevara's demolished column. What happened was that in one of the knapsacks they found a notebook that listed the name, address, weapon, and ammunition of the entire column, member by member. In addition, one member of this column, who is also a member of the PSP,[4] left his knapsack containing documents from that organization.

During the following days we crossed the San Pedro river and the Durán or Altamira, reaching a place called El Chicharrón. There an individual who had joined in Camagüey deserted. A little later, while crossing a dangerous line, José Pérez was lost. He had joined the column before leaving Oriente, and I suspect he deserted with his rifle. We crossed a somewhat dangerous road and found shelter in a rice-growing area where there are large plantations belonging to the Aguilera brothers. We had no guides and followed sporadic tracks left by Camilo. Since Sep-

3. José Moreno.
4. Pablo Rivalta.

tember 20 we have been walking almost nonstop through swampland. More than once we had to abandon the few horses that we brought. *Mazamorra*[5] began to sow havoc among the troops.

September 29. After we had left behind the last Aguilera rice field, and entered the fields of the Baraguá sugar mill, we found that the army had the route we had to cross totally blocked off. We were discovered while marching, and the rear guard repelled the soldiers with a few shots. Thinking that the shots had come from enemy soldiers who, following their invariable custom, were hiding in ambush along the way, I ordered us to wait until nightfall, thinking we would be able to pass. When I learned of the skirmish, signifying that the enemy was fully informed of our position, it was already too late to attempt the passage, since it was a dark and rainy night, and we had no knowledge at all of the enemy's position, which was heavily reinforced. It was necessary to retreat by compass, remaining in the relatively barren swampland to escape the planes that were actually launching their attack on a heavily wooded area some distance from our position.

The scouts headed by Lieutenant [Rogelio] Acevedo discovered a passageway at the far end of the enemy line, since they were not guarding a lagoon they considered impassable. We took this swampy lagoon, trying to minimize the noise of 140 men splashing through the mud. We walked nearly two kilometers until crossing the line that was almost one hundred meters from the last enemy post, whose voices we could hear. The splashing noise, which was impossible to avoid totally, and the full moon made me almost certain that the enemy was aware of our presence, but the low combat morale that the dictatorship's soldiers have demonstrated at all times made them deaf to every suspicious sound.

5. A foot disease caused by fungus.

We walked all night and part of the following day through saltwater swamps. A fourth of the men were either entirely barefoot, or their shoes were in bad shape.

October 3. At a spot close to the Baraguá sugar mill, the butcher who worked there was captured. His family was notified that nothing would happen to him, but that he would remain with us as guide for a couple of days. It seems the woman wanted a change of husbands and informed on us, leading to a visit by the B-26s with their usual cargo. There was no harm done, but we had to walk all night through a lagoon full of bushes whose spiked leaves cut the feet of some of our barefoot men. The morale of the troops was suffering under the impact of hunger and *mazamorra*. We were unable to rest at all since the soldiers were following our trail guided primarily by the planes. In every peasant we saw a potential informer, a psychological situation similar to the first days of the Sierra Maestra.

We were unable to make contact with the July 26 organization, since a couple of alleged members refused to show up when I asked for aid. All I received was money, nylons, some shoes, medicine, food, and guides from members of the PSP, who told me they had requested aid from the Movement's organization but received the following reply, which should be taken with caution, since I could not confirm it: "If Che sends us something in writing, we'll help him; if not, Che can go fuck himself."

October 7. We made contact with three guides from the Escambray who brought a string of complaints over the actions of Gutiérrez Menoyo. They informed me that Bordón had been taken prisoner and that there existed a situation that could lead to a pitched battle between the groups. It seemed to me there was a lot of dirty linen being washed in public, and I sent one of the guides back, with orders to Bordón to come meet me.[6]

That day, in an attempt to clean out the scum of the column, I ordered the discharge of anyone requesting to be released. Seven men took advantage of the offer, and I present their names as part of the negative history of this revolution: Víctor Sarduy, Juan Noguera, Ernesto Magaña, Rigoberto Solís, Oscar Macías, Teodoro Reyes, and Rigoberto Alarcón. A day earlier one man was lost, and I suspect that Pardillo, a member of Joel's platoon, deserted.[7]

Beginning at that point, enemy aircraft followed our steps mathematically, bombing the woods we had left a day earlier, while trying to cut off our pass at the Jatibonico river. In one of these bombings, a retropropulsion jet exploded in the air, news of which you will have heard over the radio. On October 10 the aircraft reached us, strafing the woods we were in. The planes left without leaving any victims.

The following day the forward detachment occupied a sugar mill that was close to a nearby rice field, and through intercepting the army's telephone conversations, we learned they knew of our situation. According to them, the location of the "rats" was pinpointed. (Even before this we had abandoned the woods and found shelter in a house surrounded by pastureland, remaining there an entire day without moving.)

According to information extracted from the army's conversations, they did not believe we were capable of walking the two leagues to the Jatibonico. Naturally, we did so that very night, swimming across the river, although getting almost all the weapons wet, and going another league farther until reaching the safety of a wooded area. The crossing of the Jatibonico was like

6. Víctor Bordón commanded a small July 26 Movement guerrilla force in Las Villas prior to the arrival of Guevara's column. During a visit to the camp of the Second National Front of the Escambray led by Eloy Gutiérrez Menoyo, Bordón was seized and held prisoner for several days. Bordón's troops were subsequently integrated into Guevara's column.
7. Rolando Pardillo had gotten separated from Guevara's column. Unable to reunite, he formed a small group of rebel combatants in the Escambray.

a symbol of the passage from darkness into light. Ramiro says it was like turning on an electric switch, and that is an accurate image. But since the day before the blue streak of the mountains could be seen in the distance, even the most reluctant hill-dweller felt a terrible longing to arrive.

We later made an exhausting day's march through the swamps, crossing rice fields and cane fields. We crossed the Zaza river, which must be one of the widest in Cuba. On the night of October 5 we crossed the last cordon of guards along the Trinidad-to-Sancti Spíritus highway and began our difficult political task.

I have heard of Vega's disaster,[8] clearly the product of inexperience, which would not have happened to Ramiro [Valdés]. But give us some time, and we will demonstrate that his presence here is positive for the revolution.

Escambray mountains, October 23, 1958

8. On the night of September 27–28, a Rebel Army column led by Jaime Vega fell into an army ambush in Camagüey province. Eighteen rebels were killed, and eleven wounded fighters were taken prisoner and subsequently murdered.

NOVEMBER 3, 1958

Letter to Enrique Oltuski

Santa Lucía
November 3, 1958

Dear Sierra:

I have just received your letter, which deeply surprised me. I now realize that what is discussed and agreed to here is not the same thing as what filters down to the *Llano*. You mention in the postscript that Diego[1] agrees with you, although when he was here he agreed with me. Could it be that Diego is unreliable, or does he simply have no opinion on the fundamental problems of the revolution?

You say that not even Fidel himself did this when he had nothing to eat. That is true. But when he had nothing to eat he was also not strong enough to carry out an action of this type.[2] When we asked for aid from the classes whose interests could suffer from the assault, they responded to us with evasions and finally betrayal. Such was the case with the rice growers during the recent offensive.

According to the person who brought me the letter, the local leaderships in the towns are threatening to resign. I agree that they should do so. Even more, I demand it now, since it is impermissible to have a deliberate boycott of a measure that would be so beneficial to the interests of the revolution.

I find myself faced with the sad necessity of reminding you that I have been named commander in chief, precisely to pro-

1. A reference to Víctor Paneque, the July 26 Movement's head of urban military action in Las Villas province.
2. Guevara had asked the *Llano* militias to assault a bank in Sancti Spíritus to obtain funds.

vide the Movement with unity of command and to improve things. Because of the fainthearts, it was not possible to carry out the attack on Fomento as we had planned. At the hour of battle, there were a ridiculous number of mix-ups; there were no militiamen to carry out the tasks assigned to them, and they left at the wrong time. Whether they resign or don't resign, I intend to sweep away, with the authority vested in me, all the weaklings from the villages surrounding the mountains. I never imagined things would come to a boycott by my own comrades.

Now I realize that the old antagonism we thought had been overcome is resurrected with the word *Llano*. You have leaders divorced from the masses stating what they think the people believe. I could ask you: Why is it that no peasant disagrees with our thesis that the land belongs to those who work it, while the landlords do?

Is this unrelated to the fact that the mass of combatants are in favor of the assault on the banks when they are all penniless? Have you never considered the economic reasons for this respect toward the most arbitrary of financial institutions? Those who make their money loaning out other people's money and speculating with it have no right to special consideration. The miserable amount they offer us is what they make from one day of exploitation. Meanwhile, the suffering people are shedding their blood in the mountains and on the plains, and suffering on a daily basis from betrayal by their false leaders.

You warn me that I bear total responsibility for the destruction of the organization. I accept this revolutionary responsibility, and I am prepared to render an account of my behavior before any revolutionary tribunal, at any moment decided by the National Directorate of the Movement. I will give an accounting of every last cent provided to the combatants of the Sierra, however it was obtained. But I will also ask for an accounting of each of the fifty thousand pesos you mention, since by Fidel's decision, in a letter I will show you when you come up, the treasury of the Escambray front belongs here.[3]

You ask me for a signed receipt, something I am not accustomed to doing among comrades. I am absolutely responsible for my acts, and my word is worth more than all the signatures in the world. If I demand signed statements from anyone, it is because I am not convinced of their honesty. It would never occur to me to ask you for such a thing, although I would ask for a hundred signatures from Gutiérrez Menoyo.

I will end by sending you revolutionary greetings, and I await your arrival together with Diego.

Che

Guevara's exchange with Oltuski on agrarian reform[4]

Guevara: When we have broadened and consolidated our territory we will implement an agrarian reform. We will divide the land among those who work it. What do you think of the agrarian reform?

Oltuski: It is indispensable. Without agrarian reform economic progress is not possible.

Guevara: Or social progress.

Oltuski: Yes social progress, of course. I have written an agrarian thesis for the Movement.

Guevara: Really? What did it say?

Oltuski: That all idle land should be given to the peasants, and that large landowners should be pressured to let them purchase the land with their own money. Then the land would be sold to

3. Oltuski had informed Guevara that the *Llano* group had accumulated over fifty thousand pesos and that part of it would be turned over to Guevara's column.

4. The following exchange, as recorded by Oltuski several years later, occurred during his visit to Guevara's camp in the Escambray mountains, several days before Guevara's letter above. It is taken from Enrique Oltuski, "Gente del Llano," in *Casa de las Américas*, January–February 1967.

the peasants at cost, with payment terms and credits to produce.

Guevara: That is a reactionary thesis! How are we going to charge those who work the land? You're just like all the other Llano people.

Oltuski: And what do you think we should do? Just give it to them? So they can destroy it as in Mexico? A man should feel that what he owns has cost him effort.

Guevara: My god, listen to what you're saying!

Oltuski: In addition, one must disguise things. Don't think that the Americans are going to sit idly by and watch us do things so openly. It is necessary to be more discreet.

Guevara: So you're one of those who believes we can make a revolution behind the backs of the Americans. That's idiotic! The revolution must be carried out in a life-and-death struggle against imperialism from the very first moment. A true revolution cannot be disguised.

NOVEMBER 7, 1958

Letter to Faure Chomón

Escambray mountains
November 7, 1958

Comrade Faure Chomón
General Secretary of the Revolutionary Directorate

Dear comrade:

The aim of this letter is to inform you of the latest developments in the Escambray mountains.

Following the appeal [for unity] by our highest leader, Dr. Fidel Castro, the difficulties that have arisen between us and the organization called the Second Front of the Escambray were reaching crisis proportions, culminating in an open act of aggression against one of my captains located in the region of San Blas.[1] This delicate situation makes it impossible to reach agreement with this organization.

In our previous meeting I was unable to comment concretely on your refusal to even talk with members of the Second Front, which was in contradiction with the unity instructions I brought from the Sierra Maestra. I now believe that at the present time the July 26 Movement is also unable to speak in a fraternal manner with this organization. This opens the way for us to hold concrete discussions on all points of interest to our respective organizations.

In official talks held with members of the Popular Socialist Party, they have openly expressed a pro-unity stance and have placed their organization in the towns and their guerrillas on

1. A reference to the detention of Víctor Bordón, mentioned in "En Route to Las Villas."

the Yaguajay front at the disposal of this unity.

I will be able to confer with you wherever you feel it most convenient. However, if it is not possible, for military reasons, to make contact with me directly, Cmdr. Ramiro Valdés, second in command of this region militarily for the July 26 Movement, is authorized to hold these talks.

I am taking advantage of this opportunity to inform you that Comrade Pompilio Viciedo has repeated his willingness to submit to trial rather than abandon our ranks.[2] For this reason he is being detained in this camp until the events are completely clarified. We would be grateful for anyone who could offer eyewitness or secondhand testimony about the event, and would appreciate their appearance at the trial that will be held after all the evidence is collected.

Revolutionary greetings,

Che
Commander in chief of the Las Villas
region for the July 26 Movement

2. Sebastián "Pompilio" Viciedo and Sindo Naranjo were local guerrilla leaders belonging to the July 26 Movement who had killed two members of the Second National Front of the Escambray during a clash.

NOVEMBER 8, 1958

Military order no. 1

The commander in chief of the Las Villas region for the July 26 Movement, acting under the powers vested in him by the National Directorate of the Movement, and after conferring with the different organizations that maintain armed bodies in the province, issues the following order:

As of this date, the area demarcated approximately by the Agabama river, the Fomento-to-Placetas road, and enemy lines is hereby constituted as territory under the administration of the July 26 Movement.

In this territory an official land register will immediately be undertaken in order to begin the distribution of land to the peasantry of the region. As of this moment, all property, both fixed and movable, belonging to servants of the dictatorship is declared confiscated, regardless of how it may have been obtained. The sole exception will be those small proprietors who are able to demonstrate that they have family responsibilities and hold no other possessions in any part of the republic. All properties greater than 30 caballerías[1] that are not devoted to intensive agricultural cultivation or animal husbandry are to be subject to investigation by the Agrarian Reform Commission of our Revolutionary Army. Every peasant who for at least two years has been paying rent, either in cash or in kind, for working a parcel of land in the territory covered by this military order is hereby declared free of all payment obligations and is invited to claim his rights over the land he works. Such claims will be attended to and studied by the above-named commission.

Any member of a revolutionary organization other than the July 26 Movement may pass through, live, and operate militar-

1. Thirty caballerías is approximately 1,000 acres, or 400 hectares.

ily in this territory. The only requirement shall be to abide by the military orders that have been or will be promulgated.

No one who is not a member of a revolutionary organization has the right to bear arms in this territory. No member of any revolutionary body is permitted to drink alcoholic beverages in public establishments. Members of this Movement who disobey this rule will be subject to trial by a council of war. Members of other organizations who do so shall receive a warning on the first violation, and for subsequent violations will be disarmed and sent to their respective command posts. Any shedding of blood due to violation of this order will fall under the jurisdiction of the Penal Code of the revolutionary army.

All commanders and officers of the organizations that operate in this territory are requested to solicit from the Movement's authorities any article of consumption or vehicle of transport they may require and that is included in the first paragraphs of this military order, with full assurance that such requirements will be dealt with in the spirit of revolutionary fraternity. This request is made in the interests of better administration of the region.

All military or civil crimes committed within the borders of the administrative territory encompassed by this order will fall under the jurisdiction of our appropriate regulations.

The commander in chief of the Las Villas
region for the July 26 Movement
Escambray, November 8, 1958

NOVEMBER 20, 1958

Letter to Alfredo Peña

Free Territory of Cuba,
November 20, 1958

Commander Alfredo Peña:[1]

I regret having to give orders that were directed against the guerrillas under your command to some extent. You have always been known as an honorable comrade, and we have never been subjected by you to the aggressiveness and mistrust that has characterized other commanders of the Second Front.

Time will show that we had valid reasons for what we did. It would be useless today to try to convince you.

With respect to Gutiérrez Menoyo, you should know that he has never answered my letters or responded to my invitation for us to meet. Nevertheless, our stance has always been that we are willing to reach as broad an agreement as possible, as we have done with the friendly organization of the Directorate.

Had you been fully informed about matters, you would know that we are not the aggressors, nor are we the ones who refuse to talk.

Hoping, for the good of Cuba, that this situation ends, I send you warm greetings.

Che
Commander in chief of the Las Villas
region for the July 26 Movement

1. A member of the general staff of the Second National Front of the Escambray, led by Eloy Gutiérrez Menoyo.

Late December 1958. *Top,* Fidel Castro with Col. Rego Rubido, Batista army's military commander in Oriente Province, meeting outside Santiago de Cuba to discuss surrender of the city; at center is Celia Sánchez. (COUNCIL OF STATE OFFICE OF HISTORICAL AFFAIRS)

Bottom, members of Rebel Army Column no. 2 during battle of Yaguajay in northern Las Villas. From left to right Camilo Cienfuegos, Ángel Frías, Ramón "Nené" López, Antonio Sánchez, Gilberto Gutiérrez. Sánchez accompanied Guevara to Bolivia in 1966-67, using nom de guerre Marcos, and was killed in battle.

INSTITUTE OF CUBAN HISTORY

COUNCIL OF STATE OFFICE OF HISTORICAL AFFAIRS

Above, members of Column no. 8 following liberation of Fomento, December 18, 1958, as they closed in on Santa Clara. From left, Hermes Peña, Mongo Martínez, Guevara, Jesús Parra, Sobeida Rodríguez, Víctor Bordón, José Ramón Silva.

Facing page, top, army locomotive destroyed during battle of Santa Clara. *Middle,* rebels guarding captured government troops in Fomento, as local residents watch. *Bottom,* Column no. 8 marching into battle in Santa Clara. The army garrison in Santa Clara surrendered to Guevara on January 1, 1959.

COUNCIL OF STATE OFFICE OF HISTORICAL AFFAIRS

BOHEMIA

GRANMA

January 1, 1959. Headline, *top,* reads "Batista flees." *This page*, working people in Havana celebrate victory, taking over the streets.

Facing page, top, former political prisoners, moments after being released from jail. *Bottom*, revolutionary citizenry stopping cars on Havana's waterfront, looking for Batista's henchmen. (PHOTOS: LEE LOCKWOOD)

26
PLYMOU

BOHEMIA

BOHEMIA

LEE LOCKWOOD

INSTITUTE OF CUBAN HISTORY

January 1, 1959.
Facing page, inset, Rebel Army contingent after arriving in Havana.

Residents of Havana destroy casino and burn its furnishings. U.S. ruling families had turned Havana into a center of gambling and prostitution, hated by Cuban working people.

Above, inset, From Palma Soriano, outside Santiago, Castro reads call for nationwide general strike to counter attempted military coup aimed at thwarting revolutionary victory. The call was broadcast over Radio Rebelde throughout Cuba. Facing Castro is July 26 Movement cadre Jorge Enrique Mendoza.

Throughout Cuba, workers massively supported call for general strike, leading to collapse of attempted coup. *This page, top,* January 2 strike rally in Havana.

Top, Castro addresses residents of Colón, January 7, 1959, one day before his Rebel Army forces reached Havana.

Bottom, Fidel Castro and Camilo Cienfuegos, standing in jeep, right to left, during the Rebel Army's "caravan of liberty" from Santiago de Cuba to Havana, January 2-8, 1959.

WIDE WORLD

GRANMA

DECEMBER 1, 1958

Pedrero Pact

To the people of Las Villas:

The disintegration of Fulgencio Batista's dictatorial government has entered its final stage. All the efforts of the dictatorship were directed to maintaining itself until the electoral farce of November 3. That date has come and gone, and it constituted a resounding slap in the face by the people to the dictatorship's candidates, whether or not they were officials.

Another date now faces the weary soldiers of the tyranny: February 24, when the presidential sash is theoretically to be transferred. But the Batista soldiers have fewer and fewer illusions. They increasingly feel in their flesh and blood the effectiveness of the people's arms.

We hereby make clear the total identification existing between the July 26 Movement and the Revolutionary Directorate in the struggle against the tyranny. Both organizations now address themselves to the people of Las Villas from the Escambray mountains, where their forces are fighting for Cuba's freedom.

The aim of the July 26 Movement and the Revolutionary Directorate is to maintain precise coordination of military action, moving toward combined operations in which combatants of the Revolutionary Directorate and the July 26 Movement will participate simultaneously. In addition, they aim to jointly utilize, for the benefit of the revolution, the lines of communication and supplies that are under the control of one or the other organization.

With regard to political administration, the liberated territory has been divided into zones under the jurisdiction of the Revolutionary Directorate and the July 26 Movement, where each organization will collect war taxes.

With regard to agrarian policy and the administration of justice, the July 26 Movement and the Revolutionary Directorate are coordinating their plans for agrarian reform and a new penal code.

This declaration summarizes the cohesion of the revolutionary movement on the Las Villas front, where the July 26 Movement and Revolutionary Directorate are fighting as brothers. It represents the purest ideals of the youth, who have borne a large part of the weight of the Cuban insurrection, shedding their blood, without which there could be no Sierra Maestra nor Sierra Escambray, nor could there have been a July 26 attack on the Moncada garrison, or a March 13 attack on the Presidential Palace.

We are aware of our debt to the homeland, and in the name of the revolutionary ideas of Frank País and José Antonio Echeverría, we call for unity of all revolutionary forces in the territory, asking them to adhere publicly to this call and to coordinate their actions on behalf of the Cuban nation.

Unity is the watchword. Together we are prepared to win or die.

Commander in chief
of Las Villas
July 26 Movement

Commander in chief
of Las Villas
Revolutionary Directorate

DECEMBER 3, 1958

Letter to Provincial Committee of July 26 Movement

Free Territory of Cuba
December 3, 1958

Provincial Committee
July 26 Movement

Comrade:

I am writing these lines to clarify a series of points involving the Movement. Above all I must inform you that on behalf of the July 26 Movement, I have signed a pact of relative unity with the Revolutionary Directorate (mimeographed copy attached).[1] In addition, in discussions between Camilo Cienfuegos and Félix Torres and leaders of the PSP, we reached an agreement whereby Félix Torres sent a public letter renouncing his independence as a guerrilla commander and putting his group—named "Máximo Gómez"— at the disposal of the July 26 Movement, with Torres holding the rank of captain. The corp chief will be Capt. Ángel Frías of my column, in the event that Camilo has to abandon the region. As a result of these developments, the only group with which we have been unable to reach any type of accord is the Second Front. Our relations with them have significantly improved in recent days, however, and they gave a good reception to Capt. Julio Chaviano, who is here at the present time.

Regarding the Yaguajay front: in talks with Camilo Cienfuegos, he told me of the complaints about the coordinator for this town. For this reason, I request he be replaced, or that precise instructions be given to him so that he carries out his assigned tasks better.

1. The Pedrero Pact, printed on the previous pages.

The coordinators for Remedios, Zuleta, and Caibarién should report to Commander Cienfuegos to discuss with him a number of questions.

At the same time, I inform you that we have completed the reorganization of the committee to coordinate urban actions. It will be made up of three leaders for now: René Rodríguez for this zone; "Macho" Parra in the zone of Yaguajay; and Eliecer Grave de Peralta in the zone of Chaviano, including the city of Santa Clara for the time being. Each action chief will be under the orders of the head of the group, and will be responsible for all urban and semiurban militias through this structure we have just created.

The revolutionary army has been divided into four groups. The first will be under my direct command; the second consists of the Yaguajay zone,[2] whose border is the highway linking Caibarién, Remedios, and Camajuaní; the third consists of Bordón's old area in the Escambray; and the fourth is the western zone. The third and fourth groups are commanded by Capts. Erasmo Peraza and Julio Chaviano.

In the next few days we will send a drawing of the insignia that the July 26 revolutionary army should use to unify identification.

The special section consisting of the school has finished training the first group of militia members, who will operate in the Fomento region.[3]

The Propaganda Section is working at full capacity, although some of the topics are a bit theoretical. I was forced to confiscate an issue of *El Miliciano* that did not meet the objective for which this publication was created. We have printed a special limited edition of a newspaper entitled *A ti soldado de la tiranía* [To you, soldier of the tyranny]. I am attaching, in addition to this, a copy of Military Order no. 5, and a small internal letter

2. Under the command of Camilo Cienfuegos.
3. Guevara had established the 'Ñ ico López" school for recruits at the Rebel Army camp at Caballete de Casas.

to members of the July 26 army.[4]

Regarding military actions: we repulsed an attempt by the dictatorship's army to take the position of El Pedrero, suffering four wounded in the attempt. The enemy retreated to Fomento along the right flank, leaving behind a tank they disabled and a large number of bullets and various other military equipment. Along the center, they were repulsed as far as Santa Lucía, and they also attempted to enter along the right flank in an enveloping maneuver, which was also repulsed as far as Santa Lucía. In reprisal, the enemy burned down twenty-one peasant homes.

The sabotage of lines of communication continues. Our forces have totally destroyed the railroad bridge over the Tuinicú river, in addition to destroying a bridge and the road on the Trinidad-to-Sancti Spíritus highway.

Two comrades have been promoted to captain: Erasmos Rodríguez and Alfonso Zayas. A number of promotions to lieutenant have been made; I do not list them here since I do not know their Christian names.

The lists of supplies being ordered for the column will be sent in the usual way. I attach the main points for the July 26 program that Comrade "Eloy" asked me for, and a letter for Fidel.

Revolutionary greetings,

Che

4. Guevara's Order no. 5 limited transportation on all highways in Las Villas.

DECEMBER 15–18, 1958

The battle of Fomento

Official Report

In the early hours of December 15, after having destroyed the Central Highway bridge over the Falcón river, thus cutting off the enemy's land route, our troops proceeded to block all access roads to Fomento. The most important road, the Fomento-to-Placetas highway, was cut off by the forces led by Captain Silva, while troops of the Revolutionary Directorate blocked the adjacent highways. At 9:00 P.M. a platoon under the command of Capt. Alfonso Zayas took the Santa Isabel sugar mill. On the 16th, at 6:30 A.M., forces under Capts. Alfonso Zayas, Manuel Hernández, and Joel Iglesias occupied positions inside the city. At 7:00 A.M., commander in chief Ernesto Guevara spoke with the city garrison's commander. Later, the battle extended to the entire city.

At 10:00 A.M. troops under the command of Capt. Manuel Hernández seized a shortwave radio unit and put it into operation to address the regime's soldiers. Comrade Wilfredo Campos was killed in this action. At 1:00 P.M. members of the same platoon forced the enemy to surrender at a spot near the CNC radio station; one hour later a squad led by Cmdr. René Rodríguez forced the garrison to surrender to our forces. Comrade Rolando Enrique Moreno, a native of Fomento and a member of that town's militia, was killed in this action. That evening the members of the army post in the city's theater building abandoned their position and surrendered to our forces. After we had taken over the city, the dictatorship turned the city into an inferno, utilizing the air force in a retaliatory attack, strafing the unarmed civilian population. This attack resulted in the deaths of a four-year-old child and several other civilians.

In this battle we suffered other irreparable losses. Our beloved captains Manuel Hernández and Joel Iglesias were seriously wounded, especially the latter, during the battle to encircle the garrison, and in the early hours of December 18, while we were tightening the encirclement, our dear comrade Mariano Pérez was mortally wounded. At 4:00 P.M. the entire garrison surrendered to our forces. That day the enemy air force concentrated its attack on nonmilitary targets. The Spanish Club was viciously strafed with .50-caliber machine gun fire. Even the Red Cross building was mercilessly attacked, despite the clearly visible Red Cross emblem on the building, where at that moment many wounded from both sides, and others who had not been involved in the battle, were being taken care of.

A total of 141 prisoners were taken—including soldiers, policemen, and informers—and a substantial amount of booty, consisting of 2 jeeps, one of them equipped with shortwave radio and receiving sets; 3 trucks, one of them armored; one 81-mm. mortar with 5 shells; one .30-caliber machine gun with tripod; 11 Garand rifles; 8 San Cristóbal rifles; 6 M-1 carbines; 13 Thompson machine guns; 96 Springfield rifles; 9 .45-caliber revolvers; 4 rifles; 5,000 rounds of .30-06 shells; 1,000 rounds of 30 M-1 caliber shells; 2,500 .22-caliber shells; 300 12-gauge shotgun shells; 250 16-gauge shotgun shells; 45 shells (.45 caliber); 24 detonators for 81-mm. mortars; 3 typewriters in good condition; 2 radios; 1 television set; 1 electric power generator; 1 shortwave unit; 145 shirts; 170 pairs of pants; 18 pairs of shoes; 10 pairs of leggings; 41 undershirts; 34 pairs of shorts; 10 raincoats; 25 knapsacks; 21 blankets; 20 towels; 4 mosquito nets; 18 sheets; 31 tin plates; 5 canteens; 1 alarm clock; 6 tents; 8 cots; 5 horse blankets; 20 pistol holsters; and 10 horses, with saddles.

The city of Fomento is the seat of the municipality of Fomento and has a population of ten thousand. It is linked to Placetas by a first-class highway; to Trinidad by a second-class highway; to Manicaragua by country roads running through Güinía de Miranda; and to Cabaiguán by country roads running through Santa Lucía, Sancti Spíritus, Pedreda, etc.

The taking of Fomento has led to the liberation of a vast territory reaching as far as the Central Highway, where the enemy strongholds of Placetas, Cabaiguán, and Sancti Spíritus are located. As a result of the actions fought these past few days, this command has awarded the following ranks: Dr. Oscar Fernández Mell (to captain); Lt. Roberto Rodríguez, head of the Suicide Squad (to captain); Lt. Orlando Pantoja Tamayo (to captain); Comrade Francisco Chacón (to lieutenant); Comrades Jesús Vázquez, Gilberto del Río, and Enrique Acevedo (to lieutenant). This command congratulates all troops under its command for their heroic behavior during the encirclement and taking of the city of Fomento, and extends congratulations to the group of war correspondents for their efficient job throughout the battle.

Ernesto Guevara
Commander in chief of the rebel forces of the
July 26 Movement in the region of Las Villas

Letter to the Red Cross

December 18, 1958
Free Territory of Cuba
Head Physician of the Red Cross
Section 23, Placetas

Distinguished doctor:

The purpose of this letter is to denounce the savage strafings of the civilian population in the city of Fomento and nearby towns—attacks that pursue no military objective whatsoever and that have resulted in the deaths of two children in the city of Fomento and the wounding of two civilians in the town of Arenas.

It is my wish that your superiors be informed of this denunciation, which I am making in defense of elementary principles of humanity, reminding you that the objective of the Red Cross is not only to pick up wounded or dead combatants but also to look after the safety and welfare of civilians in time of war. To this let us add that the people being subjected to these horrible methods of attack are not strangers, but the Cuban people themselves, from whom the respected members of your institution come.

Thanking you in advance for your efforts to humanize this so unilaterally cruel war, I remain

Yours,

Ernesto Guevara
Commander in chief of the July 26 Movement
in the region of Las Villas

JANUARY 2, 1959

To the people of Las Villas

Upon my departure from this capital and province to take on new responsibilities that the general command of our army has ordered me to assume, I express my heartfelt appreciation to this magnificent people who have given so much assistance to the revolutionary cause, and on whose soil so many of the important final battles against the tyranny have been fought. I express my wish that you offer the fullest support to the military governor of Las Villas, Capt. Calixto Morales, to rapidly normalize the institutional life of this long-suffering province.

The people of Las Villas should know that in leaving, our invasion column—enormously increased in size through the support of the sons of this land—goes full of deep personal affection and with the feeling of leaving a beloved place. I ask you to maintain the same revolutionary spirit, so that in the gigantic task of reconstruction ahead, Las Villas may continue to be in the vanguard of the revolution.

Che
Commander in chief of the July 26
Revolutionary Army, Las Villas

FEBRUARY 1961

A sin of the revolution

REVOLUTIONS ARE RADICAL AND ACCELERATED social transformations made under specific circumstances. They rarely, if ever, emerge fully ripe, and not all their details are scientifically foreseen. They are products of passion, of improvisation by human beings in their struggle for social change, and are never perfect. Our revolution was no exception. It committed errors, and some of these cost us dearly. Today one such error has been shown to us, although its repercussions have been few. Nonetheless, it demonstrates the truth of the popular sayings: "The leopard never changes his spots" and "Birds of a feather flock together."

When the troops of the invasion column reached the foothills of the Escambray—in great pain, their feet bloodied and lacerated by diseases caused by fungus, keeping themselves going on faith alone, after forty-five days on the march—they were greeted by an unusual letter. It was signed by Commander Carreras,[1] and it stated that the column of the revolutionary army under my command was prohibited from entering the Escambray without a clear explanation of what we were doing there. Before entering I was instructed to halt right there and give them an explanation. We were to halt in the open plains, under those conditions, threatened constantly with enemy encirclement, which we could escape only through our rapid movement! That was the essence of the long and insolent letter.

We continued ahead, perplexed, sorry that we were unable to wait for those who proclaimed themselves our comrades in struggle, but determined to resolve any problem and carry out

1. Jesús Carreras was a leader of the Second National Front of the Escambray, led by Eloy Gutiérrez Menoyo.

the express orders of commander in chief Fidel Castro, who had clearly ordered us to work for the unity of all combatants.

We reached the Escambray and made camp near Del Obispo peak, which is visible from Sancti Spíritus and has a cross on its summit. There we were able to establish our first camp, and we immediately looked for a house where we were supposed to find the most precious items to a guerrilla fighter: shoes. There were no shoes; they had been taken by the forces of the Second Front of the Escambray, despite having been obtained by the July 26 Movement. A storm was brewing. Nevertheless, we succeeded in staying calm, talking to some captain, who later informed us he had murdered four combatants of the people who wanted to abandon the Second Front and join the revolutionary ranks of the July 26 Movement. We had a discussion with Commander Carreras, unfriendly but not heated. He had already drunk half a bottle of liquor, which was approximately half his daily quota. He was not as gross and aggressive in person as was his missive of a few days earlier, but we saw in him an enemy.

Later we learned of Commander Peña, famous in the region for rustling the peasants' cattle. He emphatically prohibited us from attacking Güinía de Miranda, because the village belonged to his zone. When we argued that the region belonged to everyone, that it was necessary to fight, and that we had more and better weapons and more experience, he said simply that our bazooka was balanced by two hundred shotguns, and that two hundred shotguns had the same effect as a bazooka. End of discussion. Güinía de Miranda was to be taken by the Second Front, and we could not attack it. Naturally we paid no attention, but we knew we faced dangerous "allies."

After many trials and tribulations, too long to relate, where our patience was tested an infinite number of times—and where, according to the correct criticism made by Fidel, we put up with more than we should have—we reached a "truce." They permitted us to make the agrarian reform in the entire area belonging to the Second Front, as long as we permitted them to collect taxes. Collect taxes—that was the watchword!

It was a long story. Through a bloody and unrelenting struggle we occupied the principal cities of the country, and we had the support of good allies in the Revolutionary Directorate, whose men, although fewer and with less experience, did everything possible to help our common success. On January 1 the revolutionary command demanded that all troops be put under my command in Santa Clara. The Second National Front of the Escambray, through the mouth of its leader Gutiérrez Menoyo, immediately placed itself under my command. No problem whatsoever. We then gave the order for them to wait for us, because we had to work out arrangements for administering the first big city we had conquered.

During those days it was difficult to control things, and we soon learned that the Second Front, trailing after Camilo Cienfuegos, had "heroically" entered Havana. We thought it might be some maneuver to try to gain strength, to occupy something, to cause some provocation. I already knew them, although with each passing day I got to know them even better. They did in fact occupy the most important strategic positions, from their point of view—a few days later the first bill arrived from the Hotel Capri, signed by Fleitas: it was for $15,000 in food and drink for a tiny number of beneficiaries.

When it came time to give out ranks, almost a hundred captains and a large number of commanders aspired to cushy state jobs, in addition to a large and "select" group of men put forward by the inseparable Menoyo and Fleitas, who aspired to a whole series of jobs in the government. These were not particularly well-paying positions, but they had one characteristic: they had all been sources of graft in the prerevolutionary regime. Housing inspectors; tax collectors; all the places where money changed hands and passed through avid fingers—these posts were the objects of their desires. This was a part of the Rebel Army with whom we had to coexist.

From the very first days serious differences arose that sometimes culminated in violent exchanges of words. But what appeared to be revolutionary good sense on our part always prevailed, and we gave way for the sake of unity. We maintained principles. We did not permit theft, nor did we give out key positions to those we knew to be potential traitors. But we did not eliminate them; we temporized, always on behalf of some vague and poorly understood unity. *This was a sin of the revolution.*

The same sin led us to pay juicy salaries to people like Barquín, Felipe Pazos, Teté Casuso, and so many other domestic and foreign freeloaders whom the revolution kept to avoid conflict, trying to buy their silence with a tacit understanding: a salary that was already a source of sponging, from a government that they were waiting to betray. But the enemy has more money and more means of bribing than the people do. When all is said and done, what could we offer a Fleitas or a Menoyo except a position of work and sacrifice?

They lived off fairy tales of a struggle in which they did nothing, duping the people, looking for posts, always trying to get closer to where money was ripe for the picking, "inciting" in all the cabinet ministries. In this they were scorned by all pure revolutionaries. Yet we allowed them to function, albeit gritting our teeth. All this was an insult to our revolutionary conscience. Their presence constantly revealed to us our sin: the sin of laxness in the face of absence of revolutionary sprit; in the face of potential traitors; in the face of weakness of spirit, cowardice, thievery, and "cattle rustling."

Our conscience has now been cleared because they have all gone, those whom God sent to Miami, in little boats. Thank you so much, "cattle rustlers" of the Second Front. Thank you so much for relieving us of the detestable presence of self-appointed commanders, of ridiculous captains, of heroes unfamiliar with the rigors of military life but not the easy seizure of peasant homes. Thank you so much for giving us this lesson, for demonstrating to us that consciousness cannot be bought by revolutionary generosity, that we must be strict and demanding toward all. Thank you so much for showing us the need to be inflexible toward error, weakness, and bad faith. And thank you so much for allowing us to rise up, denounce, and punish, wherever it occurs, any act of vice that goes against the high ideals of the revolution.

Let the example of the Second Front, and the example of our good, dear friend, the ex-thief Prío, bring us down to reality. Let us not be ashamed to call a thief a thief, because we ourselves, as a result of what we loosely called "revolutionary tactics," referred to the thief as "ex-president" during the days when the "ex-president" did not refer to us as "contemptible communists," as he does now, but as "saviors of Cuba."

A thief is a thief, and he'll die a thief—at least the "distinguished" ones. Not the desperate person in some countries who has to steal a crust of bread so his children can eat. But the other one—the one who robs to attain women, drugs, or liquor, to satisfy the base instincts that drive him—he'll be a thief his entire life.

They're now all together over there, those who assaulted our conscience. People like Felipe Pazos, who sold his honor as if it were a gold coin, to put it at the disposal of "serious" institutions. People like Rufo López and Justo Carrillo, who took a baby step to accommodate themselves to the situation in order to get a little further. People like [José] Miró Cardona, the eternal optimist. People like the incurable thieves, complicit in murders against the people. People like the "cattle rustlers," whose "great feats" were carried out against the masses of peasants they murdered in the Escambray, sowing more terror than Batista's army itself. They are our conscience. They remind us of our sin, a sin of the revolution that must not be repeated, a lesson we must learn.

Revolutionary conduct is a mirror of revolutionary faith. When someone who calls himself a revolutionary does not behave as such, he is simply a charlatan. Let them all embrace one another: Ventura and Tony Varona, who fought so much among themselves; Prío and Batista; Gutiérrez Menoyo and Sánchez Mosquera; murderers who killed to satisfy their cravings for some immediate desire, and those who did so in the name of freedom. Open thieves and those who buy and sell honor; opportunists of every stripe; presidential candidates—a pretty package!

You have taught us a lot! Thank you so much.

PUBLISHED IN VERDE OLIVO, FEBRUARY 12, 1961

Letters *on the* Cuban Revolutionary War

JULY 6, 1956

To his parents

Mexico,
July 6, 1956
Government Jail

Dear folks:

I received your letter (Dad's) here in my new and elegant Miguel Schulz mansion, together with the visit by Petit informing me of your fears.[1] I will give you a history of the case.

Some time ago—quite a while already—I met a young Cuban leader who invited me to join his movement, dedicated to the armed liberation of his country. I of course accepted. For the last few months, I have devoted my time to the physical training of the young men who would some day have to set foot in Cuba, keeping up the false impression that I was only an instructor. On June 21 (one month after I had left my house in Mexico City, since I was living on a ranch on the outskirts), Fidel was taken prisoner together with a group of comrades. In the house was a list of addresses where we were all staying, so everyone was caught in the roundup. My papers listed me as a student of Russian at the Mexican-Russian Institute for Cultural Exchange, which was sufficient for them to consider me an important link in the organization, and Dad's friendly news agencies began to make noise all over the world.

That is a summary of past events. The future ones are divided in two: medium-term and immediate. With regard to the me-

1. Guevara was one of twenty-eight *Granma* expeditionaries and their supporters arrested by Mexican police; they were being held at the Miguel Schulz Jail in Mexico City. Guevara's parents, Ernesto Guevara Lynch and Celia de la Serna, were living in Buenos Aires, Argentina. Ulises Petit was a friend of the Guevara family.

dium term, I will state here that my future is linked to the liberation of Cuba. Either I will triumph with it, or I will die there. (This is the explanation for a rather enigmatic and romantic letter I sent to Mom a while back.) With regard to the immediate future, I can say little because I don't know what will become of me. I am at the mercy of the judge and it will be easy for them to deport me to Argentina, unless I obtain asylum in a third country, which I would consider beneficial to my political health.

In any case, whether I have to leave for a new destination, stay in this jail, or go free, Hilda[2] will return to Peru, which now has a new government that has announced a political amnesty.

For obvious reasons I will greatly reduce my correspondence. Besides, the Mexican police have the pleasant custom of censoring letters, to prevent all but the most banal, household things from being written. And no one is particularly eager to have some son of a bitch know about his intimate matters, regardless of how insignificant they may be. I ask you to give Beatriz[3] a kiss, and to explain why I am not writing, and tell her not to worry about sending newspapers for the time being.

We are just about to declare an indefinite hunger strike to protest the unjustified detentions and the tortures that some of my comrades were submitted to. The morale of the entire group is high.

For now, continue writing to the house.

If for any reason I am unable to write more—which I don't think likely—and later my number comes up, consider these lines as my farewell, not very grandiloquent but sincere. I have spent my life searching for my truth by fits and starts, and now that I'm on my way and have a baby daughter who will perpetuate me, the cycle is complete. From this time onward, I

2. Hilda Gadea, Guevara's wife. Following the end of the revolutionary war they were divorced, and Che married Aleida March in June 1959.
3. A reference to Guevara's aunt.

would not consider death a frustration. Rather, I would feel as Hikmet put it:[4] "I will bring to my grave only the sorrow of an unfinished song."

A kiss to everyone,

Ernesto

4. Nazim Hikmet (1902–1963) was a Turkish poet and dramatist.

JANUARY 28, 1957

To Hilda Gadea

January 28, 1957

Dear old lady:

From the woods of Cuba, alive and thirsting for blood, I write these fiery lines in the spirit of Martí. As though I were a real soldier (I'm filthy and in tatters at least), I am writing on top of a messkit, with a rifle at my side and a new accessory in my lips: a cigar.

The thing was difficult. As you know, after seven days packed like sardines in the now-famous *Granma,* due to the navigators we landed in a fetid mangrove swamp, and we continued our misadventures until being taken by surprise at the now-also-famous Alegría, where we were scattered like pigeons. I was wounded in the neck and remained alive thanks only to my cat lives, since a machine gun bullet struck a box of bullets I was wearing over my chest and the ricochet caught me in the neck. I walked a few days through the forest believing I was badly wounded, since the impact of the bullet had given me quite a pain in my chest.

Of the fellows you knew, only Jimmy Hirzel was killed, murdered while surrendering. My group—which includes Almeida and Ramirito, of the ones you know—spent seven days of terrible hunger and thirst until we eluded the encirclement and, with the help of peasants, once again met up with Fidel. (One of those listed as killed, still unconfirmed, is poor Ñico.)

After all kinds of problems we reorganized, armed ourselves, and attacked a garrison, killing five soldiers, wounding a few, and taking some prisoners. The army, which had assumed we were scattered, was given the biggest surprise. It extended the suspension of rights to the entire republic and for forty-five days sent elite troops on our tail. We scattered them again, and this time they suffered three dead and two wounded. The dead remained in the woods. Shortly thereafter, we captured three soldiers and took their weapons.

If one adds to all this that we've suffered no losses and the forest is ours, you can get an idea of the army's demoralization. Just when they think we're in their grasp, they see us disappear like soap through their fingers. Naturally the fight is not completely won and many battles lie ahead, but things now lean in our favor, as they will increasingly.

Now, speaking of everyone there, I want to know if you're still at home where I'm writing this to. Tell me how everyone is doing, particularly the "apple of my eye."[5] I send her the strongest hug and kiss, which should be able to vie with her bony armor. To the others, I send a hug and regards. With my precipitous departure, I left some things in Pocho's house,[6] among them photos of you and the little one. When you write, send these to me. You can write to my uncle's house, addressed to El Patojo. The letters will be delayed somewhat but should arrive.

A hug from

Chancho

5. Hildita, Guevara's first daughter.
6. A reference to Alfredo Bauer Paíz, a Guatemalan exile who Guevara had been staying with in Mexico City.

DECEMBER 9, 1957

To Fidel Castro

Sierra Maestra
December 9, 1957

Commander:

We have avenged the loss of El Hombrito, killing at least three soldiers at Alto de Conrado. The victory didn't come free of charge since we could not capture a single weapon and lost a rifle.

Alejandro Oñate was wounded in the shoulder and I caught an M-1 bullet in the instep of my foot, which is still there and for the moment completely prevents me from walking. Ramiro has taken command of the column and is going with most of the men to the place the bearer of this letter will tell you. Rapid resupply of .30-06 and .45 automatic ammunition would be helpful. I am in a safe spot, with an ambush prepared. I am very sorry not to have followed your advice, but the morale of the men had fallen quite a bit as a result of the useless flurry of activity they had been subjected to, and I considered my presence in the front line of fire to be necessary. All things considered, I took pretty good care of myself and the wound was accidental.

The beating we gave them was impressive: twelve definitive casualties, counting the killed and prisoners, not including the wounded. The result was poor in terms of acquiring weapons.

The situation is calm and there is no news of other troops in the region, except for a small garrison at Mar Verde, which I don't dare attack because of the shortage of ammunition. I enclose the proclamations produced by the "genius" of Capote, which I ordered to be distributed as widely as we are capable of.

A fraternal good-bye,

Che

JANUARY 6, 1958

To Fidel Castro

Sierra Maestra
January 6, 1958, 8:45

Fidel,

I received the letter to Prío and we are already having it printed.[7] Based on its content, I believe it is a document no less important than that of Montecristi, and it will surely be a historic model.[8] Today it will perhaps cause some problems—especially among certain top levels of industry—but, as Lenin said, principled politics is politic. The end result will be magnificent.

It is really fantastic that we can now go to Manzanillo. I already have a small column under the command of Israel operating there where you told me. I don't have any direct reports, but the indirect ones that have arrived indicate that he captured [illegible] with seven soldiers, whom he later freed. They say he has about eighty men. I intend to make him a captain, assign a teacher to him so he will learn how to read, and send him down to operate in some place. Ramiro has surely told you about my troops. Camilo is doing great in everything, and he is my right-hand man at present.

In conclusion, I repeat my congratulations on the document. I told you before that you would have the merit of demonstrating the possibilities of armed struggle in Latin America supported by the people. Now you are on the even greater road to

7. A reference to Castro's letter of December 14, 1957, in response to the Miami Pact, contained in the chapter "One Year of Armed Struggle."
8. The Montecristi manifesto, presenting a democratic program for Cuba, was issued by José Martí in 1895, at the beginning of the final war for independence from Spain.

being one of the two or three in Latin America to reach power through armed struggle of the masses.

Greetings,

Che

JANUARY 14, 1959

To Sergia Cordoví Rodríguez

Military Department of La Cabaña
Havana
January 14, 1959

Mrs. Sergia Cordoví Rodríguez
Luyanó, Havana

Dear madam:

I am writing in reply to your letter dated January 3, in which you inquire about your son Geonel Rodríguez y Cordoví.

With deep regret I must inform you that your son Geonel was killed while fighting heroically against the tyranny at the battle of Santo Domingo, the victim of an enemy mortar. He was buried with honors corresponding to his rank of captain; his grave is located at the "Julián Pérez" estate.

This office shares with you the pain over the irreparable loss of such a valiant comrade.

Sincerely yours,
Freedom or death

Ernesto "Che" Guevara
Commander in chief of the
Military Department of La Cabaña

APRIL 12, 1960

To Ernesto Sábato

Havana
April 12, 1960
Year of the Agrarian Reform

Mr. Ernesto Sábato[9]
Santos Lugares, Argentina

Dear compatriot:

It must be fifteen years now since I met your son, who should be close to twenty, and your wife at the place I believe is called "Cabalango," in Carlos Paz. Later I read your book *Uno y el universo* [One and the universe], which fascinated me. I would not have imagined that with the passage of time it would be you—someone possessing the title of writer, which for me was the most sacred thing in the world—who would be asking me for a definition, a reencountering, as you call it, based on an authority earned through various events and many subjective phenomena.

I make these preliminary remarks only to remind you that despite everything, I belong to the land of my birth, and I am still able to feel deeply all its joys, its hopes, and also its deceptions. It would be difficult to explain to you why "this" is not the "Revolution of Liberty."[10] Perhaps I should tell you that when

9. Ernesto Sábato (1911–) is one of Argentina's most prominent novelists.
10. The "Revolution of Liberty" refers to the 1955 military coup against Juan Domingo Perón, carried out with the backing of sections of the Argentine bourgeoisie that supported closer links to Washington and Wall Street. Perón was president of Argentina from 1946 to 1955 and from 1973 until his death the following year. During his first period in office, he sought to bolster his bourgeois government by offering concessions to the working

this struggle began, I viewed in the same way these words you denounce by putting them in quotation marks. I identified these words with what had occurred in Guatemala, which I had just left, defeated and somewhat deceived. And all of us felt the same way—those who participated from the beginning in this strange adventure, and those who were deepening our revolutionary feelings in contact with the peasant masses, in a close interrelationship, over two years of cruel struggle and truly great efforts.

We could not be a "Revolution of Liberty" because we were not part of a plutocratic army but of a new popular army, who took up arms to destroy the old. We could not be a "Revolution of Liberty" because our banner of struggle was not a cow but a tractor destroying the barbed wire fence around a large landed estate—which is today the insignia of our National Institute of Agrarian Reform. We could not be a "Revolution of Liberty" because our servant girls cried with happiness the day Batista fled and we entered Havana, and today they continue giving information about all the counterrevolutionary actions and all the naive conspiracies of the "Country Club" people—the same "Country Club" people you knew over there, and who occasionally shared your hatred of Peronism.

Here the submissiveness of the intellectuals had a much less subtle appearance than in Argentina. Here the intellectuals were open slaves, not disguised as indifferent as they are over there, and much less disguised as intelligent; it was simply a case of slaves to a despicable cause, without subterfuges; they simply vociferated.

But all this is merely literature. I am sending you a book, as you did to me, about Cuba's ideology;[11] it is like taking you back

---

class, while maneuvering for a better position for Argentine capital against U.S. and British imperialism. His anti-imperialist stance won him support among broad layers of working people, and his supporters took the leadership of the main trade union federation, the General Confederation of Labor (CGT).

11. Guevara's *Guerrilla Warfare: A Method.*

a year in time. Today it appears as the first fledgling attempt to draw theoretical conclusions from this revolution. This book about guerrilla warfare is eminently practical, as are, invariably, all the empirical things we do. It is little more than a schoolboy's attempt to arrange words one after another; it has no pretensions of explaining the great things you are concerned about. Nor does it explain what I intend to publish in a second book, if national and international circumstances do not compel me to pick up a rifle once again (a task I disdain as a member of government, but greet with enthusiasm as a man of adventure). Anticipating what may or may not come about (the book), I can tell you, in short, that this revolution is the most genuine work of improvisation.

In the Sierra Maestra, a communist leader who visited us, admiring such improvisation and how all the little details being worked out separately were adjusted to centralized organization, stated that it was the most perfectly organized chaos in the universe. And this revolution is the same, because it traveled much more rapidly than did its earlier ideology. For when all is said and done, Fidel Castro was a candidate for deputy on the ticket of a bourgeois party, so bourgeois and so respectable that it could just as well have been the Radical Party in Argentina. It followed the teachings of a deceased leader, Eduardo Chibás, whose ideas were much like those of Irigoyen.[12] And we who followed him were a group of men with little political preparation; only a lot of good will and an innate sense of honor. Thus we cried, "In 1956 we will be heroes or martyrs." A little earlier we had cried, or rather Fidel had cried, "Honor against money." These simple phrases summarized our simple viewpoint.

12. A leader of the left wing of the Orthodox Party and its youth organization, Castro had been a candidate of that party for the house of representatives prior to the scheduled 1952 elections, which were cancelled following Batista's March 10 coup. Castro subsequently split with the Orthodox Party and formed the July 26 Movement. Hipólito Irigoyen, a founding leader of the Argentine Radical Party, served as president of Argentina from 1916 to 1930.

The war revolutionized us. There is no more profound experience for a revolutionary than the act of war; not the isolated act of killing, or of carrying a rifle, or of undertaking a struggle of this or that type. It is the totality of the war itself, knowing that an armed man is worth something as a combat entity, and is worth as much as any other armed man, and no longer fears other armed men. It is the process of continuing to explain to the defenseless peasants how they can take up a rifle and prove to the soldiers that an armed peasant is worth as much as the best of them; of continuing to learn how the efforts of one are worthless if not surrounded by the efforts of all. It is the process of continuing to learn how revolutionary slogans have to reflect the deep aspirations of the people, and of continuing to learn from the people what their most deeply felt desires are, and to transform these into banners of political agitation. This we have all been doing, and we understood that the peasants' yearning for land was the most powerful motive of struggle that could be found in Cuba.

Fidel understood many other things and was already developing into the extraordinary leader of men he is today, into the gigantic force for unity of our people. Because Fidel, above all, is the unifier par excellence, the undisputed leader who overcomes all differences and whose disapproval sweeps things away. Often times utilizing, sometimes challenged by those with money or ambition, he is always feared by his adversaries.

In this way our revolution was born. In this way its slogans were being created, and in this way, little by little, we began drawing theoretical conclusions in the heat of these events to create our own body of ideas. When we launched our agrarian reform law in the Sierra Maestra, we had already been dividing up the land there. After understanding in practice a series of factors, we put forward our first timid law, which did not deal with the most fundamental thing: the suppression of the large landed estates.

Initially, from the standpoint of the press of the continent, we were not all that bad, for two reasons. First, because Fidel Castro is an extraordinary politician who never revealed his intentions beyond certain limits, and he knew how to win the admiration of reporters from the large media enterprises, who sympathized with him and took the easy road of sensational reporting. Secondly, because the North Americans, who are the greatest creators of tests and standards, simply applied one of their standards, marked down the results, and then rated it.

According to their rating sheet the words "We will nationalize public services," were to be read as "We will prevent this from happening if we receive a reasonable amount of support." The words "We will eliminate the system of large landed estates," were to be read as: "We will utilize the large landed estates as a good source of funding for our political campaigns, or for our personal enrichment." And so on and so forth.

It never entered their heads that what Fidel Castro and our Movement were saying so candidly and sharply was what we actually intended to do. For them we constitute the great fraud of the century: we stated the truth in an attempt to deceive. When Eisenhower says we betrayed our principles, that is partially true—from their vantage point: we betrayed the image they had of us. It is like the tale of the lying shepherd boy, but in reverse; they did not believe us, either.

Thus we are now speaking a language that is also new, because our thinking is not able to keep up with the speed we are traveling. We are in a state of continual motion, and theory moves more slowly, so slowly in fact that after writing this manual that I am now sending you—written during little bits of free time—I find that it is almost worthless here in Cuba. For our own country, on the other hand, it might be of some value, but only if it is used with intelligence, without haste or deception. I am therefore afraid of trying to describe the ideology of the movement. By the time it is published, everyone would think it was written many years earlier.

While the external situation is sharpening and international tension is growing, our revolution, for its own survival, must continue to sharpen itself. And as the revolution sharpens itself more and more, the tension is raised more and more. It is a vicious circle that seems destined to be tightened more and more until it is ready to break; we will then see how we get out of the jam. What I can assure you, though, is that the people are strong, because they have struggled and won, and they know the value of victory. They know the taste of bullets and of bombs, and also the taste of oppression. They will know how to struggle with exemplary firmness.

At the same time, I can assure you that when that time comes we will have theorized very little—despite the fact that I am now making a timid attempt along these lines—and we will have to resolve the problems with the agility given us by guerrilla life. I know that when that day comes, your weapon of intellectual honesty will fire at the enemy, our enemy, and that we will be able to count on you from over there, fighting at our side. This letter has been a bit long and not free of that small amount of posturing characteristic of simple people like us. Nevertheless, in trying to explain things to a thinker, we are also becoming something we are not: thinkers. In any case, I am at your service.

Cordially,

Ernesto Che Guevara

DECEMBER 1962

To Carlos Franqui

Comrade Carlos Franqui
Havana
Editor, *Revolución* newspaper

Comrade Franqui:

I did not like the photo supplement published the other day.[13] Allow me to tell you this very frankly and to explain why, hoping that these lines will be published as my "salvo."

Leaving aside small things that do not speak well of the newspaper's seriousness, such as those photos with a group of soldiers aiming at a supposed enemy with their eyes turned to the camera, there are fundamental errors:

1. That extract from the diary is not entirely authentic. The thing was like this: I was asked (during the war) if I had kept a diary of the invasion. I had, but in the form of very bare notes, for my personal use; and at the time I had no time to develop it. A gentleman from Santa Clara took charge of doing that (I don't remember now under what circumstances); he turned out to be quite "flamboyant" and tried to add feats by means of adjectives. What little value those four notes might have is destroyed when they lose authenticity.

2. It is false that, for me, the war took second place to meeting the needs of the peasantry. At that time winning the war was the important thing, and I believe I devoted myself to that task with all the determination I was capable of. After entering the Escambray mountains I gave two days rest to a troop that had

13. In its December 24, 1962, issue, the daily *Revolución* had published a special photo supplement entitled "Che in the Escambray: Diary of an Invasion." This letter was published in the December 29 issue.

been on the march for forty-five days under extremely difficult conditions and resumed operations, seizing Güinía de Miranda. If a mistake was made, it was in the opposite sense: little attention to the difficult task of dealing with all the "cattle rustlers" who had taken up arms in those cursed hills. Gutiérrez Menoyo and his crew vexed me to no end, and I had to put up with it to be able to devote myself to the central task: the war.

3. It is false to say that Ramiro Valdés was a "close collaborator of Che's in organizational matters." I don't know how that could have gotten by you, as editor, knowing him as well as you do.

Ramirito was at the Moncada, he was imprisoned on the Isle of Pines, he came on the *Granma* as a lieutenant, rose to captain when I was made a commander, he headed a column as a commander, he was second in command of the invasion, and then he headed the operations in the eastern sector while I marched toward Santa Clara.

I believe that historical truth must be respected: to fabricate it at whim does not lead to any good results. For that reason, and because I was an actor in that part of the drama, I made up my mind to write you these critical notes, which try to be constructive. It seems to me that if you had checked the text, the errors could have been avoided.

I wish you happy holidays and a coming year without many big headlines (because of what they bring).

Che

OCTOBER 28, 1963

To Pablo Díaz González

Havana
October 28, 1963
Year of Organization

Comrade Pablo Díaz González
Administrator
Camagüey

Pablo:

I read your article. I must thank you for how well you portray me; too well, I think. Furthermore, it seems you portray yourself pretty well too.

The first thing a revolutionary who writes history has to do is stick to the truth like a finger inside a glove. You did that, but it was a boxing glove, and that's cheating.

My advice to you: reread the article, eliminate everything you know is not true, and be careful with everything you don't know for certain is the truth.

Revolutionary greetings
Patria o muerte [Homeland or death]
Venceremos [We will win]

Commander Ernesto Che Guevara

JUNE 12, 1964

To Haydée Santamaría

June 12, 1964
Year of the Economy

Comrade Haydée Santamaría
Director, Casa de las Américas
Havana

Dear Haydée:

I instructed the Writers Union to put that money at your disposal as a compromise measure, so as not to let this trifle become a struggle over principles that are much more far-reaching.[14]

The only important thing is that I cannot accept a cent from a book that does nothing more than narrate incidents from the war. Do whatever you wish with the money.

Revolutionary greetings,
Patria o muerte
Venceremos

Commander Ernesto Che Guevara

14. A reference to royalties from the publication of the first edition of *Episodes of the Revolutionary War.*

JUNE 16, 1964

To Ezequiel Vieta

June 16, 1964
Year of the Economy

Mr. Ezequiel Vieta
Miramar, Havana

Dear comrade:

I had not really read your note. I'm a little embarrassed by how well you treated me.[15] The book is a compilation of items written with the aim of encouraging others to write down their experiences too and have them published in *Verde Olivo*. Someday I will reach the end. I never wanted the book to be published in a fragmentary way, but they paid no attention to me. I don't see how anyone who is not intimately familiar with the history of the revolution will be able to understand it.

I hope that someday you can write a review of the complete history of those two truly epic years that I had the good fortune to live through. Meanwhile, I appreciate the superlatives, although I do not share them.

Yours revolutionarily,
Patria o muerte
Venceremos

Commander Ernesto Che Guevara

15. Vieta had written a review of the first edition of *Episodes of the Revolutionary War*, published in the April 1964 issue of *La Gaceta de Cuba*. In it he had lauded Guevara's book as an "epic narrative."

APRIL 1, 1965

To Fidel Castro

Havana
Year of Agriculture

Fidel:[16]

At this moment I remember many things—when I met you in María Antonia's house, when you proposed I come along, all the tensions involved in the preparations.[17] One day they came by and asked who should be notified in case of death, and the real possibility of it struck us all. Later we knew it was true, that in a revolution one wins or dies (if it is a real one). Many comrades fell along the way to victory.

Today everything has a less dramatic tone, because we are more mature, but the event repeats itself. I feel that I have fulfilled the part of my duty that tied me to the Cuban revolution in its territory, and I say farewell to you, to the comrades, to your people, who now are mine.

I formally resign my positions in the leadership of the party, my post as minister, my rank of commander, and my Cuban citizenship. Nothing legal binds me to Cuba. The only ties are of another nature—those that cannot be broken as can appointments to posts.

Reviewing my past life, I believe I have worked with sufficient

16. This letter announcing Guevara's decision to pursue internationalist missions was delivered April 1, 1965, prior to his departure for the Congo (today Zaire) to aid revolutionary forces fighting the imperialist-installed regime. The letter was read aloud by Castro on October 3, 1965, during a televised speech introducing the members of the newly constituted Central Committee of the Communist Party of Cuba.
17. Guevara and Castro met in Mexico at the home of Cuban revolutionary María Antonia González, shortly after Castro's arrival in July 1955.

integrity and dedication to consolidate the revolutionary triumph. My only serious failing was not having had more confidence in you from the first moments in the Sierra Maestra, and not having understood quickly enough your qualities as a leader and a revolutionary.

I have lived magnificent days, and at your side I felt the pride of belonging to our people in the brilliant yet sad days of the Caribbean crisis.[18] Seldom has a statesman been more brilliant than you were in those days. I am also proud of having followed you without hesitation, of having identified with your way of thinking and of seeing and appraising dangers and principles.

Other nations of the world summon my modest efforts of assistance. I can do that which is denied you owing to your responsibility at the head of Cuba, and the time has come for us to part.

You should know that I do so with a mixture of joy and sorrow. I leave here the purest of my hopes as a builder and the dearest of those I hold dear. And I leave a people who received me as a son. That wounds a part of my spirit. I carry to new battlefronts the faith that you taught me, the revolutionary spirit of my people, the feeling of fulfilling the most sacred of duties: to fight against imperialism wherever one may be. This is a source of strength, and more than heals the deepest of wounds.

I state once more that I free Cuba from all responsibility, except that which stems from its example. If my final hour finds me under other skies, my last thought will be of this people and especially of you. I am grateful for your teaching and your example, to which I shall try to be faithful up to the final consequences of my acts.

I have always been identified with the foreign policy of our revolution, and I continue to be. Wherever I am, I will feel the responsibility of being a Cuban revolutionary, and I shall behave as such. I am not sorry that I leave nothing material to my wife and children; I am happy it is that way. I ask nothing for them,

18. A reference to the October 1962 "Cuban missile crisis."

as the state will provide them with enough to live on and receive an education.

I would have many things to say to you and to our people, but I feel they are unnecessary. Words cannot express what I would like them to, and there is no point in scribbling pages.

Hasta la victoria siempre! [Ever onward to victory!]

Patria o muerte! [Homeland or Death!]

I embrace you with all my revolutionary fervor.

Che

Glossaries *and* Charts

NOVEMBER 25–DECEMBER 2, 1956

Granma expeditionaries

Below is a list of the 82 Granma *expeditionaries, and what happened to them during the month after the landing.*

KILLED, DECEMBER 5–15, 1956 (21)

Luis Arcos
René Bedia†
Miguel Cabañas
Israel Cabrera
Noelio Capote
Félix J. Elmuza
Cándido González
Santiago (Jimmy) Hirzel
Humberto Lamothe
Antonio (Ñico) López†
Andrés Luján
Juan Manuel Márquez
José R. Martínez†
Armando Mestre†
René O. Reiné
Eduardo P. Reyes
Oscar Rodríguez
Tomás D. Royo
Miguel Saavedra
José R. Smith
Raúl Suárez

CAPTURED AND JAILED AFTER ALEGRÍA DE PÍO (21)

Gregorio Enrique Cámara†
Norberto Collado
Jaime Costa†
Arturo Chaumont
Francisco Chicola
Manuel Echevarría
José Fuentes
Mario Fuentes
Jesús Gilberto García
Norberto Godoy
César Gómez
Mario Hidalgo
Pablo Hurtado
Antonio Darío López†
Jesús Montané†
Evaristo Montes de Oca
Arnaldo Pérez
José Ponce†
Roberto Roque
Rolando Santana
Guillén Zelaya

† Veteran of July 26, 1953, Moncada and Bayamo garrison assaults

AVOIDED CAPTURE AND ESCAPED (20)

Emilio Albentosa†
Enrique Cuélez
Mario Chanes†
Pablo Díaz
Raúl Díaz*
Gino Donne
Ernesto Fernández
Arsenio García*
Gabriel Gil*†
Jesús Gómez
Armando Huau
Ramón Mejías
José Morán*
Rolando Moya
Onelio Pino
Jesús Reyes
Horacio Rodríguez*
Fernando Sánchez-Amaya
Esteban Sotolongo*
Pedro Sotto*

REGROUPED AS REBEL ARMY, DECEMBER 16–28, 1956 (20)

Juan Almeida†
Efigenio Ameijeiras
Reynaldo Benítez†
Carlos Bermúdez
Fidel Castro†
Raúl Castro†
Camilo Cienfuegos
Luis Crespo
Rafael Chao
Julio Díaz†
Calixto García†
Francisco González†
Ernesto Che Guevara
Calixto Morales
Faustino Pérez
Ciro Redondo†
René Rodríguez
Armando Rodríguez
Universo Sánchez
Ramiro Valdés†

* Reincorporated in Rebel Army, 1957

Glossary

The names of some four hundred people are mentioned by Ernesto Che Guevara in this book. The glossary contains information on the large majority of them, as well as on organizations and publications that appear in the text. Readers can also refer to the index for a listing of each reference to individuals or institutions mentioned. Where a listing includes both a paternal and maternal family name, it is alphabetized, as is the custom in Spanish, under the paternal name, which appears first. Information is current as of January 1996.

Acevedo, Enrique (1942–) – joined Column 4 of Rebel Army July 1957; later combatant in Column 8; currently brigadier general in Cuban armed forces; served on several internationalist missions in Angola.

Acevedo, Rogelio (1941–) – joined Column 4 of Rebel Army July 1957; later served as officer in Column 8; national director of revolutionary militias 1960; second in command of military mission in Angola 1975–76; currently brigadier general in Revolutionary Armed Forces and president of Cuban Institute of Civil Aeronautics.

Acosta, Clodomira (1937–1958) – member of July 26 Movement in Manzanillo; Rebel Army courier in Sierra Maestra for Column 1; captured during mission to Havana, she was tortured and murdered September 12, 1958.

Acuña, Juan Vitalio "Vilo" (1925–1967) – peasant from Sierra Maestra; joined Rebel Army April 1957; headed rear guard in Column 4 commanded by Guevara; later served in Column 3; promoted to commander November 1958; elected to Communist Party Central

Committee 1965; killed in Bolivia with Guevara where he was known as "Joaquín."

Acuña, Manuel (1908–) – joined Rebel Army at Cinco Palmas, December 1956; wounded at El Uvero May 28, 1957.

Agüero, Conte. *See* Conte Agüero, Luis

Agüero, Rivero. *See* Rivero Agüero, Andrés

Aguilera, Pedro – participant in 1953 Moncada attack; captured, tried, and acquitted; served on July 26 Movement National Directorate prior to revolutionary war.

Álamo. *See* Pérez Álamo, Dumey

Alarcón, Juventino (1930–1957) – Rebel Army combatant in Column 1; killed at Palma Mocha with rank of lieutenant, August 19, 1957.

Alarcón, Rigoberto (1932–1958) – member of Rebel Army Column 8; killed in battle in Las Villas December 9, 1958.

Albentosa, Emilio (1920–) – participant in 1953 Moncada attack; escaped arrest; *Granma* expeditionary; wounded at Alegría de Pío; avoided capture; subsequently active in July 26 Movement underground.

Almeida, Juan (1927–) – participant in 1953 Moncada attack; sentenced to 10 years in prison; released May 1955 following amnesty campaign; *Granma* expeditionary; promoted to commander of Rebel Army Column 3 in February 1958; later commanded Third Eastern Front; carried numerous responsibilities after 1959, including commander of air force, vice minister of armed forces, and vice president of Council of State and Council of Ministers; member of Communist Party Central Committee and Political Bureau since 1965.

Ameijeiras, Efigenio (1931–) – *Granma* expeditionary; finished war as commander of Rebel Army Column 6 and second in command of Second Eastern Front; later served as internationalist combatant in Algeria and Angola; currently brigadier general in Cuban armed forces.

Arbenz, Jacobo (1914–1971) – president of Guatemala 1951–54; overthrown by CIA-organized coup in 1954.

Arcos, Gustavo – participant in 1953 Moncada attack; helped organize July 26 Movement in Las Villas; worked with July 26 Movement

Committee in Exile during revolutionary war; ambassador to Belgium until 1966; broke with revolutionary movement; currently living in Havana and general secretary of antigovernment Cuban Committee for Human Rights.

Arias Sotomayor, José (1933–) – Rebel Army combatant; served in Columns 4 and 6, attaining rank of captain; later participated in fight against counterrevolutionary bands and at Bay of Pigs.

Authentic Organization – military organization set up by leaders of Authentic Party to oppose Batista following his 1952 coup.

Authentic Party (Cuban Revolutionary Party) – bourgeois-nationalist party popularly known as *auténticos;* formed in 1934, claiming to be authentic followers of José Martí s Cuban Revolutionary Party; held presidency from 1944 until 1952; led by Carlos Prío during Batista dictatorship.

Babún brothers – cement manufacturers and importers of cedar and mahogany, with large landed estates in Sierra Maestra; supporters of Batista regime, did business with Rebel Army by transporting arms and supplies.

Bandera, Teodoro (1930–1958) – Rebel Army combatant killed at El Jigüe July 19, 1958.

Barquín, Ramón – colonel in pre-1959 Cuban army; military attaché in U.S.; leader of anti-Batista conspiracy of "pure" officers; arrested April 1956 and imprisoned; released January 1, 1959; took command of army in attempted coup following Batista's flight.

Barrón, Arnaldo – headed Patriotic Club, a pro–July 26 Movement organization of Cuban exiles in New York during revolutionary war.

Batista, Fulgencio (1901–1973) – former army sergeant who helped lead military coup by junior officers in September 1933, following popular uprising that overturned Machado dictatorship a few weeks earlier; rose to chief of staff and became strongman in government in 1934, remaining in power until 1944; left office but retained base of support within army officer corps; lived in Florida 1944–48; led coup on March 10, 1952, establishing military dictatorship; fled to Dominican Republic on January 1, 1959, as revolutionary forces advanced toward Havana; died in Spain.

Bayo, Alberto (1892–1967) – general in Republican army during Spanish civil war; provided military training in Mexico to future *Granma* expeditionaries 1956; moved to Cuba after January 1, 1959, and worked for Revolutionary Armed Forces; author of *150 Questions for a Guerrilla,* published in 1955, and other books on military matters.

Beatón, Pupo and Manuel – peasants from Sierra Maestra; joined Rebel Army before battle of El Uvero in May 1957; left its ranks several months later; imprisoned November 1959 for murder of Cmdr. Cristino Naranjo; escaped to Sierra Maestra; captured and shot, 1960.

Benítez, Reynaldo (1928–) – participant in 1953 Moncada attack; sentenced to 10 years in prison; released May 1955 following amnesty campaign; *Granma* expeditionary; left Sierra for health reasons early 1957; captured March 1957; freed January 1, 1959.

Bermúdez, Carlos (1933–) – *Granma* expeditionary; Rebel Army combatant; left Sierra for health reasons; active in Havana July 26 Movement underground.

Bohemia – largest circulation Cuban weekly magazine, founded 1908; in 1955 had 255,000 readers; during 1950s the largest-circulation publication expressing anti-Batista sentiment; has continued publication since 1959.

Boldo. *See* LaRosa, Mauro

Bonito, Luis – member of July 26 National Directorate prior to revolutionary war and head of its workers section from June 1955 until May 1956.

Bordón, Víctor – member of Orthodox Youth and later July 26 Movement in Las Villas; commanded July 26 Movement guerrilla unit in Las Villas in early 1958 that was absorbed into Column 8 under Guevara in October 1958; attained rank of commander; later worked in Ministry of Construction in Matanzas.

Borrero, Marcos (1917–1958) – joined Rebel Army First Front, later captain in Column 8 under Guevara; killed at La Federal September 9, 1958.

Buch, Luis (1913–) – veteran fighter against Machado and Batista dictatorships; member of July 26 Movement in Havana and in Venezuela; following May 1958 became general coordinator of External Front of July 26 Movement; secretary to cabinet of government ministers after victory of revolution; later served as Supreme Court magistrate.

Cabrera, Francisco "Paco" (1924–1959) – member of July 26 Movement; lieutenant in Column 4; died in airplane accident in Venezuela January 27, 1959.

Cáceres, Julio Roberto "El Patojo" (1936–1962) – Guatemalan revolutionary and friend of Guevara in Mexico; moved to Cuba 1959; killed attempting to establish guerrilla front in Guatemala.

Cantillo, Eulogio – leading Cuban general under Batista; chief of operations in Oriente during May–July 1958 offensive; subsequently head of army general staff; met with Castro December 28 and agreed that Santiago de Cuba garrison would acknowledge rebel victory; broke accord by attempting to assume power after Batista fled on January 1, 1959; imprisoned by revolutionary government; went to U.S. after being amnestied.

Capote, Gilberto (1928–1958) – member of July 26 Movement in Havana; Rebel Army lieutenant in Column 4; killed at second battle of Pino del Agua, February 16, 1958.

Caracas Pact – agreement unifying opposition political currents announced July 20, 1958; signed by broad spectrum of anti-Batista opposition, including Fidel Castro for July 26 Movement; called for armed insurrection to establish a provisional government and for an end to U.S. support to Batista dictatorship.

Cardero, Gilberto (1930–) – joined Rebel Army 1957; served in Columns 1, 7, 6, and 19.

Carreras, Jesús – a leader of Second National Front of the Escambray, led by Eloy Gutiérrez Menoyo; joined armed counterrevolutionary bands in Escambray after 1959; captured and executed in 1961.

Carrillo, Justo (1912–) – headed Agricultural and Development Bank under Prío; founded bourgeois opposition Montecristi Group in 1956 with goal of encouraging military coup against Batista; went to U.S. in 1960 and helped organize counterrevolutionary activities.

Casillas, Joaquín – army colonel under Batista; notorious murderer;

head of army garrison in Santa Clara; tried and sentenced to death January 1, 1959; shot while attempting to escape.

Castillo, Eduardo "Yayo" – Rebel Army combatant; killed at Palma Mocha August 20, 1957.

Castro, Fidel (1926–) – student leader at University of Havana from mid-1940s; central organizer of revolutionary-minded Orthodox Party youth after 1947; Orthodox candidate for house of representatives in 1952 elections canceled following Batista coup; organizer of Centennial Youth, in honor of 100th anniversary of José Martí s birth in 1953; organized and led 1953 attack on Moncada garrison; sentenced to 15 years in prison; his courtroom defense speech, "History Will Absolve Me," distributed in tens of thousands of copies across Cuba, became program of revolutionary movement; released in 1955 after mass amnesty campaign; founder of July 26 Movement; organized *Granma* expedition from Mexico 1956 and commanded Rebel Army during revolutionary war; became general secretary of July 26 Movement May 1958; Cuban prime minister February 1959 to 1976; president of Council of State and Council of Ministers since 1976; commander in chief of armed forces; first secretary of Communist Party of Cuba since 1965.

Castro, Raúl (1931–) – student leader at University of Havana; participant in 1953 Moncada attack; sentenced to 13 years in prison; released May 1955 following amnesty campaign; founding member of July 26 Movement; *Granma* expeditionary; promoted to commander of Rebel Column 6 in February 1958 and headed Second Eastern Front; minister of Revolutionary Armed Forces since October 1959; vice premier 1959–76; vice president of Council of State and Council of Ministers since 1976; second secretary of Communist Party of Cuba since 1965.

Castro Mercader, Raúl (1937–) – joined Rebel Army March 1957 as part of first group of reinforcements; captain in Column 4; later served in internationalist mission in Angola; retired colonel in Cuban army.

Casuso, Teresa "Teté" – active in student movement in 1930s; lived in exile in Mexico for many years, where she collaborated with July 26 Movement; broke with revolution in early years.

Chao, Rafael (1914–) – Rebel Army combatant; fought for Spanish republic in 1936–39 civil war; *Granma* expeditionary; left Sierra May 1, 1957, for health reasons; subsequently active in July 26 Movement underground.

Chibás, Eduardo (1907–1951) – a student leader of fight against Machado dictatorship in 1920s and 1930s; founding leader of opposition Cuban People's (Orthodox) Party in 1947; elected senator in 1950; committed suicide in 1951 at conclusion of radio address as protest against government corruption.

Chibás, Raúl (1914–) – Orthodox Party leader; brother of Eduardo Chibás; signed Sierra Manifesto in June 1957; subsequently treasurer of July 26 Movement Committee in Exile; went to U.S. after triumph of revolution.

Chomón, Faure (1929–) – leader of Revolutionary Directorate and survivor of 1957 attack on Presidential Palace; organized February 1958 expedition landing in northern Camagüey; later established guerrilla detachment in Escambray mountains; collaborated with Guevara's column and signed Pedrero Pact; commander in Revolutionary Armed Forces; member of Communist Party Central Committee since 1965; has served as Cuba's ambassador to Soviet Union, Vietnam, and Ecuador.

Cienfuegos, Camilo (1932–1959) – after three months as art student in late 1949, worked in Havana garment shop as presser for three years; immigrant worker in U.S. April 1953–May 1955, participating in anti-Batista exile organizations there; returned to Cuba May 1955–March 1956; shot by police while taking part in student demonstrations against Batista in Havana; after returning to U.S., went to Mexico in fall 1956 and was one of last to sign on to *Granma* expedition; captain in Guevara's column, later promoted to commander; operated in Cauto region of Oriente province March–April 1958; headed "Antonio Maceo" Column no. 2, leading march westward from Sierra Maestra en route to Pinar del Río in late 1958; operated in northern Las Villas until end of war; became Rebel Army chief of staff January 1959; in charge of suppressing Hubert Matos mutiny in Camagüey; plane lost at sea while returning to Havana October 28, 1959.

Civic Resistance Movement – broad opposition formation initiated inside Cuba in early 1957 by July 26 Movement.

Clodomira. *See* Acosta, Clodomira

Colomé, Abelardo "Furry" (1939–) – member of July 26 Movement in Santiago de Cuba and participant in November 30, 1956, uprising; joined Rebel Army March 1957 with first group of reinforcements; served in Columns 1 and 6, ending war as commander; headed Cuban military mission in Angola 1975; currently army corps general and third-highest ranked officer in Cuban armed forces.

Confederation of Cuban Workers (CTC) – main Cuban union federation founded 1939 under leadership of Communist Party; control seized in 1950 by Eusebio Mujal, who later backed Batista; reorganized after triumph of revolution; changed name to Central Organization of Cuban Workers, with same initials, in 1961.

Conte Agüero, Luis (1924–) – bourgeois journalist and a leader of Orthodox Party; took oppositionist stand against Batista but opposed revolutionary struggle; went to U.S. in 1960.

Corynthia – name of yacht carrying Authentic Organization armed expedition; 27 combatants headed by Calixto Sánchez landed in northern Oriente May 24, 1957, met by Batista forces, apparently betrayed from within before landing; 16 were captured and executed.

Crespo, Luis (1923–) – participant in *Granma* expedition; served in Rebel Army Column 1; ended war with rank of commander.

Crucito. *See* Enríquez, Salustiano de la Cruz

Cuban People's Party. *See* Orthodox Party

Cuban Revolutionary Party. *See* Authentic Party

Cubela, Rolando (1933–) – a student leader of Revolutionary Directorate's guerrilla column in Escambray mountains; headed Federation of University Students 1959–60; attaché to Cuban embassy in Madrid in 1963, where he was recruited by CIA to assassinate Fidel Castro; sentenced to 25 years in prison in 1966; currently living in Spain.

Cuervo Navarro, Pelayo (1901–1957) – lawyer and senator; led effort to prosecute Authentic Party leaders for embezzlement during Prío administration; president of Orthodox Party following death of Eduardo Chibás; assassinated by Batista's police in Havana March 14, 1957.

de la Cruz, José "Crucito." *See* Enríquez, Salustiano de la Cruz

del Valle, Sergio (1927–) – joined guerrillas in Sierra Maestra in 1957 as combatant and physician, becoming captain in column led by Guevara; served as second in command of Camilo Cienfuegos's column; head of army general staff in 1960s; then minister of interior and of public health; member of Communist Party Central Committee since 1965 and of Political Bureau 1965–86; currently a division general in Cuban army.

Diario de la Marina – reactionary Cuban daily founded 1844, closely tied to Catholic church hierarchy; closed by revolutionary government May 13, 1960.

Díaz, Emiliano "Nano" (1936–1957) – member of Revolutionary National Action, organization led by Frank País in Santiago that joined in formation of July 26 Movement in 1955; participant in November 30, 1956, uprising; joined Rebel Army as part of March 1957 reinforcements; killed at El Uvero, with rank of lieutenant May 28, 1957.

Díaz, Epifanio (d. 1964) – peasant in Sierra Maestra who provided aid to Rebel Army.

Díaz, Julio (1929–1957) – former student activist; participant in 1953 Moncada attack; sentenced to 10 years in prison; released May 1955 following amnesty campaign; *Granma* expeditionary; captain in Rebel Army killed at El Uvero May 28, 1957.

Díaz, Raúl – *Granma* expeditionary; escaped capture at Alegría de Pío and rejoined Rebel Army February 17, 1957; combatant in Second and Third Eastern Fronts; ended war as captain.

Díaz González, Pablo (1912–1992) – *Granma* expeditionary; escaped capture after Alegría de Pío and went to Havana and then U.S.; headed Cuban Democratic Workers Committee in Exile in New York; returned to Cuba after 1959 and worked in sugar industry, tourism, and organizing international solidarity with Cuba.

Díaz Tamayo, Martín – brigadier general in Batista army; head of Military District of Oriente at time of *Granma* landing.

Doce, Lidia (1913–1958) – member of July 26 Movement in Havana; joined Rebel Army September 1957 in San Pablo de Yao near Sierra Maestra; served as courier in Columns 1 and 4; captured during mission to Havana, tortured and murdered September 12, 1958.

Domínguez, Guillermo (1932–1957) – member of July 26 Movement urban underground; joined Rebel Army March 1957 as part of first group of reinforcements; became lieutenant; captured and killed near Pino del Agua May 17, 1957.

Duque, Félix (1931–1989) – member of July 26 Movement in Camagüey and Santiago de Cuba; served in Columns 1 and 9; promoted to commander December 1958; took part in defense of Cuba during 1961 Bay of Pigs invasion and in battle against counterrevolutionary bands in Escambray.

Echeverría, José Antonio (1932–1957) – president of Federation of University Students from 1954 until his death; central leader of Revolutionary Directorate; killed March 13, 1957, in Directorate-organized attack on Presidential Palace and Radio Reloj, whose goal was assassination of Batista.

El Cubano Libre – Rebel Army newspaper produced on mimeograph machine in Sierra Maestra; established by Guevara November 1957; also name of paper published by Cuban patriots during independence wars of 19th century.

El Patojo. *See* Cáceres, Julio Roberto

Enríquez, Salustiano de la Cruz "Crucito" – Rebel Army combatant in Column 4; described by Guevara as bard of the troops; killed at first battle of Pino del Agua, September 17, 1957.

Ermus, Enrique (d. 1977) – member of July 26 Movement in Santiago de Cuba; joined Rebel Army March 1957 with first group of reinforcements; combatant in First Front; in charge of Rebel Army's jail in Puerto Malanga; rose to rank of captain.

Escalona, Dermidio – joined Rebel Army June 1957; combatant in First Front; led squad in second battle of Pino del Agua, February 24, 1958; part of forces assigned to open new front in Órganos mountains in Pinar del Río May 1958; ended war as commander.

Escalona, Enrique "Quique" – member of July 26 Movement in Manzanillo; joined Rebel Army March 1957 and rose to rank of lieutenant; wounded at El Uvero; sent to Santiago de Cuba, where he was active in July 26 Movement underground; captured and later paroled; went to U.S.; returned to Cuba 1959.

Espín, Vilma (1930–) – member Revolutionary National Action, organization led by Frank País in Santiago that joined in formation of July 26 Movement in 1955; participant in November 30, 1956, uprising; later served as July 26 Movement coordinator in Oriente province; joined Rebel Army in July 1958, serving in Second Eastern Front; president of Federation of Cuban Women since 1960; member of Communist Party Central Committee since 1965 and of Political Bureau 1980–91; member of Council of State since 1976.

Fajardo, Manuel (1932–1995) – one of first peasants to join Rebel Army in Sierra Maestra; became commander; following triumph of revolution headed Turiguano Cattle Development Plan in Ciego de Ávila and led other agricultural development projects; served on Communist Party Central Committee 1965–75.

Fajardo, Manuel "Piti" (1930–1960) – joined Rebel Army in 1958 as doctor and combatant in Columns 1 and 12, reaching rank of commander; killed in combat against counterrevolutionary forces in Escambray mountains November 29, 1960.

Fajardo, Roberto – joined Rebel Army April 1, 1957; served in Columns 1 and 32; ended war as commander.

Federation of University Students (FEU) – formed 1923 by Julio Antonio Mella, a founder of Cuba's Communist Party; José Antonio Echeverría was elected FEU president 1954; subsequently provided main cadres of Revolutionary Directorate; has continued to be main organization of university students since 1959.

Fernández, Marcelo (1932–) – a leader of July 26 urban underground; national coordinator of July 26 Movement from March 1958 to 1960; later minister of foreign trade and head of National Bank; member of Communist Party Central Committee 1965–86; economic adviser to Central Planning Commission; currently official of Cubanacán corporation.

Fernández Mell, Oscar (1931–) – captain and doctor in Guevara's Rebel Army Column 8; promoted to commander after triumph of revolution; a leader of Guevara's guerrilla effort in Congo 1965;

later served as head of general staff of Western Army, second in command of army general staff, president of Havana People's Power assembly, Cuban ambassador to Britain.

Fiallo, Ramón (1936–) – member of Orthodox Party and later July 26 Movement; served in Rebel Army Columns 1 and 6; ended war as captain.

Figueredo, Idelfredo "Chino" – combatant in Columns 1 and 4, later second in command of column in Rebel Army's Camagüey Front; ended war as captain; retired colonel in Revolutionary Armed Forces.

Fleitas, Armando – a leader of Second National Front of the Escambray, along with Eloy Gutiérrez Menoyo; went to U.S. in 1961.

Fonseca, Arquímedes (1935–) – member of July 26 Movement in Bueycito; served in Rebel Army Columns 4 and 10; ended war as first lieutenant.

Fonseca, Paulino (1932–) – joined Rebel Army March 25, 1957; served in Column 4 under Guevara's command; ended war as first lieutenant.

Franqui, Carlos (1921–) – member of Popular Socialist Party and then July 26 Movement; joined Rebel Army Column 1 in 1958; edited *El Cubano Libre;* headed Radio Rebelde late 1958; editor of daily *Revolución* 1959–63; later director of Council of State Office of Historical Affairs; left Cuba 1968 and became public opponent of revolution.

Frías, Ciro (1928–1958) – peasant from Sierra Maestra; joined Rebel Army January 1957 and became captain; member of Column 18 of Second Eastern Front led by Raúl Castro; killed at Imías April 9, 1958; posthumously promoted to commander.

Gadea, Hilda – first wife of Che Guevara; Peruvian-born, she met Guevara in Guatemala; divorced 1959; moved to Cuba after revolution and remained there until her death in 1970s.

García, Calixto (1931–) – participated in July 26, 1953, attack on Bayamo garrison; escaped and went to Costa Rica, Honduras, and Mexico; *Granma* expeditionary; finished war as commander in Rebel Army; member of Communist Party Central Committee 1965–80; currently brigadier general in Cuban armed forces.

García, Guillermo (1928–) – peasant in Sierra Maestra; member of July 26 Movement cell; helped organize regroupment of rebel forces December 1956; became combatant early 1957; promoted to commander in Third Eastern Front late 1958; member of Communist Party Central Committee since 1965 and of Political Bureau 1965–86; minister of transportation 1979–85; member of Council of State.

Geilín, Guillermo (1940–1958) – member of July 26 Movement from Cárdenas; Rebel Army fighter in Column 4; killed at El Dorado April 8, 1958.

Gil, Gabriel (1924–) – participant in Moncada attack; sentenced to 10 years in prison; released May 1955 following amnesty campaign; member of *Granma* expedition; escaped after Alegría de Pío; rejoined Rebel Army February 17, 1957; left Sierra soon after for health reasons; subsequently active in July 26 Movement underground; has served revolution in various capacities since 1959.

Gómez Ochoa, Delio (1929–) – Rebel Army fighter; after April 1958 general strike attempt became national action coordinator of July 26 Movement, based in Havana; became commander of Rebel Column 32 and of Fourth Eastern Front November 1958; led armed expedition to Dominican Republic in June 1959 by Dominican and Cuban volunteers; captured and later released; subsequently had responsibilities in agricultural sector of economy.

González, Francisco "Pancho" (1928–1994) – participant in 1953 Moncada attack; sentenced to 10 years in prison; released May 1955 following amnesty campaign; *Granma* expeditionary; left Sierra for health reasons May 25, 1957; remained in underground until January 1, 1959.

González, María Antonia (d. 1987) – Cuban living in Mexico; supporter of July 26 Movement; gave assistance to *Granma* expeditionaries; returned to Cuba 1959.

Guerra, Eutimio – peasant collaborator of Rebel Army who became traitor; executed by rebels February 17, 1957.

Guerra, Orestes (1932–) – served in Rebel Army Columns 1, 4, and 2; ended war as captain; retired colonel in Revolutionary Armed Forces.

Guevara, Ángel (1930–1958) – Rebel Army combatant in Column

4; died February 23, 1958, from wounds received at second battle of Pino del Agua.

Gutiérrez, Dalcio (d. 1958) – member of Rebel Army Column 8 under Guevara; killed at La Federal September 9, 1958.

Gutiérrez, Oniria (d. 1971) – joined Rebel Army 1957; first woman to join Column 4 commanded by Guevara; later served in Third Eastern Front.

Gutiérrez Menoyo, Eloy – leader of Second National Front of Escambray guerrilla group; refused to collaborate with Rebel Army; left Cuba for United States 1960; returned with counterrevolutionary armed band in December 1964; captured and imprisoned until 1986; currently head of Miami-based organization Cambio Cubano.

Hart, Armando (1930–) – joined Orthodox Youth 1947 in Havana; a leader of Revolutionary National Movement following Batista coup; founding member of July 26 Movement and a leader of its urban underground; imprisoned briefly 1957 and escaped; national coordinator of July 26 Movement from early 1957 to January 1958, when he was captured; imprisoned until January 1, 1959; minister of education 1959–65; Communist Party organization secretary 1965–70; minister of culture since 1976; member of Communist Party Central Committee since 1965 and of Political Bureau 1965–86.

Hernández, Juan (d. 1958) – member of Rebel Army Column 8 under Guevara; killed at Cuatro Compañeros September 14, 1958.

Hernández, Manuel (1931–1967) – sugarcane cutter and magnesium miner from Oriente; joined Rebel Army mid-1957; captain in Guevara's column during Las Villas campaign; killed in Bolivia with Guevara, where he was known as "Miguel."

Hernández, Melba (1922–) – participant in 1953 Moncada attack; jailed seven months; leader of July 26 Movement; participated in planning of *Granma* expedition from Mexico; joined Rebel Army Third Eastern Front; president of Cuban Vietnam solidarity committee during 1960s and 1970s; Cuba's ambassador to Vietnam in 1980s; currently vice president of Anti-Imperialist Tribunal of Our America; member of Communist Party Central Committee since 1986.

Hidalgo, Mario (1924–) – a leader of July 26 Movement; member of

National Directorate and head of its Youth Brigades August–October 1956; *Granma* expeditionary; captured December 1956; imprisoned until January 1, 1959.

Hirzel, Santiago "Jimmy" – *Granma* expeditionary; captured after Alegría de Pío and murdered December 8, 1956.

Humanismo – magazine published in Havana during early days of revolution.

Hurtado, Pablo (d. 1987) – *Granma* expeditionary; wounded at Alegría de Pío and captured December 14, 1956; freed January 1, 1959; took part in fight against counterrevolutionary bands; worked in petroleum industry.

Iglesias, Carlos "Nicaragua" – a leader of July 26 Movement in Santiago; arrested May 1957 and later freed by July 26 Movement commando raid; finished war as commander of Column 16; later served as head of education for Cuba's Western Army, director of National Pork Industry Plan; municipal delegate to People's Power in Havana.

Iglesias, Joel (1941–) – joined Rebel Army 1957, serving in Columns 4 and 8 under Guevara; promoted to commander; first president of Association of Rebel Youth in 1960; member of Communist Party Central Committee 1965–75; author of *De la Sierra Maestra al Escambray*, an account of Column 8's invasion of Las Villas.

Infante, Enzo (Bruno) (1930–) – member of National Directorate of July 26 Movement; served as provincial coordinator of July 26 Movement in Oriente and Camagüey; head of propaganda for July 26 Movement National Directorate until failed general strike of April 9, 1958, then became July 26 Movement coordinator in Havana province; imprisoned July 1958 to January 1, 1959; following 1959 served as adviser in Ministry of Labor; official in armed forces' Political Directorate and leader of Association of Combatants; currently retired lieutenant colonel in Cuban armed forces.

Jiménez Lage, Reynerio (d. 1987) – member of July 26 Movement and participant in November 30, 1956, uprising in Santiago de Cuba; joined Rebel Army March 1957 with first group of reinforcements; served in Columns 1, 6, and 16; after 1959 a colonel in Revolutionary Armed Forces.

July 26 Movement – founded June 1955 by Fidel Castro and other veterans of Moncada attack, youth activists from left wing of Orthodox Party, and other forces, including Revolutionary National Action in Santiago led by Frank País, and veterans of Revolutionary National Movement such as Armando Hart and Faustino Pérez in Havana; separated from Orthodox Party in March 1956; during revolutionary war composed of Rebel Army in mountains *(Sierra)* and urban underground network *(Llano);* Fidel Castro became general secretary May 1958; published *Revolución;* fused in 1961 with PSP and Revolutionary Directorate to form Integrated Revolutionary Organizations and later Communist Party of Cuba.

Labrada, Emilio – young peasant who joined Rebel Army January 30, 1957; withdrew less than three weeks later.

Laferté, Evelio – lieutenant in Batista army; captured February 1958 at second battle of Pino del Agua; joined Rebel Army March 1958; instructor at School for Recruits at Minas del Frío, formed in Sierra Maestra under Guevara's direction; served as captain in Revolutionary Armed Forces after victory of revolution.

Lamothe, Humberto (1919–1956) – *Granma* expeditionary; killed at Alegría de Pío December 5, 1956.

LaRosa, Mauro "Boldo" – member of Rebel Army First Front; later served in Column 2 under Camilo Cienfuegos.

Larrazábal, Wolfgang (1911–1970) – headed government of Venezuela, January–November 1958; gave support to Cuban rebel forces.

Leal, Mario (d. 1963) – Rebel Army combatant; wounded at El Uvero May 28, 1957; imprisoned for remainder of war.

Leyva, Eisler (1934–) – native of Niquero; founding member of July 26 Movement; member of Rebel Army, serving in Column 3; promoted to commander; at end of war was head of operations for Rebel Army general staff.

Leyva, Hermes (1938–1957) – Rebel Army combatant; killed at El Hombrito August 29, 1957.

Lidia. *See* Doce, Lidia

Liens, Raimundo (1935–1958) – Rebel Army combatant in Column 4; killed at second battle of Pino del Agua February 16, 1958.

Llada, Pardo. *See* Pardo Llada, José

Llano. *See* July 26 Movement

Llerena, Mario (1913–) – chairman and public relations director of July 26 Movement Committee in Exile, based in U.S.; quit July 26 Movement August 1958; opposed revolution after 1959 and went to U.S. in June 1960.

López, Antonio "Ñico" (1932–1956) – stevedore and member of Orthodox Youth; leader of cell of revolutionary movement led by Fidel Castro prior to Moncada assault; participant in July 26, 1953, attack on army garrison in Bayamo; escaped arrest and lived in exile in Guatemala, where he became friends with Guevara in 1954; met him again in Mexico the following year; member of July 26 Movement National Directorate and head of its Youth Brigades June 1955 to August 1956; participant in *Granma* expedition; captured after Alegría de Pío and murdered December 8, 1956.

López Fresquet, Rufo – member of bourgeois opposition to Batista; treasury minister during first year of revolutionary government; left Cuba in 1960.

Lugones, Félix "Pilón" (1934–1970) – member of July 26 Movement from Pilón; served in Rebel Army Columns 1 and 6, becoming captain; promoted to commander 1959; after triumph of revolution served as officer in National Revolutionary Police; fought U.S.-backed invasion at Bay of Pigs.

Lunes de Revolución – weekly supplement on culture and arts appearing every Monday in *Revolución*, daily newspaper of July 26 Movement; published from March 1959 to November 1961; edited by Guillermo Cabrera Infante.

Maceo, Antonio (1845–1896) – prominent military leader and strategist in Cuban wars of independence from Spain in nineteenth century; a leader of 1895–96 invasion of western provinces; a symbol of revolutionary intransigence in Cuba; killed in battle December 7, 1896.

Maceo, Mario (1938–1958) – member of first group of reinforcements sent to Sierra Maestra March 1957; served in Rebel Army Columns 1, 4, and 3; killed during mission to Santiago de Cuba, August 31, 1958.

Machado, Gerardo (1871–1939) – Cuban dictator 1925–33, closely linked to U.S. companies in Cuba; deposed by revolutionary upsurge August 12, 1933; died in United States.

Machado Ventura, José R. (1930–) – combatant and doctor in Rebel Army Second Eastern Front; minister of public health 1960–68; assisted Guevara in Congo 1965; first secretary of provincial committee of Communist Party in Matanzas 1968–70 and Havana 1971–76; member of Communist Party Central Committee since 1965 and its Political Bureau since 1975; currently member of Council of State and organizer of party's Central Committee.

Magadan, José "Pepín" (d. 1961) – member of Rebel Army; head of group assigned to obtain supplies for Rebel Army in Jibacoa region of Oriente, mid-1958.

Manals, Miguel (1937–) – joined Rebel Army March 1957 with first group of reinforcements; wounded at El Uvero May 28, 1957, and sent down from Sierra; later served in Second Eastern Front.

Manifesto of the Sierra Maestra – issued July 12, 1957, by Fidel Castro, Felipe Pazos, and Raúl Chibás; called for united effort to overthrow Batista and support Rebel Army, and outlined elements of land reform and a social program; opposed foreign interference in Cuban affairs.

Mark, Herman – North American; veteran of Korean War; instructor at Rebel Army School for Recruits at Minas del Frío 1958; captain in Guevara's Column 8; wounded during invasion of Las Villas; after triumph of revolution served as officer at La Cabaña prison.

Márquez, Juan Manuel (1915–1956) – imprisoned in 1930s for opposition to Machado dictatorship; a founding leader of Orthodox Party in 1947; joined July 26 Movement in 1955; second in command of *Granma* expedition; captured after Alegría de Pío and murdered December 16, 1956.

Martí, José (1853–1895) – Cuban national hero; noted poet, writer, speaker, and journalist; founded Cuban Revolutionary Party in 1892 to fight Spanish rule and oppose U.S. designs on Cuba; launched 1895 independence war; killed in battle; his revolutionary anti-imperialist program is part of political heritage of Cuban revolution.

Martínez Páez, Julio – rebel combatant and doctor; later served as minister of public health after revolution's triumph; currently director of Fructuoso Rodríguez Hospital.

Mas, Carlos (1939–1958) – joined Rebel Army Column 4 July 1957; promoted to captain; died July 14, 1958, from wounds received while resisting Batista army offensive.

Masetti, Jorge Ricardo (1929–1964) – journalist from Argentina who traveled to Sierra Maestra in January 1958 and joined Rebel movement; founded Cuba's Prensa Latina news service after 1959; killed while leading guerrilla group in northern Argentina.

Masferrer, Rolando (1914–1975) – pro-Batista politician and notorious gangster; organized private army of torturers and assassins named "Tigers"; fled Cuba December 31, 1958; assassinated in Miami by rivals in 1975.

Matos, Huber (1918–) – small landowner; joined Rebel Army in March 1958; commander of Column 9 of Third Front led by Juan Almeida; as military head of Camagüey province in October 1959 he was arrested for attempted counterrevolutionary mutiny; imprisoned until 1979; currently head of right-wing Cuba Independent and Democratic in United States.

Matthews, Herbert (1900–1977) – *New York Times* correspondent; first journalist to interview and photograph Fidel Castro in Sierra Maestra February 17, 1957; author of several books about Cuban revolution.

Medina, Ricardo (1936–1958) – member of Rebel Army assigned to Column 4 under Guevara; helped produce *El Cubano Libre;* killed at Minas de Bueycito March 11, 1958.

Mendoza, Eligio – joined Rebel Army in Sierra Maestra as guide; killed at El Uvero May 28, 1957.

Mendoza, Félix (1922–1995) – joined Rebel Army June 1958; member of Guevara's Column 4; later promoted to captain.

Mercader, Raúl. *See* Castro Mercader, Raúl

Meruelo, Otto – pro-Batista radio commentator; arrested 1959 for attempted murder and other charges and sentenced to 30 years imprisonment; later pardoned and left Cuba.

Mexico Pact – agreement signed August 30, 1956, between Fidel Castro for July 26 Movement and José Antonio Echeverría for Revolutionary Directorate, calling for united revolutionary action by the two groups.

Miami Pact – issued November 1, 1957, by forces including leaders of Authentic Party, Orthodox Party, Revolutionary Directorate, and others who falsely claimed document had been signed by authorized representatives of July 26 Movement; created Cuban Liberation Junta dominated by Authentic Party leader Carlos Prío; denounced by Rebel Army and July 26 Movement in letter drafted by Fidel Castro.

Miret, Pedro (1927–) – member of Military Committee that prepared 1953 Moncada attack; sentenced to 13 years in prison; released May 1955 following amnesty campaign; imprisoned in Mexico and unable to participate in *Granma* expedition; arrived in Sierra Maestra by air March 1958 and became a Rebel Army commander; minister of agriculture 1959–60; member of Communist Party Central Committee since 1965, and of Political Bureau 1975–91; currently a vice president of Council of State.

Miró Cardona, José (1902–1974) – a leader of bourgeois opposition to Batista; prime minister of Cuba, January–February 1959; went to U.S. in 1960; served as president of counterrevolutionary Revolutionary Democratic Front, and later Cuban Revolutionary Council in exile; later moved to Puerto Rico.

Moll, Gustavo (1935–1957) – member of July 26 Movement from Caimanera; joined Rebel Army March 1957 as part of first group of reinforcements; killed at El Uvero May 28, 1957.

Moncada garrison – main Cuban army garrison in Santiago de Cuba; attacked simultaneously with Bayamo garrison July 26, 1953, by 160 combatants under command of Fidel Castro, launching revolutionary armed struggle against Batista; attacks failed and over 50 revolutionaries were captured and murdered; 28 were imprisoned, amnestied May 1955.

Montané, Jesús (1923–) – a leader of 1953 Moncada attack; sentenced to 10 years in prison; released May 1955 following amnesty campaign; *Granma* expeditionary; captured after Alegría de Pío December 12, 1956, and held prisoner for remainder of war; posts held since 1959 include head of Central Committee's International Department and organizer of Central Committee; head of tourism; minister of communication; member of Communist Party Central

Committee since 1965; currently political aide to Fidel Castro.

Montecristi Group – bourgeois opposition group formed in 1956 by Justo Carrillo with goal of encouraging military coup against Batista; name taken from Montecristi Manifesto of 1895 drafted by José Martí.

Mora, Menelao (1905–1957) – veteran of anti-Machado struggle of 1930s; a leader of March 13, 1957, attack on Presidential Palace, in which he was killed.

Mora, Víctor – joined Rebel Army April 22, 1957; served as head of Camagüey front late 1958.

Morales, Calixto (1929–) – *Granma* expeditionary and Rebel Army combatant; assigned to work in Santiago underground from September 1957 to March 1958; subsequently captain in Column 8 under Guevara; in early 1960s worked with Guevara in Ministry of Industry; later in Ministry of Agriculture.

Morán, José (1929–1957) – *Granma* expeditionary; left Rebel Army February 1957; later worked for Batista; executed in Guantánamo by revolutionary fighters.

Naranjo, Cristino (1929–1959) – agricultural worker and miner; joined Rebel Army 1957, serving in Columns 1 and 4; promoted to commander; participated in suppression of attempted mutiny by Hubert Matos, October 1959; murdered by Manuel Beatón November 12, 1959.

National Workers Front (FON) – formed in Havana December 1957 at initiative of July 26 Movement and its workers section; raised demands around wages, jobs, pensions, and union rights, called for a general strike to help bring down the Batista regime; in November 1958 United National Workers Front (FONU) was formed, including trade union cadres belonging to July 26 Movement, Popular Socialist Party, Revolutionary Directorate, and other revolutionary-minded workers and unionists.

Noda, Enrique (1929–1958) – member of July 26 Movement in Havana; Rebel Army lieutenant in Column 4; killed at second battle of Pino del Agua February 16, 1958.

Nñ ez Jiménez, Antonio (1923–) – member of PSP youth group; leader of April 9, 1958, general strike action in Las Villas; cooperated in establishing Escambray front; joined Guevara's Rebel Army column on eve of battle of Santa Clara, with rank of captain; responsibilities since 1959 include executive director of National Institute of Agrarian Reform, president of Academy of Sciences, vice minister of culture, and ambassador to Peru; internationally known geographer and specialist on caves.

O Cruzeiro – weekly magazine published in Portuguese in Rio de Janeiro, and in Spanish-language international edition.

Olazábal, Luis (1926–) – member of PSP and later July 26 Movement in Manzanillo; served in Rebel Army Column 4; ended war as captain under command of Fidel Castro.

Oliva, Rigoberto (1924–1957) – Rebel Army combatant; killed at Palma Mocha August 20, 1957.

Oltuski, Enrique (1930–) – leader of July 26 Movement urban underground in Las Villas province; named minister of communications in 1959; currently vice minister of fishing industry.

Oñate, Alejandro "Cantinflas" (1936–) – Rebel Army combatant; promoted to lieutenant; served in Camilo Cienfuegos's invasion column.

Orthodox Party (Cuban People's Party) – known as *ortodoxos;* formed 1947 as populist movement on platform of opposition to imperialist domination of Cuba and government corruption; youth wing provided initial cadres for Moncada assault; official leadership moved rightward after Batista coup and party fragmented.

País, Frank (1934–1957) – vice president of Federation of University Students in Oriente; central leader of Oriente Revolutionary Action, later renamed Revolutionary National Action, which fused with Moncada veterans and other forces to form July 26 Movement in 1955; central leader of July 26 Movement in Oriente province; led November 30, 1956, Santiago de Cuba uprising; national action coordinator of July 26 Movement and head of its urban militias; murdered by Batista forces July 30, 1957.

País, Josué (1937–1957) – captain in July 26 Movement urban militia in Santiago; brother of Frank País; murdered by government troops June 30, 1957.

Palomares, Pastor (1939–1957) – joined Rebel Army April 20, 1957, serving in Column 1; killed in battle of Palma Mocha August 20, 1957.

Pantoja, Orlando (1933–1967) – early member of July 26 Movement, jailed for underground activities; joined Rebel Army October 1957; captain in Column 8 under Guevara during Las Villas campaign; killed in Bolivia with Guevara, where he was known as "Antonio."

Pardo Guerra, Benjamín "Mingolo" (1932–1958) – Rebel Army combatant; member of Column 4 and later Third Eastern Front; killed at Dos Palmas, January 4, 1958.

Pardo Guerra, Israel – joined Rebel Army June 1957; combatant in Column 4 under Guevara's command; later promoted to captain.

Pardo Guerra, Ramón "Guile" (1939–) – joined Rebel Army 1957; served in Guevara's column; member of Communist Party Central Committee 1965–86; currently division general in Cuban armed forces; head of Western Army since 1989; vice minister of armed forces.

Pardo Llada, José (1923–) – radio announcer and Orthodox Party member; participated in moderate anti-Batista activities; left Cuba in March 1961; currently lives in Colombia.

Paz, Ramón (1924–1958) – member of July 26 Movement; Rebel Army combatant in Column 1; killed in second battle of Santo Domingo July 28, 1958.

Pazos, Felipe (1912–) – head of Cuban National Bank during Prío administration; opposed Batista's coup; signed Sierra Manifesto in 1957; signed Miami Pact November 1957; president of National Bank, January–October 1959, replaced by Guevara; opposed revolutionary measures and went to U.S.

Pazos, Javier – member of July 26 Movement; son of Felipe Pazos; joined Rebel Army July 1957; captured January 1958 and imprisoned; went to U.S. in September 1960.

Pedrero Pact – agreement signed at Rebel Army camp in Pedrero December 1, 1958, between July 26 Movement and Revolutionary Directorate, calling for joint action by revolutionary forces in Las Villas.

Pena, Félix (1930–1959) – student leader; member of Orthodox Party youth; joined Revolutionary National Action, organization led by Frank País in Santiago that joined in formation of July 26 Movement in 1955; headed July 26 Movement's youth brigades in Oriente province; joined Rebel Army in March 1957; served in Column 6 under Raúl Castro; later commander of Column 18.

Pérez, Crescencio (1895–1986) – member of July 26 Movement cell in Sierra Maestra prior to *Granma* landing; one of first peasants to join Rebel Army; finished war as commander of Column 7; following triumph of the revolution carried various responsibilities as member of Revolutionary Armed Forces.

Pérez, Faustino (1920–1992) – active in revolutionary politics at University of Havana; following Batista's coup together with Armando Hart was leader of Revolutionary National Movement, most of whose members took part in formation of July 26 Movement; *Granma* expeditionary; headed July 26 Movement urban underground in Havana until April 1958; later became commander in Sierra Maestra; member of Communist Party Central Committee from 1965 until his death.

Pérez, Ignacio (1931–1958) – Rebel Army combatant; son of Crescencio Pérez; attained rank of captain; killed in Jiguaní December 19, 1958.

Pérez, Julio – member of second contingent of reinforcements to Sierra Maestra, serving in Columns 1 and 6.

Pérez, Ramón "Mongo" – peasant collaborator of Rebel Army; provided shelter to Fidel Castro and other combatants following Alegría de Pío.

Pérez Álamo, Dumey – combatant in Rebel Army Columns 4 and 9; commanded squad at second battle of Pino del Agua, February 24, 1958; later attained rank of captain.

Pérez Vidal, Ángel – headed Cuban Civic Action in New York 1953–54; a leader of Patriotic Club of July 26 Movement in New York from 1955 through revolutionary war.

Pesant, Adalberto "Beto" (1930–1958) – member of Orthodox Party; founder and organizer of July 26 Movement in Manzanillo; combatant in Column 1 of Rebel Army, with rank of captain; killed in accident at Las Mercedes August 8, 1958.

Ponce, José (1926–) – participant in 1953 Moncada attack; sentenced to 10 years in prison; released May 1955 following amnesty campaign; *Granma* expeditionary; captured December 1956 and imprisoned until January 1, 1959; commander in Revolutionary Armed Forces and later Ministry of the Interior; later served as director of National Reforestation Institute.

Popular Socialist Party (PSP) – name taken in 1944 by Communist Party of Cuba; opposed Batista coup and dictatorship but rejected political course of July 26 Movement in launching revolutionary war in 1956–57; after revolution's victory fused with July 26 Movement and Revolutionary Directorate in 1961 to form Integrated Revolutionary Organizations, and later Communist Party of Cuba in 1965.

Prío Socarrás, Carlos (1903–1977) – leader of Authentic Party; president of Cuba 1948–52; overthrown by Batista; leading figure in bourgeois opposition; instigator of Miami Pact November 1957; went to U.S. in 1961.

Pupo, Orlando – joined Rebel Army March 1957 as member of first group of reinforcements; served in Columns 1 and 6.

Quesada, Florentino (1936–1958) – member of Rebel Army Column 1; killed at second battle of Pino del Agua February 16, 1958.

Quiala, José (d. 1979) – joined Rebel Army March 1957 as part of first group of reinforcements; contributed to *El Cubano Libre;* later served in Column 6.

Quiroga, Antolín (1927–) – member of July 26 Movement in Manzanillo; combatant in Rebel Army, serving as captain in Column 9; after victory of revolution participated in fight against counter-revolutionary bands and served in internationalist mission in Angola.

Radio Rebelde – Rebel Army radio station initiated by Guevara's column; began broadcasting February 24, 1958, from Sierra Maestra; later transferred to Fidel Castro's column; in later months of war, transmissions were beamed to Venezuela for rebroadcast to Cuba.

Ramos Latour, René (Daniel) (1932–1958) – July 26 Movement national action coordinator after Frank País's death, heading urban militias; Rebel Army commander after May 1958; killed in action July 30, 1958, at end of army offensive in Sierra Maestra.

Redondo, Ciro (1931–1957) – member of Orthodox Youth; participant in 1953 Moncada attack; sentenced to 10 years in prison; released May 1955 following amnesty campaign; *Granma* expeditionary; captain in Rebel Army, serving in Guevara's column; killed at Mar Verde November 29, 1957; posthumously promoted to commander.

Revolución – national newspaper of July 26 Movement published clandestinely during fight against Batista; became daily newspaper 1959; following 1961 fusion creating Integrated Revolutionary Organizations, it became central voice of the united party and leadership of revolutionary government; in 1965 merged with *Hoy*, formerly newspaper of PSP that published daily after the revolution, to create *Granma*.

Revolutionary Directorate – formed 1955 by José Antonio Echeverría and other leaders of Federation of University Students; organized attack on Presidential Palace March 13, 1957, in which a number of central leaders, including Echeverría, were killed; organized guerrilla column in Escambray mountains in Las Villas February 1958 led by Faure Chomón, expelling Second National Front of the Escambray from the organization in mid-1958; fused with July 26 Movement and PSP in 1961 to form Integrated Revolutionary Organizations and later Communist Party of Cuba.

Revolutionary Workers Directorate – grouping of trade union activists and officials in opposition to pro-Batista leadership of Confederation of Cuban Workers; politically linked with Authentic Party.

Reyes, Emiliano (1918–1958) – Rebel Army combatant; served in Columns 1 and 3, becoming captain; killed between Santa Rita and Juguaní October 28, 1958.

Reyes, Gerardo "Yayo" (d. 1977) – member of first group of reinforcements sent to Sierra Maestra March 1957; served in Columns 1 and 6, attaining rank of captain.

Rivero, Pedro (1939–1957) – Rebel Army combatant; member of Column 4; killed at Bueycito August 1, 1957.

Rivero Agüero, Andrés (1905–) – prime minister under Batista; declared elected as president in November 1958 rump elections; fled Cuba January 1, 1959.

Rodríguez, Armando (1929–) – *Granma* expeditionary; deserted February 1957 after attack at Altos de Espinosa.

Rodríguez, Fructuoso (1933–1957) – most prominent leader of Revolutionary Directorate after José Antonio Echeverría; vice president of Federation of University Students; survivor of March 13, 1957, attack on Presidential Palace; murdered by police April 20, 1957, in massacre at 7 Humboldt St. in Havana.

Rodríguez, Geonel (1934–1958) – member of July 26 Movement at University of Havana; Rebel Army combatant, promoted to captain; helped produce *El Cubano Libre;* killed at Naranjo July 12, 1958.

Rodríguez, Léster (1927–) – participant in military support action for 1953 Moncada attack; escaped arrest; leader of July 26 Movement in Oriente, and later served as its military representative in U.S.; finished war as captain in Rebel Army's Second Eastern Front; later served as minister of steel industry, ambassador to Syria, and vice minister of economic cooperation.

Rodríguez, Luis Orlando (1912–1989) – member of Revolutionary Student Directorate in 1930; a leader of Authentic Party youth in 1940s; founding member of Orthodox Party in 1947; joined Rebel Army 1957; became editor of *El Cubano Libre* and director of Radio Rebelde; following 1959 served as interior minister January–October 1959; later spent over two decades in diplomatic service.

Rodríguez, René (1928–1990) – worked with Fidel Castro in preparations for Moncada attack; *Granma* expeditionary; participant in Guevara's column in Las Villas; head of Cuban Institute for Friendship with the Peoples for many years; member of Communist Party Central Committee from 1980 until his death.

Rodríguez, Roberto "Vaquerito" (1935–1958) – Rebel Army captain; headed Suicide Squad in Column 8 commanded by Guevara; killed in Santa Clara, December 30, 1958.

Rodríguez, William (1931–1983) – member of Orthodox Party and then July 26 Movement; joined Rebel Army June 1957, serving in Column 4; ended war as first lieutenant.

Roque, Roberto (1915–1989) – *Granma* expeditionary and second captain of ship; captured December 12, 1956, following Alegría de Pío and imprisoned; after 1959 served as a commander of Cuban navy.

Sábato, Ernesto (1911–) – one of Argentina's most prominent novelists; in 1984 chaired presidential commission investigating human rights abuses by military regime in late 1970s and early 1980s.

Saborit, Evelio (1939–1975) – member of July 26 Movement in Bayamo; joined Rebel Army June 1957; served in Columns 4 and 3; promoted to commander; after 1959 carried out various military and civilian responsibilities.

St. George, Andrew – U.S. journalist; interviewed Castro in Sierra Maestra and published articles on Rebel Army in wide-circulation magazines *Look* and *Coronet;* considered by Guevara and others to be U.S. intelligence agent.

Salvador, David (1923–) – headed July 26 Movement workers section 1957–58; general secretary of Cuban Workers Confederation 1959–60; arrested and imprisoned for counterrevolutionary activity 1960.

Sánchez, Calixto (1924–1957) – trade union leader and member of Authentic Organization; led May 1957 armed expedition to Cuba aboard *Corynthia;* captured and murdered May 28, 1957.

Sánchez, Celia (1920–1980) – a leader of amnesty campaign for Moncada prisoners in Oriente province; joined July 26 Movement in 1955, and became its central organizer in Manzanillo; organized urban supply and recruitment network for Rebel Army; first woman to become combatant in Rebel Army; member of Rebel Army general command beginning October 1957; at her death a member of Communist Party Central Committee and secretary of Council of State and Council of Ministers.

Sánchez, Universo (1929–) – *Granma* expeditionary; became Rebel Army commander; currently a retired officer of Cuban armed forces.

Sánchez Mosquera, Ángel – lieutenant in Batista's army; notorious for brutality against peasants; ended war as colonel; escaped Cuba January 1, 1959.

San Román, Dionisio – lieutenant in Cuban navy; member of anti-Batista military opposition; led uprising at Cienfuegos naval base September 5, 1957, in coordination with local July 26 Movement; captured and murdered.

Santamaría, Abel (1927–1953) – member of Orthodox Youth; in May 1952 joined with Fidel Castro and became second in command of new revolutionary movement; a leader of July 26, 1953, Moncada attack; captured, tortured, and murdered.

Santamaría, Aldo (1926–) – imprisoned 1956 as leader of July 26 Movement; brother of Abel and Haydée; joined Rebel Army 1958, serving in Fidel Castro's command post; member of Communist Party Central Committee 1965–86; currently vice admiral in Cuban navy.

Santamaría, Haydée (1922–1980) – participated in 1953 Moncada attack, in which her brother Abel was captured and murdered; imprisoned for seven months; founding leader of July 26 Movement in 1955; participant in November 30, 1956, uprising in Santiago de Cuba; carried out numerous underground and international tasks during revolutionary war; Rebel Army combatant in Column 1; director of Casa de las Américas from 1959 until her death; member of Communist Party Central Committee 1965–80.

Sardiñas, Eduardo "Lalo" (1929–) – captain in Rebel Army Column 4 under Guevara; demoted for inadvertently shooting a combatant; finished war as commander of Column 12; following victory of revolution headed up network of people's stores organized by Ministry of Defense; currently retired officer of Cuban armed forces.

Sardiñas, Guillermo (1916–1964) – Catholic priest; joined Rebel Army in June 1957 and finished war with rank of commander; following 1959 represented the revolution on a number of international delegations.

Second National Front of the Escambray – guerrilla organization in Las Villas led by Eloy Gutiérrez Menoyo; formed November 10, 1957, on initiative of Revolutionary Directorate; subsequently conducted bandit-type actions and was expelled from Directorate in mid-1958; refused to collaborate with Guevara's forces and other revolutionary units; most of its leaders joined counterrevolution after 1959.

Sierra Manifesto. *See* Manifesto of the Sierra Maestra

Sierra. *See* July 26 Movement

Silleros, Emiliano Rigoberto – Rebel Army combatant; mortally wounded at El Uvero, May 28, 1957.

Silva, José Ramón – Rebel Army captain in Column 8 led by Guevara; officer in Revolutionary Armed Forces after victory of revolution.

Sorí Marín, Humberto – Authentic Party politician; joined Rebel Army in Sierra Maestra 1957, ended war with rank of commander; minister of agriculture after revolution; later joined counterrevolutionary bands; captured and executed in 1961.

Soto, Francisco "Policeman" (1921–1957) – former member of National Police fired after Batista's coup; joined Rebel Army March 1957 as part of first group of reinforcements; killed at El Uvero, May 28, 1957.

Soto, Juan (1935–1957) – joined Rebel Army March 1957 with first group of reinforcements; killed at San Lorenzo, November 20, 1957; posthumously promoted from captain to commander.

Sotolongo, Esteban (1928–) – *Granma* expeditionary; escaped capture following Alegría de Pío; reincorporated in Rebel Army February 19, 1957; left Sierra for health reasons May 1957; worked in July 26 Movement underground until triumph of revolution.

Sotomayor. *See* Arias Sotomayor, José

Sotto, Pedro "Pedrín" (1935–1958) – joined July 26 Movement in Manzanillo 1955; *Granma* expeditionary; avoided capture after Alegría de Pío; rejoined Rebel Army March 24, 1957, as part of reinforcement group; became lieutenant in Column 6 of Second Eastern Front; killed June 26, 1958, in Moa.

Sotús, Jorge – led group of 50 Rebel reinforcements sent by Frank País March 1957; captain in Rebel Army; later broke with July 26 Movement; imprisoned for counterrevolutionary activity after victory of revolution; escaped and went to U.S.; killed in accident while organizing counterrevolutionary raid.

Student Directorate – *See* Revolutionary Directorate

Suárez, José "Pepe" (1927–) – participant in 1953 Moncada attack; sentenced to 10 years in prison; released after amnesty campaign May 1955; member of July 26 Movement National Directorate until time of *Granma* landing; subsequently active in July 26 Movement work abroad; returned to Cuba following 1959.

Suárez, Raúl (1935–1956) – helped organize July 26 Movement in Las

Villas province; *Granma* expeditionary; captured following Alegría de Pío and murdered, December 8, 1956.

Suicide Squad – elite volunteer platoon in Guevara's Column 8, assigned most difficult and hazardous missions; headed by Roberto Rodríguez, known as "Vaquerito."

Suñol, Eduardo "Eddy" (1926–1971) – member of Orthodox Party and later July 26 Movement in Santiago de Cuba; imprisoned October 1956 to May 1957; joined Rebel Army June 1957; commander of Column 14; held responsibilities in Cuban armed forces and Ministry of the Interior after 1959.

Taber, Robert – U.S. journalist; filmed interview with Fidel Castro in Sierra Maestra in 1957, with correspondent Wendell Hoffman shown on CBS-TV in May; author of *M-26: The Biography of a Revolution;* founder of U.S. Fair Play for Cuba Committee.

Tabernilla, Francisco (b. 1888) – military leader who participated in Batista's 1952 coup, subsequently becoming chief of general staff with rank of major general; fled Cuba January 1, 1959; died in United States.

Tamayo, Félix (1931–1987) – member of PSP and later July 26 Movement; joined Rebel Army Column 4; finished war with rank of lieutenant.

Tamayo, Francisco "Pancho" (1904–1960) – one of earliest peasant supporters of Rebel Army in Sierra Maestra; murdered by counterrevolutionary band led by Beatón brothers April 4, 1960.

Tamayo, Leonardo (1941–) – peasant from Sierra Maestra; joined Rebel Army mid-1957, serving in Guevara's column; member of Suicide Squad in Column 8; accompanied Guevara to Bolivia, where he was known as "Urbano"; later served in internationalist missions in Nicaragua and Angola; currently retired colonel in Ministry of the Interior.

Torres, Antonio "Ñ ico" (d. 1991) – railroad worker from Guantánamo; leader of July 26 Movement's workers section; member of Rebel Army Second Eastern Front, under Raúl Castro, heading its Workers Bureau; after 1959 an officer in Revolutionary Armed Forces.

Torres, Félix – commanded PSP guerrilla column in Yaguajay, northern Las Villas; collaborated with Camilo Cienfuegos's Rebel Army column in late 1958; currently an officer in Revolutionary Armed Forces.

Trujillo, Rafael Leónidas (1891–1961) – dictator in Dominican Republic from 1930 until his death; after 1959 organized attacks against Cuba backed by Washington; assassinated by revolutionary opponents of the dictatorship.

Urrutia Lleó, Manuel (1901–1981) – a judge at trial in Santiago de Cuba of captured *Granma* expeditionaries, where he publicly criticized Batista regime; became Cuban president January 5, 1959; opponent of land reform and other revolutionary measures; resigned July 17, 1959, in face of mounting popular opposition; later went to U.S.

Valdés, Ramiro (1932–) – participant in 1953 Moncada attack; sentenced to 10 years in prison; released May 1955 following amnesty campaign; *Granma* expeditionary; second in command of Guevara's Rebel Army Column 4, later becoming its commander; second in command and later commander of Column 8 in Las Villas; minister of interior 1961–68, 1979–87; member of Communist Party Central Committee since 1965, and of Political Bureau 1965–86.

Vallejo, René (1920–1969) – Rebel Army combatant and doctor in Column 1; during 1960s served as personal physician to Fidel Castro.

Vaquerito. *See* Rodríguez, Roberto

Varona, Antonio "Tony" (1908–1992) – a leader of Authentic Party; served two terms as senator from Camagüey; Cuban prime minister 1948–50; left Cuba after revolution; helped organize 1961 Bay of Pigs invasion.

Vega, Anselmo. *See* Verdecia Vega, Anselmo

Ventura, Esteban – colonel in Batista police; notorious torturer and murderer; fled to U.S. January 1, 1959.

Verde Olivo – weekly magazine of Revolutionary Armed Forces, published in Havana beginning 1959.

Verdecia, Ángel (1933–1958) – Rebel Army captain; killed in combat at Loma del Frío July 13, 1958.

Verdecia Vega, Anselmo (1907–1957) – agricultural worker from Niquero; active in Orthodox Party and later July 26 Movement; joined Rebel Army April 1957; killed at El Uvero May 28, 1957.

Viciedo, Sebastián "Pompilio" – veteran of fight against Machado in 1930s and of Young Cuba movement headed by revolutionary leader Antonio Guiteras; volunteer in Spanish civil war; member of Orthodox Party; underground fighter in Sancti Spíritus area; joined Rebel Army Column 8 in Las Villas in late 1958.

Villegas, Harry (1940–) – born in Yara, Oriente province; joined Rebel Army 1957; member of Guevara's personal escort in Columns 4 and 8; accompanied Guevara to Congo and Bolivia, where he was known as "Pombo"; member of general staff of Bolivian guerrilla movement; served three tours of duty in Angola in 1970s and '80s; currently brigadier general in Cuban army.

Virelles, Fernando (1924–) – Cuban immigrant in United States; Korean War veteran; joined May 1957 *Corynthia* expedition; survived and made his way to Sierra Maestra, becoming captain in Rebel Army.

Westbrook, Joe (1937–1957) – a youth leader of Revolutionary Directorate; survivor of March 13, 1957, attack on Presidential Palace; murdered by police April 20, 1957, in massacre at 7 Humboldt St. in Havana.

Weyler, Valeriano (1838–1930) – Spanish general appointed governor and captain general of Cuba in 1896 during independence war; ordered concentration of rural population in garrisoned towns, to prevent support to independence fighters.

Zayas, Alfonso (1936–) – joined Rebel Army March 1957 as part of first group of reinforcements; captain in Column 8 under Guevara; after victory of revolution served as political secretary of Western Army; first secretary of Communist Party in Las Tunas; currently an official in Youth Army of Labor.

Zenón Acosta, Julio (1912–1957) – peasant in Sierra Maestra; joined July 26 Movement in Manzanillo; became member of Rebel Army January 1957; killed at Altos de Espinosa February 9, 1957.

Glossary of weapons

The following is a brief description of weapons and ammunition mentioned in this book.

.30-06 – rifle cartridge with a .30 inch diameter, originally standardized in 1906.

.30-30 – rifle cartridge with a .30 inch diameter, designed to hold roughly 30 grains of powder.

Automatic – uses expanding gases from firing of bullet to eject empty casing, reload, recock, and continue firing shots in rapid succession until trigger is released or ammunition runs out. *See also* Semiautomatic.

Automatic rifle – assault rifle capable of firing in rapid succession; designed for use by a single combatant; fed from clips of ammunition as opposed to cartridge belts used to feed most machine guns.

Bazooka – portable, tube-like, recoilless shoulder-fired weapon whose shells are capable of piercing tanks and other armored vehicles.

Beretta – brand of weapons manufactured in Italy, ranging from pistols to submachine guns; in this book, the reference is to a pistol.

Browning – main automatic rifle used in World War II and Korean War by U.S. armed troops, often referred to as a BAR.

Caliber – diameter of bore of gun barrel, or of projectile fired from it, in inches or millimeters.

Carbine – short, light rifle, originally designed to replace pistols used by officers.

Garand – *See* M-1.

Johnson – brand of semiautomatic rifle, U.S. manufactured, World War II vintage.

M-1 – semiautomatic rifle, introduced in U.S. army in 1936; also called Garand, after designer; standard issue to U.S. soldiers in World War II, Korean War.

M-2 – submachine gun, manufactured in U.S. in early 1940s.

M-3 – submachine gun, replaced M-2 during World War II.

Machine gun – automatic weapon; tripod-mounted varieties referred to most often by Guevara are 25 to 60 pounds, and either .30- or .50-caliber; operated by more than one soldier from emplacement and prone position; fed by a cartridge belt.

Madsen – light machine gun manufactured in Denmark, World War II and postwar vintage.

Mortar – short tube cannon used to throw shells at high angle; ammunition fired by dropping shells into tube.

Revolver – pistol that fires cartridges from revolving cylinder.

San Cristóbal – automatic carbine made in Dominican Republic.

Semiautomatic – uses energy from fired bullet to eject empty casing and load next round, which must be fired manually by pulling the trigger. *Contrast to* Automatic.

Submachine gun – lightweight automatic weapon designed to use lower caliber ammunition; smaller sizes also called machine pistol.

Springfield – bolt action rifle, introduced in U.S. army in 1903; replaced by M-1 in 1936; each shot must be preceded by two separate operations, moving bolt back and forth and then pulling trigger.

Thompson – submachine gun, World War II vintage.

DECEMBER 1956 THROUGH DECEMBER 1958

Evolution of Rebel Army columns and fronts

The column was the basic operational unit of the Rebel Army, from the establishment of the first column in December 1956 in the Sierra Maestra mountains under Fidel Castro's command. Led by commanders and eventually growing to approximately 70 to 200 combatants, the columns were generally organized into platoons, led by captains, and squads, led by lieutenants.

As the Rebel Army grew in 1958, some columns were organized into companies led by captains, which often evolved into separate columns; independent detachments were organized by several fronts, as well.

As the war expanded, several additional fronts were established, primarily in Oriente and Las Villas provinces; each was composed of several columns.

The charts that follow provide an indication of the development of the Rebel Army over the two years of the revolutionary war. The list of columns and fronts at the end of this section provides more information on each of these units. The charts and list were prepared with information provided by the Council of State Office of Historical Affairs.

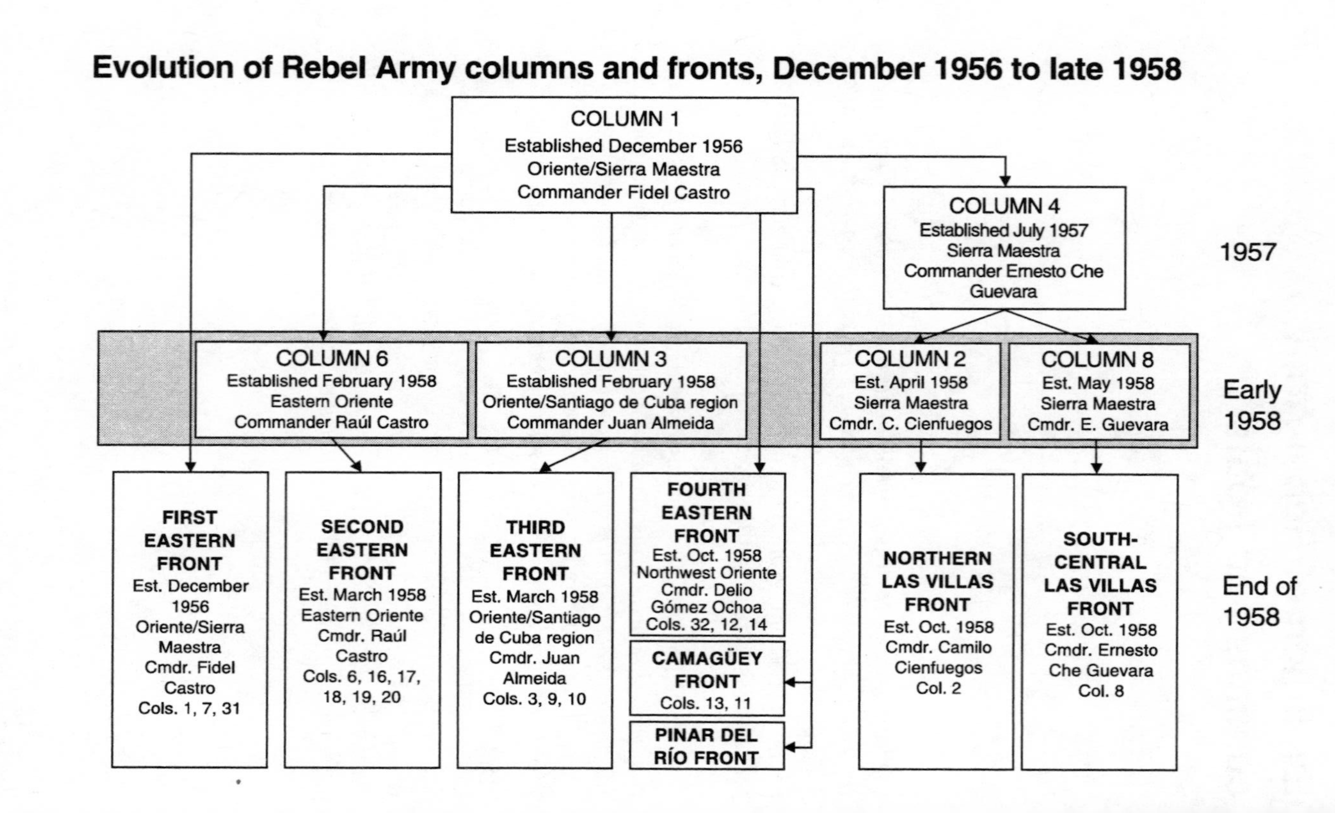
Evolution of Rebel Army columns and fronts, December 1956 to late 1958
COLUMN 1
Established December 1956
Oriente/Sierra Maestra
Commander Fidel Castro
COLUMN 4
Established July 1957
Sierra Maestra
Commander Ernesto Che Guevara
1957
COLUMN 6
Established February 1958
Eastern Oriente
Commander Raúl Castro
COLUMN 3
Established February 1958
Oriente/Santiago de Cuba region
Commander Juan Almeida
COLUMN 2
Est. April 1958
Sierra Maestra
Cmdr. C. Cienfuegos
COLUMN 8
Est. May 1958
Sierra Maestra
Cmdr. E. Guevara
Early 1958
FIRST EASTERN FRONT
Est. December 1956
Oriente/Sierra Maestra
Cmdr. Fidel Castro
Cols. 1, 7, 31
SECOND EASTERN FRONT
Est. March 1958
Eastern Oriente
Cmdr. Raúl Castro
Cols. 6, 16, 17, 18, 19, 20
THIRD EASTERN FRONT
Est. March 1958
Oriente/Santiago de Cuba region
Cmdr. Juan Almeida
Cols. 3, 9, 10
FOURTH EASTERN FRONT
Est. Oct. 1958
Northwest Oriente
Cmdr. Delio Gómez Ochoa
Cols. 32, 12, 14
CAMAGÜEY FRONT
Cols. 13, 11
PINAR DEL RÍO FRONT
NORTHERN LAS VILLAS FRONT
Est. Oct. 1958
Cmdr. Camilo Cienfuegos
Col. 2
SOUTH-CENTRAL LAS VILLAS FRONT
Est. Oct. 1958
Cmdr. Ernesto Che Guevara
Col. 8
End of 1958

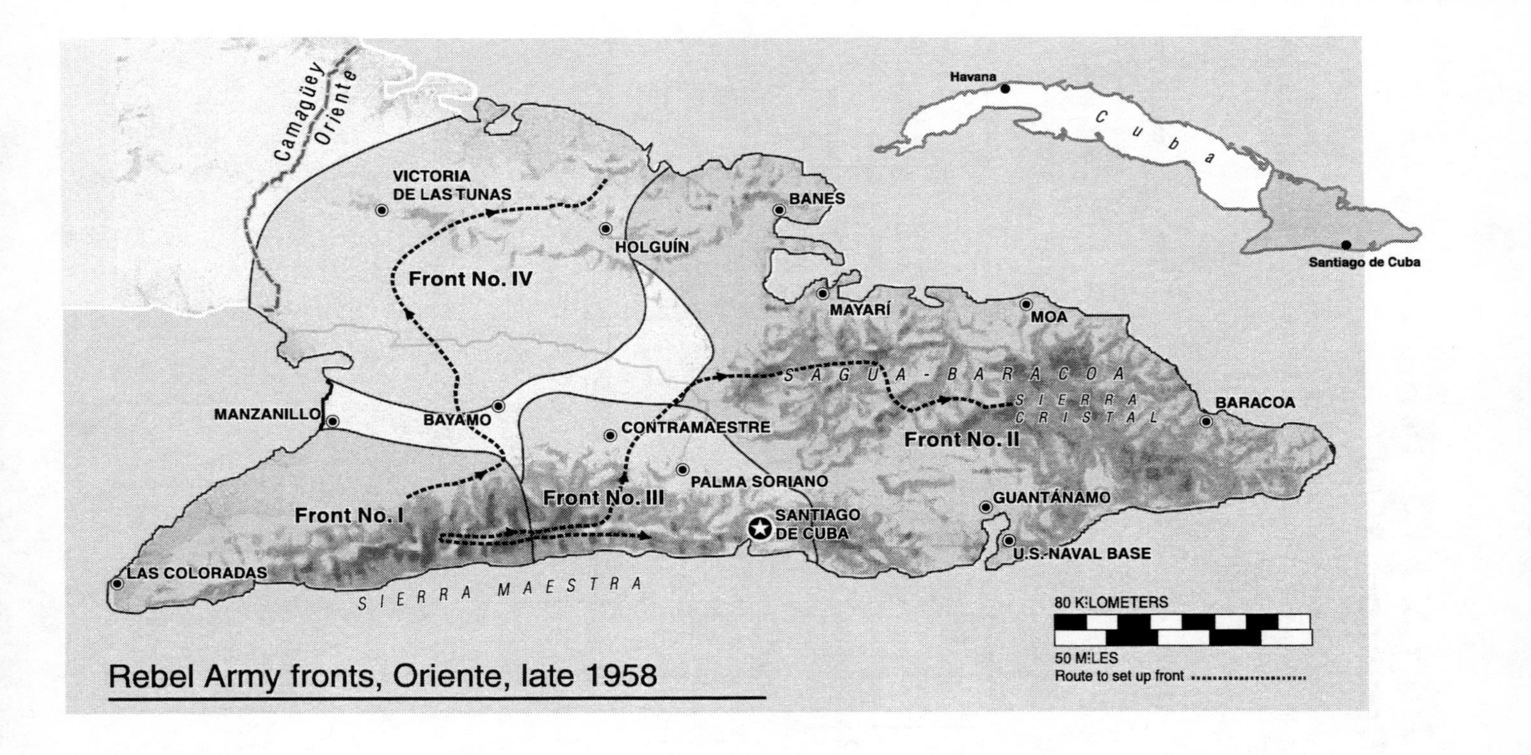

Rebel Army fronts, Oriente, late 1958

Order of battle of Rebel Army as of December 1958

Boxes contain name of column, and of commanding officer, of units of Rebel Army and other organizations as they were organized at the end of revolutionary war.

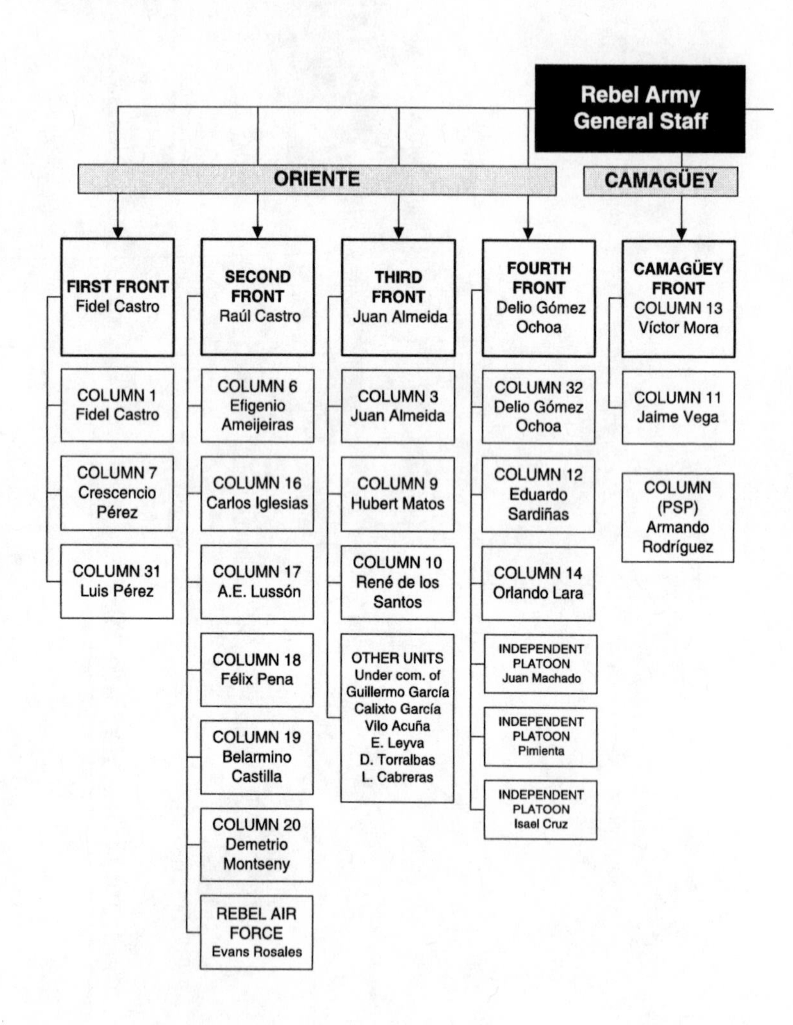

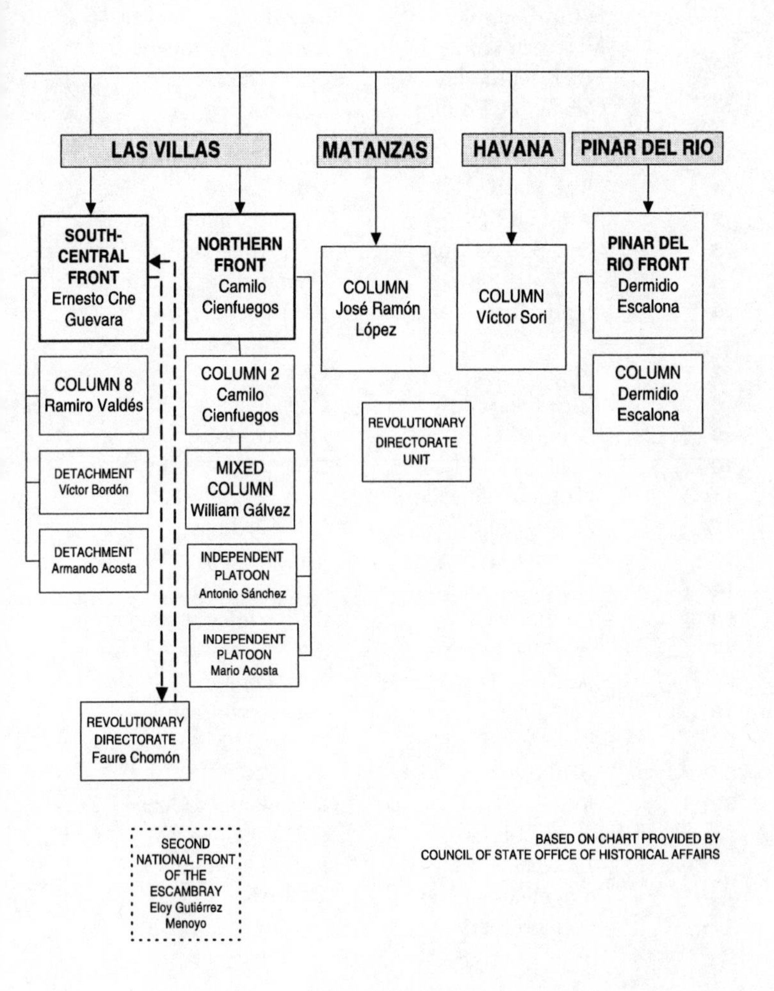

BASED ON CHART PROVIDED BY
COUNCIL OF STATE OFFICE OF HISTORICAL AFFAIRS

DECEMBER 1956–DECEMBER 1958

Columns and fronts

FRONT	NAME	COMMANDER
1	"José Martí"	Fidel Castro
2	"Frank País"	Raúl Castro
3	"Mario Muñoz"	Juan Almeida
4	"Simón Bolívar"	Delio Gómez Ochoa
	South-Central Front	Ernesto Che Guevara
	Northern Front	Camilo Cienfuegos
	Pinar del Río Front	Dermidio Escalona
	Camagüey Front	Víctor Mora

COLUMN	NAME	COMMANDER
1	"José Martí"	Fidel Castro
2	"Antonio Maceo"	Camilo Cienfuegos
3	"Santiago de Cuba"	Juan Almeida
4	—	Che Guevara / Ramiro Valdés[1]
6	"Juan Manuel Ameijeiras"	Raúl Castro / Efigenio Ameijeiras
7	"Regimiento Caracas"	Crescencio Pérez
8	"Ciro Redondo"	Che Guevara / Ramiro Valdés
9	"Antonio Guiteras"	Hubert Matos
10	"René Ramos Latour"	René de los Santos
11	"Cándido González"	Jaime Vega
12	"Simón Bolívar"	Lalo Sardiñas
13	"Ignacio Agramonte"	Víctor Mora
14	"Juan Manuel Márquez"	Orlando Lara
16	"Enrique Hart"	Carlos Iglesias
17	"Abel Santamaría"	Antonio Enrique Lussón
18	"Antonio 'Ñico' López"	Félix Pena
19	"José Tey"	Belarmino Castilla
20	"Gustavo Fraga"	Demetrio Montseny
31	"Benito Juárez"[2]	Luis Pérez
32	"José Antonio Echeverría"	Delio Gómez Ochoa
	Mixed column[3]	William Gálvez
	"Enrique Hart"	José Ramón López
	"Á ngel Ameijeiras"	Víctor Sori
	"Saíz Brothers"	Dermidio Escalona

1. Column ceased to exist mid-1958, after creation of Columns 2 and 8.
2. Became part of Column no. 1 in late November 1958.
3. Composed of troops from Rebel Army Column no. 2, the "Marcelo Salado" July 26 Movement detachment, and the "Máximo Gómez" column of the PSP.

LOCATION/FRONT	ESTABLISHED	FRONT
Sierra Maestra	December 1956	**1**
Oriente, east of Santiago	March 1958	**2**
Oriente, west of Santiago	March 1958	**3**
Oriente / Holguín area	October 1958	**4**
South-Central Las Villas	October 1958	
Northern Las Villas	October 1958	
Pinar del Río	May 1958	
Camagüey	October 1958	

		COLUMN
First Front	December 1956	**1**
Northern Las Villas	April 1958	**2**
Third Front	February 1958	**3**
Sierra Maestra	July 1957	**4**
Second Eastern Front	February 1958	**6**
First Front	March 1958	**7**
South-Central Las Villas	May 1958	**8**
Third Front	August 1958	**9**
Third Front	August 1958	**10**
Camagüey	September 1958	**11**
Fourth Front	October 1958	**12**
Camagüey	October 1958	**13**
Fourth Front	October 1958	**14**
Second Front	October 1958	**16**
Second Front	August 1958	**17**
Second Front	August 1958	**18**
Second Front	August 1958	**19**
Second Front	August 1958	**20**
First Front	October 1958	**31**
Fourth Front	October 1958	**32**
Northern Las Villas	October 1958	
Matanzas		
Havana province		
Pinar del Río		

Index

EXPAND *Your Revolutionary Library*

Malcolm X Talks to Young People

Four talks and an interview given to young people in Ghana, the United Kingdom, and the United States in the last months of Malcolm's life. This new edition contains the full 1964 talk to the Oxford Union in the UK, in print for the first time anywhere. The collection concludes with two memorial tributes by a young socialist leader to this great revolutionary. With a new preface and expanded photo display. $15 Also in Spanish.

Thomas Sankara Speaks

The Burkina Faso Revolution, 1983–87

Peasants and workers in the West African country of Burkina Faso established a popular revolutionary government and began to combat hunger, illiteracy, and economic backwardness imposed by imperialist domination. Thomas Sankara, who led that struggle, explains the example set for all of Africa. $20

What Is Surrealism?

ANDRÉ BRETON

Writings of the best-known leader of the Surrealist movement. Includes a facsimile reproduction of the 1942 Surrealist Album by André Breton. $42

Puerto Rico: Independence Is a Necessity

RAFAEL CANCEL MIRANDA

Rafael Cancel Miranda is one of five Puerto Rican Nationalists imprisoned by Washington for more than 25 years until 1979. In two interviews, he speaks out on the brutal reality of U.S. colonial domination, the campaign to free Puerto Rican political prisoners, the example of Cuba's socialist revolution, and the resurgence of the independence movement today. $3 Also in Spanish.

THE CUBAN REVOLUTION

Aldabonazo

Inside the Cuban Revolutionary Underground, 1952–58

ARMANDO HART

In this firsthand account by a historic leader of the Cuban Revolution, we meet men and women who led the urban underground in the fight against the brutal U.S.-backed tyranny in the 1950s. Together with their comrades-in-arms in the Rebel Army, they not only overthrew the dictatorship. Their revolutionary actions and example worldwide changed the history of the 20th century—and the century to come. $25 Also in Spanish.

Cuba and the Coming American Revolution

JACK BARNES

"There will be a victorious revolution in the United States before there will be a victorious counterrevolution in Cuba." That statement, made by Fidel Castro in 1961, remains as accurate today as when it was spoken. This is a book about the class struggle in the United States, where the revolutionary capacities of workers and farmers are today as utterly discounted by the ruling powers as were those of the Cuban toilers. And just as wrongly. $13 Also in Spanish and French.

Che Guevara Talks to Young People

In eight talks from 1959 to 1964, the Argentine-born revolutionary challenges youth of Cuba and the world to study, to work, to become disciplined. To join the front lines of struggles, small and large. To politicize their organizations and themselves. To become a different kind of human being as they strive together with working people of all lands to transform the world. And, along this course, to revel in the spontaneity and joy of being young. $15 Also in Spanish.

Making History
Interviews with Four Generals of Cuba's Revolutionary Armed Forces

Through the stories of four outstanding Cuban generals—Néstor López Cuba, Enrique Carreras, José Ramón Fernández, and Harry Villegas—each with close to half a century of revolutionary activity, we can see the class dynamics that shaped the Cuban Revolution and our entire epoch. $15.95 Also in Spanish.

From the Escambray to the Congo
In the Whirlwind of the Cuban Revolution

VÍCTOR DREKE

In this participant's account, Víctor Dreke describes how easy it became after the Cuban Revolution to take down a rope segregating blacks from whites at a dance in the town square, yet how enormous was the battle to transform social relations underlying all the "ropes" inherited from capitalism and Yankee domination. $17 Also in Spanish.

Dynamics of the Cuban Revolution
A Marxist Appreciation

JOSEPH HANSEN

How did the Cuban Revolution come about? Why does it represent, as Hansen puts it, an "unbearable challenge" to U.S. imperialism? What political obstacles has it overcome? Written as the revolution advanced from its earliest days. $22.95

Women's Liberation and Socialism

Cosmetics, Fashions, and the Exploitation of Women

Joseph Hansen, Evelyn Reed, Mary-Alice Waters

How big business plays on women's second-class status and social insecurities to market cosmetics and rake in profits. The introduction by Mary-Alice Waters explains how the entry of millions of women into the workforce during and after World War II irreversibly changed U.S. society and laid the basis for a renewed rise of struggles for women's emancipation. $15

Feminism and the Marxist Movement

Mary-Alice Waters

Since the founding of the modern revolutionary workers movement nearly 150 years ago, Marxists have championed the struggle for women's rights and explained the economic roots in class society of women's oppression. "The struggle for women's liberation," Waters writes, "was lifted out of the realm of the personal, the 'impossible dream,' and unbreakably linked to the progressive forces of our epoch"—the working-class struggle for power. $3.50

Marianas in Combat

Teté Puebla and the Mariana Grajales Women's Platoon in Cuba's Revolutionary War 1956–58

Teté Puebla

Brigadier General Teté Puebla, the highest-ranking woman in Cuba's Revolutionary Armed Forces, joined the struggle to overthrow the U.S.-backed dictatorship of Fulgencio Batista in 1956, when she was fifteen years old. This is her story—from clandestine action in the cities, to serving as an officer in the victorious Rebel Army's first all-women's unit—the Mariana Grajales Women's Platoon. For nearly fifty years, the fight to transform the social and economic status of women in Cuba has been inseparable from Cuba's socialist revolution. $14

Problems of Women's Liberation

Evelyn Reed

Six articles explore the social and economic roots of women's oppression from prehistoric society to modern capitalism and point the road forward to emancipation. $13

Women and the Family

Leon Trotsky

How the October 1917 Russian Revolution, the first victorious socialist revolution, transformed the fight for women's emancipation. Trotsky explains the Bolshevik government's steps to wipe out illiteracy, establish equality in economic and political life, set up child-care centers and public kitchens, guarantee the right to abortion and divorce, and more. $12

Communist Continuity and the Fight for Women's Liberation

Documents of the Socialist Workers Party 1971–86

Edited with an introduction by Mary-Alice Waters

How did the oppression of women begin? What class benefits? What social forces have the power to end the second-class status of women? Why is defense of a woman's right to choose abortion a pressing issue for the labor movement? This three-part series helps politically equip the generation of women and men joining battles in defense of women's rights today. 3 volumes. $30

To Speak the Truth

Why Washington's 'Cold War' against Cuba Doesn't End

FIDEL CASTRO, ERNESTO CHE GUEVARA

"In the coming year, our country intends to wage its great battle against illiteracy, with the ambitious goal of teaching every single illiterate person to read and write," Fidel Castro told the UN General Assembly in September 1960. A year later that task was done. In speeches before UN assemblies, two leaders of Cuba's socialist revolution present its political gains and internationalist course. They explain why Washington so hates Cuba's example and why its effort to destroy the revolution will fail. $17

Politics of Chicano Liberation

OLGA RODRIGUEZ AND OTHERS

Lessons from the rise of the Chicano movement in the United States in the 1960s and 1970s, which transformed consciousness and dealt lasting blows against the oppression of the Chicano people. Presents a fighting program for those determined to combat divisions within the working class based on language and national origin. $15.95

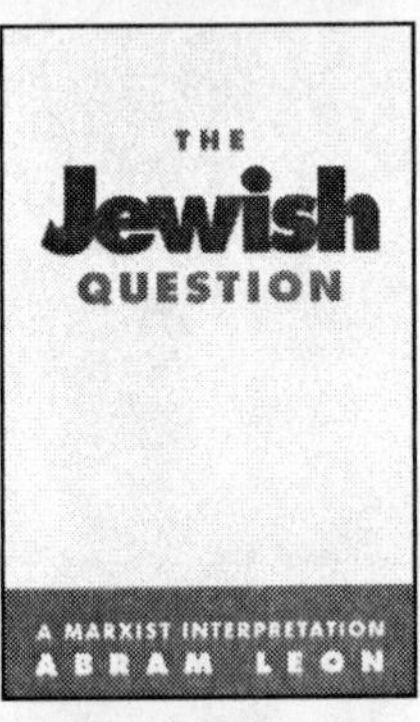

The Jewish Question

A Marxist Interpretation

ABRAM LEON

Traces the historical rationalizations of anti-Semitism to the fact that Jews—in the centuries preceding the domination of industrial capitalism—emerged as a "people-class" of merchants and moneylenders. Leon explains why the propertied rulers incite renewed Jew-hatred in the epoch of capitalism's decline. $17.95

Their Trotsky and Ours

JACK BARNES

"History has shown that small revolutionary organizations will face not only the stern test of wars and repression, but also potentially shattering opportunities that emerge unexpectedly when strikes and social struggles explode. As that happens, communist parties not only recruit. They also fuse with other workers organizations and grow into mass proletarian parties contesting to lead workers and farmers to power. This assumes that well beforehand their cadres have absorbed a world communist program and strategy, are proletarian in life and work, derive deep satisfaction from—have fun—doing politics, and have forged a leadership with an acute sense of what to do next. *Their Trotsky and Ours* is about building such a party." $15 Also in Spanish and French.

FROM THE ARSENAL OF MARXISM

The Communist Manifesto

Karl Marx, Frederick Engels

Founding document of the modern working-class movement, published in 1848. Explains why communism is derived not from preconceived principles but from *facts* and from proletarian movements that are the product of the workings of capitalism itself. $4 Also in Spanish and French.

Socialism: Utopian and Scientific

Frederick Engels

"The task of scientific socialism," wrote Frederick Engels in 1877, is "to impart to the now oppressed proletarian class a full knowledge of the momentous [revolution] it is called upon to accomplish." $4

Lenin's Final Fight

Speeches and Writings, 1922–23

V.I. Lenin

In the early 1920s Lenin waged a political battle in the Communist Party leadership in the USSR to maintain the course that had enabled workers and peasants to overthrow the tsarist empire, carry out the first socialist revolution, and begin building a world communist movement. The issues posed in this fight—from the leadership's class composition, to the worker-peasant alliance and battle against national oppression—remain central to world politics today. $19.95
Also in Spanish.

To See the Dawn

BAKU, 1920—FIRST CONGRESS OF THE PEOPLES OF THE EAST

How can peasants and workers in the colonial world achieve freedom from imperialist exploitation? By what means can working people overcome national, religious, and other divisions incited by their own ruling classes and act together for their common class interests? These questions were addressed by 2,000 delegates to the 1920 Congress of the Peoples of the East. $22

History of the Russian Revolution

Leon Trotsky

A classic account of the social, economic, and political dynamics of the first socialist revolution as told by one of its central leaders. "The history of a revolution is for us first of all a history of the forcible entrance of the masses into the realm of rulership over their own destiny," Trotsky writes. Unabridged edition, 3 volumes in one. $35.95

Fascism: What It Is and How to Fight It

Leon Trotsky

Writing in the heat of struggle against the rise of fascism in Germany, France, and Spain in the 1930s, communist leader Leon Trotsky examines the class origins and character of fascist movements. Building on foundations laid by the Communist International in Lenin's time, Trotsky advances a working-class strategy to combat and defeat this malignant danger to the labor movement and human civilization. $6

Rosa Luxemburg Speaks

Edited by Mary-Alice Waters

From her political awakening as a high school student in tsarist-occupied Poland until her murder in 1919 during the German revolution, Rosa Luxemburg acted and wrote as a proletarian revolutionist. This collection of her writings and speeches takes us inside the political battles between revolution and class collaboration that still shape the modern workers movement. $27

"Without revolutionary theor

NEW INTERNATIONAL NO. 11

U.S. Imperialism Has Lost the Cold War

Jack Barnes

Contrary to imperialist expectations at the opening of the 1990s in the wake of the collapse of regimes across Eastern Europe and the USSR claiming to be communist, the workers and farmers there have not been crushed. Nor have capitalist social relations been stabilized. The toilers remain an intractable obstacle to imperialism's advance, one the exploiters will have to confront in class battles and war. $15

NEW INTERNATIONAL NO. 7

Opening Guns of World War III: Washington's Assault on Iraq

Jack Barnes

The murderous assault on Iraq in 1990–91 heralded increasingly sharp conflicts among imperialist powers, growing instability of international capitalism, and more wars. $12

A MAGAZINE OF MARXIST POLITICS AND THEORY

here can be no revolutionary practice"

—Lenin

EW INTERNATIONAL NO. 9

he Rise and Fall of the Nicaraguan Revolution

ased on ten years of socialist journalism from inside Nicaragua, this
pecial issue recounts the achievements and worldwide impact of the
979 Nicaraguan revolution. It traces the political retreat of the
andinista National Liberation Front leadership that led to the
ownfall of the workers and farmers government in the closing years
f the 1980s. Documents of the Socialist Workers Party. $16

EW INTERNATIONAL NO. 8

he Guevara, Cuba, and the Road to Socialism

rticles by Ernesto Che Guevara, Carlos Rafael Rodríguez, Carlos
'ablada, Mary-Alice Waters, Steve Clark, Jack Barnes
xchanges from the early 1960s and today on the political
erspectives defended by Guevara as he helped lead working people to
dvance the transformation of economic and social relations in Cuba.
10

EW INTERNATIONAL NO. 6

Vashington's 50-year Domestic Contra Operation

s the U.S. rulers prepared to smash working-class resistance and join
he interimperialist slaughter of World War II, the federal political
olice apparatus as it exists today was born, together with vastly
xpanded executive powers of the imperial presidency. This article
lescribes the consequences for the labor, Black, antiwar, and other
ocial movements and how communists have fought to defend
vorkers rights against government and employer attacks. $16

Do you have a friend, coworker, or relative whose first language is Spanish, French, Swedish, or Icelandic?
If so, many issues of New International are available as Nueva Internacional, Nouvelle Internationale, Ny International, and Nýtt Alþjóðlegt.

See full listing at www.pathfinderpress.com

CAPITALISM'S LONG HOT WINTER HAS BEGUN

BY JACK BARNES

One of capitalism's infrequent, long winters has begun, explains Jack Barnes. We have entered the opening stages of what will be decades of economic and social crises and class battles. With the "acceleration of imperialism's drive toward war, it's going to be a long, hot winter. Even more important, slowly but surely and explosively, it will be one that breeds a scope and depth of resistance not previously seen by revolutionary-minded militants throughout today's world."

New International no. 12 also includes: "Their Transformation and Ours," draft theses, Socialist Workers Party National Committee, and "Crisis, Boom, and Revolution: 1921 Reports by V.I. Lenin and Leon Trotsky." $16

OUR POLITICS START WITH THE WORLD

BY JACK BARNES

The huge economic and cultural inequalities between imperialist and semicolonial countries, and among classes within almost every country, are produced, reproduced, and accentuated by the workings of capitalism. For vanguard workers to build parties able to lead a successful revolutionary struggle for power in our own countries, says Jack Barnes, our activity must be guided by a strategy to close this gap. "We are part of an international class that itself has no homeland. That's not a slogan. That's not a moral imperative. It is a recognition of the class reality of economic, social, and political life in the imperialist epoch."

New International no. 13 also includes: "Farming, Science, and the Working Classes" by Steve Clark and "Capitalism, Labor, and Nature," an exchange between Richard Levins and Steve Clark. $14

NEW INTERNATIONAL

A MAGAZINE OF MARXIST POLITICS AND THEORY

ORDER FROM WWW.PATHFINDERPRESS.COM